I0372739

Advanced Durgā Pūjā

5950 Highway 128
Napa, CA 94558 USA
Communications: Phone and Fax 1-707-966-2802
E-Mail swamiji@shreemaa.org
Please visit us on the World Wide Web at
http://www.shreemaa.org

ISBN 978-1-877795-15-1
Library of Congress Catalog Card Number
CIP 2001 126147

Advanced Durgā Pūjā
Swami Satyananda Saraswati
1. Hindu Religion. 2. Worship. 3. Spirituality.
4. Philosophy. I. Saraswati, Swami Satyananda;

Saṁskṛta and Computer Layout
by Swami Adaityananda Saraswati

Table of Contents

yantra	1
Introduction	2
devatā praṇām	3
dhyānam	5
ācamana	14
saṅkalpa	18
gaṇeśa pūjā	23
puṇyā havācana, svasti vācana	26
gāyatrī viddhi	34
sāmānyārghya	46
puṣpa śuddhi	49
kalaśa sthāpana	50
prāṇa pratiṣṭhā	62
viśeṣārghya	70
bhūta śuddhi	73
kara śuddhi	74
bhūtāpsāraṇa	75
aghamārṣaṇa	76
agni prajvālitaṁ	77
mātṛkā pūjā	84
nava durgā pūjā (1)	92
nava patrikā pūjā	99
nava durgā pūjā (2)	103
yantra pūjā	107
sarvato bhadramaṇḍala devatā sthāpanam	116
aṣṭāśakti pūjā	130
nava grahaṇa pūjā	134
yoginī pūjā	139
astra pūjā	147
bāhya mātrikā nyāsa	152
mātṛkā nyāsa	158
aṅga pūjā	164
pīṭha nyāsa	167
āvāhaṇa	172
prāṇa pratiṣṭhā	174
stapana	178
pūjā naivedya	181
durgā pūjā	200
durgā dvātriṁśannāma mālā	206
śrī durgāṣṭottara śatanāma stotram	209
durgā dakārādisahasranāmastotram	217
durgā dakārādisahasranāmavali	259

durgā cālīsā 412
shree maa pūjā 421
puṣpāñjalī 422
praṇām 423
aśīrbād 426
visārjaṇa 427
appendix
chandi yajna paddhoti 429

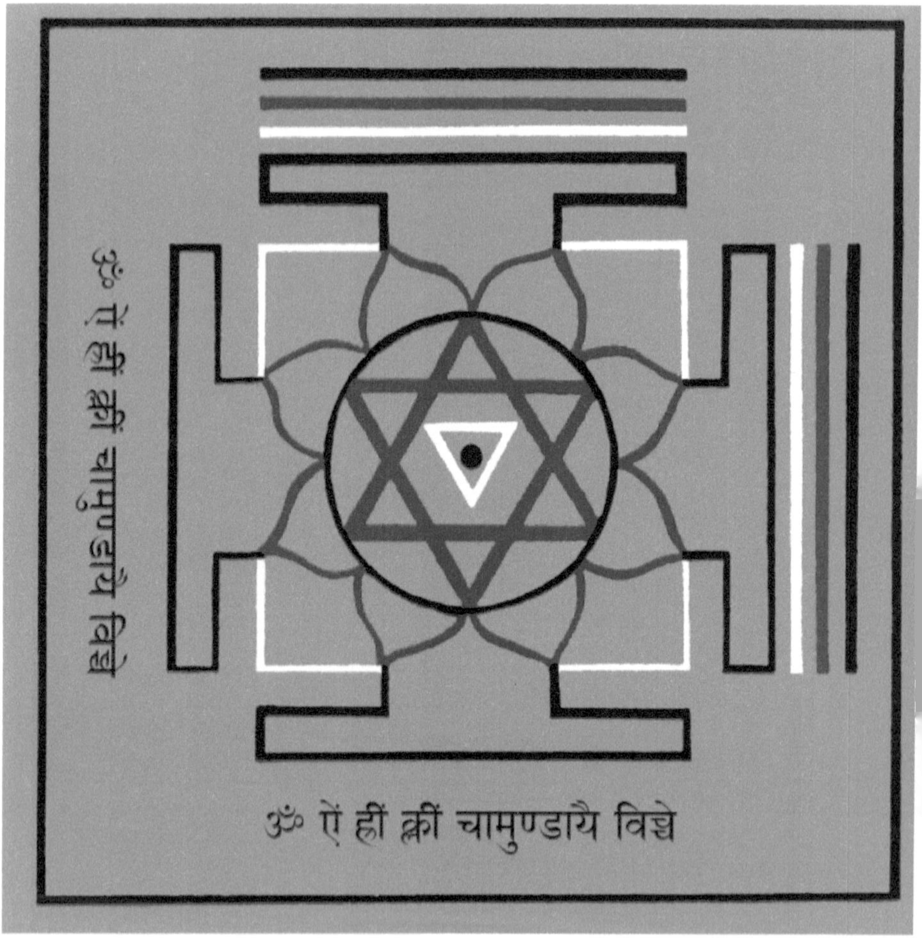
ॐ ऐं ह्रीं क्लीं चामुण्डायै विच्चे
ॐ ऐं ह्रीं क्लीं चामुण्डायै विच्चे

Introduction

Durgam means confusion, obstacles, attachments which hinder our greatest success. Durgā takes away the durgam, guiding us beyond all confusion to the place of stillness, clarity, and understanding.

She is the female image of Infinite Energy, the form of the Divine Mother of the Universe. She is usually depicted with somewhere between four arms and a thousand, all forms indicative of the immensity of Her power. The main deity of this puja has ten arms, with hands holding ten weapons, representing ten forms of discipline with which sadhus come closer to Her.

She delivers everything She has promised: bhukti - mukti, enjoyment and liberation. She gives wealth, both materially and spiritually, accompanied by wisdom, love, good health, and energy. That is Her promise. She does exactly what She says!

This puja is a guided meditation into the presence of Durgā. It contains four parts: Invitation, invocation, offering, and union, and most often they are interconnected, so that we are in union while we are offering our invocation. It is very similar to the harmony of the yogas: Dhyān, Jñāna, Bhakti, and Karma. They are not separate or distinct. They are all interconnected and mutually dependent upon one another.

All of these four Yogas will unite in all the four parts of the worship, so when we sit for puja, we will be sitting in an āsana, performing prāṇāyām, bringing our senses to a focus, restraining the wandering of the mind, all the steps of aṣṭaṅga yoga will join in our communion.

This is the goal of worship, it is the blessing of pūjā. Shree Maa joins me is requesting Durgā to send blessings to all devotees everywhere, and we pray that this book will assist you in enhancing your capacity of worship.

Shree Maa and Swami Satyananda Saraswati, Devi Mandir, Fairfield, 2015

देवता प्रणाम्
devatā praṇām

श्रीमन्महागणाधिपतये नमः

śrīmanmahāgaṇādhipataye namaḥ
We bow to the Respected Great Lord of Wisdom.

लक्ष्मीनारायणाभ्यां नमः

lakṣmīnārāyaṇābhyāṁ namaḥ
We bow to Lakṣmī and Nārāyaṇa, The Goal of all Existence and the Perceiver of all.

उमामहेश्वराभ्यां नमः

umāmaheśvarābhyāṁ namaḥ
We bow to Umā and Maheśvara, She who protects existence, and the Great Consciousness or Seer of all.

वाणीहिरण्यगर्भाभ्यां नमः

vāṇīhiraṇyagarbhābhyāṁ namaḥ
We bow to Vāṇī and Hiraṇyagarbha, Sarasvatī and Brahmā, who create the cosmic existence.

शचीपुरन्दराभ्यां नमः

śacīpurandarābhyāṁ namaḥ
We bow to Śacī and Purandara, Indra and his wife, who preside over all that is divine.

मातापितृभ्यां नमः

mātāpitṛbhyāṁ namaḥ
We bow to the Mothers and Fathers.

इष्टदेवताभ्यो नमः

iṣṭadevatābhyo namaḥ
We bow to the chosen deity of worship.

कुलदेवताभ्यो नमः

kuladevatābhyo namaḥ

We bow to the family deity of worship.

ग्रामदेवताभ्यो नमः

grāmadevatābhyo namaḥ

We bow to the village deity of worship.

वास्तुदेवताभ्यो नमः

vāstudevatābhyo namaḥ

We bow to the particular household deity of worship.

स्थानदेवताभ्यो नमः

sthānadevatābhyo namaḥ

We bow to the established deity of worship.

सर्वेभ्यो देवेभ्यो नमः

sarvebhyo devebhyo namaḥ

We bow to all the Gods.

सर्वेभ्यो ब्राह्मणेभ्यो नमः

sarvebhyo brāhmaṇebhyo namaḥ

We bow to all the Knowers of divinity.

dhyānam

खड्गं चक्रगदेषुचापपरिघाञ्छूलं भुशुण्डीं शिरः
शङ्खं संदधतीं करैस्त्रिनयनां सर्वाङ्गभूषावृताम् ।
नीलाश्मद्युतिमास्यपाददशकां सेवे महाकालिकां
यामस्तौत्स्वपिते हरौ कमलजो हन्तुं मधुं कैटभम् ॥

khaḍgaṁ cakra gadeṣu cāpa
parighāñ chūlaṁ bhuśuṇḍīṁ śiraḥ
śaṅkhaṁ saṁdadhatīṁ karai
strinayanāṁ sarvāṅga bhūṣāvṛtām |
nīlāś madyutimāsya pāda
daśakāṁ seve mahākālikāṁ
yāmastaut svapite harau
kamalajo hantuṁ madhuṁ kaiṭabham ||

Bearing in Her ten hands the sword of worship, the discus of revolving time, the club of articulation, the bow of determination, the iron bar of restraint, the pike of attention, the sling, the head of egotism and the conch of vibrations, She has three eyes and displays ornaments on all Her limbs. Shining like a blue gem, She has ten faces. I worship that Great Remover of Darkness whom the lotus-born Creative Capacity praised in order to slay Too Much and Too Little when the Supreme Consciousness was asleep.

अक्षस्रक्परशुं गदेषुकुलिशं पद्मं धनुः कुण्डिकां
दण्डं शक्तिमसिं च चर्म जलजं घण्टां सुराभाजनम् ।
शूलं पाशसुदर्शने च दधतीं हस्तैः प्रसन्नाननां
सेवे सैरिभमर्दिनीमिह महालक्ष्मीं सरोजस्थिताम् ॥

akṣasrak paraśuṁ gadeṣu
kuliśaṁ padmaṁ dhanuḥ kuṇḍikāṁ
daṇḍaṁ śaktīm asiṁ ca carma
jalajaṁ ghaṇṭāṁ surābhājanam |
śūlaṁ pāśa sudarśane ca
dadhatīṁ hastaiḥ prasannānanāṁ
seve sairibha mardinī
miha mahālakṣmīṁ sarojasthitām ||

She with the beautiful face, the Destroyer of the Great Ego, is seated upon the lotus of Peace. In Her hands She holds the rosary of alphabets, the battle axe of good actions, the club of articulation, the arrow of speech, the thunderbolt of illumination, the lotus of peace, the bow of determination, the water-pot of purification, the staff of discipline, energy, the sword of worship, the shield of faith, the conch of vibrations, the bell of continuous tone, the wine cup of joy, the pike of concentration, the net of unity and the discus of revolving time named Excellent Intuitive Vision. I worship that Great Goddess of True Wealth.

घण्टाशूलहलानि शङ्खमुसले चक्रं धनुः सायकं
हस्ताब्जैर्दधतीं घनान्तविलसच्छीतांशुतुल्यप्रभाम् ।
गौरीदेहसमुद्भवां त्रिजगतामाधारभूतां महा-
पूर्वामत्र सरस्वतीमनुभजे शुम्भादिदैत्यार्दिनीम् ॥

ghaṇṭā śūla halāni śaṅkha
musale cakraṁ dhanuḥ sāyakaṁ
hastābjair dadhatīṁ ghanānta
vilasacchītāṁ śutulya prabhām ।
gaurīdeha samudbhavāṁ
trijagatām ādhārabhūtāṁ mahā-
pūrvāmatra sarasvatīm
anubhaje śumbhādi daityārdinīm

Bearing in Her lotus hands the bell of continuous tone, the pike of concentration, the plow sowing the seeds of the Way of Truth to Wisdom, the conch of vibrations, the pestle of refinement, the discus of revolving time, the bow of determination and the arrow of speech, whose radiance is like the moon in autumn, whose appearance is most beautiful, who is manifested from the body of She Who is Rays of Light, and is the support of the three worlds, I worship that Great Goddess of All-Pervading Knowledge, who destroyed Self-Conceit and other thoughts.

या चण्डी मधुकैटभादिदैत्यदलनी या माहिषोन्मूलिनी
या धूम्रेक्षणचण्डमुण्डमथनी या रक्तबीजाशनी ।
शक्तिः शुम्भनिशुम्भदैत्यदलनी या सिद्धिदात्री परा
सा देवी नवकोटीमूर्तिसहिता मां पातु विश्वेश्वरी ॥

yā caṇḍī madhukaiṭabhādidaityadalanī yā māhiṣonmūlinī
yā dhūmrekṣaṇacaṇḍamuṇḍamathanī yā raktabījāśanī
śaktiḥ śumbhaniśumbhadaityadalanī yā siddhidātrī parā
sā devī navakoṭīmūrtisahitā māṁ pātu viśveśvarī

That Caṇḍī, who slays the negativities of Too Much and Too Little and other Thoughts; Who is the origin of the Great Ego, and the Destroyer of Sinful Eyes, Passion and Anger, and the Seed of Desire; the Energy that tears asunder Self-Conceit and Self-Deprecation, the Grantor of the highest attainment of perfection: may that Goddess who is represented by ninety million divine images, the Supreme Lord of the Universe, remain close and protect me.

ॐ अग्निर्ज्योतिर्ज्योतिरग्निः स्वाहा ।
सूर्यो ज्योतिर्ज्योतिः सूर्यः स्वाहा ।
अग्निर्वर्चो ज्योतिर्वर्चः स्वाहा ।
सूर्यो वर्चो ज्योतिर्वर्चः स्वाहा ।
ज्योतिः सूर्यः सूर्यो ज्योतिः स्वाहा ॥

oṁ agnir jyotir jyotir agniḥ svāhā
sūryo jyotir jyotiḥ sūryaḥ svāhā
agnir varco jyotir varcaḥ svāhā
sūryo varco jyotir varcaḥ svāhā
jyotiḥ sūryaḥ sūryo jyotiḥ svāhā

oṁ The Divine Fire is the Light, and the Light is the Divine Fire; I am One with God! The Light of Wisdom is the Light, and the Light is the Light of Wisdom; I am One with God! The Divine Fire is the offering, and the Light is the Offering; I am One with God!
The Light of Wisdom is the Offering, and the Light is the Light of Wisdom; I am One with God!

(Wave light)

ॐ अग्निर्ज्योती रविर्ज्योतिश्चन्द्रो ज्योतिस्तथैव च ।
ज्योतिषामुत्तमो देवि दीपोऽयं प्रतिगृह्यताम् ॥
एष दीपः ॐ ह्रीं श्रीं दुं दुर्गायै नमः ॥

oṁ agnirjyotī ravirjyotiścandro jyotistathaiva ca
jyotiṣāmuttamo devi dīpo-yaṁ pratigṛhyatām
eṣa dīpaḥ oṁ hrīṁ śrīṁ duṁ durgāyai namaḥ

oṁ The Divine Fire is the Light, the Light of Wisdom is the Light, the Light of Devotion is the Light as well. The Light of the Highest Bliss, Oh Goddess, is in the Light which we offer, the Light which we request you to accept. With the offering of Light Oṁ I bow to the Goddess, Durgā, the Grantor of Increase, who Removes all Difficulties.

(Wave incense)

ॐ वनस्पतिरसोत्पन्नो गन्धात्ययी गन्ध उत्तमः ।
आघ्रेयः सर्वदेवानां धूपोऽयं प्रतिगृह्यताम् ॥
एष धूपः ॐ ह्रीं श्रीं दुं दुर्गायै नमः ॥

oṁ vanaspatirasotpanno gandhātyayī gandha uttamaḥ
āghreyaḥ sarvadevānāṁ dhūpo-yaṁ pratigṛhyatām
eṣa dhūpaḥ oṁ hrīṁ śrīṁ duṁ durgāyai namaḥ

oṁ Spirit of the Forest, from you is produced the most excellent of scents. The scent most pleasing to all the Gods, that scent we request you to accept. With the offering of fragrant scent Oṁ I bow to the Goddess, Durgā, the Grantor of Increase, who Removes all Difficulties.

ārātrikam

ॐ चन्द्रादित्यौ च धरणी विद्युदग्निस्तथैव च ।
त्वमेव सर्वज्योतीषिं आरात्रिकं प्रतिगृह्यताम् ॥
ॐ ह्रीं श्रीं दुं दुर्गायै नमः आरात्रिकं समर्पयामि

oṁ candrādityau ca dharaṇī vidyudagnistathaiva ca
tvameva sarvajyotīṣiṁ ārātrikaṁ pratigṛhyatām
oṁ hrīṁ śrīṁ duṁ durgāyai namaḥ ārātrikaṁ samarpayāmi

All knowing as the Moon, the Sun and the Divine Fire, you alone are all light, and this light we request you to accept. With the offering of light Oṁ I bow to the Goddess, Durgā, the Grantor of Increase, who Removes all Difficulties.

ॐ पयः पृथिव्यां पय ओषधीषु
पयो दिव्यन्तरिक्षे पयो धाः ।
पयःस्वतीः प्रदिशः सन्तु मह्यम् ॥

oṁ payaḥ pṛthivyāṁ paya oṣadhīṣu
payo divyantarikṣe payo dhāḥ
payaḥsvatīḥ pradiśaḥ santu mahyam

oṁ Earth is a reservoir of nectar, all vegetation is a reservoir of nectar, the divine atmosphere is a reservoir of nectar, and also above. May all perceptions shine forth with the sweet taste of nectar for us.

ॐ अग्निर्देवता वातो देवता सूर्यो देवता चन्द्रमा देवता
वसवो देवता रुद्रो देवता ऽदित्या देवता मरुतो देवता विश्वे
देवा देवता बृहस्पतिर्देवतेन्द्रो देवता वरुणो देवता ॥

oṁ agnirdevatā vāto devatā sūryo devatā candramā devatā vasavo devatā rudro devatā-dityā devatā maruto devatā viśve devā devatā bṛhaspatirdevatendro devatā varuṇo devatā

oṁ The Divine Fire (Light of Purity) is the shining God, the Wind is the shining God, the Sun (Light of Wisdom) is the shining God, the Moon (Lord of Devotion) is the shining God, the Protectors of the Wealth are the shining Gods, the Relievers of Sufferings are the shining Gods, the Sons of the Light are the shining Gods; the Emancipated seers (Maruts) are the shining Gods, the Universal Shining Gods are the shining Gods, the Guru of the Gods is the shining God, the Ruler of the Gods is the shining God, the Lord of Waters is the shining God.

ॐ भूर्भुवः स्वः ।
तत् सवितुर्वरेण्यम् भर्गो देवस्य धीमहि ।
धियो यो नः प्रचोदयात् ॥

oṁ bhūr bhuvaḥ svaḥ
tat savitur vareṇyam bhargo devasya dhīmahi
dhiyo yo naḥ pracodayāt

oṁ the Infinite Beyond Conception, the gross body, the subtle body and the causal body; we meditate upon that Light of Wisdom which is the Supreme Wealth of the Gods. May it grant to us increase in our meditations.

ॐ भूः

oṁ bhūḥ

oṁ the gross body

ॐ भुवः

oṁ bhuvaḥ

oṁ the subtle body

ॐ स्वः

oṁ svaḥ

oṁ the causal body

ॐ महः

oṁ mahaḥ

oṁ the great body of existence

ॐ जनः

oṁ janaḥ

oṁ the body of knowledge

ॐ तपः

oṁ tapaḥ

oṁ the body of light

ॐ सत्यं

oṁ satyaṁ
oṁ the body of Truth

ॐ तत् सवितुर्वरेण्यम् भर्गो देवस्य धीमहि ।
धियो यो नः प्रचोदयात् ॥

oṁ tat savitur vareṇyam bhargo devasya dhīmahi
dhiyo yo naḥ pracodayāt
oṁ we meditate upon that Light of Wisdom which is the Supreme Wealth of the Gods. May it grant to us increase in our meditations.

ॐ आपो ज्योतीरसोमृतं ब्रह्म भूर्भुवस्स्वरोम् ॥

oṁ āpo jyotīrasomṛtaṁ brahma bhūrbhuvassvarom
May the divine waters luminous with the nectar of immortality of Supreme Divinity fill the earth, the atmosphere and the heavens.

ॐ मां माले महामाये सर्वशक्तिस्वरूपिणि ।
चतुर्वर्गस्त्वयि न्यस्तस्तस्मान्मे सिद्धिदा भव ॥

oṁ māṁ māle mahāmāye sarvaśaktisvarūpiṇi
catur vargas tvayi nyastas tasmān me siddhidā bhava
oṁ My Rosary, The Great Measurement of Consciousness, containing all energy within as your intrinsic nature, give to me the attainment of your Perfection, fulfilling the four objectives of life.

ॐ अविघ्नं कुरु माले त्वं गृह्णामि दक्षिणे करे ।
जपकाले च सिद्ध्यर्थं प्रसीद मम सिद्धये ॥

oṁ avighnaṁ kuru māle tvaṁ gṛhṇāmi dakṣiṇe kare
japakāle ca siddhyarthaṁ prasīda mama siddhaye
oṁ Rosary, You please remove all obstacles. I hold you in my right hand. At the time of recitation be pleased with me. Allow me to attain the Highest Perfection.

ॐ अक्षमालाधिपतये सुसिद्धिं देहि देहि
सर्वमन्त्रार्थसाधिनि साधय साधय सर्वसिद्धिं परिकल्पय
परिकल्पय मे स्वाहा ॥

oṁ akṣa mālā dhipataye susiddhiṁ dehi dehi sarva mantrārtha sādhini sādhaya sādhaya sarva siddhiṁ parikalpaya parikalpaya me svāhā

oṁ Rosary of rudrākṣa seeds, my Lord, give to me excellent attainment. Give to me, give to me. Illuminate the meanings of all mantras, illuminate, illuminate! Fashion me with all excellent attainments, fashion me! I am One with God!

एते गन्धपुष्पे ॐ गं गणपतये नमः

ete gandhapuṣpe oṁ gaṁ gaṇapataye namaḥ

With these scented flowers oṁ we bow to the Lord of Wisdom, Lord of the Multitudes.

एते गन्धपुष्पे ॐ आदित्यादिनवग्रहेभ्यो नमः

ete gandhapuṣpe oṁ ādityādi navagrahebhyo namaḥ

With these scented flowers oṁ we bow to the Sun, the Light of Wisdom, along with the nine planets.

एते गन्धपुष्पे ॐ शिवादिपञ्चदेवताभ्यो नमः

ete gandhapuṣpe oṁ śivādipañcadevatābhyo namaḥ

With these scented flowers oṁ we bow to Śiva, the Consciousness of Infinite Goodness, along with the five primary deities (Śiva, Śakti, Viṣṇu, Gaṇeśa, Sūrya).

एते गन्धपुष्पे ॐ इन्द्रादिदशदिक्पालेभ्यो नमः

ete gandhapuṣpe oṁ indrādi daśadikpālebhyo namaḥ

With these scented flowers oṁ we bow to Indra, the Ruler of the Pure, along with the Ten Protectors of the ten directions.

एते गन्धपुष्पे ॐ मत्स्यादिदशावतारेभ्यो नमः

ete gandhapuṣpe oṁ matsyādi daśāvatārebhyo namaḥ
With these scented flowers oṁ we bow to Viṣṇu, the Fish, along with the Ten Incarnations which He assumed.

एते गन्धपुष्पे ॐ प्रजापतये नमः

ete gandhapuṣpe oṁ prajāpataye namaḥ
With these scented flowers oṁ we bow to the Lord of All Created Beings.

एते गन्धपुष्पे ॐ नमो नारायणाय नमः

ete gandhapuṣpe oṁ namo nārāyaṇāya namaḥ
With these scented flowers oṁ we bow to the Perfect Perception of Consciousness.

एते गन्धपुष्पे ॐ सर्वेभ्यो देवेभ्यो नमः

ete gandhapuṣpe oṁ sarvebhyo devebhyo namaḥ
With these scented flowers oṁ we bow to All the Gods.

एते गन्धपुष्पे ॐ सर्वाभ्यो देवीभ्यो नमः

ete gandhapuṣpe oṁ sarvābhyo devībhyo namaḥ
With these scented flowers oṁ we bow to All the Goddesses.

एते गन्धपुष्पे ॐ श्री गुरवे नमः

ete gandhapuṣpe oṁ śrī gurave namaḥ
With these scented flowers oṁ we bow to the Guru.

एते गन्धपुष्पे ॐ ब्राह्मणेभ्यो नमः

ete gandhapuṣpe oṁ brāhmaṇebhyo namaḥ
With these scented flowers oṁ we bow to All Knowers of Wisdom.

Tie a piece of string around right middle finger or wrist.

ॐ कुशासने स्थितो ब्रह्मा कुशे चैव जनार्दनः ।
कुशे ह्याकाशवद् विष्णुः कुशासन नमोऽस्तु ते ॥

oṁ kuśāsane sthito brahmā kuśe caiva janārdanaḥ
kuśe hyākāśavad viṣṇuḥ kuśāsana namo-stu te

Brahmā is in the shining light (or kuśa grass), in the shining light resides Janārdana, the Lord of Beings. The Supreme all-pervading Consciousness, Viṣṇu, resides in the shining light. Oh Repository of the shining light, we bow down to you, the seat of kuśa grass.

आचमन

ācamana

ॐ केशवाय नमः स्वाहा

oṁ keśavāya namaḥ svāhā

We bow to the one of beautiful hair.

ॐ माधवाय नमः स्वाहा

oṁ mādhavāya namaḥ svāhā

We bow to the one who is always sweet.

ॐ गोविन्दाय नमः स्वाहा

oṁ govindāya namaḥ svāhā

We bow to He who is one-pointed light.

ॐ विष्णुः ॐ विष्णुः ॐ विष्णुः

oṁ viṣṇuḥ oṁ viṣṇuḥ oṁ viṣṇuḥ

oṁ Consciousness, oṁ Consciousness, oṁ Consciousness.

ॐ तत् विष्णोः परमं पदम् सदा पश्यन्ति सूरयः ।
दिवीव चक्षुराततम् ॥

oṁ tat viṣṇoḥ paramaṁ padam sadā paśyanti sūrayaḥ
divīva cakṣurā tatam

oṁ That Consciousness of the highest station, who always sees the Light of Wisdom, give us Divine Eyes.

ॐ तद् विप्र स पिपानोव जुविग्रन्सो सोमिन्द्रते ।
विष्णुः तत् परमं पदम् ॥

oṁ tad vipra sa pipānova juvigranso somindrate
viṣṇuḥ tat paramaṁ padam

oṁ That twice-born teacher who is always thirsty for accepting the nectar of devotion, Oh Consciousness, you are in that highest station.

ॐ अपवित्रः पवित्रो वा सर्वावस्थां गतोऽपि वा ।
यः स्मरेत् पुण्डरीकाक्षं स बाह्याभ्यन्तरः शुचिः ॥

oṁ apavitraḥ pavitro vā sarvāvasthāṁ gato-pi vā
yaḥ smaret puṇḍarīkākṣaṁ sa bāhyābhyantaraḥ śuciḥ

oṁ The Impure and the Pure reside within all objects. Who remembers the lotus-eyed Consciousness is conveyed to radiant beauty.

ॐ सर्वमङ्गलमाङ्गल्यम् वरेण्यम् वरदं शुभं ।
नारायणं नमस्कृत्य सर्वकर्माणि कारयेत् ॥

oṁ sarva maṅgala māṅgalyam
vareṇyam varadaṁ śubhaṁ
nārāyaṇaṁ namaskṛtya sarvakarmāṇi kārayet

All the Welfare of all Welfare, the highest blessing of Purity and Illumination, with the offering of respect we bow down to the Supreme Consciousness who is the actual performer of all action.

ॐ सूर्य्यश्चमेति मन्त्रस्य ब्रह्मा ऋषिः प्रकृतिश्छन्दः आपो देवता आचमने विनियोगः ॥

oṁ sūryyaścameti mantrasya brahmā ṛṣiḥ
prakṛtiśchandaḥ āpo devatā ācamane viniyogaḥ

oṁ these are the mantras of the Light of Wisdom, the Creative Capacity is the Seer, Nature is the meter, the divine flow of waters is the deity, being applied in washing the hands and rinsing the mouth.

Draw the asana yantra with some drops of water and/or sandal paste at the front of your seat. Place a flower on the bindu in the middle.

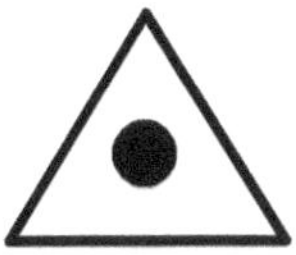

ॐ आसनस्य मन्त्रस्य मेरुपृष्ठ ऋषिः सुतलं छन्दः कूर्म्मो
देवता आसनोपवेशने विनियोगः ॥

oṁ āsanasya mantrasya merupṛṣṭha ṛṣiḥ sutalaṁ chandaḥ kūrmmo devatā āsanopaveśane viniyogaḥ
Introducing the mantras of the Purification of the seat. The Seer is He whose back is Straight, the meter is of very beautiful form, the tortoise who supports the earth is the deity. These mantras are applied to make the seat free from obstructions.

एते गन्धपुष्पे ॐ ह्रीं आधारशक्तये कमलासनाय नमः ॥

ete gandhapuṣpe oṁ hrīṁ ādhāraśaktaye kamalāsanāya namaḥ
With these scented flowers oṁ hrīṁ we bow to the Primal Energy situated in this lotus seat.

ॐ पृथ्वि त्वया धृता लोका देवि त्वं विष्णुना धृता ।
त्वञ्च धारय मां नित्यं पवित्रं कुरु चासनम् ॥

oṁ pṛthvi tvayā dhṛtā lokā devi tvaṁ viṣṇunā dhṛtā tvañca dhāraya māṁ nityaṁ pavitraṁ kuru cāsanam
oṁ Earth! You support the realms of the Goddess. You are supported by the Supreme Consciousness. Also bear me eternally and make pure this seat.

ॐ गुरुभ्यो नमः

oṁ gurubhyo namaḥ
oṁ I bow to the Guru.

ॐ परमगुरुभ्यो नमः

oṁ paramagurubhyo namaḥ
oṁ I bow to the Guru's Guru.

ॐ परापरगुरुभ्यो नमः

oṁ parāparagurubhyo namaḥ
oṁ I bow to the Gurus of the lineage.

ॐ परमेष्ठिगुरुभ्यो नमः

oṁ parameṣṭhigurubhyo namaḥ
oṁ I bow to the Supreme Gurus.

ॐ गं गणेशाय नमः

oṁ gaṁ gaṇeśāya namaḥ
oṁ I bow to the Lord of Wisdom.

ॐ अनन्ताय नमः

oṁ anantāya namaḥ
oṁ I bow to the Infinite One.

ॐ ऐं ह्रीं क्लीं चामुण्डायै विच्चे

oṁ aiṁ hrīṁ klīṁ cāmuṇḍāyai vicce
oṁ Creation, Circumstance, Transformation are known by Consciousness.

ॐ नमः शिवाय

oṁ namaḥ śivāya
oṁ I bow to the Consciousness of Infinite Goodness.

Clap hands 3 times and snap fingers in the ten directions (N S E W NE SW NW SE UP DOWN) repeating

ॐ ह्रीं श्रीं दुं दुर्गायै नमः

oṁ hrīṁ śrīṁ duṁ durgāyai namaḥ
Oṁ I bow to the Goddess, Durgā, the Grantor of Increase, who Removes all Difficulties.

सङ्कल्प
saṅkalpa

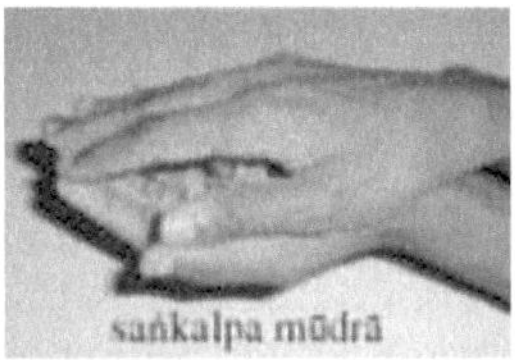

विष्णुः ॐ तत् सत् । ॐ अद्य जम्बूद्वीपे ( ) देशे ( ) प्रदेशे ( ) नगरे ( ) मन्दिरे ( ) मासे ( ) पक्षे ( ) तिथौ ( ) गोत्र श्री ( ) कृतैतत् श्रीदुर्गा कामः पूजाकर्माहं करिष्ये ॥

viṣṇuḥ oṁ tat sat oṁ adya jambūdvīpe (Country) deśe (State) pradeśe (City) nagare (Name of house or temple) mandire (month) māse (śukla or kṛṣṇa) pakṣe (name of day) tithau (name of) gotra śrī (your name) gotra śrī (your name) kṛtaitat śrī durgā kāmaḥ pūjā karmāhaṁ kariṣye

The Consciousness Which Pervades All, oṁ That is Truth. Presently, on the Planet Earth, Country of (Name), State of (Name), City of (Name), in the Temple of (Name), (Name of Month) Month, (Bright or Dark) fortnight, (Name of Day) Day, (Name of Sādhu Family), Śrī (Your Name) is performing the worship for the satisfaction of the Respected Durgā.

ॐ यज्जाग्रतो दूरमुदेति दैवं तदु सुप्तस्य तथैवैति ।
दूरङ्गमं ज्योतिषां ज्योतिरेकं तन्मे मनः शिवसङ्कल्पमस्तु ॥

oṁ yajjāgrato dūramudeti
daivaṁ tadu suptasya tathaivaiti
dūraṅgamaṁ jyotiṣāṁ jyotirekaṁ
tanme manaḥ śiva saṅkalpamastu

May our waking consciousness replace pain and suffering with divinity as also our awareness when asleep. Far extending be our radiant aura of light, filling our minds with light. May that be the firm determination of the Consciousness of Infinite Goodness.

या गुङ्गूर्या सिनीवाली या राका या सरस्वती ।
ईन्द्राणीमह्व ऊतये वरुणानीं स्वस्तये ॥

yā guṅgūryā sinīvālī yā rākā yā sarasvatī
īndrāṇīmahva ūtaye varuṇānīṁ svastaye

May that Goddess who wears the Moon of Devotion protect the children of Devotion. May that Goddess of All-Pervading Knowledge protect us. May the Energy of the Rule of the Pure rise up. Oh Energy of Equilibrium grant us the highest prosperity.

ॐ स्वस्ति न इन्द्रो वृद्धश्रवाः स्वस्ति नः पूषा विश्ववेदाः ।
स्वस्ति नस्तार्क्ष्यो अरिष्टनेमिः स्वस्ति नो बृहस्पतिर्दधातु ॥

oṁ svasti na indro vṛddhaśravāḥ
svasti naḥ pūṣā viśvavedāḥ
svasti nastārkṣyo ariṣṭanemiḥ
svasti no bṛhaspatirdadhātu

The Ultimate Prosperity to us, Oh Rule of the Pure, who perceives all that changes; the Ultimate Prosperity to us, Searchers for Truth, Knowers of the Universe; the Ultimate Prosperity to us, Oh Divine Being of Light, keep us safe; the Ultimate Prosperity to us, Oh Spirit of All-Pervading Delight, grant that to us.

ॐ गणानां त्वा गणपतिꣳ हवामहे
प्रियाणां त्वा प्रियपतिꣳ हवामहे
निधीनां त्वा निधिपतिꣳ हवामहे वसो मम ।
आहमजानि गर्भधमा त्वमजासि गर्भधम् ॥

oṁ gaṇānāṁ tvā gaṇapati guṁ havāmahe
priyāṇāṁ tvā priyapati guṁ havāmahe
nidhīnāṁ tvā nidhipati guṁ havāmahe vaso mama
āhamajāni garbbhadhamā tvamajāsi garbbhadham

We invoke you with offerings, Oh Lord of the Multitudes; we invoke you with offerings, Oh Lord of Love; we invoke you with offerings, Oh Guardian of the Treasure. Sit within me, giving birth to the realm of the Gods within me; yes, giving birth to the realm of the Gods within me.

ॐ गणानां त्वा गणपतिꣳ हवामहे
कविं कवीनामुपमश्रवस्तमम् ।
ज्येष्ठराजं ब्रह्मणां ब्रह्मणस्पत
आ नः शृण्वन्नूतिभिः सीद सादनम् ॥

oṁ gaṇānāṁ tvā gaṇapati guṁ havāmahe
kaviṁ kavīnāmupamaśravastamam
jyeṣṭharājaṁ brahmaṇāṁ brahmaṇaspata
ā naḥ śṛṇvannūtibhiḥ sīda sādanam

We invoke you with offerings, Oh Lord of the Multitudes, Seer among Seers, of unspeakable grandeur. Oh Glorious King, Lord of the Knowers of Wisdom, come speedily hearing our supplications and graciously take your seat amidst our assembly.

ॐ अदितिर्द्यौरदितिरन्तरिक्षमदितिर्माता स पिता स
पुत्रः । विश्वे देवा अदितिः पञ्च जना
अदितिर्जातमदितिर्जनित्वम् ॥

oṁ aditir dyauraditirantarikṣamaditirmātā
sa pitā sa putraḥ
viśve devā aditiḥ pañca janā
aditirjātamaditirjanitvam

The Mother of Enlightenment pervades the heavens; the Mother of Enlightenment pervades the atmosphere; the Mother of Enlightenment pervades Mother and Father and child. All Gods of the Universe are pervaded by the Mother, the five forms of living beings, all Life. The Mother of Enlightenment, She is to be known.

ॐ त्वं स्त्रीस्त्वं पुमानसि त्वं कुमार अत वा कुमारी ।
त्वं जिर्नो वन्देन वञ्चसि त्वं जातो भवसि विश्वतोमुखः ॥

oṁ tvaṁ strīstvaṁ pumānasi
tvaṁ kumāra ata vā kumarī
tvaṁ jirno vandena vañcasi
tvaṁ jāto bhavasi viśvatomukhaḥ

You are Female, you are Male; you are a young boy, you are a young girl. You are the word of praise by which we are singing; you are all creation existing as the mouth of the universe.

ॐ अम्बेऽम्बिकेऽम्बालिके न मा नयति कश्चन ।
ससस्त्यश्वकः सुभद्रिकां काम्पीलवासिनीम् ॥

oṁ ambe-ambike-mbālike na mā nayati kaścana
sasastyaśvakaḥ subhadrikāṁ kāmpīlavāsinīm

Mother of the Perceivable Universe, Mother of the Conceivable Universe, Mother of the Universe of Intuitive Vision, lead me to that True Existence. As excellent crops (or grains) are harvested, so may I be taken to reside with the Infinite Consciousness.

ॐ शान्ता द्यौः शान्तापृथिवी शान्तमिदमुर्वन्तरिक्षम् ।
शान्ता उदन्वतिरापः शान्ताः नः शान्त्वोषधीः ॥

oṁ śāntā dyauḥ śāntā pṛthivī śāntam idamurvantarikṣam
śāntā udanvatirāpaḥ śāntāḥ naḥ śāntvoṣadhīḥ

Peace in the heavens, Peace on the earth, Peace upwards and permeating the atmosphere; Peace upwards, over, on all sides and further; Peace to us, Peace to all vegetation;

ॐ शान्तानि पूर्वरूपाणि शान्तं नोऽस्तु कृताकृतम् ।
शान्तं भूतं च भव्यं च सर्वमेव शमस्तु नः ॥

oṁ śāntāni pūrva rūpāṇi śāntaṁ no-stu kṛtākṛtam
śāntaṁ bhūtaṁ ca bhavyaṁ ca sarvameva śamastu naḥ

Peace to all that has form, Peace to all causes and effects; Peace to all existence, and to all intensities of reality including all and everything; Peace be to us.

ॐ पृथिवी शान्तिरन्तरिक्षं शान्तिर्द्यौः

शान्तिरापः शान्तिरोषधयः शान्तिः वनस्पतयः शान्तिर्विश्वे मे

देवाः शान्तिः सर्वे मे देवाः शान्तिर्ब्रह्म शान्तिरापः शान्तिः

सर्वं शान्तिरेधि शान्तिः शान्तिः सर्व शान्तिः सा मा शान्तिः

शान्तिभिः ॥

oṁ pṛthivī śāntir antarikṣaṁ śāntir dyauḥ
śāntir āpaḥ śāntir oṣadhayaḥ śāntiḥ vanaspatayaḥ śāntir viśve me devāḥ śāntiḥ sarve me devāḥ śāntir brahma śāntirāpaḥ śāntiḥ sarvaṁ śāntiredhi śāntiḥ śāntiḥ sarva śāntiḥ sā mā śāntiḥ śāntibhiḥ

Let the earth be at Peace, the atmosphere be at Peace, the heavens be filled with Peace. Even further may Peace extend, Peace be to waters, Peace to all vegetation, Peace to All Gods of the Universe, Peace to All Gods within us, Peace to Creative Consciousness, Peace be to Brilliant Light, Peace to All, Peace to Everything, Peace, Peace, altogether Peace, equally Peace, by means of Peace.

ताभिः शान्तिभिः सर्वशान्तिभिः समया मोहं यदिह घोरं

यदिह क्रूरं यदिह पापं तच्छान्तं

तच्छिवं सर्वमेव समस्तु नः ॥

tābhiḥ śāntibhiḥ sarva śāntibhiḥ samayā mohaṁ yadiha ghoraṁ yadiha krūraṁ yadiha pāpaṁ tacchāntaṁ tacchivaṁ sarvameva samastu naḥ

Thus by means of Peace, altogether one with the means of Peace, Ignorance is eliminated, Violence is eradicated, Improper Conduct is eradicated, Confusion (sin) is eradicated, all that is, is at Peace, all that is perceived, each and everything, altogether for us,

ॐ शान्तिः शान्तिः शान्तिः ॥

oṁ śāntiḥ śāntiḥ śāntiḥ

oṁ Peace, Peace, Peace

गणेश पूजा

gaṇeśa pūjā

worship of gaṇeśa

ॐ विश्वेशं माधवं ढुण्ढिं दण्डपाणिं च भैरवम् ।
वन्दे काशीं गुहां गङ्गां भवानीं मणिकर्णिकाम् ॥

oṁ viśveśaṁ mādhavaṁ ḍhuṇḍhiṁ
daṇḍapāṇiṁ ca bhairavam
vande kāśīṁ guhāṁ gaṅgāṁ
bhavānīṁ maṇikarṇikām

Oṁ the Lord of the Universe, Lord Viṣṇu Mādhava, who holds the club in his hand and is fearless, worships He Who dwells in the cave at Benaris, who holds aloft the Gaṅgā, who is the Lord of the Universe, He who wears jeweled earrings.

gaṇeśa gāyatrī

ॐ तत् पुरुषाय विद्महे वक्रतुण्डाय धीमहि ।
तन्नो दन्ती प्रचोदयात् ॥

oṁ tatpuruṣāya vidmahe vakratuṇḍāya dhīmahi
tanno dantī pracodayāt

Oṁ we meditate on that Perfect Consciousness, we contemplate the One with a broken tooth. May that One with the Great Tusk grant us increase.

एते गन्धपुष्पे ॐ गं गणपतये नमः

ete gandhapuṣpe oṁ gaṁ gaṇapataye namaḥ

With these scented flowers oṁ we bow to the Lord of Wisdom, Lord of the Multitudes.

gaṇeśa dhyānam
meditation

ॐ सुमुखश्चैकदन्तश्च कपिलो गजकर्णकः ।
लम्बोदरश्च विकटो विघ्ननाशो विनायकः ॥

oṁ sumukhaścaika dantaśca kapilo gaja karṇakaḥ
lambodaraśca vikaṭo vighnanāśo vināyakaḥ

Oṁ He has a beautiful face with only one tooth (or tusk), of red color with elephant ears; with a big belly and a great tooth he destroys all obstacles. He is the Remover of Obstacles.

धूम्रकेतुर्गणाध्यक्षो भालचन्द्रो गजाननः ।
द्वादशैतानि नामानि यः पठेच्छृणुयादपि ॥

dhūmraketurgaṇādhyakṣo bhāla candro gajānanaḥ
dvādaśaitāni nāmāni yaḥ paṭhecchṛṇu yādapi

With a grey banner, the living spirit of the multitudes, having the moon on his forehead, with an elephant's face. Whoever will recite or listen to these twelve names

विद्यारम्भे विवाहे च प्रवेशे निर्गमे तथा ।
संग्रामे संकटे चैव विघ्नस्तस्य न जायते ॥

vidyārambhe vivāhe ca praveśe nirgame tathā
saṁgrāme saṁkate caiva vighnastasya na jāyate

at the time of commencing studies, getting married, or on entering or leaving any place; on a battlefield of war, or in any difficulty, will overcome all obstacles.

शुक्लाम्बरधरं देवं शशिवर्णं चतुर्भुजम् ।
प्रसन्नवदनं ध्यायेत् सर्वविघ्नोपशान्तये ॥

śuklāmbaradharaṁ devaṁ śaśivarṇaṁ caturbhujam
prasannavadanaṁ dhyāyet sarvavighnopaśāntaye

Wearing a white cloth, the God has the color of the moon and four arms. That most pleasing countenance is meditated on who gives peace to all difficulties.

अभीप्सितार्थसिद्ध्यर्थं पूजितो यः सुरासुरैः ।
सर्वविघ्नहरस् तस्मै गणाधिपतये नमः ॥

abhīpsitārtha siddhyartharh pūjito yaḥ surā suraiḥ
sarvavighna haras tasmai gaṇādhipataye namaḥ

For gaining the desired objective, or for the attainment of perfection, he is worshipped by the Forces of Union and the Forces of Division alike. He takes away all difficulties, and therefore, we bow down in reverance to the Lord of the Multitudes.

वक्रतुण्ड महाकाय सूर्यकोटिसमप्रभ ।
अविघ्नं कुरु मे देव सर्वकार्येषु सर्वदा ॥

vakratuṇḍa mahākāya sūrya koṭi samaprabha
avighnaṁ kuru me deva sarva kāryeṣu sarvadā

With a broken (or bent) tusk, a great body shining like a million suns, make us free from all obstacles, Oh God. Always remain (with us) in all actions.

एकदन्तं महाकायं लम्बोदरं गजाननम् ।
विघ्ननाशकरं देवं हेरम्बं प्रणामाम्यहम् ॥

ekadantaṁ mahākāyaṁ lambodaraṁ gajānanam
vighnanāśakaraṁ devaṁ herambaṁ praṇāmāmyaham

With one tooth, a great body, a big belly and an elephant's face, he is the God who destroys all obstacles to whom we are bowing down with devotion.

मल्लिकादि सुगन्धीनि मालित्यादीनि वै प्रभो ।
मयाऽहृतानि पूजार्थं पुष्पाणि प्रतिगृह्यताम् ॥

mallikādi sugandhīni mālityādīni vai prabho
mayā-hṛtāni pūjārthaṁ puṣpāṇi pratigṛhyatām

Various flowers, such as mallikā and others of excellent scent, are being offered to you, Our Lord. All these flowers have come from the devotion of our hearts for your worship. Please accept them.

एते गन्धपुष्पे ॐ गं गणपतये नमः

ete gandhapuṣpe oṁ gaṁ gaṇapataye namaḥ
With these scented flowers oṁ we bow to the Lord of Wisdom, the Lord of the Multitudes.

puṇyā havācana, svasti vācana
proclamation of merits and eternal blessings

ॐ शान्तिरस्तु

oṁ śāntirastu
oṁ Peace be unto you.

ॐ पुष्टिरस्तु

oṁ puṣṭirastu
oṁ Increase or Nourishment be unto you.

ॐ तुष्टिरस्तु

oṁ tuṣṭirastu
oṁ Satisfaction be unto you.

ॐ वृद्धिरस्तु

oṁ vṛddhirastu
oṁ Positive Change be unto you.

ॐ अविघ्नमस्तु

oṁ avighnamastu
oṁ Freedom from Obstacles be unto you.

ॐ आयुष्यमस्तु

oṁ āyuṣyamastu
oṁ Life be unto you.

ॐ आरोग्यमस्तु

oṁ ārogyamastu
oṁ Freedom from Disease be unto you.

ॐ शिवमस्तु

oṁ śivamastu
oṁ Consciousness of Infinite Goodness be unto you.

ॐ शिवकर्माऽस्तु

oṁ śivakarmā-stu
oṁ Consciousness of Infinite Goodness in all action be unto you.

ॐ कर्मसमृद्धिरस्तु

oṁ karmasamṛddhirastu
oṁ Progress or Increase in all action be unto you.

ॐ धर्मसमृद्धिरस्तु

oṁ dharmasamṛddhirastu
oṁ Progress and Increase in all Ways of Truth be unto you.

ॐ वेदसमृद्धिरस्तु

oṁ vedasamṛddhirastu
oṁ Progress or Increase in all Knowledge be unto you.

ॐ शास्त्रसमृद्धिरस्तु

oṁ śāstrasamṛddhirastu
oṁ Progress or Increase in Scriptures be unto you.

ॐ धन-धान्यसमृद्धिरस्तु

oṁ dhana-dhānyasamṛddhirastu
oṁ Progress or Increase in Wealth and Grains be unto you.

ॐ इष्टसम्पदस्तु

oṁ iṣṭasampadastu
oṁ May your beloved deity be your wealth.

ॐ अरिष्टनिरसनमस्तु

oṁ ariṣṭanirasanamastu

oṁ May you remain safe and secure, without any fear.

ॐ यत्पापं रोगमशुभमकल्याणं तद्दूरे प्रतिहतमस्तु

oṁ yatpāpaṁ rogamaśubhamakalyāṇaṁ taddūre pratihatamastu

oṁ May sin, sickness, impurity, and that which is not conducive unto welfare, leave from you.

ॐ ब्रह्म पुण्यमहर्यच्च सृष्ट्युत्पादनकारकम् ।
वेदवृक्षोद्भवं नित्यं तत्पुण्याहं ब्रुवन्तु नः ॥

oṁ brahma puṇyamaharyacca sṛṣṭyutpādanakārakam
vedavṛkṣodbhavaṁ nityaṁ tatpuṇyāhaṁ bruvantu naḥ

The Creative Capacity with the greatest merit, the Cause of the Birth of Creation, eternally has its being in the tree of Wisdom. May His blessing of merit be bestowed upon us.

भो ब्राह्मणाः ! मया क्रियमाणस्य दुर्गापूजनाख्यस्य कर्मणः
पुण्याहं भवन्तो ब्रुवन्तु ॥

bho brāhmaṇāḥ! mayā kriyamāṇasya durgāpūjanākhyasya karmaṇaḥ puṇyāhaṁ bhavanto bruvantu

Oh Brahmiṇs! My sincere effort is to perform the worship of Durgā. Let these activities yield merit.

ॐ पुण्याहं ॐ पुण्याहं ॐ पुण्याहं ॥

oṁ puṇyāhaṁ oṁ puṇyāhaṁ oṁ puṇyāhaṁ

oṁ Let these activities yield merit.

ॐ अस्य कर्मणः पुण्याहं भवन्तो ब्रुवन्तु ॥

oṁ asya karmaṇaḥ puṇyāhaṁ bhavanto bruvantu

oṁ Let these activities yield merit.

ॐ पुण्याहं ॐ पुण्याहं ॐ पुण्याहं ॥

oṁ puṇyāhaṁ oṁ puṇyāhaṁ oṁ puṇyāhaṁ

oṁ Let these activities yield merit (3 times).

पृथिव्यामुद्धृतायां तु यत्कल्याणं पुरा कृतम् ।
ऋषिभिः सिद्धगन्धर्वैस्तत्कल्याणं ब्रुवन्तु नः ॥

pṛthivyāmuddhṛtāyāṁ tu yatkalyāṇaṁ purā kṛtam
ṛṣibhiḥ siddha gandharvaistatkalyāṇaṁ bruvantu naḥ

With the solidity of the earth, let supreme welfare be. May the Ṛṣis, the attained ones and the celestial singers bestow welfare upon us.

भो ब्राह्मणाः ! मया क्रियमाणस्य दुर्गापूजनाख्यस्य कर्मणः
कल्याणं भवन्तो ब्रुवन्तु ॥

bho brāhmaṇāḥ! mayā kriyamāṇasya
durgāpūjanākhyasya karmaṇaḥ kalyāṇaṁ
bhavanto bruvantu

Oh Brahmiṇs! My sincere effort is to perform the worship of Durgā. Let these activities bestow welfare.

ॐ कल्याणं ॐ कल्याणं ॐ कल्याणं

oṁ kalyāṇaṁ oṁ kalyāṇaṁ oṁ kalyāṇaṁ

oṁ Let these activities bestow welfare (3 times).

सागरस्य तु या ऋद्धिर्महालक्ष्म्यादिभिः कृता ।
सम्पूर्णा सुप्रभावा च तामृद्धिं प्रब्रुवन्तु नः ॥

sāgarasya tu yā ṛddhirmahālakṣmyādibhiḥ kṛtā
sampūrṇā suprabhāvā ca tāmṛddhiṁ prabruvantu naḥ

May the ocean yield Prosperity, as it did when the Great Goddess of True Wealth and others were produced; fully and completely giving forth excellent lustre, may Prosperity be unto us.

भो ब्राह्मणाः ! मया क्रियमाणस्य दुर्गापूजनाख्यस्य कर्मणः

ऋद्धिं भवन्तो ब्रुवन्तु ॥

bho brāhmaṇāḥ! mayā kriyamāṇasya durgāpūjanākhyasya karmaṇaḥ ṛddhiṁ bhavanto bruvantu

Oh Brahmiṇs! My sincere effort is to perform the worship of Durgā. Let these activities bestow Prosperity.

ॐ कर्म ऋध्यताम् ॐ कर्म ऋध्यताम् ॐ कर्म ऋध्यताम्

oṁ karma ṛdhyatām oṁ karma ṛdhyatām oṁ karma ṛdhyatām

oṁ Let these activities bestow Prosperity (3 times).

स्वस्तिरस्तु याविनाशाख्या पुण्यकल्याणवृद्धिदा ।

विनायकप्रिया नित्यं तां च स्वस्तिं ब्रुवन्तु नः ॥

svastirastu yā vināśākhyā puṇya kalyāṇa vṛddhidā vināyakapriyā nityaṁ tāṁ ca svastiṁ bruvantu naḥ

Let the Eternal Blessings which grant changes of indestructible merit and welfare be with us. May the Lord who removes all obstacles be pleased and grant to us Eternal Blessings.

भो ब्राह्मणाः ! मया क्रियमाणस्य दुर्गापूजनाख्यस्य कर्मणः

स्वस्तिं भवन्तो ब्रुवन्तु ॥

bho brāhmaṇāḥ! mayā kriyamāṇasya durgāpūjanākhyasya karmaṇaḥ svastiṁ bhavanto bruvantu

Oh Brahmiṇs! My sincere effort is to perform the worship of Durgā. Let these activities bestow Eternal Blessings.

ॐ आयुष्मते स्वस्ति ॐ आयुष्मते स्वस्ति

ॐ आयुष्मते स्वस्ति

oṁ āyuṣmate svasti oṁ āyuṣmate svasti oṁ āyuṣmate svasti

oṁ May life be filled with Eternal Blessings (3 times).

ॐ स्वस्ति न इन्द्रो वृद्धश्रवाः स्वस्ति नः पूषा विश्ववेदाः ।
स्वस्ति नस्तार्क्ष्यो अरिष्टनेमिः स्वस्ति नो बृहस्पतिर्दधातु ॥

oṁ svasti na indro vṛddhaśravāḥ
svasti naḥ pūṣā viśvavedāḥ
svasti nastārkṣyo ariṣṭanemiḥ
svasti no bṛhaspatirdadhātu

The Eternal Blessings to us, Oh Rule of the Pure, who perceives all that changes; the Eternal Blessings to us, Searchers for Truth, Knowers of the Universe; the Eternal Blessings to us, Oh Divine Being of Light, keep us safe; the Eternal Blessings to us, Oh Spirit of All-Pervading Delight, grant that to us.

समुद्रमथनाज्ज्ञाता जगदानन्दकारिका ।
हरिप्रिया च माङ्गल्या तां श्रियं च ब्रुवन्तु नः ॥

samudramathnājjātā jagadānandakārikā
haripriyā ca māṅgalyā tāṁ śriyaṁ ca bruvantu naḥ

Who was born from the churning of the ocean, the cause of bliss to the worlds, the beloved of Viṣṇu and Welfare Herself, may Śrī, the Highest Respect, be unto us.

भो ब्राह्मणाः ! मया क्रियमाणस्य दुर्गापूजनाख्यस्य कर्मणः
श्रीरस्त्विति भवन्तो ब्रुवन्तु ॥

bho brāhmaṇāḥ! mayā kriyamāṇasya
durgāpūjanākhyasya karmaṇaḥ śrīrastviti
bhavanto bruvantu

Oh Brahmiṇs! My sincere effort is to perform the worship of Durgā. Let these activities bestow the Highest Respect.

ॐ अस्तु श्रीः ॐ अस्तु श्रीः ॐ अस्तु श्रीः

oṁ astu śrīḥ oṁ astu śrīḥ oṁ astu śrīḥ

oṁ Let these activities bestow the Highest Respect (3 times).

ॐ श्रीश्च ते लक्ष्मीश्च पत्न्यावहोरात्रे पार्श्वे नक्षत्राणि
रूपमश्विनौ व्यात्तम्। इष्णन्निषाणामुं म इषाण
सर्वलोकं म इषाण ॥

oṁ śrīśca te lakṣmīśca patnyāvahorātre pārśve nakṣatrāṇi rūpamaśvinau vyāttam
iṣṇanniṣāṇāmuṁ ma iṣāṇa sarvalokaṁ ma iṣāṇa

oṁ the Highest Respect to you, Goal of all Existence, wife of the full and complete night (the Unknowable One), at whose sides are the stars, and who has the form of the relentless search for Truth. Oh Supreme Divinity, Supreme Divinity, my Supreme Divinity, all existence is my Supreme Divinity.

मृकण्डसूनोरायुर्यद्ध्रुवलोमशयोस्तथा।
आयुषा तेन संयुक्ता जीवेम शरदः शतम् ॥

mṛkaṇḍasūnorāyuryaddhruvalomaśayostathā
āyuṣā tena saṁyuktā jīvema śaradaḥ śatam

As the son of Mṛkaṇḍa, Mārkaṇḍeya, found imperishable life, may we be united with life and blessed with a hundred autumns.

शतं जीवन्तु भवन्तः

śataṁ jīvantu bhavantaḥ

May a hundred autumns be unto you.

शिवगौरीविवाहे या या श्रीरामे नृपात्मजे।
धनदस्य गृहे या श्रीरस्माकं साऽस्तु सद्मनि ॥

śiva gaurī vivāhe yā yā śrīrāme nṛpātmaje
dhanadasya gṛhe yā śrīrasmākaṁ sā-stu sadmani

As the imperishable union of Śiva and Gaurī, as the soul of kings manifested in the respected Rāma, so may the Goddess of Respect forever be united with us and always dwell in our house.

ॐ अस्तु श्रीः ॐ अस्तु श्रीः ॐ अस्तु श्रीः

oṁ astu śrīḥ oṁ astu śrīḥ oṁ astu śrīḥ

May Respect be unto you.

प्रजापतिर्लोकपालो धाता ब्रह्मा च देवराट् ।
भगवाञ्छाश्वतो नित्यं नो वै रक्षन्तु सर्वतः ॥

prajāpatirlokapālo dhātā brahmā ca devarāṭ
bhagavāñchāśvato nityaṁ no vai rakṣantu sarvataḥ
The Lord of all beings, Protector of the worlds, Creator, Brahmā, Support of the Gods; may the Supreme Lord be gracious eternally and always protect us.

ॐ भगवान् प्रजापतिः प्रियताम्

oṁ bhagavān prajāpatiḥ priyatām
May the Supreme Lord, Lord of all beings, be pleased.

आयुष्मते स्वस्तिमते यजमानाय दाशुषे ।
श्रिये दत्ताशिषः सन्तु ऋत्विग्भिर्वेदपारगैः ॥

āyuṣmate svastimate yajamānāya dāśuṣe
śriye dattāśiṣaḥ santu ṛtvigbhirvedapāragaiḥ
May life and eternal blessings be unto those who perform this worship and to those who assist. May respect be given to the priests who impart this wisdom.

ॐ स्वस्तिवाचनसमृद्धिरस्तु

oṁ svastivācanasamṛddhirastu
oṁ May this invocation for eternal blessings find excellent prosperity.

gāyatrī viddhi

system of worship with gāyatrī

ॐ प्रजापतिर्ऋषिर्गायित्रीछन्दोऽग्निर्देवता व्याहृति होमे विनियोगः ।

oṁ prajāptirṛṣirgāyatrī chando-gnirdevatā vyāhṛti home viniyogaḥ

Oṁ The Lord of Creation is the Seer, Gāyatrī is the meter (24 syllables to the verse), Purification is the Divinity, the Proclamations of Delight are applied in offering.

ॐ भूः स्वाहा ॥

oṁ bhūḥ svāhā

Oṁ Gross Perception.

ॐ प्रजापतिर्ऋषिरुष्णिक्छन्दोवायुर्देवता व्याहृति होमे विनियोगः ।

oṁ prajāpatirṛṣiruṣṇik chando vāyurdevatā vyāhṛti home viniyogaḥ

The Lord of Creation is the Seer, Uṣṇik is the meter (28 syllables to the verse), Emancipation is the Divinity, the Proclamations of Delight are applied in offering.

ॐ भुवः स्वाहा ॥

oṁ bhuvaḥ svāhā

Oṁ Subtle Perception.

ॐ प्रजापतिर्ऋषिरनुष्टुपछन्दः सूर्योदेवता व्याहृति होमे विनियोगः ।

oṁ prajāpitirṛṣiranuṣṭup chandaḥ sūryodevatā vyāhṛti home viniyogaḥ

The Lord of Creation is the Seer, Anuṣṭup is the meter (32 syllables to the verse), The Light of Wisdom is the Divinity, the Proclamations of Delight are applied in offering.

ॐ स्वः स्वाहा ॥

oṁ svaḥ svāhā
Oṁ Intuitive Perception.

ॐ प्रजापतिर्ऋषिर्बृहती छन्दः प्रजापतिर्देवता महाव्याहृति होमे विनियोगः ।

oṁ prajāpatirṛṣirbṛhatī chandaḥ prajāpatirdevatā mahāvyāhṛti home viniyogaḥ
The Lord of Creation is the Seer, Bṛhatī is the meter (40 syllables to the verse), The Lord of Creation is the Divinity, the Great (full, complete) Proclamations of Delight are applied in offering.

ॐ भूर्भुवः स्वः स्वाहा ॥

oṁ bhūrbhuvaḥ svaḥ svāhā
Oṁ Gross Perception, oṁ Subtle Perception, oṁ Intuitive Perception.

ॐ गायत्र्या विश्वामित्रऋषिर्गायित्री छन्दः सवितादेवता गायत्री जपे विनियोगः ॥

oṁ gāyatryā viśvāmitraṛṣirgāyatrī chandaḥ savitādevatā gāyatrī jape viniyogaḥ
The Gāyatrī (Mantra), The Friend of the Universe is the Seer, Gāyatrī is the meter (24 syllables to the verse), The Daughter of Light is the Divinity, the Gāyatrī (mantra) is applied in recitation.

Holding tattva mudrā, touch head:

विश्वामित्र ऋषये नमः

viśvāmitra ṛṣaye namaḥ touch head
To the Seer, Friend of the Universe, I bow.

गायत्री छन्दःसे नमः

gāyatrī chandaḥse namaḥ touch mouth
To the Meter, Gāyatrī (24 syllables to the verse), I bow.

सवित्रीदेवतायै नमः

savitrīdevatāyai namaḥ touch heart
To the Divinity, the Daughter of the Light, I bow.

aṅga nyāsa
establishment in the body

ॐ हृदयाय नमः

oṁ hṛdayāya namaḥ touch heart
Oṁ in the heart, I bow.

ॐ भूः शिरसे स्वाहा

oṁ bhūḥ śirase svāhā top of head
Oṁ Gross Perception on the top of the head, I am One with God!

ॐ भुवः शिखायै वषट्

oṁ bhuvaḥ śikhāyai vaṣaṭ back of head
Oṁ Subtle Perception on the back of the head, Purify!

ॐ स्वः कवचाय हुं

oṁ svaḥ kavacāya huṁ cross both arms
Oṁ Intuitive Perception crossing both arms, Cut the Ego!

ॐ भूर्भुवः स्वः नेत्रत्रयाय वौषट्

oṁ bhūrbhuvaḥ svaḥ netratrayāya vauṣaṭ touch three eyes
Oṁ Gross Perception, Subtle Perception, Intuitive Perception in the three eyes, Ultimate Purity!

ॐ भूर्भुवः स्वः करतल कर पृष्ठाभ्यां अस्त्राय फट्

oṁ bhūrbhuvaḥ svaḥ karatal kar pṛṣṭābhyāṁ astrāya phaṭ
Oṁ I bow to Gross Perception, Subtle Perception, Intuitive Perception with the weapon of Virtue.
roll hand over hand front and back and clap

ॐ भूः हृदयाय नमः

oṁ bhūḥ hṛdayāya namaḥ touch heart

Oṁ Gross Perception in the heart, I bow.

ॐ भुवः शिरसे स्वाहा

oṁ bhuvaḥ śirase svāhā top of head

Oṁ Subtle Perception on the top of the head, I am One with God!

ॐ स्वः शिखायै वषट्

oṁ svaḥ śikhāyai vaṣaṭ back of head

Oṁ Intuitive Perception on the back of the head, Purify!

ॐ तत् सवितुर्वरेण्यम् कवचाय हुं

oṁ tat saviturvareṇyam kavacāya huṁ cross both arms

Oṁ That Light of Wisdom that is the Supreme crossing both arms, Cut the Ego!

ॐ भर्गो देवस्य धीमहि नेत्रत्रयाय वौषट्

oṁ bhargo devasya dhīmahi netratrayāya vauṣaṭ touch three eyes

Oṁ Wealth of the Gods, we meditate in the three eyes, Ultimate Purify!

roll hand over hand front and back and clap saying:

ॐ धियो यो नः प्रचोदयात् ॐ करतल कर पृष्ठाभ्यां अस्त्राय फट्

oṁ dhiyo yo naḥ pracodayāt oṁ karatal kar pṛṣṭābhyāṁ astrāya phaṭ

Oṁ May it grant to us increase in our meditations with the weapon of Virtue.

ॐ तत् सवितुर्हृदयाय नमः

oṁ tat saviturhṛdayāya namaḥ touch heart
Oṁ That Light of Wisdom in the heart, I bow.

ॐ वरेण्यम् शिरसे स्वाहा

oṁ vareṇyam śirase svāhā top of head
Oṁ That is the Supreme on the top of the head, I am One with God!

ॐ भर्गो देवस्य शिखायै वषट्

oṁ bhargo devasya śikhāyai vaṣaṭ back of head
Oṁ Wealth of the Gods on the back of the head, Purify!

ॐ धीमहि कवचाय हुं

oṁ dhīmahi kavacāya huṁ cross both arms
Oṁ We meditate crossing both arms, Cut the Ego!

ॐ धियो योनः नेत्रत्रयाय वौषट्

oṁ dhiyo yo naḥ netratrayāya vauṣaṭ touch three eyes
Oṁ May it grant to us increase in Ultimate Purity in the three eyes

ॐ प्रचोदयात् ॐ करतलकरपृष्ठाभ्यां अस्त्राय फट्

oṁ pracodayāt oṁ karatal kar pṛṣṭhābhyāṁ astrāya phaṭ
Oṁ Increase in our meditations with the weapon of Virtue.
roll hand over hand front and back and clap

ॐ भूर्भुवः स्वः । तत् सवितुर्वरेण्यम् भर्गो देवस्य धीमहि
धियो योनः प्रचोदयात् ॐ ॥

oṁ bhūrbhuvaḥ svaḥ
tat saviturvareṇyam bhargo devasya dhīmahi
dhiyo yo naḥ pracodayāt oṁ
Oṁ the Infinite Beyond Conception, the gross body, the subtle body and the causal body; we meditate on that Light of Wisdom that is the Supreme Wealth of the Gods. May it grant to us increase in our meditations.

महेश-वदनोत्पन्ना विष्णोर्हृदय सम्भवा ।

ब्रह्मणा समनुज्ञाता गच्छ देवि यथेच्छया ॥

maheśa-vadanotpannā viṣṇorhṛdaya sambhavā
brahmaṇā samanujñātā gaccha devi yathecchayā

Arisen from Maheśvara, The Great Seer of All, residing in the heart of the Consciousness that Pervades All, equally in the Wisdom of the Creative Capacity, the Goddess moves according to Her desire.

ātmarakṣa

protection of the soul

ॐ जातवेदस ईत्यस्य काश्यप ऋषिस्त्रिष्टुप् छन्दोऽग्निर्देवता

आत्मरक्षायां जपे विनियोगः ।

oṁ jātavedasa ītyasya kāśyapa ṛṣistriṣṭup chando-gnirdevatā ātmarakṣāyāṁ jape viniyogaḥ

Oṁ the mantra beginning, "The Knower of All," etc., Kaśyapa is the Seer, Triṣṭup is the meter (44 syllables to the verse), Agni is the divinity, for the protection of the soul these mantras are applied in recitation.

ॐ जातवेदसे सुनवाम सोममरातीयतोनि दहाति वेदः ।

स नः पर्षदति दुर्गाणि विश्वा नावेव सिन्धुं दुरितात्यग्निः ॥

oṁ jātavedase sunavāma somam
arātīyatoni dahāti vedaḥ
sa naḥ parṣadati durgāṇi viśvā
nāveva sindhuṁ duritātyagniḥ

Oṁ We worship the Knower of All with the offering of Love and Devotion. May the God of Purity reduce all enmity in the universe to ashes, and as an excellent oarsman, may he steer our ship across the sea of pain and confusion to the shores of Liberation.

ॐ दुर्गे दुर्गे रक्षाणि हुं फट् स्वाहा ॥

oṁ durge durge rakṣāṇi huṁ phaṭ svāhā

Oṁ Reliever of Difficulties, Reliever of Difficulties, Protect us, Cut the Ego! Purify! I am One with God!

ॐ अं हुं फट् स्वाहा ॥

oṁ aṁ huṁ phaṭ svāhā
Oṁ Aṁ (Creation, Beginning) Cut the Ego! Purity! I am One with God!

rudropasthāna

the establishment of the reliever of sufferings

ॐ ऋतमित्यस्य कालाग्निरुद्र ऋषिरनुष्टुप् छन्दोरुद्रो देवता रुद्रोपस्थाने विनियोगः ।

oṁ ṛtamityasya kālāgnirudra ṛṣiranuṣṭup chandorudro devatā rudropasthāne viniyogaḥ
Oṁ "Whose sole form is the Entire Universe," the Reliever of Sufferings, Purifier of Time (or Purifier in Time) is the Seer, Anuṣṭup is the meter (32 syllables to the verse), the establishment of the Reliever of Sufferings is the application.

ॐ ऋतं सत्यं परं ब्रह्म पुरुषं कृष्णपिङ्गलम् ।
ऊर्द्ध्वरेतं विरूपाक्षं विश्वरूपं नमो नमः ॥

oṁ ṛtaṁ satyaṁ paraṁ brahmā puruṣaṁ kṛṣṇapiṅgalam ūrdvaretaṁ virūpākṣaṁ viśvarūpaṁ namo namaḥ
Oṁ The Supreme Consciousness whose sole form is the Entire Universe, and Infinite Wisdom and Truth, who, for the advancement of Devotion, assumes the form of Consciousness both male and female (Umā, Maheśvara: Consciousness and Nature); whose one half is dark and the other half light, whose semen rises up, and who is the form of the universe, with three eyes, to that Universal Form, again and again we bow down in devotion.

एते गन्धपुष्पे ॐ ब्रह्मणे नमः

ete gandhapuṣpe oṁ brahmaṇe namaḥ
With these scented flowers oṁ we bow to Creative Consciousness.

एते गन्धपुष्पे ॐ ब्राह्मणेभ्यो नमः

ete gandhapuṣpe oṁ brāhmaṇebhyo namaḥ
With these scented flowers oṁ we bow to the Knowers of Divine Wisdom.

एते गन्धपुष्पे ॐ आचार्येभ्यो नमः

ete gandhapuṣpe oṁ ācāryebhyo namaḥ

With these scented flowers oṁ we bow to the Teachers of Divine Wisdom.

एते गन्धपुष्पे ॐ ऋषिभ्यो नमः

ete gandhapuṣpe oṁ ṛṣibhyo namaḥ

With these scented flowers oṁ we bow to the Seers of Divine Wisdom.

एते गन्धपुष्पे ॐ देवेभ्यो नमः

ete gandhapuṣpe oṁ devebhyo namaḥ

With these scented flowers oṁ we bow to the Exemplifiers of Divine Wisdom.

एते गन्धपुष्पे ॐ वेदेभ्यो नमः

ete gandhapuṣpe oṁ vedebhyo namaḥ

With these scented flowers oṁ we bow to the Wisdom of Divine Wisdom.

एते गन्धपुष्पे ॐ वायवे नमः

ete gandhapuṣpe oṁ vāyave namaḥ

With these scented flowers oṁ we bow to Emancipation.

एते गन्धपुष्पे ॐ मृत्यवे नमः

ete gandhapuṣpe oṁ mṛtyave namaḥ

With these scented flowers oṁ we bow to Transformation (moving beyond, death).

एते गन्धपुष्पे ॐ विष्णवे नमः

ete gandhapuṣpe oṁ viṣṇave namaḥ

With these scented flowers oṁ we bow to That which Pervades All.

एते गन्धपुष्पे ॐ वैश्रवणाय नमः

ete gandhapuṣpe oṁ vaiśravaṇāya namaḥ
With these scented flowers oṁ we bow to the Universal Being.

एते गन्धपुष्पे ॐ उपजाय नमः

ete gandhapuṣpe oṁ upajāya namaḥ
With these scented flowers oṁ we bow to The Cause of All.

ॐ भूर्भुवः स्वः । तत् सवितुर्वरेण्यम् भर्गो देवस्य धीमहि ।
धियो यो नः प्रचोदयात् ॐ ॥

oṁ bhūrbhuvaḥ svaḥ tat saviturvareṇyam bhargo devasya dhīmahi dhiyo yo naḥ pracodayāt oṁ
Oṁ the Infinite Beyond Conception, the gross body, the subtle body and the causal body; we meditate on that Light of Wisdom that is the Supreme Wealth of the Gods. May it grant to us increase in our meditations.

kumārī pūjā
worship of the ever pure one

ॐ कुमारीमृग्वेदयुतां ब्रह्मरूपां विचिन्तायेत् ।
हंसस्थितां कुशहस्तां सूर्यमण्डल संस्थितां ॥

oṁ kumārīmṛgvedayutāṁ brahmarūpāṁ vicintāyet
haṁsasthitāṁ kuśahastāṁ sūryamaṇḍala saṁsthitāṁ
Oṁ We contemplate the Goddess of Purity, embodiment of the Ṛg Veda, the form of Supreme Divinity. Situated upon the swan, with kuśa grass in Her hand, She is situated in the regions of the sun.

ॐ कुमारीं कमलारुढां त्रिनेत्रां चन्द्रशेखराम् ।
तप्तकाञ्चनवर्णाभां नानालङ्कार भूषिताम् ॥

oṁ kumārīṁ kamalāruḍhāṁ
trinetrām candraśekharām
taptakāñcaṇa varnabhāṁ nānālaṅkāra bhūṣitām
Oṁ Kumāri has an orange color with three eyes and the Moon on Her head. Of the color of melted gold, She displays various ornaments.

रक्ताम्बरपरीधानां रक्तमाल्याणुलेपनाम् ।
वामेनाभयदां ध्यायेद्दक्षिणेन वरप्रदाम् ॥

raktāmbāra parīdhanāṁ raktamālyāṇulepanām
vāmenābhayadāṁ dhyāyeddakṣiṇena varapradām
She wears a red cloth and a red mālā or garland. With Her left hand She gives us freedom from fear, and with Her right hand She grants boons.

ॐ सर्वाभीष्टप्रधे देवि सर्वापद्विनिवारिनि ।
सर्वशान्तिकरे देवि नमस्तेऽस्तु कुमारिके ॥

oṁ sarvabhīṣṭapradhe devi sarvāpadvinivārini
sarvaśānti kare devi namaste-stu kumārike
Oṁ Grant fulfillment of all desires, oh Goddess. Remove all obstacles. Cause all Peace, oh Goddess. We bow to you, to Kumāri.

ब्रह्मी महेश्वरी रौद्री रूप त्रितय धारिणि ।
अभयञ्च वरं देहि नारायणि नमोऽस्तु ते ॥

brahmī maheśvarī raudrī rūpa tritaya dhāriṇi
abhayañca varaṁ dehi nārāyaṇi namo-stu te
Creative Energy, the Energy of the Great Seer of All, the Energy of the Terrible One; She wears three forms. Give freedom from fear and boons; Exposer of Consciousness, we bow to you.

ॐ कौं कौमार्यै नमः

oṁ kauṁ kaumaryai namaḥ
Oṁ kauṁ we bow to the Goddess of Purity.

ॐ सावित्री विष्णुरूपाञ्च तार्क्ष्यस्थां पीतवाससिं ।
युवतीञ्च यजुर्वेद सूर्यमण्डल संस्थितां ॥

oṁ sāvitrī viṣṇurūpāñca tārkṣyasthāṁ pītavāsasiṁ
yuvatīñca yajurveda sūryamaṇḍala saṁsthitāṁ
Oṁ Goddess of Light in the form of Viṣṇu, radiating light of yellow color; appearing in a youthful form as the Yājur Veda, She is situated in the regions of the sun.

ॐ सरस्वती शिवरूपाञ्च वृद्धा वृषभ वहिनीं ।
सूर्यमण्डल मध्यस्थां सामवेद समायुतां ॥

oṁ sarasvatī śivarūpāñca vṛddhā vṛṣabha vahinīṁ
sūryamaṇḍala madhyasthāṁ sāmaveda samāyutāṁ

Oṁ Sarasvati is in the form of Śiva, appearing as an old woman riding upon a bull. Situated in the middle of the regions of the sun, She is united with the Sāma Veda.

gāyatrī saṁpūṭ

gāyatrī with oṁ before and after

ॐ भूर्भुवः स्वः ॐ तत् सवितुर्वरेण्यम् ॐ भर्गो देवस्य धीमहि ॐ धियो यो नः प्रचोदयात् ॐ ॥

oṁ bhūrbhuvaḥ svaḥ oṁ tat saviturvareṇyam oṁ bhargo devasya dhīmahi oṁ dhiyo yo naḥ pracodayāt oṁ

Oṁ the Infinite Beyond Conception, the gross body, the subtle body and the causal body; oṁ we meditate on that Light of Wisdom oṁ that is the Supreme Wealth of the Gods. Oṁ may it grant to us increase in our meditations.

ॐ भूर्भुवः स्वः तत् सवितुर्वरेण्यम् ॐ भर्गो देवस्य धीमहि ॐ धियो यो नः प्रचोदयात् ॐ ॥

oṁ bhūrbhuvaḥ svaḥ tat saviturvareṇyam oṁ bhargo devasya dhīmahi oṁ dhiyo yo naḥ pracodayāt oṁ

Oṁ the Infinite Beyond Conception, the gross body, the subtle body and the causal body; we meditate on that Light of Wisdom oṁ that is the Supreme Wealth of the Gods. Oṁ may it grant to us increase in our meditations oṁ.

ॐ भूर्भुवः स्वः तत् सवितुर्वरेण्यम् भर्गो देवस्य धीमहि ॐ धियो यो नः प्रचोदयात् ॐ ॥

oṁ bhūrbhuvaḥ svaḥ tat saviturvareṇyam bhargo devasya dhīmahi oṁ dhiyo yo naḥ pracodayāt oṁ

Oṁ the Infinite Beyond Conception, the gross body, the subtle body and the causal body; we meditate on that Light of Wisdom that is the Supreme Wealth of the Gods. Oṁ may it grant to us increase in our meditations oṁ.

ॐ भूर्भुवः स्वः तत् सवितुर्वरेण्यम् भर्गो देवस्य धीमहि
धियो यो नः प्रचोदयात् ॐ ॥

oṁ bhūrbhuvaḥ svaḥ
tat saviturvareṇyam bhargo devasya dhīmahi
dhiyo yo naḥ pracodayāt oṁ

Oṁ the Infinite Beyond Conception, the gross body, the subtle body and the causal body; aie meditate upon that Light of Wisdom that is the Supreme Wealth of the Gods. May it grant to us increase in our meditations oṁ.

आगच्छ वरदे देवि जप्ये मे सन्निधा भव ।
गायन्तं त्रायसे यस्माद् गायत्री त्वमतः स्मृता ॥

āgaccha varade devi japye me sannidhā bhava
gāyaṇtaṁ trāyase yasmād gāyatrī tvamataḥ smṛtā

Come, granting boons, oh Goddess, and be situated in me while I continue meditation and prayer. The three forms of wisdom are remembered in you, Gāyatrī.

आयाहि वरदे देवि त्र्यक्षरे ब्रह्मवादिनि ।
गायत्री छन्दसां मातर्ब्रह्मयोनि नमोऽस्तु ते ॥

āyāhi varade devi tryakṣare brahmavādini
gāyatrī chandasāṁ mātarbrahmayoni namo-stu te

Come, granting boons, oh Goddess, the three letters of the word of the Supreme Divinity. Oh Mother, in the rhythm of Gāyatrī (24 syllables to the verse) we bow to you as the womb of creation.

sāmānyārghya

purification of water

Draw the yantra on the plate or space for worship with sandal paste and/or water. Offer rice on the yantra for each of the four mantras.

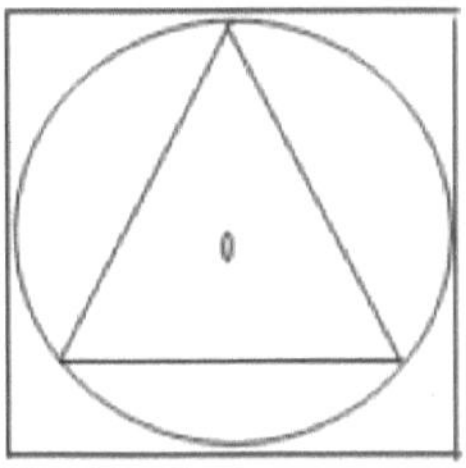

ॐ आधारशक्तये नमः

oṁ ādhāra śaktaye namaḥ

oṁ we bow to the Primal Energy

ॐ कूर्म्माय नमः

oṁ kūrmmāya namaḥ

oṁ we bow to the Support of the Earth

ॐ अनन्ताय नमः

oṁ anantāya namaḥ

oṁ we bow to Infinity

ॐ पृथिव्यै नमः

oṁ pṛthivyai namaḥ

oṁ we bow to the Earth

Place an empty water pot on the bindu in the center of the yantra when saying Phaṭ.

स्थां स्थीं स्थिरो भव फट्

sthāṁ sthīṁ sthiro bhava phaṭ

Be Still in the Gross Body! Be Still in the Subtle Body! Be Still in the Causal Body! Purify!

Fill the pot with water while chanting the mantra.

ॐ गङ्गे च जमुने चैव गोदावरि सरस्वति ।

नर्मदे सिन्धु कावेरि जलऽस्मिन् सन्निधिं कुरु ॥

oṁ gaṅge ca jamune caiva godāvari sarasvati
narmade sindhu kāveri jale-asmin sannidhiṁ kuru

oṁ the Ganges, Jamunā, Godāvarī, Sarasvatī, Narmadā, Sindhu, Kāverī, these waters are mingled together.

The Ganges is the Iḍā, Jamunā is the Piṅgalā, the other five rivers are the five senses. The land of the seven rivers is within the body as well as outside.

Offer Tulasī leaves into water

ॐ ऐं ह्रीं क्लीं श्रीं वृन्दावनवासिन्यै स्वाहा

oṁ aiṁ hrīṁ klīṁ śrīṁ vṛndāvanavāsinyai svāhā

oṁ Wisdom, Māyā, Increase, to She who resides in Vṛndāvana, I am One with God!

Offer 3 flowers into the water pot with the mantras

एते गन्धपुष्पे ॐ अं अर्कमण्डलाय द्वादशकलात्मने नमः

ete gandhapuṣpe oṁ aṁ arkamaṇḍalāya dvādaśakalātmane namaḥ

With these scented flowers oṁ "A" we bow to the twelve aspects of the realm of the sun. Tapinī, Tāpinī, Dhūmrā, Marīci, Jvālinī, Ruci, Sudhūmrā, Bhoga-dā, Viśvā, Bodhinī, Dhārinī, Kṣamā; Containing heat, Emanating heat, Smoky, Ray-producing, Burning, Lustrous, Purple or Smoky-red, Granting enjoyment, Universal, Which makes known, Productive of Consciousness, Which supports, Which forgives.

एते गन्धपुष्पे ॐ उं सोममण्डलाय षोडशकलात्मने नमः

ete gandhapuṣpe oṁ uṁ somamaṇḍalāya ṣoḍaśakalātmane namaḥ

With these scented flowers oṁ "U" we bow to the sixteen aspects of the realm of the moon. Amṛtā, Prāṇadā, Puṣā, Tuṣṭi, Puṣṭi, Rati, Dhṛti, Śaśinī, Candrikā, Kānti, Jyotsnā, Śrī, Prīti, Aṅgadā, Pūrṇā, Pūrṇāmṛtā; Nectar, Which sustains life, Which supports, Satisfying, Nourishing, Playful, Constancy, Unfailing, Producer of Joy, Beauty enhanced by love, Light, Grantor of Prosperity, Affectionate, Purifying the body, Complete, Full of Bliss.

एते गन्धपुष्पे ॐ मं वह्निमण्डलाय दशकलात्मने नमः

ete gandhapuṣpe oṁ maṁ vahnimaṇḍalāya daśakalātmane namaḥ

With these scented flowers oṁ "M" we bow to the ten aspects of the realm of fire: Dhūmrā, Arciḥ, Jvalinī, Śūkṣmā, Jvālinī, Visphuliṅginī, Suśrī, Surūpā, Kapilā, Havya-Kavya-Vahā; Smoky Red, Flaming, Shining, Subtle, Burning, Sparkling, Beautiful, Well-formed, Tawny, The Messenger to Gods and Ancestors.

ॐ ह्रीं श्रीं दुं दुर्गायै नमः

oṁ hrīṁ śrīṁ duṁ durgāyai namaḥ

Oṁ I bow to the Goddess, Durgā, the Grantor of Increase, who Removes all Difficulties.

Wave hands in matsyā, dhenu and aṅkuśa mudrās while chanting this mantra.

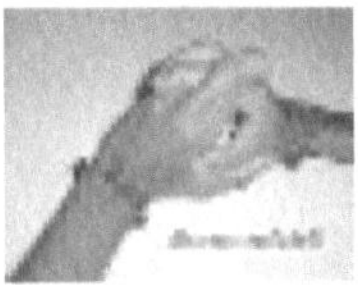

ॐ गङ्गे च जमुने चैव गोदावरि सरस्वति ।
नर्मदे सिन्धु कावेरि जलेऽस्मिन् सन्निधिं कुरु ॥

oṁ gaṅge ca jamune caiva godāvari sarasvati
narmade sindhu kāveri jale-asmin sannidhiṁ kuru

oṁ the Ganges, Jamunā, Godāvarī, Sarasvatī, Narmadā, Sindhu, Kāverī, these waters are mingled together.

ॐ ह्रीं श्रीं दुं दुर्गायै नमः

oṁ hrīṁ śrīṁ duṁ durgāyai namaḥ

Oṁ I bow to the Goddess, Durgā, the Grantor of Increase, who Removes all Difficulties.

Sprinkle water over all articles to be offered, then throw some drops of water over your shoulders while repeating the mantra.

अमृताम् कुरु स्वाहा

amṛtām kuru svāhā

Make this immortal nectar! I am One with God!

puṣpa śuddhi

purification of flowers

Wave hands over flowers with prārthanā mudrā while chanting first line, and with dhenu mudrā while chanting second line of this mantra.

ॐ पुष्प पुष्प महापुष्प सुपुष्प पुष्पसम्भवे ।
पुष्पचयावकीर्णे च हुं फट् स्वाहा ॥

oṁ puṣpa puṣpa mahāpuṣpa
supuṣpa puṣpa sambhave
puṣpa cayāvakīrṇe ca huṁ phaṭ svāhā

oṁ Flowers, flowers, Oh Great Flowers, excellent flowers; flowers in heaps and scattered about, cut the ego, purify, I am One with God!

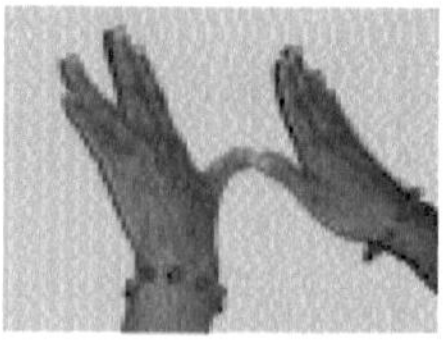

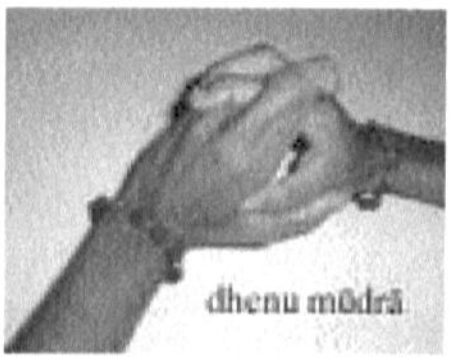

kara śuddhi

purification of hands

ॐ ऐं रं अस्त्राय फट्

oṁ aiṁ raṁ astrāya phaṭ

oṁ Wisdom, the divine fire, with the weapon, Purify !

kalaśa sthāpan

establishment of the pot

touch earth

ॐ भूरसि भूमिरस्यदितिरसि

विश्वधारा विश्वस्य भुवनस्य धर्त्री ।

पृथिवीं यच्छ पृथिवीं दृंह पृथिवीं मा हिंसीः ॥

oṁ bhūrasi bhūmirasyaditirasi viśvadhārā
viśvasya bhuvanasya dhartrī
pṛthivīṁ yaccha pṛthivīṁ dṛṁha pṛthivīṁ mā hiṁsīḥ

You are the object of sensory perception; you are the Goddess who distributes the forms of the earth. You are the Producer of the Universe, the Support of all existing things in the universe. Control (or sustain) the earth, firmly establish the earth, make the earth efficient in its motion.

give rice

ॐ धान्यमसि धिनुहि देवान् धिनुहि यज्ञं ।

धिनुहि यज्ञपतिं धिनुहि मां यज्ञन्यम् ॥

oṁ dhānyamasi dhinuhi devān dhinuhi yajñaṁ
dhinuhi yajñapatiṁ dhinuhi māṁ yajñanyam

You are the grains which satisfy and gladden the Gods, gladden the sacrifice, gladden the Lord of Sacrifice. Bring satisfaction to us through sacrifice.

place pot

ॐ आजिघ्र कलशं मह्या त्वा विशन्त्विन्दवः ।

पुनरूर्जा निवर्त्तस्व सा नः सहस्रं धुक्ष्वोरुधारा पयस्वतीः

पुनर्मा विशताद्रयिः ॥

oṁ ājigghra kalaśaṁ mahyā tvā viśantvindavaḥ
punarūrjā nivarttasva sā naḥ sahasraṁ dhukṣvorudhārā
payasvatīḥ punarmā viśatādrayiḥ

Cause the effulgent fire of perception to enter into your highly honored container for renewed nourishment. Remaining there, let it increase in thousands, so that upon removal, abounding in spotlessly pure strength, it may come flowing into us.

pour water

ॐ वरुणस्योत्तम्भनमसि वरुणस्य स्कम्भसर्जनी स्थो ।
वरुणस्य ऋतसदन्यसि । वरुणस्य ऋतसदनमसि ।
वरुणस्य ऋतसदनमासीद ॥

oṁ varuṇasyottambhanamasi varuṇasya skambhasarjanī stho
varuṇasya ṛtasadanyasi varuṇasya ṛtasadanamasi varuṇasya ṛtasadanamāsīda

You, Waters, are declared the Ultimate of waters established in all creation begotten, abiding in waters as the eternal law of truth; always abiding in waters as the eternal law of truth, and forever abiding in waters as the eternal law of truth.

place wealth

ॐ धन्वना गा धन्वनाजिं जयेम
धन्वना तीव्राः समद्रो जयेम ।
धनुः शत्रोरपकामं कृणोति धन्वना सर्वाः प्रदिशो जयेम ॥

oṁ dhanvanā gā dhanvanājiṁ jayema
dhanvanā tīvrāḥ samadro jayema
dhanuḥ śatrorapakāmaṁ kṛṇoti
dhanvanā sarvāḥ pradiśo jayema

Let wealth, even abundance, be victorious. Let wealth be sufficient as to be victorious over the severe ocean of existence. As a bow to protect us safe from the enemies of desire, let it be victorious to illuminate all.

place fruit

ॐ याः फलिनीर्याऽअफलाऽअपुष्पा याश्च पुष्पिणीः ।
बृहस्पतिप्रसूतास्ता नो मुञ्चन्त्वंहसः ॥

oṁ yāḥ phalinīryā-aphalā-apuṣpā yāśca puṣpiṇīḥ
bṛhaspatiprasūtāstā no muñcantvaṁhasaḥ

That which bears fruit, and that which bears no fruit; that without flowers and that with flowers as well. To we who exist born of the Lord of the Vast, set us FREE! ALL THIS IS GOD!

red powder

ॐ सिन्धोरिव प्राध्वने शूघनासो वातप्रमियः पतयन्ति यह्वाः । घृतस्य धारा अरुषो न वाजी काष्ठा भिन्दन्नूर्मिभिः पिन्वमानः ॥

oṁ sindhoriva prādhvane śūghanāso vātapramiyaḥ patayanti yahvāḥ ghṛtasya dhārā aruṣo na vājī kāṣṭhā bhindannūrmibhiḥ pinvamānaḥ

The pious mark of red vermilion symbolizing the ocean of love placed prominently upon the head above the nose bursting forth, allows the vibrance of youth to fly. As the stream of ghee pours into the flames, those spirited steeds of the Divine Fire consume the logs of wood increasing the will and self-reliance of the worshiper.

ॐ सिन्दूरमरुणाभासं जपाकुसुमसन्निभम् ।
पूजिताऽसि मया देवि प्रसीद परमेश्वरि ॥
ॐ ह्रीं श्रीं दुं दुर्गायै नमः सिन्दूरं समर्पयामि

oṁ sindūramaruṇābhāsaṁ japākusumasannibham pūjitā-si mayā devi prasīda parameśvari oṁ hrīṁ śrīṁ duṁ durgāyai namaḥ sindūraṁ samarpayāmi

This red colored powder indicates Love, who drives the chariot of the Light of Wisdom, with which we are worshiping our Lord. Please be pleased, Oh Great Seer of All. With this offering of red colored powder Oṁ I bow to the Goddess, Durgā, the Grantor of Increase, who Removes all Difficulties.

kuṅkum

ॐ कुङ्कुमं कान्तिदं दिव्यं कामिनीकामसम्भवम् ।
कुङ्कुमेनाऽर्चिते देवि प्रसीद परमेश्वरि ॥
ॐ ह्रीं श्रीं दुं दुर्गायै नमः कुङ्कुमं समर्पयामि

oṁ kuṅkumaṁ kāntidaṁ divyaṁ
kāminī kāmasambhavam
kuṅkumenā-rcite devi prasīda parameśvari
oṁ hrīṁ śrīṁ duṁ durgāyai namaḥ kuṅkumaṁ samarpayāmi

You are being adorned with this divine red powder, which is made more beautiful by the love we share with you, and is so pleasing. Oh Lord, when we present this red powder be pleased, Oh Supreme Ruler of All. With this offering of red colored powder Oṁ I bow to the Goddess, Durgā, the Grantor of Increase, who Removes all Difficulties.

sandal paste

ॐ श्रीखण्डचन्दनं दिव्यं गन्धाढ्यं सुमनोहरम् ।
विलेपनं च देवेशि चन्दनं प्रतिगृह्यताम् ॥
ॐ ह्रीं श्रीं दुं दुर्गायै नमः चन्दनं समर्पयामि

oṁ śrīkhaṇḍacandanaṁ divyaṁ
gandhāḍhyaṁ sumano haram
vilepanaṁ ca deveśi candanaṁ pratigṛhyatām
oṁ hrīṁ śrīṁ duṁ durgāyai namaḥ candanaṁ samarpayāmi

You are being adorned with this beautiful divine piece of sandal wood, ground to a paste which is so pleasing. Please accept this offering of sandal paste, Oh Supreme Sovereign of all the Gods. With the offering of sandal paste Oṁ I bow to the Goddess, Durgā, the Grantor of Increase, who Removes all Difficulties.

turmeric

ॐ हरिद्रारञ्जिता देवि सुख-सौभाग्यदायिनि ।

तस्मात्त्वं पूजयाम्यत्र दुःखशान्तिं प्रयच्छ मे ॥

ॐ ह्रीं श्रीं दुं दुर्गायै नमः हरिद्रां समर्पयामि

oṁ haridrārañjitā devi sukha saubhāgyadāyini
tasmāttvaṁ pūjayāmyatra duḥkha śāntiṁ prayaccha me
oṁ hrīṁ śrīṁ duṁ durgāyai namaḥ haridrāṁ samarpayāmi

Oh Lord, you are being gratified by this turmeric, the giver of comfort and beauty. When you are worshiped like this, then you must bestow upon us the greatest peace. With the offering of turmeric Oṁ I bow to the Goddess, Durgā, the Grantor of Increase, who Removes all Difficulties.

milk bath

ॐ कामधेनुसमुद्भूतं सर्वेषां जीवनं परम् ।

पावनं यज्ञहेतुश्च स्नानार्थं प्रतिगृह्यताम् ॥

ॐ ह्रीं श्रीं दुं दुर्गायै नमः पयस्नानं समर्पयामि

oṁ kāmadhenu samudbhūtaṁ sarveṣāṁ jīvanaṁ param
pāvanaṁ yajña hetuśca snānārthaṁ pratigṛhyatām
oṁ hrīṁ śrīṁ duṁ durgāyai namaḥ paya snānaṁ samarpayāmi

Coming from the ocean of being, the Fulfiller of all Desires, Grantor of Supreme Bliss to all souls. For the motive of purifying or sanctifying this holy union, we request you to accept this bath. With this offering of milk for your bath Oṁ I bow to the Goddess, Durgā, the Grantor of Increase, who Removes all Difficulties.

yogurt bath

ॐ पयसस्तु समुद्भूतं मधुराम्लं शशिप्रभम् ।

दध्यानितं मया दत्तं स्नानार्थं प्रतिगृह्यताम् ॥

ॐ ह्रीं श्रीं दुं दुर्गायै नमः दधिस्नानं समर्पयामि

oṁ payasastu samudbhūtaṁ madhurāmlaṁ śaśiprabham
dadhyānitaṁ mayā dattaṁ snānārthaṁ pratigṛhyatām
oṁ hrīṁ śrīṁ duṁ durgāyai namaḥ dadhi snānaṁ samarpayāmi

Derived from milk from the ocean of being, sweet and pleasing like the glow of the moon, let these curds eternally be our ambassador, as we request you to accept this bath. With this offering of yogurt for your bath Oṁ I bow to the Goddess, Durgā, the Grantor of Increase, who Removes all Difficulties.

ghee bath

ॐ नवनीतसमुत्पन्नं सर्वसन्तोषकारकम् ।
घृतं तुभ्यं प्रदास्यामि स्नानार्थं प्रतिगृह्यताम् ॥
ॐ ह्रीं श्रीं दुं दुर्गायै नमः घृतस्नानं समर्पयामि

oṁ navanīta samutpannaṁ sarvasantoṣakārakam
ghṛtaṁ tubhyaṁ pradāsyāmi snānārthaṁ pratigṛhyatām
oṁ hrīṁ śrīṁ duṁ durgāyai namaḥ ghṛta snānaṁ samarpayāmi

Freshly prepared from the ocean of being, causing all fulfillment, we offer this delightful ghee (clarified butter) and request you to accept this bath. With this offering of ghee for your bath Oṁ I bow to the Goddess, Durgā, the Grantor of Increase, who Removes all Difficulties.

honey bath

ॐ तरुपुष्पसमुद्भूतं सुस्वादु मधुरं मधु ।
तेजोपुष्टिकरं दिव्यं स्नानार्थं प्रतिगृह्यताम् ॥
ॐ ह्रीं श्रीं दुं दुर्गायै नमः मधुस्नानं समर्पयामि

oṁ tarupuṣpa samudbhūtam susvādu madhuraṁ madhu
tejo puṣṭikaraṁ divyaṁ snānārtham pratigṛhyatām
oṁ hrīṁ śrīṁ duṁ durgāyai namaḥ madhu snānaṁ samarpayāmi

Prepared from flowers of the ocean of being, enjoyable as the sweetest of the sweet, causing the fire of divine nourishment to burn swiftly, we request you to accept this bath. With this offering of honey for your bath Oṁ I bow to the Goddess, Durgā, the Grantor of Increase, who Removes all Difficulties.

sugar bath

ॐ इक्षुसारसमुद्भूता शर्करा पुष्टिकारिका ।

मलापहारिका दिव्या स्नानार्थं प्रतिगृह्यताम् ॥

ॐ ह्रीं श्रीं दुं दुर्गायै नमः शर्करास्नानं समर्पयामि

oṁ ikṣusāra samudbhūtā śarkarā puṣṭikārikā
malāpahārikā divyā snānārthaṁ pratigṛhyatām
oṁ hrīṁ śrīṁ duṁ durgāyai namaḥ śarkarā snānaṁ samarpayāmi

From the lake of sugar-cane, from the ocean of being, which causes the nourishment of sugar to give divine protection from all impurity, we request you to accept this bath. With this offering of sugar for your bath Oṁ I bow to the Goddess, Durgā, the Grantor of Increase, who Removes all Difficulties.

five nectars bath

ॐ पयो दधि घृतं चैव मधु च शर्करायुतम् ।

पञ्चामृतं मयाऽऽनीतं स्नानार्थं प्रतिगृह्यताम् ॥

ॐ ह्रीं श्रीं दुं दुर्गायै नमः पञ्चामृतस्नानं समर्पयामि

oṁ payo dadhi ghṛtaṁ caiva madhu ca śarkarāyutam
pañcāmṛtaṁ mayā--nītaṁ snānārthaṁ pratigṛhyatām
oṁ hrīṁ śrīṁ duṁ durgāyai namaḥ pañcāmṛta snānaṁ samarpayāmi

Milk, curd, ghee and then honey and sugar mixed together; these five nectars are our ambassador, as we request you to accept this bath. With this offering of five nectars for your bath Oṁ I bow to the Goddess, Durgā, the Grantor of Increase, who Removes all Difficulties.

scented oil

ॐ नानासुगन्धिद्रव्यं च चन्दनं रजनीयुतम् ।

उद्वर्तनं मया दत्तं स्नानार्थं प्रतिगृह्यताम् ॥

ॐ ह्रीं श्रीं दुं दुर्गायै नमः उद्वर्तनस्नानं समर्पयामि

oṁ nānāsugandhidravyaṁ ca candanaṁ rajanīyutam
udvartanaṁ mayā dattaṁ snānārthaṁ pratigṛhyatām
oṁ hrīṁ śrīṁ duṁ durgāyai namaḥ udvartana snānaṁ samarpayāmi

oṁ With various beautifully smelling ingredients, as well as the scent of sandal, we offer you this scented oil, Oh Lord. With this offering of scented oil Oṁ I bow to the Goddess, Durgā, the Grantor of Increase, who Removes all Difficulties.

scent bath

गन्धद्वारां दुराधर्षां नित्यपुष्टां करीषिणीम् ।
ईश्वरीं सर्वभूतानां तामिहोपह्वये श्रियम् ॥
ॐ ह्रीं श्रीं दुं दुर्गायै नमः गन्धस्नानं समर्पयामि

gandhadvārāṁ durādharṣāṁ nityapuṣṭāṁ karīṣiṇīm
īśvarīṁ sarvabhūtānāṁ tāmihopahvaye śriyam
oṁ hrīṁ śrīṁ duṁ durgāyai namaḥ gandha snānaṁ samarpayāmi

She is the cause of the scent which is the door to religious ecstasy, unconquerable (never-failing), continually nurturing for all time. May we never tire from calling that manifestation of the Highest Respect, the Supreme Goddess of all existence. With this offering of scented bath Oṁ I bow to the Goddess, Durgā, the Grantor of Increase, who Removes all Difficulties.

water bath

ॐ गङ्गे च जमुने चैव गोदावरि सरस्वति ।
नर्मदे सिन्धु कावेरि स्नानार्थं प्रतिगृह्यताम् ॥
ॐ ह्रीं श्रीं दुं दुर्गायै नमः गङ्गास्नानं समर्पयामि

oṁ gaṅge ca jamune caiva godāvari sarasvati
narmade sindhu kāveri snānārthaṁ pratigṛhyatām
oṁ hrīṁ śrīṁ duṁ durgāyai namaḥ gaṅgā snānaṁ samarpayāmi

Please accept the waters from the Gaṅges, the Jamunā, Godāvarī, Sarasvatī, Narmadā, Sindhu and Kāverī, which have been provided for your bath. With this offering of Ganges bath waters Oṁ I bow to the Goddess, Durgā, the Grantor of Increase, who Removes all Difficulties.

cloth

ॐ शीतवातोष्णसंत्राणं लज्जायै रक्षणं परं ।

देहालंकरणं वस्त्रं अथ शान्तिं प्रयच्छ मे ॥

ॐ ह्रीं श्रीं दुं दुर्गायै नमः वस्त्रं समर्पयामि

oṁ śīta vātoṣṇa saṁ trāṇaṁ lajjāyai rakṣaṇaṁ paraṁ
dehālaṅkaraṇaṁ vastraṁ atha śāntiṁ prayaccha me
oṁ hrīṁ śrīṁ duṁ durgāyai namaḥ vastraṁ samarpayāmi

To take away the cold and the wind and to fully protect your modesty, we adorn your body with this cloth, and thereby find the greatest Peace. With this offering of wearing apparel Oṁ I bow to the Goddess, Durgā, the Grantor of Increase, who Removes all Difficulties.

sacred thread

ॐ यज्ञोपवीतं परमं पवित्रं प्रजापतेर्यत् सहजं पुरस्तात् ।

आयुष्यमग्रं प्रतिमुञ्च शुभ्रं यज्ञोपवीतं बलमस्तु तेजः ॥

oṁ yajñopavītaṁ paramaṁ pavitraṁ
prajāpateryat sahajaṁ purastāt
āyuṣyamagraṁ pratimuñca śubhraṁ
yajñopavītaṁ balamastu tejaḥ

Oṁ the sacred thread of the highest purity is given by Prajāpati, the Lord of Creation, for the greatest facility. You bring life and illuminate the greatness of liberation. Oh sacred thread, let your strength be of radiant light.

शमो दमस्तपः शौचं क्षान्तिरार्जवमेव च ।

ज्ञानं विज्ञानमास्तिक्यं ब्रह्मकर्म स्वभावजम् ॥

śamo damastapaḥ śaucaṁ kṣāntirārjavameva ca
jñānaṁ vijñānamāstikyaṁ brahmakarma svabhāvajam

Peacefulness, self-control, austerity, purity of mind and body, patience and forgiveness, sincerity and honesty, wisdom, knowledge, and self-realization, are the natural activities of a Brahmaṇa.

नवभिस्तन्तुभिर्युक्तं त्रिगुणं देवतामयं ।

उपवीतं मया दत्तं गृहाण त्वं सुरेश्वरि ॥

ॐ ह्रीं श्रीं दुं दुर्गायै नमः यज्ञोपवीतं समर्पयामि

navamiṣṭantubhiryuktaṁ triguṇaṁ devatā mayaṁ
upavītaṁ mayā dattaṁ gṛhāṇa tvaṁ sureśvari
oṁ hrīṁ śrīṁ duṁ durgāyai namaḥ yajñopavītaṁ samarpayāmi

With nine desirable threads all united together, exemplifying the three guṇas (or three qualities of harmony of our deity), this sacred thread will be our ambassador. Oh Ruler of the Gods, please accept. With this offering of a sacred thread Oṁ I bow to the Goddess, Durgā, the Grantor of Increase, who Removes all Difficulties.

rudrākṣa

त्र्यम्बकं यजामहे सुगन्धिं पुष्टिवर्द्धनम् ।

उर्व्वारुकमिव बन्धनान्मृत्योर्म्मुक्षीयमामृतात् ॥

ॐ ह्रीं श्रीं दुं दुर्गायै नमः रुद्राक्षं समर्पयामि

tryambakaṁ yajāmahe sugandhiṁ puṣṭivarddhanam
urvvārukamiva bandhanānmṛtyormmukṣīyamāmṛtāt
oṁ hrīṁ śrīṁ duṁ durgāyai namaḥ rudrākṣaṁ samarpayāmi

We adore the Father of the three worlds, of excellent fame, Grantor of Increase. As a cucumber is released from its bondage to the stem, so may we be freed from Death to dwell in immortality. With this offering of rudrākṣa Oṁ I bow to the Goddess, Durgā, the Grantor of Increase, who Removes all Difficulties.

mālā

ॐ मां माले महामाये सर्वशक्तिस्वरूपिणि ।

चतुर्वर्गस्त्वयि न्यस्तस्तस्मान्मे सिद्धिदा भव ॥

ॐ ह्रीं श्रीं दुं दुर्गायै नमः मालां समर्पयामि

oṁ māṁ māle mahāmāye sarvaśaktisvarūpiṇi
caturvargastvayi nyastastasmānme siddhidā bhava
oṁ hrīṁ śrīṁ duṁ durgāyai namaḥ mālāṁ samarpayāmi

Oṁ my rosary, the Great Limitation of Consciousness, containing all energy within as your intrinsic nature, fulfilling the four desires of men, give us the attainment of your perfection. With this offering of a mālā Oṁ I bow to the Goddess, Durgā, the Grantor of Increase, who Removes all Difficulties.

rice

अक्षतान् निर्मलान् शुद्धान् मुक्ताफलसमन्वितान् ।
गृहाणेमान् महादेवि देहि मे निर्मलां धियम् ॥
ॐ ह्रीं श्रीं दुं दुर्गायै नमः अक्षतान् समर्पयामि

akṣatān nirmalān śuddhān muktāphalasamanvitān
gṛhāṇemān mahādevi dehi me nirmalāṁ dhiyam
oṁ hrīṁ śrīṁ duṁ durgāyai namaḥ akṣatān samarpayāmi

Oh Great Lord, please accept these grains of rice, spotlessly clean, bestowing the fruit of liberation, and give us a spotlessly clean mind. With the offering of grains of rice Oṁ I bow to the Goddess, Durgā, the Grantor of Increase, who Removes all Difficulties.

flower garland

शङ्ख-पद्मजपुष्पादि शतपत्रैर्विचित्रताम् ।
पुष्पमालां प्रयच्छामि गृहाण त्वं सुरेश्वरि ॥
ॐ ह्रीं श्रीं दुं दुर्गायै नमः पुष्पमालां समर्पयामि

śaṅkha-padma japuṣpādi śatapatrairvicitratām
puṣpamālāṁ prayacchāmi gṛhāṇa tvaṁ sureśvari
oṁ hrīṁ śrīṁ duṁ durgāyai namaḥ puṣpamālāṁ samarpayāmi

We offer you this garland of flowers with spiraling lotuses, other flowers and leaves. Be pleased to accept it, Oh Ruler of All Gods. With the offering of a garland of flowers Oṁ I bow to the Goddess, Durgā, the Grantor of Increase, who Removes all Difficulties.

flower

मल्लिकादि सुगन्धीनि मालित्यादीनि वै प्रभो ।

मयाऽहृतानि पूजार्थं पुष्पाणि प्रतिगृह्यताम् ॥

ॐ ह्रीं श्रीं दुं दुर्गायै नमः पुष्पम् समर्पयामि

mallikādi sugandhīni mālityādīni vai prabho
mayā-hṛtāni pūjārthaṁ puṣpāṇi pratigṛhyatām
oṁ hrīṁ śrīṁ duṁ durgāyai namaḥ puṣpam samarpayāmi

Various flowers such as mallikā and others of excellent scent, are being offered to you, our Lord. All these flowers have come from the devotion of our hearts for your worship. Be pleased to accept them. With the offering of flowers Oṁ I bow to the Goddess, Durgā, the Grantor of Increase, who Removes all Difficulties.

sthirī karaṇa

establishment of stillness

ॐ सर्वतीर्थमयं वारि सर्वदेवसमन्वितम् ।

इमं घटं समागच्छ तिष्ठ देवगणैः सह ॥

oṁ sarvatīrthamayaṁ vāri sarvadevasamanvitam
imaṁ ghaṭaṁ samāgaccha tiṣṭha devagaṇaiḥ saha

All the places of pilgrimage as well as all of the Gods, all are placed within this container. Oh Multitude of Gods, be established within!

lelihānā mudrā

(literally, sticking out or pointing)

स्थां स्थीं स्थिरो भव वीड्वङ्ग आशुर्भव वाज्यर्वन् ।

पृथुर्भव सुषदस्त्वमग्नेः पुरीषवाहनः ॥

sthāṁ sthīṁ sthiro bhava
vīḍvaṅga āśurbhava vājyarvan
pṛthurbhava suṣadastvamagneḥ purīṣavāhanaḥ

Be Still in the Gross Body! Be Still in the Subtle Body! Be Still in the Causal Body! Quickly taking in this energy and shining forth as the Holder of Wealth, oh Divine Fire, becoming abundant, destroy the current of rubbish from the face of this earth.

prāṇa pratiṣṭhā
establishment of life

ॐ अं आं ह्रीं क्रों यं रं लं वं शं षं सं हों हं सः

oṁ aṁ āṁ hrīṁ kroṁ yaṁ raṁ laṁ vaṁ śaṁ ṣaṁ saṁ hoṁ haṁ saḥ

oṁ The Infinite Beyond Conception, Creation (the first letter), Consciousness, Māyā, the cause of the movement of the subtle body to perfection and beyond; the path of fulfillment: control, subtle illumination, one with the earth, emancipation, the soul of peace, the soul of delight, the soul of unity (all this is I), perfection, Infinite Consciousness, this is I.

ॐ ह्रीं श्रीं दुं दुर्गायै नमः प्राणा इह प्राणाः

oṁ hrīṁ śrīṁ duṁ durgāyai namaḥ prāṇā iha prāṇāḥ

Oṁ I bow to the Goddess, Durgā, the Grantor of Increase, who Removes all Difficulties. You are the life of this life!

ॐ अं आं ह्रीं क्रों यं रं लं वं शं षं सं हों हं सः

oṁ aṁ āṁ hrīṁ kroṁ yaṁ raṁ laṁ vaṁ śaṁ ṣaṁ saṁ hoṁ haṁ saḥ

oṁ The Infinite Beyond Conception, Creation (the first letter), Consciousness, Māyā, the cause of the movement of the subtle body to perfection and beyond; the path of fulfillment: control, subtle illumination, one with the earth, emancipation, the soul of peace, the soul of delight, the soul of unity (all this is I), perfection, Infinite Consciousness, this is I.

ॐ ह्रीं श्रीं दुं दुर्गायै नमः जीव इह स्थितः

oṁ hrīṁ śrīṁ duṁ durgāyai namaḥ jīva iha sthitaḥ

Oṁ I bow to the Goddess, Durgā, the Grantor of Increase, who Removes all Difficulties. You are situated in this life (or individual consciousness).

ॐ अं आं ह्रीं क्रों यं रं लं वं शं षं सं हों हं सः

oṁ aṁ āṁ hrīṁ kroṁ yaṁ raṁ laṁ vaṁ śaṁ ṣaṁ saṁ hoṁ haṁ saḥ

oṁ The Infinite Beyond Conception, Creation (the first letter), Consciousness, Māyā, the cause of the movement of the subtle body to perfection and beyond; the path of fulfillment: control, subtle illumination, one with the earth, emancipation, the soul of peace, the soul of delight, the soul of unity (all this is I), perfection, Infinite Consciousness, this is I.

ॐ ह्रीं श्रीं दुं दुर्गायै नमः सर्वेन्द्रियाणि

oṁ hrīṁ śrīṁ duṁ durgāyai namaḥ sarvendriyāṇi

Oṁ I bow to the Goddess, Durgā, the Grantor of Increase, who Removes all Difficulties. You are all these organs (of action and knowledge).

ॐ अं आं ह्रीं क्रों यं रं लं वं शं षं सं हों हं सः

oṁ aṁ āṁ hrīṁ kroṁ yaṁ raṁ laṁ vaṁ śaṁ ṣaṁ saṁ hoṁ haṁ saḥ

oṁ The Infinite Beyond Conception, Creation (the first letter), Consciousness, Māyā, the cause of the movement of the subtle body to perfection and beyond; the path of fulfillment: control, subtle illumination, one with the earth, emancipation, the soul of peace, the soul of delight, the soul of unity (all this is I), perfection, Infinite Consciousness, this is I.

ॐ ह्रीं श्रीं दुं दुर्गायै नमः वाग् मनस्त्वक्चक्षुः-श्रोत्र-घ्राण-प्राणा इहागत्य सुखं चिरं तिष्ठन्तु स्वाहा

oṁ hrīṁ śrīṁ duṁ durgāyai namaḥ vāg manastvakcakṣuḥ śrotra ghrāṇa prāṇā ihāgatya sukhaṁ ciraṁ tiṣṭhantu svāhā

Oṁ I bow to the Goddess, Durgā, the Grantor of Increase, who Removes all Difficulties. You are all these vibrations, mind, sound, eyes, ears, tongue, nose and life force. Bring forth infinite peace and establish it forever, I am One with God!

kara nyāsa
establishment in the hands

ॐ ह्रां अंगुष्ठाभ्यां नमः
oṁ hrāṁ aṅguṣṭhābhyāṁ namaḥ thumb forefinger
Oṁ hrāṁ in the thumb I bow.

ॐ ह्रीं तर्जनीभ्यां स्वाहा
oṁ hrīṁ tarjanībhyāṁ svāhā thumb forefinger
Oṁ hrīṁ in the forefinger, I am One with God!

ॐ ह्रूं मध्यमाभ्यां वषट्
oṁ hrūṁ madhyamābhyāṁ vaṣaṭ thumb middlefinger
Oṁ hrūṁ in the middle finger, Purify!

ॐ ह्रैं अनामिकाभ्यां हुं
oṁ hraiṁ anāmikābhyāṁ huṁ thumb ring finger
Oṁ hraiṁ in the ring finger, Cut the Ego!

ॐ ह्रौं कनिष्ठिकाभ्यां बौषट्
oṁ hrauṁ kaniṣṭhikābhyāṁ vauṣaṭ thumb little finger
Oṁ hrauṁ in the little finger, Ultimate Purity!

Roll hand over hand forwards while reciting karatal kar,
and backwards while chanting pṛṣṭhābhyāṁ,
then clap hands when chanting astrāya phaṭ.

ॐ ह्रः करतल कर पृष्ठाभ्यां अस्त्राय फट् ॥
oṁ hraḥ karatal kar pṛṣṭhābhyāṁ astrāya phaṭ
Oṁ hraḥ I bow with the weapon of Virtue.

ॐ ह्रीं श्रीं दुं दुर्गायै नमः
oṁ hrīṁ śrīṁ duṁ durgāyai namaḥ
Oṁ I bow to the Goddess, Durgā, the Grantor of Increase, who Removes all Difficulties.

aṅga nyāsa

establishment in the body

Holding tattva mudrā, touch heart.

ॐ ह्रां हृदयाय नमः

oṁ hrāṁ hṛdayāya namaḥ touch heart

Oṁ hrāṁ in the heart, I bow.

Holding tattva mudrā, touch top of head.

ॐ ह्रीं शिरसे स्वाहा

oṁ hrīṁ śirase svāhā top of head

Oṁ hrīṁ on the top of the head, I am One with God!

With thumb extended, touch back of head.

ॐ ह्रूं शिखायै वषट्

oṁ hrūṁ śikhāyai vaṣaṭ back of head

Oṁ hrūṁ on the back of the head, Purify!

Holding tattva mudrā, cross both arms.

ॐ ह्रैं कवचाय हुं

oṁ hraiṁ kavacāya huṁ

Oṁ hraiṁ crossing both arms, Cut the Ego!

Holding tattva mudrā, touch two eyes and in between at once with three middle fingers.

ॐ ह्रौं नेत्रत्रयाय वौषट्

oṁ hrauṁ netratrayāya vauṣaṭ touch three eyes

Oṁ hrauṁ in the three eyes, Ultimate Purity!

Roll hand over hand forwards while reciting karatal kar, and backwards while chanting pṛṣṭhābhyāṁ, then clap hands when chanting astrāya phaṭ.

ॐ ह्रः करतल कर पृष्ठाभ्यां अस्त्राय फट् ॥

oṁ hraḥ karatal kar pṛṣṭhābhyāṁ astrāya phaṭ

Oṁ hraḥ I bow with the weapon of Virtue.

ॐ ह्रीं श्रीं दुं दुर्गायै नमः

oṁ hrīṁ śrīṁ duṁ durgāyai namaḥ
Oṁ I bow to the Goddess, Durgā, the Grantor of Increase, who Removes all Difficulties

japa

prāṇa pratiṣṭhā sūkta
hymn of the establishment of life

ॐ अस्यै प्राणाः प्रतिष्ठन्तु अस्यै प्राणाः क्षरन्तु च ।
अस्यै देवत्वमर्चायै मामहेति कश्चन ॥

oṁ asyai prāṇāḥ pratiṣṭhantu
asyai prāṇāḥ kṣarantu ca
asyai devatvamārcāyai māmaheti kaścana
Thus has the life force been established in you, and thus the life force has flowed into you. Thus to you, God, offering is made, and in this way make us shine.

कलाकला हि देवानां दानवानां कलाकलाः ।
संगृह्य निर्मितो यस्मात् कलशस्तेन कथ्यते ॥

kalākalā hi devānāṁ dānavānāṁ kalākalāḥ
saṁgṛhya nirmito yasmāt kalaśastena kathyate
All the Gods are Fragments of the Cosmic Whole. Also all the asuras are Fragments of the Cosmic Whole. Thus we make a house to contain all these energies.

कलशस्य मुखे विष्णुः कण्ठे रुद्रः समाश्रितः ।
मूले त्वस्य स्थितो ब्रह्मा मध्ये मातृगणाः स्मृताः ॥

kalaśasya mukhe viṣṇuḥ kaṅṭhe rudraḥ samāśritaḥ
mūle tvasya sthito brahmā madhye mātṛgaṇāḥ smṛtāḥ
In the mouth of the pot is Viṣṇu, in the neck resides Rudra. At the base is situated Brahmā, and in the middle we remember the multitude of Mothers.

कुक्षौ तु सागराः सप्त सप्तद्वीपा च मेदिनी ।
अर्जुनी गोमती चैव चन्द्रभागा सरस्वती ॥

kukṣau tu sāgarāḥ sapta saptadvīpā ca medinī
arjunī gomatī caiva candrabhāgā sarasvatī
In the belly are the seven seas and the seven islands of the earth. The rivers Arjunī, Gomatī, Candrabhāgā, Sarasvatī;

कावेरी कृष्णवेणा च गङ्गा चैव महानदी ।
ताप्ती गोदावरी चैव माहेन्द्री नर्मदा तथा ॥

kāverī kṛṣṇaveṇā ca gaṅgā caiva mahānadī
tāptī godāvarī caiva māhendrī narmadā tathā
Kāverī, Kṛṣṇaveṇā and the Gaṅges and other great rivers; the Tāptī, Godāvarī, Māhendrī and Narmadā.

नदाश्च विविधा जाता नद्यः सर्वास्तथापराः ।
पृथिव्यां यानि तीर्थानि कलशस्थानि तानि वै ॥

nadāśca vividhā jātā nadyaḥ sarvāstathāparāḥ
pṛthivyāṁ yāni tīrthāni kalaśasthāni tāni vai
The various rivers and the greatest of beings born, and all the respected places of pilgrimage upon the earth, are established within this pot.

सर्वे समुद्राः सरितस्तीर्थानि जलदा नदाः ।
आयान्तु मम शान्त्यर्थं दुरितक्षयकारकाः ॥

sarve samudrāḥ saritastīrthāni jaladā nadāḥ
āyāntu mama śāntyarthaṁ duritakṣayakārakāḥ
All of the seas, rivers, and waters from all the respected places of pilgrimage have been brought for the peace of that which is bad or wicked.

ऋग्वेदोऽथ यजुर्वेदः सामवेदो ह्यथर्वणः ।
अङ्गैश्च सहिताः सर्वे कलशं तु समाश्रिताः ॥

ṛgvedo-tha yajurvedaḥ sāmavedo hyatharvaṇaḥ
aṅgaiśca sahitāḥ sarve kalaśaṁ tu samāśritāḥ
The Ṛg Veda, the Yajur Veda, Sāma Veda and the Atharva Veda, along with all of their limbs, are assembled together in this pot.

अत्र गायत्री सावित्री शान्तिः पुष्टिकरी तथा ।
आयान्तु मम शान्त्यर्थं दुरितक्षयकारकाः ॥

atra gāyatrī sāvitrī śāntiḥ puṣṭikarī tathā
āyāntu mama śāntyarthaṁ duritakṣayakārakāḥ
Here Gāyatrī, Sāvitrī, Peace and Increase have been brought for the peace of that which is bad or wicked.

देवदानवसंवादे मथ्यमाने महोदधौ ।
उत्पन्नोऽसि तदा कुम्भ विधृतो विष्णुना स्वयम् ॥

deva dānava saṁvāde mathyamāne mahodadhau
utpanno-si tadā kumbha vidhṛto viṣṇunā svayam
The Gods and asuras speaking together are the great givers of churning to the mind. Rise to the top of this pot to separate them from what is actually Viṣṇu, Himself.

त्वत्तोये सर्वतीर्थानि देवाः सर्वे त्वयि स्थिताः ।
त्वयि तिष्ठन्ति भूतानि त्वयि प्राणाः प्रतिष्ठिताः ॥

tvattoye sarvatīrthāni devāḥ sarve tvayi sthitāḥ
tvayi tiṣṭhanti bhūtāni tvayi prāṇāḥ pratiṣṭhitāḥ
Within you are all the pilgrimage places. All the Gods are situated within you. All existence is established within you. All life is established within you.

शिवः स्वयं त्वमेवासि विष्णुस्त्वं च प्रजापतिः ।
आदित्या वसवो रुद्रा विश्वेदेवाः सपैतृकाः ॥

śivaḥ svayaṁ tvamevāsi viṣṇustvaṁ ca prajāpatiḥ
ādityā vasavo rudrā viśvedevāḥ sapaitṛkāḥ
You alone are Śiva; you are Brahmā and Viṣṇu, the sons of Aditi, Finders of the Wealth, Rudra, the Universal Deities and the ancestors.

त्वयि तिष्ठन्ति सर्वेऽपि यतः कामफलप्रदाः ।
त्वत्प्रसादादिमं यज्ञं कर्तुमीहे जलोद्भव ।
सान्निध्यं कुरु मे देव प्रसन्नो भव सर्वदा ॥

tvayi tiṣṭhanti sarve-pi yataḥ kāmaphalapradāḥ
tvatprasādādimaṁ yajñaṁ kartumīhe jalodbhava
sānnidhyaṁ kuru me deva prasanno bhava sarvadā
All and everything has been established in you, from whence you grant the fruits of desires. From you comes the blessed fruit of the sacrifice performed with excellence. May those riches increase. Manifest your presence within us, Lord. Always be pleased.

नमो नमस्ते स्फटिकप्रभाय सुश्वेतहाराय सुमङ्गलाय ।
सुपाशहस्ताय झषासनाय जलाधिनाथाय नमो नमस्ते ॥

namo namaste sphaṭikaprabhāya
suśvetahārāya sumaṅgalāya
supāśahastāya jhaṣāsanāya
jalādhināthāya namo namaste
We bow, we bow to He who shines like crystal, to He who emits excellent clarity and excellent welfare. With the net of unity in his hand, who takes the form of a fish, to the Lord of all waters and that which dwells within, we bow, we bow!

पाशपाणे नमस्तुभ्यं पद्मिनीजीवनायक ।
पुण्याहवाचनं यावत् तावत्त्वं सन्निधौ भव ॥

pāśapāṇe namastubhyaṁ padminījīvanāyaka
puṇyāhavācanaṁ yāvat tāvattvaṁ sannidhau bhava

We bow to He with the net of unity in his hand, Seer of the Life of the Lotus One. With this meritorious invocation, please make your presence manifest.

viśeṣārghya

establishment of the conch shell offering

Draw the yantra on the plate or space for worship with sandal paste and/or water. Offer rice on the yantra for each of the four mantras.

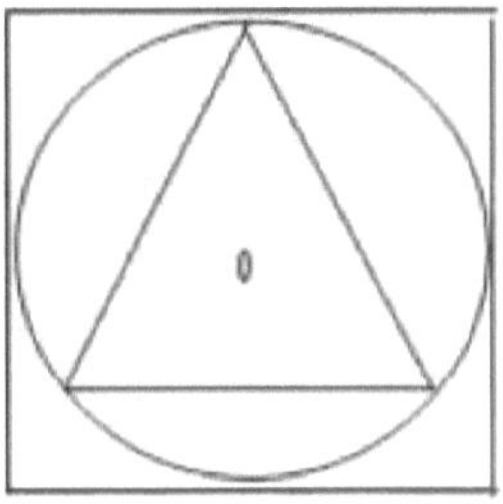

ॐ आधारशक्तये नमः

oṁ ādhāraśaktaye namaḥ

oṁ we bow to the Primal Energy

ॐ कूर्म्माय नमः

oṁ kūrmmāya namaḥ

oṁ we bow to the Support of the Earth

ॐ अनन्ताय नमः

oṁ anantāya namaḥ

oṁ we bow to Infinity

ॐ पृथिव्यै नमः

oṁ pṛthivyai namaḥ

oṁ we bow to the Earth

Place a conch shell on the bindu in the center of the yantra when saying Phaṭ.

स्थां स्थीं स्थिरो भव फट्

sthāṁ sthīṁ sthiro bhava phaṭ

Be Still in the Gross Body! Be Still in the Subtle Body! Be Still in the Causal Body! Purify!

Fill conch shell with water while chanting the mantra.

ॐ गङ्गे च जमुने चैव गोदावरि सरस्वति ।

नर्मदे सिन्धु कावेरि जलेऽस्मिन् सन्निधिं कुरु ॥

oṁ gaṅge ca jamune caiva godāvari sarasvati narmade sindhu kāveri jale-asmin sannidhiṁ kuru

oṁ the Ganges, Jamunā, Godāvarī, Sarasvatī, Narmadā, Sindhu, Kāverī, these waters are mingled together.

Offer Tulasī leaves into water

ॐ ऐं ह्रीं क्लीं श्रीं वृन्दावनवासिन्यै स्वाहा

oṁ aiṁ hrīṁ klīṁ śrīṁ vṛndāvanavāsinyai svāhā

oṁ Wisdom, Māyā, Increase, to She who resides in Vṛndāvana, I am One with God!

Offer 3 flowers into the water pot with the mantras

एते गन्धपुष्पे ॐ अं अर्कमण्डलाय द्वादशकलात्मने नमः

ete gandhapuṣpe oṁ aṁ arkamaṇḍalāya dvādaśakalātmane namaḥ

With these scented flowers oṁ "A" we bow to the twelve aspects of the realm of the sun. Tapinī, Tāpinī, Dhūmrā, Marīci, Jvālinī, Ruci, Sudhūmrā, Bhoga-dā, Viśvā, Bodhinī, Dhārinī, Kṣamā; Containing heat, Emanating heat, Smoky, Ray-producing, Burning, Lustrous, Purple or Smoky-red, Granting enjoyment, Universal, Which makes known, Productive of Consciousness, Which supports, Which forgives.

एते गन्धपुष्पे ॐ उं सोममण्डलाय षोडशकलात्मने नमः

ete gandhapuṣpe oṁ uṁ somamaṇḍalāya ṣoḍaśakalātmane namaḥ

With these scented flowers oṁ "U" we bow to the sixteen aspects of the realm of the moon. Amṛtā, Prāṇadā, Puṣā, Tuṣṭi, Puṣṭi, Rati, Dhṛti, Śaśinī, Caṇḍrikā, Kānti, Jyotsnā, Śrī, Prīti, Aṅgadā, Pūrṇā, Pūrṇāmṛta; Nectar, Which sustains life, Which supports, Satisfying, Nourishing, Playful, Constancy, Unfailing, Producer of Joy, Beauty enhanced by love, Light, Grantor of Prosperity, Affectionate, Purifying the body, Complete, Full of Bliss.

एते गन्धपुष्पे ॐ मं वह्निमण्डलाय दशकलात्मने नमः

ete gandhapuṣpe oṁ maṁ vahnimaṇḍalāya daśakalātmane namaḥ

With these scented flowers oṁ "M" we bow to the ten aspects of the realm of fire: Dhūmrā, Arciḥ, Jvalinī, Śūkṣmā, Jvālinī, Visphūliṅginī, Suśrī, Surūpā, Kapilā, Havya-Kavya-Vahā; Smoky Red, Flaming, Shining, Subtle, Burning, Sparkling, Beautiful, Well-formed, Tawny, The Messenger to Gods and Ancestors.

एते गन्धपुष्पे हुं

ete gandhapuṣpe huṁ

With these scented flowers huṁ

ॐ ह्रीं श्रीं दुं दुर्गायै नमः

oṁ hrīṁ śrīṁ duṁ durgāyai namaḥ

Oṁ I bow to the Goddess, Durgā, the Grantor of Increase, who Removes all Difficulties.

Wave hands in matsyā, dhenu and aṅkuśa mudrās while chanting this mantra.

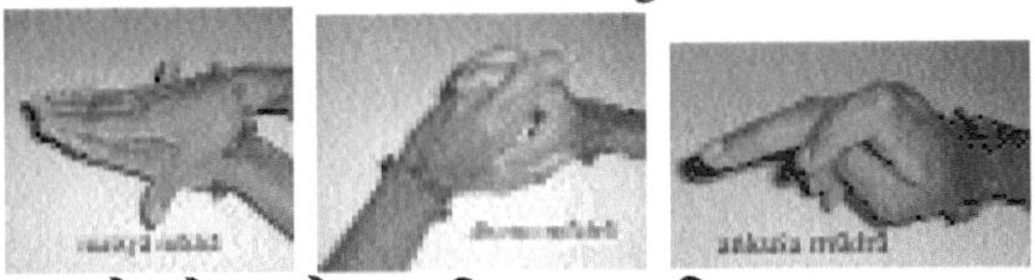

ॐ गङ्गे च जमुने चैव गोदावरि सरस्वति ।
नर्मदे सिन्धु कावेरि जलेऽस्मिन् सन्निधिं कुरु ॥

oṁ gaṅge ca jamune caiva godāvari sarasvati narmade sindhu kāveri jale-asmin sannidhiṁ kuru

oṁ the Ganges, Jamunā, Godāvarī, Sarasvatī, Narmadā, Sindhu, Kāverī, these waters are mingled together.

ॐ ह्रीं श्रीं दुं दुर्गायै नमः

oṁ hrīṁ śrīṁ duṁ durgāyai namaḥ

Oṁ I bow to the Goddess, Durgā, the Grantor of Increase, who Removes all Difficulties.

Sprinkle water over all articles to be offered, then throw some drops of water over your shoulders while repeating the mantra.

अमृतम् कुरु स्वाहा

amṛtam kuru svāhā

Make this immortal nectar! I am One with God!

bhūta śuddhi

purification of the elements

Pronounce each Bījā sixteen times in its proper location:

लं	**Mulādhāra**	(1st Cakra)	**Laṁ**	Indra	Earth
वं	**Swādiṣṭhana**	(2nd Cakra)	**Vaṁ**	Varuṇa	Water
रं	**Maṇipura**	(3rd Cakra)	**Raṁ**	Agni	Fire
यं	**Anahata**	(4th Cakra)	**Yaṁ**	Vāyu	Air
हं	**Viśuddha**	(5th Cakra)	**Haṁ**	Soma	Ether
ॐ	**Āgnyā**	(6th Cakra)	**Oṁ**	Īśvara	The Ultimate

Then move up and down the Suṣumṇa through the cakras, pronouncing each Bījā once, and feeling its presence in its proper location.

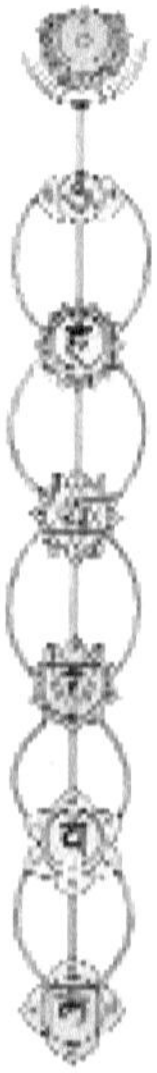

ॐ लं वं रं यं हं ॐ

oṁ laṁ vaṁ raṁ yaṁ haṁ oṁ

oṁ Earth, Water, Fire, Air, Ether, The Ultimate.

ॐ हं यं रं वं लं ॐ

oṁ haṁ yaṁ raṁ vaṁ laṁ oṁ

oṁ The Ultimate, Ether, Air, Fire, Water, Earth.

ॐ मूलशृङ्गाटाच्छिरः सुषुम्नापथेन जीवशिवं परमशिवपदे योजयामि स्वाहा ॥

oṁ mūlaśṛṅgāṭācchiraḥ suṣumnāpathena jīvaśivaṁ paramaśivapade yojayāmi svāhā

Piercing the triangular junction (yantra) situated in the Mulādhāra, the center of energy between the genital and the rectum, I direct the auspicious life force upwards by way of the Suṣumna, the subtle canal which transmits nerve impulses along the spinal column, to unite in Supreme Bliss, I am One with God!

ॐ यं लिङ्गशरीरं शोषय शोषय स्वाहा ॥

oṁ yaṁ liṅgaśarīraṁ śoṣaya śoṣaya svāhā
oṁ Yaṁ (Vāyu, Air, the Spirit of Emancipation) in the subtle body, purify, purify, I am One with God!

ॐ रं सङ्कोचशरीरं दह दह स्वाहा ॥

oṁ raṁ saṅkocaśarīraṁ daha daha svāhā
oṁ Raṁ (Agni, Fire, the Purifying Light of Wisdom) in the limited body, burn, burn, I am One with God!

ॐ परमशिव सुषुम्नापथेन मूलशृङ्गाटमुल्लसोल्लस
ज्वल ज्वल प्रज्वल प्रज्वल सोऽहं हंसः स्वाहा ॥

oṁ paramaśiva suṣumnāpathena mūlaśṛṅgāṭa mullasollasa jvala jvala prajvala prajvala so-haṁ haṁsaḥ svāhā
Oh Supreme Bliss, filling the path of the Suṣumna from the triangular junction in the Mulādhāra, dancing brilliantly, shine, shine, radiate, radiate, That is I, I am That, I am One with God!

kara śuddhi

wipe your hands with a flower

ॐ ऐं रं अस्त्राय फट्

oṁ aiṁ raṁ astrāya phaṭ
oṁ Wisdom, the Subtle Body of Light, with this weapon, Purify!

tap ground three times with fist or heel

फट् फट् फट्

phaṭ phaṭ phaṭ
Purify! Purify! Purify!

bhūtāpsāraṇa

dispersion of inimical energies

Bhūta has a number of meanings, which makes the following verses to play on the words, switching meanings even while using the same word. Its noun forms mean variously: a purified being, a good being; created thing, world; uncanny being, spirit, ghost, goblin; past, fact, reality, actual occurence; welfare; elements, especially as applied to the five gross elements of earth, water, fire, air and ether (See Bhūta Śuddhi). Here we are calling upon the friendly or the good Bhūtas to destroy obstacles created by unfriendly or bad Bhūtas.

ॐ अपसर्पन्तु ते भूता ये भूता भुवि संस्थिताः ।
ये भूता विघ्नकर्त्तारस्ते नश्यन्तु शिवज्ञया ॥

oṁ apasarpantu te bhūtā ya bhūtā bhuvi saṁsthitāḥ
ye bhūtā vighnakarttāraste naśyantu śivajñayā

We consign to you friendly spirits, friendly spirits that are situated on this earth plane, the activity of destroying any obstacles placed by unfriendly spirits, by order of the Wisdom of Infinite Goodness.

ॐ भूतप्रेतपिशाचाश्च दानवा राक्षसाश्च ये ।
शान्तिं कुर्वन्तु ते सर्वे ईमं गृह्वतु मद्बलिम् ॥

oṁ bhūtapretapiśācāśca dānavā rākṣasāśca ye
śāntiṁ kurvantu te sarve īmaṁ gṛhvatu madbalim

Hey ghosts, goblins, demons, unfriendly spirits and various forms of negativity projecting egos: you have been made entirely at peace. Please accept this offering from me.

ॐ वेतालाश्च पिशाचाश्च राक्षसाश्च सरीसुपाः ।
अपसर्पन्तु ते सर्वे नारसिंहेन ताढिताः ॥

oṁ vetālāśca piśācāśca rākṣasāśca sarīsupāḥ
apasarpantu te sarve nārasiṁhena taḍhitāḥ

Other demons, goblins, various forms of negativity projecting egos, creeping and crawling things: I consign to you completely the striking blows of Nārasiṁha, Viṣṇu in His incarnation of man-lion.

aghamārṣaṇa

internal cleaning

Perform Jāl Neti taking water from the Samanyārghya into the left palm. Inhale it through the Iḍa or left nostril, and bring it all the way up into the Āgnyā Cakra, then expel it through the Piṅgalā or right nostril. Blow out the nasal passages so that they are clean.

ॐ ऋतमित्यस्य ऋक्त्रयस्याघमर्षण

ऋषिरनष्टुप्छन्दोभाववृत्तं देवतामश्वमेधावभृथे विनियोगः ॥

oṁ ṛtamityasya ṛktrayasyāghamarṣaṇa ṛṣiranaṣṭupchandobhāvavṛttaṁ devatāmaśvaedhāvabhṛthe viniyogaḥ

Introducing the three Mantras which begin with "From Truth...", etc., Internal Cleaning is the Seer, Anuṣṭup is the meter (32 syllables to the verse), Who Changes the Intensity of Reality is the divinity, equal in merit to the horse sacrifice, this practice is offered in application.

ॐ ऋतं च सत्यं चाभीद्धात्तपसोऽध्यजायत ।

ततो रत्र्यजायत ततः समुद्रोऽर्णवः ॥

oṁ ṛtaṁ ca satyaṁ cābhīddhāttapaso-dhyajāyata tato ratryajāyata tataḥ samudro-rṇavaḥ

From truth, from the Imperishable Truth, the Performers of Tapasya, or strict spiritual discipline, have come. Then came forth the night, and then the sea of objects and relationships, with the multitude of its waves.

समुद्रार्णवादधि संवत्सरो अजायत ।

अहोरात्राणिविदधद्विश्वस्य भिषतो वशी ॥

samudrārṇavādadhi saṁvatsaro ajāyata ahorātrāṇividadhadiśvasya bhiṣato vaśī

From the fluctuations of the waves on the sea, the years came forth. The night transformed into day, and the universe took birth.

सूर्या चन्द्रमसौ धाता यथापूर्वमकल्पयत् ।
दिवं च पृथिवीं चान्तरिक्षमथो स्वः ॥

sūryā candramasau dhātā yathāpūrvamakalpayat
divaṁ ca pṛthivīṁ cāntarikṣamatho svaḥ

The Sun and the Moon gave forth their lights in accordance with the command of the Creator. And the earth, the atmosphere and the heavens were His Own.

jāl netī, prāṇāyāma
cleaning of the sinuses, control of breath

agni prajvālitaṁ
enkindling the sacred fire

agni gāyatrī

ॐ वैश्वानराय विद्महे लालिलय धीमहे ।
तन्नो अग्निः प्रचोदयात् ॐ ॥

oṁ vaisvānarāya vidmahe lālilaya dhīmahe
tanno agniḥ pracodayāt oṁ

Oṁ We meditate upon the All-Pervading Being, we contemplate the Luminous One who is the final resting place of all. May that Divine Fire, the Light of Meditation, grant us increase.

upasaṁhara mudrā

ह्वयाम्यग्निं प्रथमं स्वस्तये ।
ह्वयामि मित्रावरुणाविहावसे ।
ह्वयामि रात्रीं जगतो निवेशनीं ।
ह्वयामि देवं सवितारमूतये ॥

hvayāmyagniṁ prathamaṁ svastaye
hvayāmi mitrā varuṇā vihāvase
hvayāmi rātrīṁ jagato niveṣanīṁ
hvayāmi devaṁ savitāramūtaye

I am calling you, Agni, the Divine Fire, the Light of Meditation, first to grant success. I am calling you Friendship and the Continuous Flow of Equilibrium also to receive this offering. I am calling the

Night of Duality who covers the universe. I am calling the Light of Wisdom, the Divine Being, to rise up within us.

हिरण्यगर्भः समवर्तताग्रे भूतस्य जातः पतिरेक आसीत् ।
स दाधार पृथिवीं द्यामुतेमां कस्मै देवाय हविषा विधेम ॥

hiranyagarbhaḥ samavartatāgre
bhūtasya jātaḥ patireka āsīt
sa dādhāra pṛthivīṁ dyāmutemāṁ
kasmai devāya haviṣā vidhema

Oh Golden Womb, You are the One Eternal Existence from which all beings born on the earth have come forth. You always bear the earth and all that rises upon it. (You tell us) to which God shall we offer our knowledge and attention?

यथा विद्वां अरंकरद् विश्वेभ्यो यजतेभ्यः ।
अयमग्ने त्वे अपि यं यज्ञं चकृमा वयम् ॥

yathā vidvāṁ araṁkarad viśvebhyoḥ yajatebhyaḥ
ayamagne tve api yaṁ yajñaṁ cakṛmā vayam

Through knowledge of this Eternal Cause, all beings born in the universe have come forth. It is in you, Oh Agni, Oh Light of Meditation, in the flame of sacrifice, that this constant movement will find rest.

त्वमग्ने प्रथमो अङ्गिरा ऋषिर्देवो देवानामभवः शिवः सखा ।
तव व्रते कवयो विद्मनापसोऽजायन्त मरुतो भ्राजदृष्टयः ॥

tvamagne prathamo aṅgirā ṛṣirdevo
devānāmabhavaḥ śivaḥ sakhā
tava vrate kavayo vidmanāpaso-
jāyanta maruto bhrājadṛṣṭayaḥ

You, Oh Divine Light of Meditation, are the first among the performers of spiritual discipline, a Seer, a God; your name became one with all the Gods. You are the friend of Śiva, the Consciousness of Infinite Goodness. Through devotion to you, all the inspired poets (Ṛṣis who propound Vedic Knowledge, or Wisdom of Universality) come to Divine Knowledge, as did the Maruts (the 49 Gods of severe penance) did come forth from your worship.

त्वं मुखं सर्वदेवानां सप्तार्चिर्हविरद्मते ।
आगच्छ भगवनग्ने यज्ञेऽस्मिन् सन्निधा भव ॥

tvaṁ mukhaṁ sarvadevānāṁ saptārcirhaviradmate
āgaccha bhagavanagne yajñe-smin sannidhā bhava

You are the mouth of all the Gods, with your seven tongues you accept the offerings. Come here, Oh Lord Divine Fire, and take your seat in the midst of our sacrifice.

ॐ वैश्वानर जातवेद इहावह लोहिताक्ष सर्व कर्माणि
साधय स्वाहा ॥

oṁ vaiśvānara jātaveda ihāvaha lohitākṣa sarva karmāṇi sādhaya svāhā

oṁ Oh Universal Being, Knower of All, come here with your red eyes. All of our Karma burn it! I AM ONE WITH GOD!

ॐ अग्नीमिळे पुरोहितं यज्ञस्य देवमृत्विजम् ।
होतारं रत्न धातमम् ॥

oṁ agnīmiḷe purohitaṁ yajñasya devamṛtvijam
hotāraṁ ratna dhātamam

Oh Agni, Light of Meditation, you are the Priest of Sacrifice, serving the offering of the divine nectar of Immortality. You give jewels to those who offer.

ॐ अग्नि प्रज्वलितं वन्दे जातवेदं हुताशनम् ।
सुवर्णवर्णममलं समिद्धं विश्वतो मुखम्

oṁ agni prajvalitaṁ vande jātavedaṁ hutāśanam
suvarṇavarṇamamalaṁ samiddhaṁ viśvato mukham

We lovingly adore the Divine Fire, Light of Meditation, sparkling, flaming brightly, knower of all, recipient of our offerings. With His excellent golden color, everywhere His omnipresent mouths are devouring oblations.

ॐ अग्नये नमः

oṁ agnaye namaḥ
oṁ We bow to the Divine Fire.

अग्ने त्वं चण्डिकानामसि

agne tvaṁ caṇḍikānāmasi
Oh Divine Fire, we are now calling you by the name Caṇḍi, She who Tears Apart Thoughts.

ॐ वागीश्वरी मृतुस्नातां नीलेन्दीवरलोचनाम् ।
वागीश्वरेण संयुक्तां क्रीडाभाव समन्विताम् ॥

oṁ vāgīśvarī mṛtu-snātāṁ nīlendīvaralocanām
vāgīśvareṇa saṁyuktaṁ krīḍābhāva samanvitam
The Supreme Goddess of Speech, dear Mother Saraswati, has just completed Her bath following Her monthly course of menstruation. With eyes of blue, bestowing boons, She moves into union with Vāgīṣvara, Brahma, the Lord of All Vibrations, and together they create the bhāva or intensity of reality, the attitude which unites all.

एते गन्धपुष्पे ॐ ह्रीं वागीश्वर्यै नमः

ete gandhapuṣpe oṁ hrīṁ vāgīśvaryai namaḥ
With these scented flowers oṁ we bow to the Supreme Goddess of Speech, or all Vibrations.

एते गन्धपुष्पे ॐ ह्रीं वागीश्वराय नमः

ete gandhapuṣpe oṁ hrīṁ vāgīśvarāya namaḥ
With these scented flowers oṁ we bow to the Supreme Lord of Speech, or all Vibrations.

एते गन्धपुष्पे ॐ अग्नेर्हिरण्यादि सप्तजिह्वाभ्यो नमः

ete gandhapuṣpe oṁ agnerhiraṇyādi saptajihvābhyo namaḥ

With these scented flowers oṁ we bow to the seven tongues of the Divine Fire, like golden, etc.

1. Kālī	Black
2. Karālī	Increasing, formidable
3. Mano-javā	Swift as thought
4. Su-Lohitā	Excellent shine
5. Sudhūmra-Varnā	Purple
6. Ugrā or Sphulingīnī	Fearful
7. Pradīptā	Giving light

एते गन्धपुष्पे ॐ सहस्रार्चिषे हृदयाय नमः

ete gandhapuṣpe oṁ sahasrārciṣe hṛdayāya namaḥ

With these scented flowers oṁ we bow to the heart from which emanates a thousand rays.

इत्याद्यग्ने षदङ्गेभ्यो नमः

ityādyagne ṣadaṅgebhyo namaḥ

In this way establish the Divine Fire in the six centers of the body.

एते गन्धपुष्पे ॐ अग्नये जातवेदसे इत्यद्याष्टमूर्त्तिभ्यो नमः

ete gandhapuṣpe oṁ agnaye jātavedase ityadyaṣṭa mūrttibhyo namaḥ

With these scented flowers oṁ we bow to the Divine Fire, the Knower of All, etc, in His eight forms for worship.

1. Jāta-Veda	Knower of All
2. Sapta-Jihva	Seven tongued
3. Vaiśvānara	Universal Being
4. Havyā-Vāhana	Carrier of Oblations
5. Aśwodara-Ja	Fire of Stomach, lower areas
6. Kaumāra Tejaḥ	From which the son of Śiva is born
7. Viśva-Mukha	Which can devour the universe
8. Deva-Mukha	The mouth of the Gods

एते गन्धपुष्पे ॐ ब्राह्म्यद्यष्टशक्तिभ्यो नमः

ete gandhapuṣpe oṁ brāhmyadyaṣṭaśaktibhyo namaḥ

With these scented flowers oṁ we bow to the eight Śaktis or Energies, like Brāhmī, etc.

1. Brāhmī	Creative Energy
2. Nārāyaṇī	Exposer of Consciousness
3. Māheśvarī	Energy of the Seer of All
4. Cāmuṇḍā	Slayer of Passion & Meanness
5. Kaumārī	The Ever Pure One
6. Aparājitā	The Unconquerable
7. Vārāhī	The Boar of Sacrifice
8. Nārasiṁhī	The Man-lion of Courage

एते गन्धपुष्पे ॐ पद्माद्यष्टनिधिभ्यो नमः

ete gandhapuṣpe oṁ padmādyaṣṭa nidhibhyo namaḥ

With these scented flowers oṁ we bow to the eight Treasures of the Lord of Wealth, like Padma, etc.

1. Padma	The lotus of Peace
2. Mahā-Padma	The great lotus of universal Peace
3. Śaṅkha	The conch of all vibrations
4. Makara	The emblem of Love
5. Kacchapa	Tortoise, the emblem of support
6. Mukunda	The Crest gem
7. Nanda	Bliss
8. Nīla	The blue light within like a Sapphire

एते गन्धपुष्पे ॐ इन्द्रादि लोकपालेभ्यो नमः

ete gandhapuṣpe oṁ indrādi lokapālebhyo namaḥ

With these scented flowers oṁ we bow to Indra and the Protectors of the Ten Directions.

1. Indra	East
2. Agni	South-East
3. Yama	South
4. Nairrita	South-West
5. Varuṇa	West
6. Vāyu	North-West
7. Kuvera (Soma)	North
8. Īśāna	North-East
9. Brahmā	Above
10. Viṣṇu (Ananta)	Below

एते गन्धपुष्पे ॐ वज्राद्यस्त्रेभ्यो नमः

ete gandhapuṣpe oṁ vajrādyastrebhyo namaḥ
With these scented flowers oṁ we bow to the Thunderbolt and other weapons.

1. Vajra	Indra's thunderbolt
2. Śakti	Agni's spear, dart, energy
3. Daṇḍa	Yama's staff
4. Khaḍga	Nairrita's sword
5. Pāśa	Varuṇa's net or noose
6. Aṅkuśa	Vāyu's hook
7. Gadā	Kuvera's mace
8. Triśūla	Īśāna's trident
9. Padma or Kamaṇḍelu	Brahma's lotus or begging bowl
10. Cakra	Viṣṇu's discus

एते गन्धपुष्पे ॐ वह्निचैतन्याय नमः

ete gandhapuṣpe oṁ vahni caintanyāya namaḥ
With these scented flowers oṁ we bow to the Consciousness of the Divine Fire.

एते गन्धपुष्पे ॐ अग्नि मूर्त्तये नमः

ete gandhapuṣpe oṁ agni mūrttaye namaḥ

With these scented flowers oṁ we bow to the Image of the Divine Fire, the Light of Meditation.

ॐ अग्नये नमः

oṁ agnaye namaḥ
oṁ we bow to the Divine Fire.

रं रं रं रं रं

raṁ raṁ raṁ raṁ raṁ
R The Subtle Body; a Consciousness ; ṁ Perfection
Raṁ The manifestation of Perfection in the Subtle Body of Consciousness.

japa

mātṛkā pūjā

worship of gaṇeśa and the sixteen mothers

समीपे मातृवर्गस्य सर्वविघ्नहरं सदा ।
त्रैलोक्य वन्दितं देवं गणेशं स्थापयाम्यहम् ॥

samīpe mātṛvargasya sarvavighnaharaṁ sadā
trailokya vanditaṁ devaṁ gaṇeśaṁ sthāpayāmyaham

Situated before the group of Mothers, He always removes all obstacles. He is the God praised by all the Three worlds; I establish Gaṇeśa, the Lord of Wisdom.

ॐ भूर्भुवः स्वः गणपतये नमः । गणपतिमावाहयामि स्थापयामि ॥

oṁ bhūrbhuvaḥ svaḥ gaṇapataye namaḥ
gaṇapatimāvāhayāmi sthāpayāmi

Oṁ the Infinite Beyond Conception, the gross body, the subtle body and the causal body. I bow to Gaṇeśa. I invite Gaṇeśa and establish Him within.

हेमाद्रितनयां देवीं वरदां शङ्करप्रियाम् ।
लम्बोदरस्य जननीं गौरीमावाहयाम्यहम् ॥

hemādritanayāṁ devīṁ varadāṁ śaṅkarapriyām
lambodarasya jananīṁ gaurīmāvāhayāmyaham

The Goddess is the daughter of the snowy mountain, She gives boons and is the beloved of Śiva. With a big stomach, She is the Mother (of existence). I invite Gaurī, She who is Rays of Light.

ॐ भूर्भुवः स्वः गौर्यै नमः । गौरीमावाहयामि स्थापयामि ॥

oṁ bhūrbhuvaḥ svaḥ gauryai namaḥ
gaurīmāvāhayāmi sthāpayāmi

Oṁ the Infinite Beyond Conception, the gross body, the subtle body and the causal body. I bow to Gaurī. I invite Gaurī and establish Her within.

पद्मावं पद्मवदनां पद्मनाभोरुसंस्थिताम् ।
जगत्प्रियां पद्मवासां पद्मामावाहयाम्यहम् ॥

padmāvaṁ padmavadanāṁ padmanābhorusaṁsthitām
jagatpriyāṁ padmavāsāṁ padmāmāvāhayāmyaham
Favorable as a lotus, with a lotus-like mouth, situated in the navel of a lotus. She is beloved of the universe, resident of the lotus. I invite Padma, She who is the Lotus (the wealth of Peace and Love).

ॐ पद्मायै नमः पद्मामावाहयामि स्थापयामि ॥

oṁ padmāyai namaḥ padmāmāvāhayāmi sthāpayāmi
Oṁ I bow to Padma. I invite Padma and establish Her within.

दिव्यरूपां विशालाक्षीं शुचि कुण्डल धारिणीम् ।
रक्तमुक्ताद्यलङ्कारां शचीमावाहयाम्यहम् ॥

divyarūpāṁ viśālākṣīṁ śuci kuṇḍala dhāriṇīm
raktamuktādyalaṅkārāṁ śacīmāvāhayāmyaham
The form of divinity, the goal of the universe, She wears earrings, which shine with purity. Her ornaments are of red pearls. I invite Śacī, the Goddess of Purity.

ॐ शच्ये नमः शचीमावाहयामि स्थापयामि ॥

oṁ śacye namaḥ śacīmāvāhayāmi sthāpayāmi
Oṁ I bow to Śacī. I invite Śacī and establish Her within.

विश्वेऽस्मिन् भूरिवरदां जरां निर्जरसेविताम् ।
बुद्धिप्रबोधिनीं सौम्यां मेधामावाहयाम्यहम् ॥

viśve-smin bhūrivaradāṁ jarāṁ nirjarasevitām
buddhiprabodhinīṁ saumyāṁ medhāmāvāhayāmyaham
She gives boons to the aged of this universe, to the aged She gives the service of freedom from wasting away. To the Intellect She is known as the Beautiful. I invite Medhā, the Intellect of Love.

ॐ मेधायै नमः मेधामावाहयामि स्थापयामि ॥

oṁ medhāyai namaḥ medhāmāvāhayāmi sthāpayāmi
Oṁ I bow to Medhā. I invite Medhā and establish Her within.

जगत्सृष्टिकरीं धात्रीं देवीं प्रणवमातृकाम् ।
वेदगर्भां यज्ञमयीं सावित्रीं स्थापयाम्यहम् ॥

jagatsṛṣṭikarīṁ dhātrīṁ devīṁ praṇavamātṛkām
vedagarbhāṁ yajñamayīṁ sāvitrīṁ sthāpayāmyaham
She is the Goddess who is the Cause, the Giver of Birth to the perceivable universe, the Mother of the Praṇava, oṁ. The Vedas came from Her womb. She is sacrifice incarnate. I establish Sāvitrī, the Goddess of the Light.

ॐ सावित्र्यै नमः सावित्रीमावाहयामि स्थापयामि ॥

oṁ sāvitryai namaḥ sāvitrīmāvāhayāmi sthāpayāmi
Oṁ I bow to Sāvitrī. I invite Sāvitrī and establish Her within.

सर्वास्त्रधारिणीं देवीं सर्वाभरणभूषिताम् ।
सर्वदेवस्तुतां वन्द्यां विजयां स्थापयाम्यहम् ॥

sarvāstradhāriṇīṁ devīṁ sarvābharaṇabhūṣitām
sarvadevastutāṁ vandyāṁ vijayāṁ sthāpayāmyaham
She is the Goddess who holds all weapons, and She shines with all ornaments. All the Gods sing Her praises and hymns. I establish Vijayā, the Goddess of Victory.

ॐ विजयायै नमः विजयामावाहयामि स्थापयामि ॥

oṁ vijayāyai namaḥ vijayāmāvāhayāmi sthāpayāmi
Oṁ I bow to Vijayā. I invite Vijayā and establish Her within.

सुरारिमथिनीं देवीं देवानामभयप्रदाम् ।
त्रैलोक्य वन्दितां शुभ्रां जयामावाहयाम्यहम् ॥

surārimathinīṁ devīṁ devānāmabhayapradām
trailokya vanditāṁ śubhrāṁ jayāmāvāhayāmyaham

She is the Goddess who is the staff of the Gods, whose name removes fear from the Gods. She is the manifestation of excellence who is praised in the three worlds. I invite Jayā, Conquest.

ॐ जयायै नमः जयामावाहयामि स्थापयामि ॥

oṁ jayāyai namaḥ jayāmāvāhayāmi sthāpayāmi
Oṁ I bow to Jayā. I invite Jayā and establish Her within.

मयूरवाहनां देवीं खड्ग-शक्ति-धनुर्धराम् ।
आवाहयेद् देवसेनां तारकासुरमर्दिनीम् ॥

mayūravāhanāṁ devīṁ khaḍga-śakti-dhanurdharām
āvāhayed devasenāṁ tārakāsuramardinīm
She is the Goddess who rides upon a peacock, holding aloft a sword, energy and a bow. I invite the Commander of the forces of the Gods, the Slayer of Tārakāsura, the Illuminator of Duality.

ॐ देवसेनायै नमः देवसेनामावाहयामि स्थापयामि ॥

oṁ devasenāyai namaḥ devasenāmāvāhayāmi sthāpayāmi
Oṁ I bow to the Commander of the forces of the Gods. I invite the commander of the forces of the Gods and establish Her within.

अग्रजा सर्वदेवानां कव्यार्थं या प्रतिष्ठिता ।
पितॄणां तृप्तिदां देवीं स्वधामावाहयाम्यहम् ॥

agrajā sarvadevānāṁ kavyārthaṁ yā pratiṣṭitā
pitṝṇāṁ tṛptidāṁ devīṁ svadhāmāvāhayāmyaham
She is the first born of all the Gods, and was established first by the ancient poets. She is the Goddess who gives pleasure to the ancestors. I invite Svadhā, One's own Giving.

ॐ स्वधायै नमः स्वधामावाहयामि स्थापयामि ॥

oṁ svadhāyai namaḥ svadhāmāvāhayāmi sthāpayāmi
Oṁ I bow to Svadhā. I invite Svadhā and establish Her within.

हविर्गृत्वा महादत्ता देवेभ्यो या प्रयच्छति ।
तां दिव्यरूपां वरदां स्वाहामावाहयाम्यहम् ॥

havirgṛtvā mahādattā devebhyo yā prayacchati
tāṁ divyarūpāṁ varadāṁ svāhāmāvāhayāmyaham

The Great Giver of oblations with ghee, which are essential for the Gods. You give blessings in the form of divinity. I invite Svāhā, I am One with God!

ॐ स्वाहायै नमः स्वाहामावाहयामि स्थापयामि ॥

oṁ svāhāyai namaḥ svāhāmāvāhayāmi sthāpayāmi

Oṁ I bow to Svāhā. I invite Svāhā and establish Her within.

आवाहयाम्यहम् मातृः सकलाः लोकपूजिताः ।
सर्वकल्याणरूपिण्यो वरदा दिव्यभूषणाः ॥

āvāhayāmyaham mātṝḥ sakalāḥ lokapūjitāḥ
sarvakalyāṇarūpiṇyo varadā divyabhūṣaṇāḥ

I invite the Mother who is worshipped throughout the three worlds. She is the form of all welfare, and She gives blessings that shine with divinity.

ॐ मातृभ्यो नमः मातृः आवाहयामि स्थापयामि ॥

oṁ mātṛbhyo namaḥ mātṝḥ āvāhayāmi sthāpayāmi

Oṁ I bow to the Mothers. I invite the Mothers and establish them within.

आवाहयेल्लोकमातृर्जयन्तीप्रमुखाः शुभाः ।
नानाऽभीष्टप्रदाः शान्ताः सर्वलोकहितावहाः ॥

āvāhayellokamātṝrjayantīpramukhāḥ śubhāḥ
nānā-bhīṣṭapradāḥ śāntāḥ sarvalokahitāvahāḥ

I invite the Mothers of the Universe, who shine before every Victory! They give various kinds of supremacy and peace, and invite the joy of all the worlds.

ॐ लोकमातृभ्यो नमः लोकमातृः आवाहयामि स्थापयामि ॥

oṁ lokamātṛbhyo namaḥ lokamātṝḥ āvāhayāmi sthāpayāmi

Oṁ I bow to the Mothers of the Universe. I invite the Mothers of the Universe and establish them within.

सर्वहर्षकरीं देवीं भाक्तानामभयप्रदाम् ।
हर्षोत्फुल्लास्यकमलां धृतिमावाहयाम्यहम् ॥

sarvaharṣakarīṁ devīṁ bhāktānāmabhayapradām
harṣotphullāsyakamalāṁ dhṛtimāvāhayāmyaham

The Goddess is the Cause of all gladness. To devotees who take Her name She grants freedom from fear. She is the blossom of the lotus of Gladness. I invite Dhṛti, Constancy.

ॐ धृत्यै नमः धृतिमावाहयामि स्थापयामि ॥

oṁ dhṛtyai namaḥ dhṛtimāvāhayāmi sthāpayāmi

Oṁ I bow to Dhṛti. I invite Dhṛti and establish Her within.

पोषयन्तीं जगत्सर्वं स्वदेहप्रभवैर्नवैः ।
शाकैः फलैर्जलैरत्नैः पुष्टिमावाहयाम्यहम् ॥

poṣayantīṁ jagatsarvaṁ svadehaprabhavairnavaiḥ
śākaiḥ phalairjalairatnaiḥ puṣṭimāvāhayāmyaham

She who gives prosperity (abundance) to the entire universe, bringing forth from Her own body vegetables, fruits, water and gems. I invite Puṣṭi, Increase.

ॐ पुष्ट्यै नमः पुष्टिमावाहयामि स्थापयामि ॥

oṁ puṣṭyai namaḥ puṣṭimāvāhayāmi sthāpayāmi

Oṁ I bow to Puṣṭi. I invite Puṣṭi and establish Her within.

देवैराराधितां देवीं सदा सन्तोषकारिणीम् ।
प्रसादसुमुखीं देवीं तुष्टिमावाहयाम्यहम् ॥

devairārādhitāṁ devīṁ sadā santoṣakāriṇīm
prasādasumukhīṁ devīṁ tuṣṭimāvāhayāmyaham
She is the Goddess who pleases the Gods, always the cause of satisfaction. From the excellent face of the Goddess comes blessings. I invite Tuṣṭi, Satisfaction.

ॐ तुष्ट्यै नमः तुष्टिमावाहयामि स्थापयामि ॥

oṁ tuṣṭyai namaḥ tuṣṭimāvāhayāmi sthāpayāmi
Oṁ I bow to Tuṣṭi. I invite Tuṣṭi and establish Her within.

पत्तने नगरे ग्रामे विपिने पर्वते गृहे ।
नानाजातिकुलेशानीं दुर्गामावाहयाम्यहम् ॥

pattane nagare grāme vipine parvate gṛhe
nānājātikuleśānīṁ durgāmāvāhayāmyaham
In the air, in the city, in the village, in the woods, on the mountains, in a house, She is the Supreme Ruler of the family in various forms of birth. I invite Durgā, the Reliver of Difficulties.

ॐ आत्मनः कुलदेवतायै नमः आत्मनः
कुलदेवतामावाहयामि स्थापयामि ॥

oṁ ātmanaḥ kuladevatāyai namaḥ ātmanaḥ
kuladevatāmāvāhayāmi sthāpayāmi
Oṁ I bow to the soul who is the Goddess of the Family. I invite the soul who is the Goddess of the Family and establish Her within.

ॐ गौरी पद्मा शची मेधा सावित्री विजया जया ।
देवसेना स्वधा स्वाहा मातरो लोकमातरः ॥

oṁ gaurī padmā śacī medhā sāvitrī vijayā jayā
devasenā svadhā svāhā mātaro lokamātaraḥ
Oṁ Gaurī, Padmā, Śacī, Medhā, Sāvitrī, Vijayā, Jayā; Devasenā, Svadhā, Svāhā, Mātaro, Lokamātaraḥ,

धृतिः पुष्टिस्तथा तुष्टिः आत्मनः कुलदेवताः ।
गणेशेनाधिका ह्येता वृद्धौ पूज्यास्तु षौडश ॥

dhṛtiḥ puṣṭistathā tuṣṭiḥ ātmanaḥ kuladevatāḥ
gaṇeśenādhikā hyetā vṛddhau pūjyāstu ṣauḍaśa
Dhṛti, Puṣṭi and then Tuṣṭi, and the soul who is the Goddess of the Family; with Gaṇeśa situated before, we make worship of the sixteen.

आयुरारोग्यमैश्वर्यं ददध्वं मातरो मम ।
निर्विघ्नं सर्वकार्येषु कुरुध्वं सगणाधिपाः ॥

āyurārogyamaiśvaryaṁ dadadhvaṁ mātaro mama
nirvighnaṁ sarvakāryeṣu kurudhvaṁ sagaṇādhipāḥ
Give us life and freedom from disease, imperishable qualities, oh my Mothers. Make all desired effects free from obstacles with your multitudes.

ॐ गणपत्यादि कुलदेवतान्त मातृभ्यो नमः ॥

oṁ gaṇapatyādi kuladevatānta mātṛbhyo namaḥ
Oṁ I bow to Gaṇeśa and the other members of the family of Goddesses and Mothers.

nava durgā pūjā (1)

worship of the nine forms of durgā (1)

ॐ भूर्भुवः स्वः शैलपुत्रि इहा गच्छ इहतिष्ट शैलपुत्र्यै नमः ।
शैलपुत्रीमावाहयामि स्थापयामि नमः ।
पाध्यादिभिः पूजनम्बिधाय ॥

oṁ bhūrbhuvaḥ svaḥ śailaputri ihā gaccha ihatiṣṭa śailaputryai namaḥ śailputrīmāvāhayāmi sthāpayāmi namaḥ pādhyādibhiḥ pūjanambidhāya

Oṁ the Infinite Beyond Conception, the gross body, the subtle body and the causal body. Goddess of Inspiration, come here, stay here. I bow to the Goddess of Inspiration. I invite the Goddess of Inspiration and establish Her within. You are being worshipped with water for washing your feet.

ॐ जगत्पूज्ये जगद्वन्ध्ये सर्वशक्ति स्वरूपिणि ।
पूजां गृहाण कौमारि जगन्मातर्नमोऽस्तु ते ॥

oṁ jagatpūjye jagadvandhye sarvaśakti svarūpiṇi pūjāṁ gṛhāṇa kaumāri jaganmātarnamo-stu te

Oṁ You are worshipped in the world, praised in the world, as the intrinsic nature of all energy. Oh Ever Pure One, please accept this worship. We bow to you, oh Mother of the universe.

ॐ भूर्भुवः स्वः ब्रह्मचारिणि इहा गच्छ इहतिष्ट ब्रह्मचारिण्यै
नमः । ब्रह्मचारिणीमावाहयामि स्थापयामि नमः ।
पाध्यादिभिः पूजनम्बिधाय ॥

oṁ bhūrbhuvaḥ svaḥ brahmacāriṇi ihā gaccha ihatiṣṭa brahmacāriṇyai namaḥ brahmacāriṇīmāvāhayāmi sthāpayāmi namaḥ pādhyādibhiḥ pūjanambidhāya

Oṁ the Infinite Beyond Conception, the gross body, the subtle body and the causal body. Goddess of Learning, come here, stay here. I bow to the Goddess of Learning. I invite the Goddess of Learning and establish Her within. You are being worshipped with water for washing your feet.

ॐ त्रिपुरां त्रिगुणाधारां मार्गज्ञान स्वरूपिणीम् ।
त्रैलोक्य वन्दितां देवीं त्रिमुर्तिं पूजयाम्यहम् ॥

oṁ tripurāṁ triguṇādhārāṁ mārgajñāna svarūpiṇīm trailokya vanditāṁ devīṁ trimurtiṁ pūjayāmyaham

Oṁ You are the residence of the three cities, the support of the three guṇas, the intrinsic nature of the road to Wisdom. The Goddess who is praised in the three worlds, oh Image of the Three, I am worshipping you.

ॐ भूर्भुवः स्वः चन्द्रघंटे इहा गच्छ इहतिष्ठ चन्द्रघंटायै नमः । चन्द्रघंटामावाहयामि स्थापयामि नमः ।
पाध्यादिभिः पूजनम्बिधाय ॥

oṁ bhūrbhuvaḥ svaḥ caṇdraghaṇṭe ihā gaccha ihatiṣṭa candraghaṇṭāyai namaḥ candraghaṇṭāmāvāhayāmi sthāpayāmi namaḥ pādhyādibhiḥ pūjanambidhāya

Oṁ the Infinite Beyond Conception, the gross body, the subtle body and the causal body. Goddess of Practice, come here, stay here. I bow to the Goddess of Practice. I invite the Goddess of Practice and establish Her within. You are being worshipped with water for washing your feet.

ॐ कालिकां तु कलातीतां कल्याण हृदयां शिवाम् ।
कल्याण जननीं नित्यं कल्याणीं पूजयाम्यहम् ॥

oṁ kālikāṁ tu kalātītāṁ kalyāṇa hridayāṁ śivām kalyāṇa jananīṁ nityaṁ kalyāṇīṁ pūjayāmyaham

Oṁ You divide Time, but remain beyond division, Welfare in the heart of Lord Śiva. Always grant Welfare, oh Divine Mother, I worship the Goddess of Welfare.

ॐ भूर्भुवः स्वः कुष्माण्ड इहा गच्छ इहतिष्ठ कुष्माण्डायै नमः । कुष्माण्डामावाहयामि स्थापयामि नमः । पाध्यादिभिः पूजनम्बिधाय ॥

oṁ bhūrbhuvaḥ svaḥ kuṣmāṇḍa ihā gaccha ihatiṣṭa kuṣmāṇḍāyai namaḥ kuṣmāṇḍāmāvāhayāmi sthāpayāmi namaḥ pādhyādibhiḥ pūjanambidhāya

Oṁ the Infinite Beyond Conception, the gross body, the subtle body and the causal body. Goddess of Refinement, come here, stay here. I bow to the Goddess of Refinement. I invite the Goddess of Refinement and establish Her within. You are being worshipped with water for washing your feet.

ॐ अणिमादि गुणोदारां मकराकार चक्षुसम् ।
अनन्त शक्ति भेदां तां कामाक्षीं पूजयाम्यहम् ॥

oṁ aṇimādi guṇodārāṁ makarākāra cakṣusam
ananta śakti bhedāṁ tāṁ kāmākṣīṁ pūjayāmyaham

Oṁ You give rise to the qualities of every atom, the eyes that perceive all form. You distinguish the infinite energy, oh Eyes of Desire, I am worshipping you.

ॐ भूर्भुवः स्वः स्कन्दमातः इहा गच्छ इहतिष्ठ स्कन्दमात्रे नमः । स्कन्दमातरमावाहयामि स्थापयामि नमः । पाध्यादिभिः पूजनम्बिधाय ॥

oṁ bhūrbhuvaḥ svaḥ skandamātaḥ ihā gaccha ihatiṣṭa skandamātre namaḥ skandamātaramāvāhayāmi sthāpayāmi namaḥ pādhyādibhiḥ pūjanambidhāya

Oṁ the Infinite Beyond Conception, the gross body, the subtle body and the causal body. Goddess who Nurtures Divinity, come here, stay here. I bow to the Goddess who Nurtures Divinity. I invite the Goddess who Nurtures Divinity and establish Her within. You are being worshipped with water for washing your feet.

ॐ चण्डवीरां चण्डमायां चण्डमुण्ड प्रभञ्जनीम् ।
तां नमामि च देवेशीं चण्डिकां पूजयाम्यहम् ॥

oṁ caṇḍavīrāṁ caṇḍamāyāṁ
caṇḍamuṇḍa prabhañjanīm
tāṁ namāmi ca deveśīṁ caṇḍikāṁ pūjayāmyaham

Oṁ you are the warrior against anger, the limitation of anger, the stupidity of anger you cut asunder. I bow to Her, the Supreme Goddess, I worship She who Tears Apart Thoughts.

ॐ भूर्भुवः स्वः कात्यायनि इहा गच्छ इहतिष्ट कात्यायन्यै
नमः । कात्यायनीमावाहयामि स्थापयामि नमः ।
पाध्यादिभिः पूजनम्बिधाय ॥

oṁ bhūrbhuvaḥ svaḥ kātyāyani ihā gaccha ihatiṣṭa kātyāyanyai namaḥ kātyāyanīmāvāhayāmi sthāpayāmi namaḥ pādhyādibhiḥ pūjanambidhāya

Oṁ the Infinite Beyond Conception, the gross body, the subtle body and the causal body. Goddess who is Ever Pure, come here, stay here. I bow to the Goddess who is Ever Pure. I invite the Goddess who is Ever Pure and establish Her within. You are being worshipped with water for washing your feet.

ॐ सुखानन्द करीं शान्तां सर्व देवैर्नमस्कृताम् ।
सर्व भूतात्मिकां देवीं शाम्भवीं पूजयाम्यहम् ॥

oṁ sukhānanda karīṁ śāntāṁ
sarva devairnamaskṛtām
sarva bhūtātmikāṁ devīṁ
śāmbhavīṁ pūjayāmyaham

Oṁ the Bliss of happiness, Cause of Peace, all the Gods continually bow to you. You are the soul of all existence, oh Goddess, you who belong to Śiva, I worship you.

ॐ भूर्भुवः स्वः कालरात्रि इहा गच्छ इहतिष्ठ कालरात्र्यै नमः । कालरात्रीमावाहयामि स्थापयामि नमः । पाध्यादिभिः पूजनम्बिधाय ॥

oṁ bhūrbhuvaḥ svaḥ kālarātri ihā gaccha ihatiṣṭa kālarātryai namaḥ kālarātrīmāvāhayāmi sthāpayāmi namaḥ pādhyādibhiḥ pūjanambidhāya

Oṁ the Infinite Beyond Conception, the gross body, the subtle body and the causal body. Dark Night (surrendering the ego), come here, stay here. I bow to the Dark Night. I invite the Dark Night and establish Her within. You are being worshipped with water for washing your feet.

ॐ चण्डवीरां चण्डमायां रक्तबीज प्रभञ्जनीम् ।
तां नमामि च देवेशीं गायत्रीं पूजयाम्यहम् ॥

oṁ caṇḍavīrāṁ caṇḍamāyāṁ
raktabīja prabhañjanīm
tāṁ namāmi ca deveśīṁ gāyatrīṁ pūjayāmyaham

Oṁ you are the warrior against anger, the limitation of anger, you cut asunder the Seed of Desire. I bow to Her, the Supreme Goddess. I worship Gāyatrī, the three forms of wisdom.

ॐ भूर्भुवः स्वः महागौरि इहा गच्छ इहतिष्ठ महागौर्यै नमः । महागौरीमावाहयामि स्थापयामि नमः । पाध्यादिभिः पूजनम्बिधाय ॥

oṁ bhūrbhuvaḥ svaḥ mahāgauri ihā gaccha ihatiṣṭa mahāgauryai namaḥ mahāgaurīmāvāhayāmi sthāpayāmi namaḥ pādhyādibhiḥ pūjanambidhāya

Oṁ the Infinite Beyond Conception, the gross body, the subtle body and the causal body. The Great Radiant Light, come here, stay here. I bow to the Great Radiant Light. I invite the Great Radiant Light and establish Her within. You are being worshipped with water for washing your feet.

ॐ सुन्दरीं स्वर्णवर्णाङ्गीं सुख सौभाग्यदायिनीम् ।
सन्तोष जननीं देवीं सुभद्रां पूजयाम्यहम् ॥

oṁ sundarīṁ svarṇavarṇāṅgīṁ
sukha saubhāgyadāyinīm
santoṣa jananīṁ devīṁ subhadrāṁ pūjayāmyaham

Oṁ Beautiful with a golden-colored body, bestower of happiness and beauty. Oh Mother of the Universe, the Goddess of Contentment, I worship the Excellent of excellence.

ॐ भूर्भुवः स्वः सिद्धिदे इहा गच्छ इहतिष्ट सिद्धिदायै नमः ।
सिद्धिदामावाहयामि स्थापयामि नमः । पाध्यादिभिः
पूजनम्बिधाय ॥

oṁ bhūrbhuvaḥ svaḥ siddhide ihā gaccha ihatiṣṭa
siddhidāyai namaḥ siddhidāmāvāhayāmi sthāpayāmi
namaḥ pādhyādibhiḥ pūjanambidhāya

Oṁ the Infinite Beyond Conception, the gross body, the subtle body and the causal body. The Grantor of Perfection, come here, stay here. I bow to the Grantor of Perfection. I invite the Grantor of Perfection and establish Her within. You are being worshipped with water for washing your feet.

ॐ दुर्गमे दुस्तरेकार्ये भयदुर्ग विनाशिनि ।
पूजयामि सदा भक्त्या दुर्गां दुर्गतिनाशिनीम् ॥

oṁ durgame dustarekārye bhayadurga vināśini
pūjayāmi sadā bhaktyā durgāṁ durgatināśinīm

Oṁ You are the Destroyer of fear from difficulties for me, from the effects of wickedness. I always worship with devotion the Reliever of Difficulties, who destroys all difficulties.

ॐ प्रथमं शैलपुत्री च द्वितीयं ब्रह्मचारिणी ।
तृतीयं चन्द्रघण्टेति कूष्माण्डेति चतुर्थकम् ॥

oṁ prathamaṁ śailaputrī ca dvitīyaṁ brahmacāriṇī
tṛtīyaṁ candraghaṇṭeti kūṣmāṇḍeti caturthakam

Oṁ First is the Goddess of Inspiration, and second the Goddess of Learning; third is the Goddess of Practice, the Goddess of Refinement is fourth.

पञ्चमं स्कन्दमातेति षष्ठं कात्यायनीति च ।
सप्तमं कालरात्रीति महागौरीति चाष्टमम् ॥

pañcamaṁ skandamāteti ṣaṣṭhaṁ kātyāyanīti ca
saptamaṁ kālarātrīti mahāgaurīti cāṣṭamam
Fifth is the Goddess who Nurtures Divinity, sixth is the One Who is Ever Pure; seventh is the Goddess of the Dark Night of Surrendering the Ego, the Goddess of the Great Radiant Light is eighth.

नवमं सिद्धिदात्री च नवदुर्गाः प्रकीर्तिताः ।
उक्तान्येतानि नामानि ब्रह्मणैव महात्मना ॥

navamaṁ siddhidātrī ca navadurgāḥ prakīrtitāḥ
uktānyetāni nāmāni brahmaṇaiva mahātmanā
Ninth is the Goddess who Grants Perfection. The nine Durgās, Relievers of Difficulties, have been enumerated, and these names have been revealed by the great soul of the Supreme Himself.

श्री दुर्गायै नमः ॥

śrī durgāyai namaḥ
We bow to the Respected Reliever of Difficulties

nava patrikā pūjā

worship of the nine containers of divinity

ॐ दुर्गे देवि समागच्छ सान्निध्यमिह कल्पय ।
रम्भारूपेण सर्वत्र शान्तिं कुरु नमोऽस्तु ते ॥

oṁ durge devi samāgaccha sānnidhyamiha kalpaya
rambhārūpeṇa sarvatra śāntiṁ kuru namo-stu te

Oṁ Oh Goddess Durgā, come here and reside in my thoughts. In the form of beauty everywhere make peace. I bow to you.

ॐ रम्भाधिष्ठात्र्यै ब्रह्माण्यै नमः

oṁ rambhādhiṣṭhātryai brahmāṇyai namaḥ

Oṁ thus is sung a hymn to Beauty. I bow to the Creative Energy.

महिषासुरयुद्धेषु कच्वीभूतासि सुव्रते ।
मम चानुग्रहार्थाय आगतागि हरप्रिये ॥

mahiṣāsurayuddheṣu kacvībhūtāsi suvrate
mama cānugrahārthāya āgatāgi harapriye

In the battle with the Great Ego, you shined upon all existence, oh One of Excellent Vows. For the purpose of my advancement, come oh Beloved of God.

ॐ कच्व्यधिष्ठात्र्यै कालिकायै नमः

oṁ kacvyadhiṣṭhātryai kālikāyai namaḥ

Oṁ thus is sung a hymn to the Shining One. I bow to She who is Beyond Time.

हरिद्रे वरदे देवि उमारूपासि सुव्रते ।
मम विघ्नविनाशाय प्रसीद त्वं हरप्रिये ॥

haridre varade devi umārūpāsi suvrate
mama vighnavināśāya prasīda tvaṁ harapriye

Oh Goddess covered in tumeric, in the form of Umā you give boons, oh One of Excellent Vows. Destroy all of my obstacles. You be pleased, oh Beloved of God.

ॐ हरिद्राधिष्ठात्र्यै दुर्गायै नमः

oṁ haridrādhiṣṭhātryai durgāyai namaḥ
Oṁ thus is sung a hymn to the Goddess covered in tumeric. I bow to the Reliever of Difficulties.

निशुम्भशुम्भमथने सेन्द्रैर्दैवगणैः सह ।
जयन्ति पूजितासि त्वमस्माकं वरदा भव ॥

niśumbhaśumbhamathane sendrairdaivagaṇaiḥ saha
jayanti pūjitāsi tvamasmākaṁvaradā bhava
You destroy Self-Deprecation and Self-Conceit along with the multitude of the armies of the Gods. You are being worshipped along with those who are victorious. Give us boons.

ॐ जयन्त्याधिष्ठात्र्यै कौमार्यै नमः

oṁ jayantyādhiṣṭhātryai kaumāryai namaḥ
Oṁ thus is sung a hymn to the Goddess of Victory. I bow to the Ever Pure One.

महादेवप्रियकरो वासुदेवप्रियः सदा ।
उमाप्रीतिकरो वृक्षो बिल्वरूप नमोऽस्तु ते ॥

mahādevapriyakaro vāsudevapriyaḥ sadā
umāprītikaro vṛkṣo bilvarūpa namo-stu te
She is the beloved of Mahādeva (Śiva), and She is always beloved of Vāsudeva (Viṣṇu). Umā loves this tree. In the form of Bilva I bow to you.

ॐ बिल्वाधिष्ठात्र्यै शिवायै नमः

bilvādhiṣṭātryai śivāyai namaḥ
Oṁ thus is sung a hymn to the Bilva. I bow to Śivā (Divine Mother).

दाढिमि त्वः पुरा युद्धे रक्तबिजस्य सम्मुखे ।
उमाकार्यं कृतं यस्मात्तस्मात्त्वं रक्ष मां सदा ॥

dāḍhimi tvaḥ purā yuddhe raktabijasya sammukhe
umākāryaṁ kṛtaṁ yasmāttasmāttaṁ rakṣa māṁ sadā

You fought with the multitudes of Raktabijas facing you. In order to perform the work of Umā, always protect me.

ॐ दाढिम्यधिष्ठात्र्यै रक्तदन्तिकायै नमः

oṁ dāḍhimyadhiṣṭhātryai raktadantikāyai namaḥ
Oṁ thus is sung a hymn to the Multitudes. I bow to She with Red Teeth.

हरप्रीतिकरो वृक्षोह्यशोकः शोकनाशनः ।
दुर्गाप्रीतिकरो यस्मान्मामशोकं सदा कुरु ॥

harapritikaro vṛkṣohyaśokaḥ śokanāśanaḥ
durgāprītikaro yasmānmāmaśokaṁ sadā kuru
Hara (Śiva) loves this tree, yesterday's grief and all grief it destroys. Durgā especially loves this, so make me eternally free from grief.

ॐ अशोकाधिष्ठात्र्यै शोकरहितायै नमः

oṁ aśokādhiṣṭhātryai śokarahitāyai namaḥ
Oṁ thus is sung a hymn to Freedom from Grief. I bow to She who makes us free from grief.

यस्य पत्रे वसेदेवी मानवृक्षः शचीप्रियः ।
मम चानुग्रहार्थाय पूजां गृह्व प्रसीद मे ॥

yasya patre vasedevī mānavṛkṣaḥ śacīpriyaḥ
mama cānugrahārthāya pūjāṁ gṛhva prasīda me
Upon this leaf from the tree of thought the Goddess sits, the beloved of Sacī (Indra's wife). For the purpose of my progress please accept my worship and be pleased with me.

ॐ मानाधिष्ठात्र्यै चामुण्डायै नमः

oṁ mānādhiṣṭhātryai cāmuṇḍāyai namaḥ
Oṁ thus is sung a hymn to Thoughts. I bow to She who moves in the paradigm of Consciousness.

जगतः प्राणरक्षार्थं ब्रह्मणा निर्मितं पुरा ।

उमाप्रीतिकरं धान्यं तस्मात्त्वं रक्ष मां सदा ॥

jagataḥ prāṇarakṣārthaṁ brahmaṇā nirmitaṁ purā
umāprītikaraṁ dhānyaṁ tasmāttvaṁ rakṣa māṁ sadā
This giving of wealth is beloved by Umā. It protects the life force of the perceivable universe and proves the validity of the Supreme Divinity. Please protect me always.

ॐ धान्याधिष्ठात्र्यै महालक्ष्म्यै नमः

oṁ dhānyādhiṣṭhātryai mahālakṣmyai namaḥ
Oṁ thus is sung a hymn to the Giving of Wealth. I bow to the Great Goddess of True Wealth.

nava durgā pūjā (2)

worship of the nine forms of durgā (2)

चतुर्मुखीं जगद्धात्रीं हंसरूढां वरप्रदाम् ।
सृष्टिरूपां महाभागां ब्रह्माणीं तां नमाम्यहम् ॥

caturmukhīṁ jagaddhātrīṁ haṁsarūḍhāṁ varapradām
sṛṣṭirūpāṁ mahābhāgāṁ brahmāṇīṁ tāṁ namāmyaham

She has four faces, the Progenitress of the Universe who rides upon a swan and grants boons. She is the form of creation, of great parts. We bow to Her, to Brahmāṇī.

ॐ ह्रीं श्रीं ब्रह्माण्यै नमः

oṁ hrīṁ śrīṁ brahmāṇyai namaḥ

Oṁ Māyā, Increase, I bow to the Creative Energy.

वृषारूढां शुभां शुभ्रां त्रिनेत्रां वरदां शिवाम् ।
माहेश्वरीं नमाम्यद्य सृष्टिसंहारकारिणीम् ॥

vṛṣārūḍhāṁ śubhāṁ śubhrāṁ
trinetrāṁ varadāṁ śivām
māheśvarīṁ namāmyadya sṛṣṭisaṁhārakāriṇīm

She rides upon a buffalo, shining radiantly, She is Śivā with three eyes and She grants boons. We bow to Māheśvarī, the Great Seer of All, who is the cause of the dissolution of the creation.

ॐ ह्रीं श्रीं माहेश्वर्यै नमः

oṁ hrīṁ śrīṁ māheśvaryai namaḥ

Oṁ Māyā, Increase, I bow to the Great Seer of All.

कौमारीं पीतवसनां मयूरवरवाहनाम् ।
शक्तिहस्तां महाभागां नमामि वरदां सदा ॥

kaumārīṁ pītavasanāṁ mayūravaravāhanām
śaktihastāṁ mahābhāgāṁ namāmi varadāṁ sadā

Kumārī, the Ever Pure One, is of a yellow color. She rides upon a peacock, with energy in Her hands, of great parts. I bow to She who always grants boons.

ॐ ह्रीं श्रीं कौमार्यै नमः

oṁ hrīṁ śrīṁ kaumāryai namaḥ
Oṁ Māyā, Increase, I bow to the Ever Pure One.

शङ्खचक्रगदापद्मधारिणीं कृष्णरूपिणीम् ।
स्थितिरूपां खगेन्द्रस्थां वैष्णवीं तां नमाम्यहम् ॥

śaṅkhacakragadāpadmadhāriṇīṁ kṛṣṇarūpiṇīm sthitirūpāṁ khagendrasthāṁ vaiṣṇavīṁ tāṁ namāmyaham
She holds the conch shell, discus, club and lotus. As the intrinsic nature of Kṛṣṇa, She is the form of Circumstances. Situated with the king of swords, She is Vaiṣṇavī, the Energy pervading all existence. We bow to Her.

ॐ ह्रीं श्रीं वैष्णव्यै नमः

oṁ hrīṁ śrīṁ vaiṣṇavyai namaḥ
Oṁ Māyā, Increase, I bow to the Energy pervading all existence.

वराहरूपिणीं देवीं दंष्ट्रोद्धृतवसुन्दराम् ।
शुभदां पीतवसनां वाराहीं तां नमाम्यहम् ॥

varāharūpiṇīṁ devīṁ daṁṣṭroddhṛtavasundarām śubhadāṁ pītavasanāṁ vārāhīṁ tāṁ namāmyaham
She is the Goddess who appears as a boar. Her great teeth are beautiful. She is the Giver of Purity, of yellow color. We bow to Her, to Vārāhī, the Boar of Sacrifice.

ॐ ह्रीं श्रीं वाराह्यै नमः

oṁ hrīṁ śrīṁ vārāhyai namaḥ
Oṁ Māyā, Increase, I bow to the Boar of Sacrifice.

नृसिंहरूपिणीं देवीं दैत्यदानवदर्पहाम् ।
शुभां शुभप्रदां शुभ्रां नारसिंहीं नमाम्यहम् ॥

**nṛsiṁharūpiṇīṁ devīṁ daityadānavadarpahām
śubhāṁ śubhapradāṁ śubhrāṁ nārasiṁhīṁ namāmyaham**

She is the Goddess who appears as the man-lion, the reflection of the forces of duality and animalism. She shines and gives forth the radiance of Her shine. We bow to Nārasiṁhī, the man-lion of courage.

ॐ ह्रीं श्रीं नारसिंह्यै नमः

oṁ hrīṁ śrīṁ nārasiṁhyai namaḥ

Oṁ Māyā, Increase, I bow to Nārasiṁhī, the man-lion of courage.

इन्द्राणीं गजकूम्भस्थां सहस्रानयनोज्ज्वलाम् ।
नमामि वरदां देवीं सर्वदेवनमस्कृताम् ॥

**indrāṇīṁ gajakūmbhasthāṁ sahasrānayanojjalām
namāmi varadāṁ devīṁ sarvadevanamaskṛtām**

Indrāṇī, the Energy of the Rule of the Pure, sits upon the shoulders of an elephant, with a thousand eyes shining. I bow to the Goddess who gives boons, and to whom all the Gods also bow as well.

ॐ ह्रीं श्रीं इन्द्राण्यै नमः

oṁ hrīṁ śrīṁ indrāṇyai namaḥ

Oṁ Māyā, Increase, I bow to Indrāṇī, the Energy of the Rule of the Pure.

चामुण्डां चण्डमथनीं मुण्डमाल्योपशोभिताम् ।
अटटहासमूदितां नमाम्यात्मविभूतये ॥

**cāmuṇḍāṁ caṇḍamathanīṁ muṇḍamālopaśobhitām
aṭaṭahāsamūditāṁ namāmyātmavibhūtaye**

The Slayer of Passion and Meaness, who churns Passion, shines forth with a garland of skulls. She emits a loud laugh. I bow to the soul who manifests in existence.

ॐ ह्रीं श्रीं चामुण्डायै नमः

oṁ hrīṁ śrīṁ cāmuṇḍāyai namaḥ
Oṁ Māyā, Increase, I bow to the Slayer of Passion and Meaness.

कात्यायनीं दशभूजां महिषासुरमर्दिनीम् ।
प्रसन्नवदनां देवीं वरदां तां नमाम्यहम् ॥

kātyāyanīṁ daśabhūjāṁ mahiṣāsuramardinīm
prasannavadanāṁ devīṁ varadāṁ tāṁ namāmyaham
The Ever Pure One has ten arms, the Slayer of the Great Ego. She is the Goddess with the pleased face. We bow to Her, the Giver of Boons.

ॐ ह्रीं श्रीं कात्यायन्यै नमः

oṁ hrīṁ śrīṁ kātyāyanyai namaḥ
Oṁ Māyā, Increase, I bow to the Ever Pure One.

चण्डिके नवदुर्गे त्वं महादेवमनोरमे ।
पूजां समस्तां संगृह्य रक्ष मां त्रिदशेश्वरि ॥

caṇḍike navadurge tvaṁ mahādevamanorame
pūjāṁ samastāṁ saṁgṛhya rakṣa māṁ tridaśeśvari
You Who Tear Apart Thoughts and the other nine Durgās are the beauty of Śiva. Please accept this all-encompassing worship and protect me, oh Supreme among the three qualities.

ॐ ह्रीं श्रीं चण्डिकायै नमः

oṁ hrīṁ śrīṁ caṇḍikāyai namaḥ
Oṁ Māyā, Increase, I bow to She Who Tears Apart Thoughts.

ॐ ह्रीं श्रीं नवदुर्गायै नमः

oṁ hrīṁ śrīṁ navadurgāyai namaḥ
Oṁ Māyā, Increase, I bow to the Nine forms of Durgā.

yantra pūjā

worship of the yantra

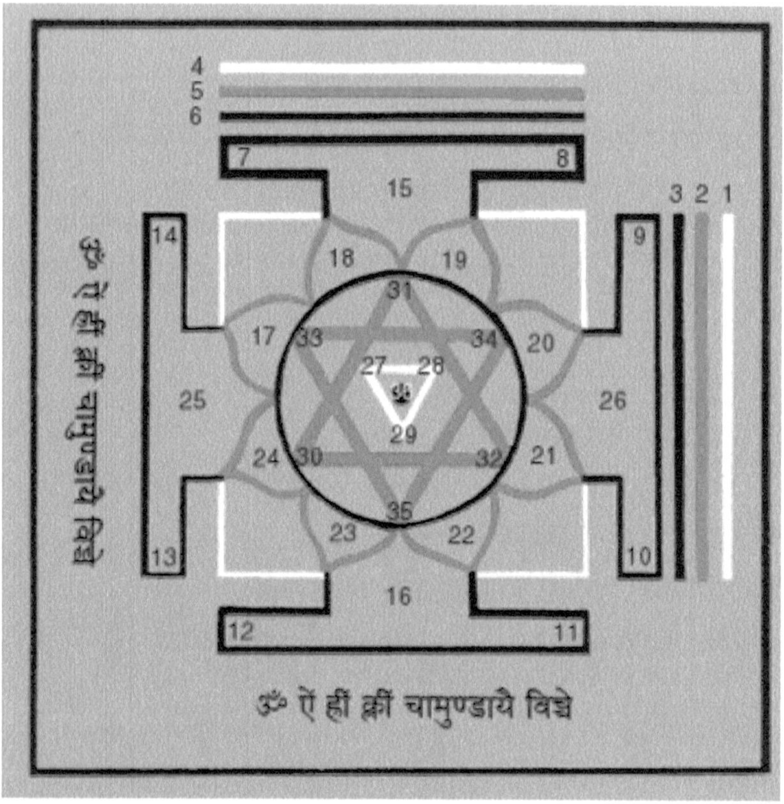

सोभयस्यास्य देवस्य विग्रहो यन्त्र कल्पणा ।
विना यन्त्रेण चेत्पूजा देवता न प्रसीदति ॥

sobhayasyāsya devasya vigraho yantra kalpaṇā
vinā yantreṇa cetpūjā devatā na prasīdati

We contemplate the form of the yantra which depicts the radiance of the Gods. Without using the yantra in the worship of consciousness the Gods are not as pleased.

यन्त्र मन्त्रमयं प्रहुर्देवता मन्त्ररूपिणी ।
यन्त्रेणापूजितो देवः सहसा न प्रसीदति ।
सर्वेषामपि मन्त्रणां यन्त्र पूजा प्रशस्यते ॥

yantra mantramayaṁ prahurdevatā mantrarūpiṇī
yantreṇāpūjito devaḥ sahasā na prasīdati
sarveṣāmapi mantraṇāṁ yantra pūjā praśasyate

The yantra conveys the objective meaning of the mantra, while the deity is the form of the mantra. By worshiping the deity by means of the yantra, the deity is completely satisfied. To attain all the bliss of the mantra, the worship of the yantra is highly recommended.

ततः स्थण्डिलमध्ये तु हसौःगर्भं त्रिकोणकम् ।
षट्कोणं तद्वहिर्वृत्तां ततोऽष्टदलपङ्कजम् ।
भूपुरं तद्वहिर्विद्वान् विलिखेद्यन्त्रमुत्तमम् ॥

tataḥ sthaṇḍilamadhye tu hasauḥgarbhaṁ trikoṇakam
ṣaṭkoṇaṁ tadvahirvṛttāṁ tato-ṣṭadalapaṅkajam
bhūpuraṁ tadvahirvidvān vilikhedhyantramuttamam

In the center of the place of worship is the single point which contains ha and sauḥ, Śiva and Śakti without distinction. Thereafter comes the three cornered equalateral triangle. Then six angles, outside of which is a circle, followed by eight lotus petals. The four doors are outside, and in this way the wise will draw the most excellent yantra.

- 1 -

ॐ मुकुन्दाय नमः

oṁ mukundāya namaḥ
oṁ I bow to the Giver of Liberation.

- 2 -

ॐ ईशनाय नमः

oṁ īśanāya namaḥ
oṁ I bow to the Ruler of All.

- 3 -

ॐ पुरन्दराय नमः

oṁ purandarāya namaḥ
oṁ I bow to the Giver of Completeness.

- 4 -

ॐ ब्रह्मणे नमः

oṁ brahmaṇe namaḥ
oṁ I bow to the Creative Consciousness.

- 5 -

ॐ वैवस्वताय नमः

oṁ vaivasvatāya namaḥ
oṁ I bow to the Universal Radiance.

- 6 -

ॐ इन्दवे नमः

oṁ indave namaḥ
oṁ I bow to the Ruler of Devotion.

- 7 -

ॐ आधारशक्तये नमः

oṁ ādhāraśaktaye namaḥ
oṁ I bow to the primal energy which sustains existence.

- 8 -

ॐ कुर्म्माय नमः

oṁ kurmmāya namaḥ
oṁ I bow to the Tortoise which supports creation.

\- 9 -

ॐ अनन्ताय नमः

oṁ anantāya namaḥ
oṁ I bow to Infinity (personified as a thousand hooded snake who stands upon the Tortoise holding aloft the worlds).

\- 10 -

ॐ पृथिव्यै नमः

oṁ pṛthivyai namaḥ
oṁ I bow to the Earth.

\- 11 -

ॐ क्षीरसमूद्राय नमः

oṁ kṣīrasamūdrāya namaḥ
oṁ I bow to the milk ocean, or ocean of nectar, the infinite expanse of existence from which all manifested.

\- 12 -

ॐ श्वेतद्वीपाय नमः

oṁ śvetadvīpāya namaḥ
oṁ I bow to the Island of Purity, which is in the ocean.

\- 13 -

ॐ मणिमन्दपाय नमः

oṁ maṇimandapāya namaḥ
oṁ I bow to the Palace of Gems, which is on the island, the home of the Divine Mother.

\- 14 -

ॐ कल्पवृक्षाय नमः

oṁ kalpavṛkṣāya namaḥ
oṁ I bow to the Tree of Fulfillment, which satisfies all desires, growing in the palace courtyard.

\- 15 -

ॐ मणिवेदिकायै नमः

oṁ maṇivedikāyai namaḥ
oṁ I bow to the altar containing the gems of wisdom.

- 16 -

ॐ रत्नसिंहासनाय नमः

oṁ ratnasiṁhāsanāya namaḥ
oṁ I bow to the throne of the jewel.

- 17 -

ॐ धर्म्माय नमः

oṁ dharmmāya namaḥ
oṁ I bow to the Way of Truth and Harmony.

- 18 -

ॐ ज्ञानाय नमः

oṁ jñānāya namaḥ
oṁ I bow to Wisdom.

- 19 -

ॐ वैराग्याय नमः

oṁ vairāgyāya namaḥ
oṁ I bow to Detachment.

- 20 -

ॐ ईश्वर्ज्याय नमः

oṁ īśvarjyāya namaḥ
oṁ I bow to the Imperishable Qualities.

- 21 -

ॐ अधर्म्माय नमः

oṁ adharmmāya namaḥ
oṁ I bow to Disharmony.

- 22 -

ॐ अज्ञानाय नमः

oṁ ajñānāya namaḥ
oṁ I bow to Ignorance.

- 23 -

ॐ अवैराग्याय नमः

oṁ avairāgyāya namaḥ
oṁ I bow to Attachment.

- 24 -

ॐ अनीश्वर्ज्याय नमः

oṁ anīśvarjyāya namaḥ
oṁ I bow to the Transient.

- 25 -

ॐ अनन्ताय नमः

oṁ anantāya namaḥ
oṁ I bow to the Infinite.

- 26 -

ॐ पद्माय नमः

oṁ padmāya namaḥ
oṁ I bow to the Lotus.

- 27 -

अं अर्कमण्डलाय द्वादशकलात्मने नमः

aṁ arkamaṇḍalāya dvādaśakalātmane namaḥ
"A" we bow to the twelve aspects of the realm of the sun. Tapinī, Tāpinī, Dhūmrā, Marīci, Jvālinī, Ruci, Sudhūmrā, Bhoga-dā, Viśvā, Bodhinī, Dhārinī, Kṣamā; Containing heat, Emanating heat, Smoky, Ray-producing, Burning, Lustrous, Purple or Smoky-red, Granting enjoyment, Universal, Which makes known, Productive of Consciousness, Which supports, Which forgives.

- 28 -

उं सोममण्डलाय षोडशकलात्मने नमः

uṁ somamaṇḍalāya ṣoḍaśakalātmane namaḥ
"U" we bow to the sixteen aspects of the realm of the moon. Amṛtā, Prāṇadā, Puṣā, Tuṣṭi, Puṣṭi, Rati, Dhṛti, Śaśinī, Candrikā, Kānti, Jyotsnā, Śrī, Prīti, Aṅgadā, Pūrṇā, Pūrṇāmṛtā; Nectar, Which sustains life, Which supports, Satisfying, Nourishing, Playful, Constancy, Unfailing, Producer of Joy, Beauty enhanced by love, Light, Grantor of Prosperity, Affectionate, Purifying the body, Complete, Full of Bliss.

- 29 -

मं वह्निमण्डलाय दशकलात्मने नमः

maṁ vahnimaṇḍalāya daśakalātmane namaḥ
"M" we bow to the ten aspects of the realm of fire: Dhūmrā, Arciḥ, Jvalinī, Śūkṣmā, Jvālinī, Visphuliṅginī, Suśrī, Surūpā, Kapilā, Havya-Kavya-Vahā; Smoky Red, Flaming, Shining, Subtle,

Burning, Sparkling, Beautiful, Well-formed, Tawny, The Messenger to Gods and Ancestors.

- 30 -

ॐ सं सत्त्वाय नमः

oṁ saṁ sattvāya namaḥ
oṁ I bow to activity, execution, light, knowledge, being.

- 31 -

ॐ रं रजसे नमः

oṁ raṁ rajase namaḥ
oṁ I bow to desire, inspiration, becoming.

- 32 -

ॐ तं तमसे नमः

oṁ taṁ tamase namaḥ
oṁ I bow to wisdom, to the darkness which exposes light, to rest.

- 33 -

ॐ आं आत्मने नमः

oṁ āṁ ātmane namaḥ
oṁ I bow to the Soul.

- 34 -

ॐ अं अन्तरात्मने नमः

oṁ aṁ antarātmane namaḥ
oṁ I bow to the Innermost Soul.

- 35 -

ॐ पं परमात्मने नमः

oṁ paṁ paramātmane namaḥ
oṁ I bow to the Universal Soul, or the Consciousness which exceeds manifestation.

- 36 -

ॐ ह्रीं ज्ञानात्मने नमः

oṁ hrīṁ jñānātmane namaḥ
oṁ I bow to the Soul of Infinite Wisdom.

Place yantra on altar.

ॐ ह्रीं श्रीं दुं दुर्गायै नमः फट्

oṁ hrīṁ śrīṁ duṁ durgāyai namaḥ phaṭ

Oṁ I bow to the Goddess, Durgā, the Grantor of Increase, who Removes all Difficulties, Purify!

ॐ यन्त्रराजाय विद्महे महायन्त्राय धीमहे ।

तन्नो यन्त्रः प्रचोदयात् ॥

oṁ yantrarājāya vidmahe mahāyantrāya dhīmahe tanno yantraḥ pracodayāt

oṁ we meditate upon the King of Yantras, contemplate the greatest yantra. May that yantra grant us increase.

ॐ ह्रीं श्रीं दुं दुर्गायै नमः सिन्दूरं समर्पयामि

oṁ hrīṁ śrīṁ duṁ durgāyai namaḥ sindūraṁ samarpayāmi

With this offering of red colored powder Oṁ I bow to the Goddess, Durgā, the Grantor of Increase, who Removes all Difficulties.

ॐ यन्त्रराजाय विद्महे महायन्त्राय धीमहे ।

तन्नो यन्त्रः प्रचोदयात् ॥

oṁ yantrarājāya vidmahe mahāyantrāya dhīmahe tanno yantraḥ pracodayāt

oṁ we meditate upon the King of Yantras, contemplate the greatest yantra. May that yantra grant us increase.

ॐ ह्रीं श्रीं दुं दुर्गायै नमः कुङ्कुमं समर्पयामि

oṁ hrīṁ śrīṁ duṁ durgāyai namaḥ kuṅkumaṁ samarpayāmi

With this offering of red colored powder Oṁ I bow to the Goddess, Durgā, the Grantor of Increase, who Removes all Difficulties.

ॐ परमेश्वराय विद्महे परातत्त्वाय धीमहे ।
तन्नो ब्रह्माः प्रचोदयात् ॥

oṁ parameśvarāya vidmahe parātattvāya dhīmahe tanno brahmāḥ pracodayāt

oṁ we meditate upon the Highest Supreme Divinity, contemplate the Highest Principle. May that Supreme Divinity grant us increase.

ॐ ह्रीं श्रीं दुं दुर्गायै नमः अक्षतान् समर्पयामि

oṁ hrīṁ śrīṁ duṁ durgāyai namaḥ akṣatān samarpayāmi

With the offering of grains of rice Oṁ I bow to the Goddess, Durgā, the Grantor of Increase, who Removes all Difficulties.

सर्वतो भद्रमण्डल देवता स्थापनम

sarvato bhadramaṇḍala devatā sthāpanam

Establishment of the Excellent Circle of Deities

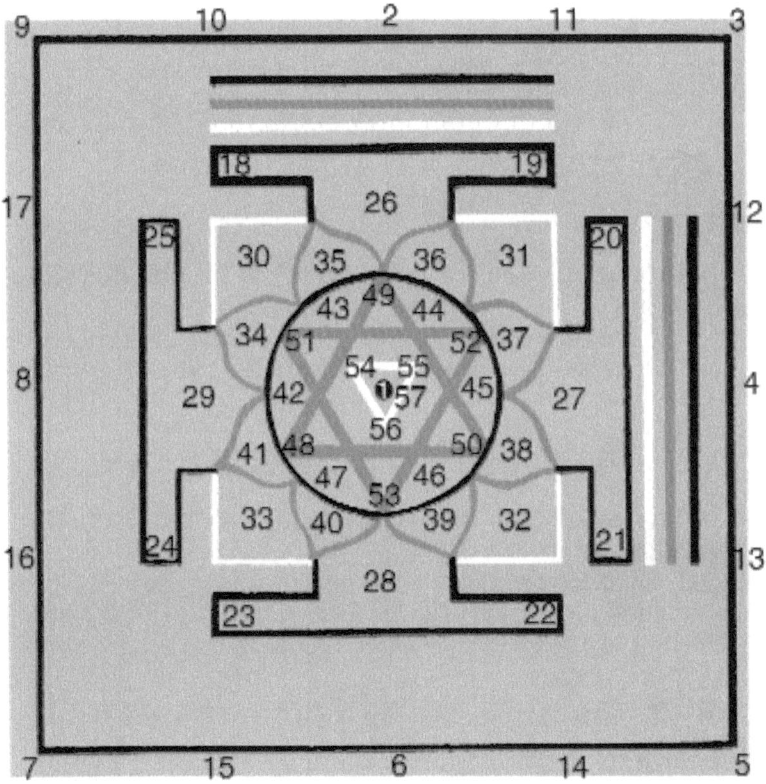

\- 1 -

ॐ भूर्भुवः स्वः ब्रह्मणे नमः ब्रह्मणमावाहयामि स्थापयामि

oṁ bhūrbhuvaḥ svaḥ brahmaṇe namaḥ
brahmaṇamāvāhayāmi sthāpayāmi

oṁ the Infinite Beyond Conception, the gross body, the subtle body and the causal body, we bow to the Creative Consciousness (Center). We invoke you, invite you and establish your presence.

\- 2 -

ॐ भूर्भुवः स्वः सोमाय नमः सोममावाहयामि स्थापयामि

oṁ bhūrbhuvaḥ svaḥ somāya namaḥ somamāvāhayāmi sthāpayāmi

oṁ the Infinite Beyond Conception, the gross body, the subtle body and the causal body, we bow to the Lord of Devotion (N). We invoke you, invite you and establish your presence.

\- 3 -

ॐ भूर्भुवः स्वः ईशानाय नमः ईशानमावाहयामि स्थापयामि

oṁ bhūrbhuvaḥ svaḥ īśānāya namaḥ īśānamāvāhayāmi sthāpayāmi

oṁ the Infinite Beyond Conception, the gross body, the subtle body and the causal body, we bow to the Ruler of All (NE). We invoke you, invite you and establish your presence.

\- 4 -

ॐ भूर्भुवः स्वः इन्द्राय नमः इन्द्रमावाहयामि स्थापयामि

oṁ bhūrbhuvaḥ svaḥ indrāya namaḥ indramāvāhayāmi sthāpayāmi

oṁ the Infinite Beyond Conception, the gross body, the subtle body and the causal body, we bow to the Rule of the Pure (E). We invoke you, invite you and establish your presence.

\- 5 -

ॐ भूर्भुवः स्वः अग्नये नमः अग्निमावाहयामि स्थापयामि

oṁ bhūrbhuvaḥ svaḥ agnaye namaḥ agnimāvāhayāmi sthāpayāmi

oṁ the Infinite Beyond Conception, the gross body, the subtle body and the causal body, we bow to the Divine Fire (SE). We invoke you, invite you and establish your presence.

\- 6 -

ॐ भूर्भुवः स्वः यमाय नमः यममावाहयामि स्थापयामि

oṁ bhūrbhuvaḥ svaḥ yamāya namaḥ yamamāvāhayāmi sthāpayāmi

oṁ the Infinite Beyond Conception, the gross body, the subtle body and the causal body, we bow to the Supreme Controller (S). We invoke you, invite you and establish your presence.

- 7 -

ॐ भूर्भुवः स्वः निर्ऋतये नमः निर्ऋतिमावाहयामि स्थापयामि

oṁ bhūrbhuvaḥ svaḥ nirṛtaye namaḥ nirṛtimāvāhayāmi sthāpayāmi

oṁ the Infinite Beyond Conception, the gross body, the subtle body and the causal body, we bow to the Destroyer (SW). We invoke you, invite you and establish your presence.

- 8 -

ॐ भूर्भुवः स्वः वरुणाय नमः वरुणमावाहयामि स्थापयामि

oṁ bhūrbhuvaḥ svaḥ varuṇāya namaḥ varuṇamāvāhayāmi sthāpayāmi

oṁ the Infinite Beyond Conception, the gross body, the subtle body and the causal body, we bow to the Lord of Equilibrium (W). We invoke you, invite you and establish your presence.

- 9 -

ॐ भूर्भुवः स्वः वायवे नमः वायुमावाहयामि स्थापयामि

oṁ bhūrbhuvaḥ svaḥ vāyave namaḥ vāyumāvāhayāmi sthāpayāmi

oṁ the Infinite Beyond Conception, the gross body, the subtle body and the causal body, we bow to the Lord of Liberation (NW). We invoke you, invite you and establish your presence.

- 10 -

ॐ भूर्भुवः स्वः अष्टवसुभ्यो नमः अष्टवसुन् आवाहयामि स्थापयामि

oṁ bhūrbhuvaḥ svaḥ aṣṭavasubhyo namaḥ aṣṭavasun āvāhayāmi sthāpayāmi

oṁ the Infinite Beyond Conception, the gross body, the subtle body and the causal body, we bow to the Eight Lords of Benificence. We invoke you, invite you and establish your presence.

- 11 -

ॐ भूर्भुवः स्वः एकादशरुद्रेभ्यो नमः
एकादशरुद्रानावाहयामि स्थापयामि

oṁ bhūrbhuvaḥ svaḥ ekādaśarudrebhyo namaḥ ekādaśarudrānāvāhayāmi sthāpayāmi

oṁ the Infinite Beyond Conception, the gross body, the subtle body and the causal body, we bow to the Eleven Relievers from Sufferings. We invoke you, invite you and establish your presence.

- 12 -

ॐ भूर्भुवः स्वः द्वादशादित्येभ्यो नमः
द्वादशादित्यानावाहयामि स्थापयामि

oṁ bhūrbhuvaḥ svaḥ dvādaśādityebhyo namaḥ dvādaśādityānāvāhayāmi sthāpayāmi

oṁ the Infinite Beyond Conception, the gross body, the subtle body and the causal body, we bow to the Twelve Sons of Light. We invoke you, invite you and establish your presence.

- 13 -

ॐ भूर्भुवः स्वः अश्विभ्यां नमः अश्विनौ आवाहयामि
स्थापयामि

oṁ bhūrbhuvaḥ svaḥ aśvibhyāṁ namaḥ aśvinau āvāhayāmi sthāpayāmi

oṁ the Infinite Beyond Conception, the gross body, the subtle body and the causal body, we bow to the Two Horses of Pure Desire. We invoke you, invite you and establish your presence.

- 14 -

ॐ भूर्भुवः स्वः सपैतृकविश्वेभ्यो देवेभ्यो नमः सपैतृकविश्वान्
देवानावाहयामि स्थापयामि

oṁ bhūrbhuvaḥ svaḥ sapaitṛkaviśvebhyo devebhyo namaḥ sapaitṛkaviśvān devānāvāhayāmi sthāpayāmi

oṁ the Infinite Beyond Conception, the gross body, the subtle body and the causal body, we bow to the Ancestors along with the Shining Ones of the Universe. We invoke you, invite you and establish your presence.

- 15 -

ॐ भूर्भुवः स्वः सप्तयक्षेभ्यो नमः सप्तयक्षानावाहयामि स्थापयामि

oṁ bhūrbhuvaḥ svaḥ saptayakṣebhyo namaḥ saptayakṣānāvāhayāmi sthāpayāmi

oṁ the Infinite Beyond Conception, the gross body, the subtle body and the causal body, we bow to the Energy which brings the good and bad of wealth. We invoke you, invite you and establish your presence.

- 16 -

ॐ भूर्भुवः स्वः अष्टकुलनागेभ्यो नमः अष्टकुलनागानावाहयामि स्थापयामि

oṁ bhūrbhuvaḥ svaḥ aṣṭakulanāgebhyo namaḥ aṣṭakulanāgānāvāhayāmi sthāpayāmi

oṁ the Infinite Beyond Conception, the gross body, the subtle body and the causal body, we bow to the Family of eight snakes. We invoke you, invite you and establish your presence.

- 17 -

ॐ भूर्भुवः स्वः गन्धर्वाऽप्सरोभ्यो नमः गन्धर्वाऽप्सरसः आवाहयामि स्थापयामि

oṁ bhūrbhuvaḥ svaḥ gandharvā-psarobhyo namaḥ gandharvā-psarasaḥ āvāhayāmi sthāpayāmi

oṁ the Infinite Beyond Conception, the gross body, the subtle body and the causal body, we bow to the celestial musicians and heavenly maidens. We invoke you, invite you and establish your presence.

- 18 -

ॐ भूर्भुवः स्वः स्कन्दाय नमः स्कन्दमावाहयामि स्थापयामि

oṁ bhūrbhuvaḥ svaḥ skandāya namaḥ skandamāvāhayāmi sthāpayāmi

oṁ the Infinite Beyond Conception, the gross body, the subtle body and the causal body, we bow to the God of War. We invoke you, invite you and establish your presence.

- 19 -

ॐ भूर्भुवः स्वः वृषभाय नमः वृषभमावाहयामि स्थापयामि

oṁ bhūrbhuvaḥ svaḥ vṛṣabhāya namaḥ vṛṣabhamāvāhayāmi sthāpayāmi

oṁ the Infinite Beyond Conception, the gross body, the subtle body and the causal body, we bow to the Bull of Discipline, Conveyance of Śiva - Nandi. We invoke you, invite you and establish your presence.

- 20 -

ॐ भूर्भुवः स्वः शूलाय नमः शूलमावाहयामि स्थापयामि

oṁ bhūrbhuvaḥ svaḥ śūlāya namaḥ śūlamāvāhayāmi sthāpayāmi

oṁ the Infinite Beyond Conception, the gross body, the subtle body and the causal body, we bow to the Spear of Concentration. We invoke you, invite you and establish your presence.

- 21 -

ॐ भूर्भुवः स्वः महाकालाय नमः महाकालमावाहयामि स्थापयामि

oṁ bhūrbhuvaḥ svaḥ mahākālāya namaḥ mahākālamāvāhayāmi sthāpayāmi

oṁ the Infinite Beyond Conception, the gross body, the subtle body and the causal body, we bow to the Great Time. We invoke you, invite you and establish your presence.

- 22 -

ॐ भूर्भुवः स्वः दक्षादि सप्तगणेभ्यो नमः दक्षादि सप्तगणानावाहयामि स्थापयामि

oṁ bhūrbhuvaḥ svaḥ dakṣādi saptagaṇebhyo namaḥ dakṣādi saptagaṇānāvāhayāmi sthāpayāmi

oṁ the Infinite Beyond Conception, the gross body, the subtle body and the causal body, we bow to Ability and the other seven qualities. We invoke you, invite you and establish your presence.

- 23 -

ॐ भूर्भुवः स्वः दुर्गायै नमः दुर्गामावाहयामि स्थापयामि

oṁ bhūrbhuvaḥ svaḥ durgāyai namaḥ durgāmāvāhayāmi sthāpayāmi

oṁ the Infinite Beyond Conception, the gross body, the subtle body and the causal body, we bow to the Reliever of Difficulties. We invoke you, invite you and establish your presence.

- 24 -

ॐ भूर्भुवः स्वः विष्णवे नमः विष्णुमावाहयामि स्थापयामि

oṁ bhūrbhuvaḥ svaḥ viṣṇave namaḥ viṣṇumāvāhayāmi sthāpayāmi

oṁ the Infinite Beyond Conception, the gross body, the subtle body and the causal body, we bow to the All-Pervading Consciousness. We invoke you, invite you and establish your presence.

- 25 -

ॐ भूर्भुवः स्वः स्वधायै नमः स्वधामावाहयामि स्थापयामि

oṁ bhūrbhuvaḥ svaḥ svadhāyai namaḥ svadhāmāvāhayāmi sthāpayāmi

oṁ the Infinite Beyond Conception, the gross body, the subtle body and the causal body, we bow to the Ancestors. We invoke you, invite you and establish your presence.

- 26 -

ॐ भूर्भुवः स्वः मृत्युरोगेभ्यो नमः मृत्युरोगानावाहयामि स्थापयामि

oṁ bhūrbhuvaḥ svaḥ mṛtyurogebhyo namaḥ mṛtyurogānāvāhayāmi sthāpayāmi

oṁ the Infinite Beyond Conception, the gross body, the subtle body and the causal body, we bow to the Spirit of deadly illnesses. We invoke you, invite you and establish your presence.

- 27 -

ॐ भूर्भुवः स्वः गणपतये नमः गणपतिमावाहयामि स्थापयामि

oṁ bhūrbhuvaḥ svaḥ gaṇapataye namaḥ gaṇapatimāvāhayāmi sthāpayāmi

oṁ the Infinite Beyond Conception, the gross body, the subtle body and the causal body, we bow to the Lord of the Multitudes.

We invoke you, invite you and establish your presence.

- 28 -

ॐ भूर्भुवः स्वः अद्भ्यो नमः अपः आवाहयामि स्थापयामि

oṁ bhūrbhuvaḥ svaḥ adbhyo namaḥ apaḥ āvāhayāmi sthāpayāmi

oṁ the Infinite Beyond Conception, the gross body, the subtle body and the causal body, we bow to Acts of Sacrifice. We invoke you, invite you and establish your presence.

- 29 -

ॐ भूर्भुवः स्वः मरुद्भ्यो नमः मरुतः आवाहयामि स्थापयामि

oṁ bhūrbhuvaḥ svaḥ marudbhyo namaḥ marutaḥ āvāhayāmi sthāpayāmi

oṁ the Infinite Beyond Conception, the gross body, the subtle body and the causal body, we bow to the Shining Ones. We invoke you, invite you and establish your presence.

- 30 -

ॐ भूर्भुवः स्वः पृथिव्यै नमः पृथ्वीमावाहयामि स्थापयामि

oṁ bhūrbhuvaḥ svaḥ pṛthivyai namaḥ pṛthvīmāvāhayāmi sthāpayāmi

oṁ the Infinite Beyond Conception, the gross body, the subtle body and the causal body, we bow to the Earth. We invoke you, invite you and establish your presence.

- 31 -

ॐ भूर्भुवः स्वः गङ्गादिनदीभ्यो नमः गङ्गादिनदीः आवाहयामि स्थापयामि

oṁ bhūrbhuvaḥ svaḥ gaṅgādinadībhyo namaḥ gaṅgādinadīḥ āvāhayāmi sthāpayāmi

oṁ the Infinite Beyond Conception, the gross body, the subtle body and the causal body, we bow to the Ganges and other rivers.
We invoke you, invite you and establish your presence.

- 32 -

ॐ भूर्भुवः स्वः सप्तसागरेभ्यो नमः सप्तसागरानावाहयामि स्थापयामि

oṁ bhūrbhuvaḥ svaḥ saptasāgarebhyo namaḥ saptasāgarānāvāhayāmi sthāpayāmi

oṁ the Infinite Beyond Conception, the gross body, the subtle body and the causal body, we bow to the Seven Seas. We invoke you, invite you and establish your presence.

- 33 -

ॐ भूर्भुवः स्वः मेरवे नमः मेरुमावाहयामि स्थापयामि

oṁ bhūrbhuvaḥ svaḥ merave namaḥ merumāvāhayāmi sthāpayāmi

oṁ the Infinite Beyond Conception, the gross body, the subtle body and the causal body, we bow to Mount Meru. We invoke you, invite you and establish your presence.

- 34 -

ॐ भूर्भुवः स्वः गदाय नमः गदामावाहयामि स्थापयामि

oṁ bhūrbhuvaḥ svaḥ gadāya namaḥ gadāmāvāhayāmi sthāpayāmi

oṁ the Infinite Beyond Conception, the gross body, the subtle body and the causal body, we bow to the Club. We invoke you, invite you and establish your presence.

- 35 -

ॐ भूर्भुवः स्वः त्रिशूलाय नमः त्रिशूलमावाहयामि स्थापयामि

oṁ bhūrbhuvaḥ svaḥ triśūlāya namaḥ triśūlamāvāhayāmi sthāpayāmi

oṁ the Infinite Beyond Conception, the gross body, the subtle body and the causal body, we bow to the Trident. We invoke you, invite you and establish your presence.

- 36 -

ॐ भूर्भुवः स्वः वज्राय नमः वज्रमावाहयामि स्थापयामि

oṁ bhūrbhuvaḥ svaḥ vajrāya namaḥ vajramāvāhayāmi sthāpayāmi

oṁ the Infinite Beyond Conception, the gross body, the subtle body and the causal body, we bow to the Thunderbolt. We invoke you, invite you and establish your presence.

- 37 -

ॐ भूर्भुवः स्वः शक्तये नमः शक्तिमावाहयामि स्थापयामि

oṁ bhūrbhuvaḥ svaḥ śaktaye namaḥ śaktimāvāhayāmi sthāpayāmi

oṁ the Infinite Beyond Conception, the gross body, the subtle body and the causal body, we bow to Energy. We invoke you, invite you and establish your presence.

- 38 -

ॐ भूर्भुवः स्वः दण्डाय नमः दण्डमावाहयामि स्थापयामि

oṁ bhūrbhuvaḥ svaḥ daṇḍāya namaḥ daṇḍamāvāhayāmi sthāpayāmi

oṁ the Infinite Beyond Conception, the gross body, the subtle body and the causal body, we bow to the Staff. We invoke you, invite you and establish your presence.

- 39 -

ॐ भूर्भुवः स्वः खड्गाय नमः खड्गमावाहयामि स्थापयामि

oṁ bhūrbhuvaḥ svaḥ khaḍgāya namaḥ khaḍgamāvāhayāmi sthāpayāmi

oṁ the Infinite Beyond Conception, the gross body, the subtle body and the causal body, we bow to the Sword. We invoke you, invite you and establish your presence.

- 40 -

ॐ भूर्भुवः स्वः पाशाय नमः पाशमावाहयामि स्थापयामि

oṁ bhūrbhuvaḥ svaḥ pāśāya namaḥ pāśamāvāhayāmi sthāpayāmi

oṁ the Infinite Beyond Conception, the gross body, the subtle body and the causal body, we bow to the Net. We invoke you, invite you and establish your presence.

- 41 -

ॐ भूर्भुवः स्वः अङ्कुशाय नमः अङ्कुशमावाहयामि स्थापयामि

oṁ bhūrbhuvaḥ svaḥ aṅkuśāya namaḥ aṅkuśamāvāhayāmi sthāpayāmi

oṁ the Infinite Beyond Conception, the gross body, the subtle body and the causal body, we bow to the Goad. We invoke you, invite you and establish your presence.

- 42 -

ॐ भूर्भुवः स्वः गौतमाय नमः गौतममावाहयामि स्थापयामि

oṁ bhūrbhuvaḥ svaḥ gautamāya namaḥ gautamamāvāhayāmi sthāpayāmi

oṁ the Infinite Beyond Conception, the gross body, the subtle body and the causal body, we bow to Ṛṣi Gautam. We invoke you, invite you and establish your presence.

- 43 -

ॐ भूर्भुवः स्वः भरद्वाजाय नमः भरद्वाजमावाहयामि स्थापयामि

oṁ bhūrbhuvaḥ svaḥ bharadvājāya namaḥ bharadvājamāvāhayāmi sthāpayāmi

oṁ the Infinite Beyond Conception, the gross body, the subtle body and the causal body, we bow to Ṛṣi Bharadvāj. We invoke you, invite you and establish your presence.

- 44 -

ॐ भूर्भुवः स्वः विश्वामित्राय नमः विश्वामित्रमावाहयामि स्थापयामि

oṁ bhūrbhuvaḥ svaḥ viśvāmitrāya namaḥ viśvāmitramāvāhayāmi sthāpayāmi

oṁ the Infinite Beyond Conception, the gross body, the subtle body and the causal body, we bow to Ṛṣi Viśvāmitra we invoke you, invite you and establish your presence.

- 45 -

ॐ भूर्भुवः स्वः कश्यपाय नमः कश्यपमावाहयामि स्थापयामि

oṁ bhūrbhuvaḥ svaḥ kaśyapāya namaḥ kaśyapamāvāhayāmi sthāpayāmi

oṁ the Infinite Beyond Conception, the gross body, the subtle body and the causal body, we bow to Ṛṣi Kaśyapa.
We invoke you, invite you and establish your presence.

- 46 -

ॐ भूर्भुवः स्वः जमदग्नये नमः जमदग्निमावाहयामि स्थापयामि

oṁ bhūrbhuvaḥ svaḥ jamadagnaye namaḥ jamadagnimāvāhayāmi sthāpayāmi

oṁ the Infinite Beyond Conception, the gross body, the subtle body and the causal body, we bow to Ṛṣi Jamadagni. We invoke you, invite you and establish your presence.

- 47 -

ॐ भूर्भुवः स्वः वसिष्ठाय नमः वसिष्ठमावाहयामि स्थापयामि

oṁ bhūrbhuvaḥ svaḥ vasiṣṭhāya namaḥ vasiṣṭhamāvāhayāmi sthāpayāmi

oṁ the Infinite Beyond Conception, the gross body, the subtle body and the causal body, we bow to Ṛṣi Vaṣiṣṭha. We invoke you, invite you and establish your presence.

- 48 -

ॐ भूर्भुवः स्वः अत्रये नमः अत्रिमावाहयामि स्थापयामि

oṁ bhūrbhuvaḥ svaḥ atraye namaḥ atrimāvāhayāmi sthāpayāmi

oṁ the Infinite Beyond Conception, the gross body, the subtle body and the causal body, we bow to Ṛṣi Atri. We invoke you, invite you and establish your presence.

- 49 -

ॐ भूर्भुवः स्वः अरुन्धत्यै नमः अरुन्धतीमावाहयामि स्थापयामि

oṁ bhūrbhuvaḥ svaḥ arundhatyai namaḥ arundhatīmāvāhayāmi sthāpayāmi

oṁ the Infinite Beyond Conception, the gross body, the subtle body and the causal body, we bow to Devi Arundati, wife of Vaṣiṣṭha, example of purity. We invoke you, invite you and establish your presence.

- 50 -

ॐ भूर्भुवः स्वः ऐन्द्र्यै नमः ऐन्द्रीमावाहयामि स्थापयामि

oṁ bhūrbhuvaḥ svaḥ aindryai namaḥ aindrīmāvāhayāmi sthāpayāmi

oṁ the Infinite Beyond Conception, the gross body, the subtle body and the causal body, we bow to Aindri, the energy of the Rule of the Pure. We invoke you, invite you and establish your presence.

- 51 -

ॐ भूर्भुवः स्वः कौमार्य्यै नमः कौमारीमावाहयामि स्थापयामि

oṁ bhūrbhuvaḥ svaḥ kaumāryyai namaḥ kaumārīmāvāhayāmi sthāpayāmi

oṁ the Infinite Beyond Conception, the gross body, the subtle body and the causal body, we bow to Kumari, the energy of the ever pure one. We invoke you, invite you and establish your presence.

- 52 -

ॐ भूर्भुवः स्वः ब्राह्म्यै नमः ब्राह्मीमावाहयामि स्थापयामि

oṁ bhūrbhuvaḥ svaḥ brāhmyai namaḥ brāhmīmāvāhayāmi sthāpayāmi

oṁ the Infinite Beyond Conception, the gross body, the subtle body and the causal body, we bow to Brahmi, the energy of Creative Consciousness. We invoke you, invite you and establish your presence.

- 53 -

ॐ भूर्भुवः स्वः वाराह्यै नमः वाराहीमावाहयामि स्थापयामि

oṁ bhūrbhuvaḥ svaḥ vārāhyai namaḥ vārāhīmāvāhayāmi sthāpayāmi

oṁ the Infinite Beyond Conception, the gross body, the subtle body and the causal body, we bow to Varāhi, the energy of the Boar of Sacrifice. We invoke you, invite you and establish your presence.

- 54 -

ॐ भूर्भुवः स्वः चामुण्डायै नमः चामुण्डामावाहयामि स्थापयामि

oṁ bhūrbhuvaḥ svaḥ cāmuṇḍāyai namaḥ cāmuṇḍāmāvāhayāmi sthāpayāmi

oṁ the Infinite Beyond Conception, the gross body, the subtle body and the causal body, we bow to Camuṇḍa, the Conquerer of Passion and Meaness. We invoke you, invite you and establish your presence.

- 55 -

ॐ भूर्भुवः स्वः वैष्णव्यै नमः वैष्णवीमावाहयामि स्थापयामि

oṁ bhūrbhuvaḥ svaḥ vaiṣṇavyai namaḥ vaiṣṇavīmāvāhayāmi sthāpayāmi

oṁ the Infinite Beyond Conception, the gross body, the subtle body and the causal body, we bow to Vaiṣṇāvi, the energy of All-Pervading Consciousness. We invoke you, invite you and establish your presence.

- 56 -

ॐ भूर्भुवः स्वः माहेश्वर्यै नमः माहेश्वरीमावाहयामि स्थापयामि

oṁ bhūrbhuvaḥ svaḥ māheśvaryai namaḥ māheśvarīmāvāhayāmi sthāpayāmi

oṁ the Infinite Beyond Conception, the gross body, the subtle body and the causal body, we bow to Maheśvarī, the energy of the Supreme Sovereign. We invoke you, invite you and establish your presence.

- 57 -

ॐ भूर्भुवः स्वः वैनायक्यै नमः वैनायकीमावाहयामि स्थापयामि

oṁ bhūrbhuvaḥ svaḥ vaināyakyai namaḥ vaināyakīmāvāhayāmi sthāpayāmi

oṁ the Infinite Beyond Conception, the gross body, the subtle body and the causal body, we bow to Vainākī, the energy of excellent conduct. We invoke you, invite you and establish your presence.

aṣṭāśakti pūjā

worship of the eight forms of passion

ऊग्रचण्डा तु वरदा मध्याह्नार्कसमप्रभा ।
सा मे सदास्तु वरदा तस्यै नित्यं नमो नमः ॥

ūgracaṇḍā tu varadā madhyāhnārkasamaprabhā
sā me sadāstu varadā tasyai nityaṁ namo namaḥ

The Terrible Slayer of Passion, Giver of Boons, who shines within the middle of the Sun. May He always give to me boons. Therefore, I always bow and bow.

ॐ ह्रीं श्रीं ऊग्रचण्डायै नमः

oṁ hrīṁ śrīṁ ūgracaṇḍāyai namaḥ

Oṁ Māyā, Increase, I bow to the Terrible Slayer of Passion.

प्रचण्डे पुत्रदे नित्यं प्रचण्डगणसंस्थिते ।
सर्वानन्दकरे देवि तुभ्यं नित्यं नमो नमः ॥

pracaṇḍe putrade nityaṁ pracaṇḍagaṇasaṁsthite
sarvānandakare devi tubhyaṁ nityaṁ namo namaḥ

Whose Nature Removes Passion, always give children. Situated with the multitude of what preceds Passion, oh Goddess, cause all bliss. I always bow to you and bow to you.

ॐ ह्रीं श्रीं प्रचण्डायै नमः

oṁ hrīṁ śrīṁ pracaṇḍāyai namaḥ

Oṁ Māyā, Increase, I bow to She Whose Nature Removes Passion.

लक्ष्मीस्त्वं सर्वभूतानां सर्वभूताभयप्रदा ।
देवि त्वं सर्वकार्येषु वरदा भव सर्वदा ॥

lakṣmīstvaṁ saravabhūtānāṁ sarvabhūtābhayapradā
devi tvaṁ sarvakāryeṣu varadā bhava sarvadā
You are Lakṣmī, all existence; you grant freedom from fear to all existence. Oh Goddess, you reside within all effects. Always give boons.

ॐ ह्रीं श्रीं चण्डोग्रायै नमः

oṁ hrīṁ śrīṁ caṇḍogrāyai namaḥ
Oṁ Māyā, Increase, I bow to She Who Slays Passion.

या सिद्धिरिति नाम्ना च देवेशवरदायिनी ।
कलिकल्मषनाशाय नमामि चण्डनायिकाम् ॥

yā siddhiriti nāmnā ca deveśavaradāyinī
kalikalmaṣanāśāya namāmi caṇḍanāyikām
Her name brings perfection, and She is the Supreme among the Gods who grants boons. I bow down to She who destroys the iniquities of darkness, the Leader of Passion.

ॐ ह्रीं श्रीं चण्डनायिकायै नमः

oṁ hrīṁ śrīṁ caṇḍanāyikāyai namaḥ
Oṁ Māyā, Increase, I bow to the Leader of Passion.

देवि चण्डात्मिके चण्डि चण्डारिविजयप्रदे ।
धर्मार्थमोक्षदे दुर्गे नित्यं मे वरदा भव ॥

devi caṇḍātmike caṇḍi caṇḍārivijayaprade
dharmārthamokṣade durge nityaṁ me varadā bhava
Oh Goddess, to the soul of She Who Tears Apart Passion, She Who Tears Apart Thought, and She Who Conquers over Passion; hey Durgā, give me the boons of the Ideal of Perfection, the necessities for physical sustenance and Liberation.

ॐ ह्रीं श्रीं चण्डायै नमः

oṁ hrīṁ śrīṁ caṇḍāyai namaḥ
Oṁ Māyā, Increase, I bow to She who Conquers over Passion.

या सृष्टिस्थितिसंहारगुणत्रयसमन्विता ।
या परा परमा शक्तिश्चण्डवत्यै नमो नमः ॥

yā sṛṣṭisthitisaṁhāraguṇatrayasamanvitā
yā parā paramā śaktiścaṇḍavatyai namo namaḥ
Hers are creation, preservation and dissolution; the three qualities are equally present. To She who is Higher than the Highest Energy, to the Spirit of Passion I bow, I bow.

ॐ ह्रीं श्रीं चण्डवत्यै नमः

oṁ hrīṁ śrīṁ caṇḍavatyai namaḥ
Oṁ Māyā, Increase, I bow to the Spirit of Passion.

चण्डरूपात्मिका चण्डा चण्डनायकनायिका ।
सर्वसिद्धिप्रदा देवी तस्यै नित्यं नमो नमः ॥

caṇḍarūpātmikā caṇḍā caṇḍanāyakanāyikā
sarvasiddhipradā devī tasyai nityaṁ namo namaḥ
The form of the soul of Passion, She who Conquers over Passion, the Leader of the Leaders of Passion, oh Goddess, give all attainments of perfection. Therefore, always I bow, I bow.

ॐ ह्रीं श्रीं चण्डरूपायै नमः

oṁ hrīṁ śrīṁ caṇḍarūpāyai namaḥ
Oṁ Māyā, Increase, I bow to the Form of Passion.

बालार्कारुणनयना सर्वदा भक्तवत्सला ।
चण्डासुरस्य मथनी वरदा त्वतिचण्डिका ॥

bālārkāruṇanayanā sarvadā bhaktavatsalā
caṇḍāsurasya mathanī varadā tvaticaṇḍikā
You have the Strength of the Sun and are always compassionate to devotees. The Warrior of Passion has a churning rod.

Give boons, oh you who Tear Apart Extreme Passion.

ॐ ह्रीं श्रीं अतिचण्डिकायै नमः

oṁ hrīṁ śrīṁ aticaṇḍikāyai namaḥ
Oṁ Māyā, Increase, I bow to You who Tears Apart Extreme Passion.

ऊग्रचण्डा प्रचण्डा च चण्डोग्रा चण्डनायिका ।
चण्डा चण्डवती चैव चण्डरूपातिचण्डिका ॥

ūgracaṇḍā pracaṇḍā ca caṇḍogrā caṇḍanāyikā
caṇḍā caṇḍavatī caiva caṇḍarūpāticaṇḍikā
The Terrible Slayer of Passion, Whose Nature Removes Passion, She Who Slays Passion, the Leader of Passion, She Who Conquers Over Passion, the Spirit of Passion, the Form of Passion and She who Tears Apart Extreme Passion.

ॐ ह्रीं श्रीं अष्टाशक्तिभ्यो नमः

oṁ hrīṁ śrīṁ aṣṭāśaktibhyo namaḥ
Oṁ I bow to the eight forms of energy

नव ग्रहण पूजा

nava grahaṇa pūjā

worship of the nine planets

ॐ जबाकुसुम सङ्काशं काश्यपेयं महाद्युतिम् ।
तमोऽरिं सर्वपापघ्नं प्रनतोऽस्मि दिवाकरम् ॥
ॐ ह्रीं ह्रीं सूर्याय नमः

oṁ jabākusuma saṅkāśaṁ
kāśyapeyaṁ mahādyutim
tamo-riṁ sarvapāpaghnaṁ
pranato-smi divākaram
oṁ hrīṁ hrīṁ sūryāya namaḥ

Oṁ Crimson red like a hybiscus flower, the Great Light shines onto the earth, removing all the darkness and eradicating sin. We bow down with devotion to that Shining Light. Oṁ we bow to the Sun, Light of Wisdom, Dispeller of Ignorance.

दधि मुख तुषाराभं क्षीरोदार्णसम्भवम् ।
नमामि शशिनम् सोमम् शम्भोर्मुकुट भुषनम् ॥
ॐ ऐं क्लीं सोमाय नमः

dadhi mukha tuṣārābhaṁ
kṣīrodārṇasambhavam
namāmi śaśinam somam
śambhormukuṭa bhuṣanam
oṁ aiṁ klīṁ somāya namaḥ

Creamy white like a container of curds and most pleasing, the Moon is born from the churning of the milk ocean. We bow down to the effulgent emblem of devotion, which is an ornament on the crown of Lord Śiva. Oṁ we bow to the Moon, emblem of devotion.

धरणीगर्भसम्भुतम् विद्युत्कान्ति समप्रभम् ।
कुमारं शक्तिहस्तं च तं मङ्गलम् प्रनमाम्यहम् ॥
ॐ हुं श्रीं मङ्गलाय नमः

dharaṇīgarbhasambhutam
vidyutkānti samaprabham
kumāraṁ śaktihastaṁ ca
taṁ maṅgalam pranamāmyaham
oṁ huṁ śrīṁ maṅgalāya namaḥ

Supporting the womb of all existence, Mars shines forth with the radiance of beauty enhanced by love, the son wielding energy in his hand. We bow down to Mars, Bearer of Welfare. Oṁ we bow down to Mars, Bearer of Welfare.

प्रियङ्गुकलिकश्यामम् रूपेणाऽप्रतिमं बुधम् ।
सौम्यं सौम्यगुणोपेतं तं बुधम् प्रनमाम्यहम् ॥
ॐ ऐं स्त्रीं श्रीं बुद्धाय नमः

priyaṅgukalikaśyāmam
rūpeṇā-pratimaṁ budham
saumyaṁ saumyaguṇopetaṁ
taṁ budham pranamāmyaham
oṁ aiṁ strīṁ śrīṁ budhāya namaḥ

Whose beloved body is dark like darkness, whose image is like the form of Intelligence, whose qualities are most beautiful, to that Mercury, emblem of Intelligence, we bow down in devotion. Oṁ we bow down to Mercury, the emblem of Intelligence.

देवानां च ऋषिनां च गुरुं काञ्चनसन्निभम् ।
बुद्धि भुतं त्रिलोकेशम् तं नमामि बृहास्पतिम् ॥
ॐ ह्रीं क्लीं हुं बृहस्पतये नमः

devānāṁ ca ṛṣināṁ ca
guruṁ kāñcana sannibham
buddhi bhutaṁ trilokeśam
taṁ namāmi bṛhāspatim
oṁ hrīṁ klīṁ huṁ bṛhaspataye namaḥ

The Guru of the Gods and also the ṛṣis, who is like the highest wealth, who is the most intelligent of all beings, to that Jupiter, Guru of the Gods, we bow down in devotion. Oṁ we bow down to the Guru of the Gods.

हिम कुन्द मृणालाभं दैत्यानां परमं गुरुम् ।
सर्वशास्त्रप्रवक्तारं भार्गवम् प्रनमाम्यहम् ॥
ॐ ह्रीं श्रीं शुक्राय नमः

hima kunda mṛṇālābhaṁ
daityānāṁ paramaṁ gurum
sarvaśāstrapravaktāraṁ
bhārgavam pranamāmyaham
oṁ hrīṁ śrīṁ śukrāya namaḥ

Like sandal and jasmine that have been crushed, the foremost Guru of the forces of duality, who expounds all the scriptures; to that descendant of Bṛgu we bow down in devotion. Oṁ we bow down to Venus, the emblem of love and attachment.

नीलाम्बुजसमाभासं रविपुत्रं यमाग्रजम् ।
छायामार्तण्डसम्भूतं तं नमामि शनैश्चरम् ॥
ॐ ऐं ह्रीं श्रीं शनैश्चराय नमः

nīlāmbujasamābhāsaṁ
raviputraṁ yamāgrajam
chāyāmārtaṇḍasambhūtaṁ
taṁ namāmi śanaiścaram
oṁ aiṁ hrīṁ śrīṁ śanaiścarāya namaḥ

Looking like a blue cloud, the son of the Sun, he is foremost of those who control. He can even put his shadow over the glorious sun. To that Saturn, emblem of control, we bow down in devotion. Oṁ we bow down to Saturn, the emblem of control.

अर्द्धकायं महावीर्यं चन्द्रादित्यविमर्दनम् ।
सिंहिकागर्भ सम्भूतं तं राहु प्रनमाम्यहम् ॥
ॐ ऐं ह्रीं राहवे नमः

arddhakāyaṁ mahāvīryaṁ candrādityavimardanam
siṁhikāgarbha sambhūtaṁ taṁ rāhu pranamāmyaham
oṁ aiṁ hrīṁ rāhave namaḥ

The great warrior divides even the sun and moon in half. He is born from the womb of Siṁhikā, and we bow down in devotion to the North Node, who commands direction. Oṁ we bow down to the North Node, who commands direction.

पालाशपुष्प सङ्काशं तारकाग्रहमस्तकम् ।
रौद्रं रौद्रात्मकं घोरं तं केतु प्रनमाम्यहम् ॥
ॐ ह्रीं ऐं केतवे नमः

pālāśapuṣpa saṅkāśaṁ tārakāgrahamastakam
raudraṁ raudrātmakaṁ ghoraṁ
taṁ ketu pranamāmyaham
oṁ hrīṁ aiṁ ketave namaḥ

Red like a pālāśa flower, who makes the starry-eyed constellation to set; he is terrible and awsome to see, and we bow down in devotion to the South Node, who presents obstacles. Oṁ we bow down to the South Node, who presents obstacles.

ब्रह्मा मुरारिस्त्रिपुरान्तकारी भानुः शशी भूमिसुतो बुधश्च ।
गुरुश्च शुक्रः शनि राहु केतवः सर्वे ग्रहा शान्तिकरा भवन्तु ॥

brahmā murāristripurāntakārī
bhānuḥ śaśī bhūmisuto budhaśca
guruśca śukraḥ śani rāhu ketavaḥ
sarve grahā śāntikarā bhavantu

Brahmā, Viṣṇu and Śiva always contemplate the Sun, Moon, Earth, Mercury, Jupiter, Venus, Saturn, the North and South Nodes. May all the constellations remain in Peace.

ॐ नव ग्रहेभ्योः नमः

oṁ nava grahebhyoḥ namaḥ

Oṁ we bow to the nine planets.

yoginī pūjā

worship of the sixty-four yoginīs

1. ॐ ह्रीं श्रीं ब्रह्माण्यै नमः

oṁ hrīṁ śrīṁ brahmāṇyai namaḥ
Oṁ Māyā, Increase, I bow to Creative Energy.

2. ॐ ह्रीं श्रीं चण्डिकायै नमः

oṁ hrīṁ śrīṁ caṇḍikāyai namaḥ
Oṁ Māyā, Increase, I bow to She who Tears Apart Thoughts.

3. ॐ ह्रीं श्रीं रौद्र्यै नमः

oṁ hrīṁ śrīṁ raudryai namaḥ
Oṁ Māyā, Increase, I bow to Fearful One.

4. ॐ ह्रीं श्रीं गौर्यै नमः

oṁ hrīṁ śrīṁ gauryai namaḥ
Oṁ Māyā, Increase, I bow to She who is Rays of Light.

5. ॐ ह्रीं श्रीं इन्द्राण्यै नमः

oṁ hrīṁ śrīṁ indrāṇyai namaḥ
Oṁ Māyā, Increase, I bow to the Energy of the Rule of the Pure.

6. ॐ ह्रीं श्रीं कौमार्यै नमः

oṁ hrīṁ śrīṁ kaumāryai namaḥ
Oṁ Māyā, Increase, I bow to the Ever Pure One.

7. ॐ ह्रीं श्रीं भैरव्यै नमः

oṁ hrīṁ śrīṁ bhairavyai namaḥ
Oṁ Māyā, Increase, I bow to the Fearless One.

8. ॐ ह्रीं श्रीं दुर्गायै नमः

oṁ hrīṁ śrīṁ durgāyai namaḥ
Oṁ Māyā, Increase, I bow to the Reliever of Difficulties

9. ॐ ह्रीं श्रीं नरसिंह्यै नमः

oṁ hrīṁ śrīṁ narasiṁhyai namaḥ
Oṁ Māyā, Increase, I bow to the Man-Lion of Courage.

10. ॐ ह्रीं श्रीं कालिकायै नमः

oṁ hrīṁ śrīṁ kālikāyai namaḥ
Oṁ Māyā, Increase, I bow to She Who is Beyond Time.

11. ॐ ह्रीं श्रीं चामुण्डायै नमः

oṁ hrīṁ śrīṁ cāmuṇḍāyai namaḥ
Oṁ Māyā, Increase, I bow to She Who Conquers Over Passion and Meanness.

12. ॐ ह्रीं श्रीं शिवदूत्यै नमः

oṁ hrīṁ śrīṁ śivadūtyai namaḥ
Oṁ Māyā, Increase, I bow to She Who Sends Śiva as an ambassador.

13. ॐ ह्रीं श्रीं वाराह्यै नमः

oṁ hrīṁ śrīṁ vārāhyai namaḥ
Oṁ Māyā, Increase, I bow to the Boar of Sacrifice.

14. ॐ ह्रीं श्रीं कौशिक्यै नमः

oṁ hrīṁ śrīṁ kauśikyai namaḥ
Oṁ Māyā, Increase, I bow to She Who Manifests from Within.

15. ॐ ह्रीं श्रीं माहेश्वर्यै नमः

oṁ hrīṁ śrīṁ māheśvaryai namaḥ
Oṁ Māyā, Increase, I bow to the Great Seer of All.

16. ॐ ह्रीं श्रीं शाङ्कर्यै नमः

oṁ hrīṁ śrīṁ śāṅkaryai namaḥ
Oṁ Māyā, Increase, I bow to the Cause of Peace

17. ॐ ह्रीं श्रीं जयन्त्यै नमः

oṁ hrīṁ śrīṁ jayantyai namaḥ
Oṁ Māyā, Increase, I bow to Victory.

18. ॐ ह्रीं श्रीं सर्वमङ्गलायै नमः

oṁ hrīṁ śrīṁ sarvamaṅgalāyai namaḥ
Oṁ Māyā, Increase, I bow to She Who is All Welfare.

19. ॐ ह्रीं श्रीं काल्यै नमः

oṁ hrīṁ śrīṁ kālyai namaḥ
Oṁ Māyā, Increase, I bow to She Who is Beyond Time.

20. ॐ ह्रीं श्रीं करालिन्यै नमः

oṁ hrīṁ śrīṁ karālinyai namaḥ
Oṁ Māyā, Increase, I bow to She with the Gaping Mouth.

21. ॐ ह्रीं श्रीं मेधायै नमः

oṁ hrīṁ śrīṁ medhāyai namaḥ
Oṁ Māyā, Increase, I bow to the Intellect of Love.

22. ॐ ह्रीं श्रीं शिवायै नमः

oṁ hrīṁ śrīṁ śivāyai namaḥ
Oṁ Māyā, Increase, I bow to the Energy of Śiva.

23. ॐ ह्रीं श्रीं साकम्भर्यै नमः

oṁ hrīṁ śrīṁ sākambharyai namaḥ
Oṁ Māyā, Increase, I bow to She Who Nourishes with Vegetables.

24. ॐ ह्रीं श्रीं भीमायै नमः

oṁ hrīṁ śrīṁ bhīmāyai namaḥ
Oṁ Māyā, Increase, I bow to She Who is Fearless.

25. ॐ ह्रीं श्रीं शान्तायै नमः

oṁ hrīṁ śrīṁ śāntāyai namaḥ
Oṁ Māyā, Increase, I bow to Peace.

26. ॐ ह्रीं श्रीं भ्रामर्यै नमः

oṁ hrīṁ śrīṁ bhrāmaryai namaḥ
Oṁ Māyā, Increase, I bow to She Who is like a Bee.

27. ॐ ह्रीं श्रीं रुद्राण्यै नमः

oṁ hrīṁ śrīṁ rudrāṇyai namaḥ
Oṁ Māyā, Increase, I bow to She Who Relieves the Sufferings of all.

28. ॐ ह्रीं श्रीं अम्बिकायै नमः

oṁ hrīṁ śrīṁ ambikāyai namaḥ
Oṁ Māyā, Increase, I bow to the Divine Mother.

29. ॐ ह्रीं श्रीं क्षमायै नमः

oṁ hrīṁ śrīṁ kṣamāyai namaḥ
Oṁ Māyā, Increase, I bow to Patient Forgiveness.

30. ॐ ह्रीं श्रीं धात्र्यै नमः

oṁ hrīṁ śrīṁ dhātryai namaḥ
Oṁ Māyā, Increase, I bow to the Creatress.

31. ॐ ह्रीं श्रीं स्वाहायै नमः

oṁ hrīṁ śrīṁ svāhāyai namaḥ
Oṁ Māyā, Increase, I bow to the oblation 'I Am One with God!'

32. ॐ ह्रीं श्रीं स्वधायै नमः

oṁ hrīṁ śrīṁ svadhāyai namaḥ
Oṁ Māyā, Increase, I bow to the Oblations to the Ancestors.

33. ॐ ह्रीं श्रीं अपर्णायै नमः
oṁ hrīṁ śrīṁ aparṇāyai namaḥ
Oṁ Māyā, Increase, I bow to She Who is Indivisible.

34. ॐ ह्रीं श्रीं महोदर्यै नमः
oṁ hrīṁ śrīṁ mahodaryai namaḥ
Oṁ Māyā, Increase, I bow to She with the Big Belly.

35. ॐ ह्रीं श्रीं घोररूपायै नमः
oṁ hrīṁ śrīṁ ghorarūpāyai namaḥ
Oṁ Māyā, Increase, I bow to the Form of Whiteness.

36. ॐ ह्रीं श्रीं महाकाल्यै नमः
oṁ hrīṁ śrīṁ mahākālyai namaḥ
Oṁ Māyā, Increase, I bow to the Great She Who is Beyond Time.

37. ॐ ह्रीं श्रीं भद्रकाल्यै नमः
oṁ hrīṁ śrīṁ bhadrakālyai namaḥ
Oṁ Māyā, Increase, I bow to the Excellent One Who is Beyond Time.

38. ॐ ह्रीं श्रीं कपालिन्यै नमः
oṁ hrīṁ śrīṁ kapālinyai namaḥ
Oṁ Māyā, Increase, I bow to She Who Wears Skulls.

39. ॐ ह्रीं श्रीं क्षेमङ्कर्यै नमः
oṁ hrīṁ śrīṁ kṣemaṅkaryai namaḥ
Oṁ Māyā, Increase, I bow to She Who Destroys.

40. ॐ ह्रीं श्रीं ऊग्रचण्डायै नमः
oṁ hrīṁ śrīṁ ūgracaṇḍāyai namaḥ
Oṁ Māyā, Increase, I bow to the Terrible Slayer of Passion.

41. ॐ ह्रीं श्रीं चण्डोग्रायै नमः

oṁ hrīṁ śrīṁ caṇḍogrāyai namaḥ
Oṁ Māyā, Increase, I bow to She Who Slays Passion.

42. ॐ ह्रीं श्रीं चण्डनायिकायै नमः

oṁ hrīṁ śrīṁ caṇḍanāyikāyai namaḥ
Oṁ Māyā, Increase, I bow to the Leader of Passion.

43. ॐ ह्रीं श्रीं चण्डायै नमः

oṁ hrīṁ śrīṁ caṇḍāyai namaḥ
Oṁ Māyā, Increase, I bow to She Who Slays Passion.

44. ॐ ह्रीं श्रीं चण्डवत्यै नमः

oṁ hrīṁ śrīṁ caṇḍavatyai namaḥ
Oṁ Māyā, Increase, I bow to the Spirit of Passion.

45. ॐ ह्रीं श्रीं चण्डयै नमः

oṁ hrīṁ śrīṁ caṇḍyai namaḥ
Oṁ Māyā, Increase, I bow to She Who Tears Apart Extreme Passion.

46. ॐ ह्रीं श्रीं महामोहायै नमः

oṁ hrīṁ śrīṁ mahāmohāyai namaḥ
Oṁ Māyā, Increase, I bow to She Who Covers the World with Ignorance.

47. ॐ ह्रीं श्रीं महामायायै नमः

oṁ hrīṁ śrīṁ mahāmāyāyai namaḥ
Oṁ Māyā, Increase, I bow to She Who is the Great Māyā.

48. ॐ ह्रीं श्रीं प्रियङ्कर्यै नमः

oṁ hrīṁ śrīṁ priyaṅkaryai namaḥ
Oṁ Māyā, Increase, I bow to She Who Causes Love.

49. ॐ ह्रीं श्रीं बलविकरण्यै नमः

oṁ hrīṁ śrīṁ balavikaraṇyai namaḥ
Oṁ Māyā, Increase, I bow to She Who is Extremely Powerful.

50. ॐ ह्रीं श्रीं बलप्रमथन्यै नमः

oṁ hrīṁ śrīṁ balapramathanyai namaḥ
Oṁ Māyā, Increase, I bow to She Who is the Strength of Disembodied Spirits.

51. ॐ ह्रीं श्रीं मदनोन्मथन्यै नमः

oṁ hrīṁ śrīṁ madanonmathanyai namaḥ
Oṁ Māyā, Increase, I bow to She Who Churns with Love.

52. ॐ ह्रीं श्रीं सर्वभूतदमन्यै नमः

oṁ hrīṁ śrīṁ sarvabhūtadamanyai namaḥ
Oṁ Māyā, Increase, I bow to She Who Controls All Existence.

53. ॐ ह्रीं श्रीं उमायै नमः

oṁ hrīṁ śrīṁ umāyai namaḥ
Oṁ Māyā, Increase, I bow to the Mother of Protection.

54. ॐ ह्रीं श्रीं तारायै नमः

oṁ hrīṁ śrīṁ tārāyai namaḥ
Oṁ Māyā, Increase, I bow to She Who Shines like a Star.

55. ॐ ह्रीं श्रीं महानिद्रायै नमः

oṁ hrīṁ śrīṁ mahānidrāyai namaḥ
Oṁ Māyā, Increase, I bow to She Who is the Great Sleep.

56. ॐ ह्रीं श्रीं विजायायै नमः

oṁ hrīṁ śrīṁ vijāyāyai namaḥ
Oṁ Māyā, Increase, I bow to Victory.

57. ॐ ह्रीं श्रीं जयायै नमः

oṁ hrīṁ śrīṁ jayāyai namaḥ
Oṁ Māyā, Increase, I bow to Conquest.

58. ॐ ह्रीं श्रीं शैलपुत्र्यै नमः

oṁ hrīṁ śrīṁ śailaputryai namaḥ
Oṁ Māyā, Increase, I bow to the Goddess of Inspiration.

59. ॐ ह्रीं श्रीं ब्रह्मचारिण्यै नमः

oṁ hrīṁ śrīṁ brahmacāriṇyai namaḥ
Oṁ Māyā, Increase, I bow to the Goddess of Learning.

60. ॐ ह्रीं श्रीं चण्डघण्टायै नमः

oṁ hrīṁ śrīṁ caṇḍaghaṇṭāyai namaḥ
Oṁ Māyā, Increase, I bow to the Goddess of Practice.

61. ॐ ह्रीं श्रीं कूष्माण्डायै नमः

oṁ hrīṁ śrīṁ kūṣmāṇḍāyai namaḥ
Oṁ Māyā, Increase, I bow to the Goddess of Refinement.

62. ॐ ह्रीं श्रीं स्कन्दमात्र्यै नमः

oṁ hrīṁ śrīṁ skandamātryai namaḥ
Oṁ Māyā, Increase, I bow to the Goddess Who Nurtures Divinity.

63. ॐ ह्रीं श्रीं कात्यायन्यै नमः

oṁ hrīṁ śrīṁ kātyāyanyai namaḥ
Oṁ Māyā, Increase, I bow to the Goddess Who is Ever Pure.

64. ॐ ह्रीं श्रीं कालरात्र्यै नमः

oṁ hrīṁ śrīṁ kālarātryai namaḥ
Oṁ Māyā, Increase, I bow to the Goddess of the Great Night of Surrendering the Ego.

ॐ ह्रीं श्रीं महागौर्यै नमः

oṁ hrīṁ śrīṁ mahāgauryai namaḥ
Oṁ Māyā, Increase, I bow to the Goddess of the Great Radiant Light.

ॐ ह्रीं श्रीं कोटियोगिनीभ्यो नमः

oṁ hrīṁ śrīṁ koṭiyoginībhyo namaḥ
Oṁ Māyā, Increase, I bow to the tens of millions of Goddesses.

astra pūjā
worship of the weapons of war

ॐ सर्वायुधानां प्रथमो निमितस्त्वं पिनाकिना ।
शूलात् सारं समाकृष्य कृत्वा मुष्ठि ग्रहं शुभम् ॥

oṁ sarvāyudhānāṁ prathamo nimitastvaṁ pinākinā
śūlāt sāraṁ samākṛṣya kṛtvā muṣṭi grahaṁ śubham
Oṁ First among all the implements of war is the trident. From the trident the ocean of existence comes together. Make a fist and accept the radiance.

ॐ त्रिशूलाय नमः

oṁ triśūlāya namaḥ
Oṁ I bow to the trident.

असिर्विशसनः खड्गस्तीक्ष्नधारो दुरासदः ।
श्रीगर्भो विजयश्चैव धर्मपाल नमोऽस्तु ते ॥

asirviśasanaḥ khaṅgastīkṣnadhāro durāsadaḥ
śrīgarbho vijayaścaiva dharmapāla namo-stu te
The sword that protects the universe, you hold aloft the sharp blade against iniquity. In the respected womb of Victory, only to protect dharma, I bow down to you.

ॐ खड्गाय नमः

oṁ khaḍgāya namaḥ
Oṁ I bow to the sword.

चक्र त्वं विष्णुरूपोऽसि विष्णुपानौ सदा स्थितः ।
देवीहस्तस्थितो नित्यं शुदर्शन नमोऽस्तु ते ॥

cakra tvaṁ viṣṇurūpo-si viṣṇupānau sadā sthitaḥ
devīhastasthito nityaṁ śudarśana namo-stu te
Oh Discus, you are of the form of Viṣṇu, and you always reside in Viṣṇu's hands. Always stay in the hands of the Goddess. Excellent Intuitive Vision, I bow to you.

ॐ चक्राय नमः

oṁ cakrāya namaḥ
Oṁ I bow to the discus.

सर्वायुधानां श्रेष्ठोऽसि दैत्यसेनानिसूदनः ।
भयेभ्यः सर्वतो रक्ष तीक्ष्नबाण नमोऽस्तु ते ॥

sarvāyudhānāṁ śreṣṭo-si daityasenānisūdanaḥ
bhayebhyaḥ sarvato rakṣa tīkṣnabāṇa namo-stu te
You are the ultimate of all implements of war, eradicating the armies of duality. Always protect from all fear. I bow to the arrows.

ॐ तीक्ष्नबाणाय नमः

oṁ tīkṣnabāṇāya namaḥ
Oṁ I bow to the sharp arrows.

शक्तिस्त्वं सर्वदेवानां गुहस्य च विशेषतः ।
शक्तिरूपेण सर्वत्र रक्षां कुरु नमोऽस्तु ते ॥

śaktistvaṁ sarvadevānāṁ guhasya ca viśeṣataḥ
śaktirūpeṇa sarvatra rakṣāṁ kuru namo-stu te
You are the energy of all the Gods, especially hidden. By means of this energy always protect me. I bow to you.

ॐ शक्तये नमः

oṁ śaktaye namaḥ
Oṁ I bow to Energy.

षष्ठिरूपेण खेट त्वं वैरिसंहारकारकः ।
देवीहस्तस्थितो नित्यं मम रक्षां कुरुष्व च ॥

ṣaṣṭirūpeṇa kheṭa tvaṁ vairisaṁhārakārakaḥ
devīhastasthito nityaṁ mama rakṣāṁ kuruṣva ca

With the form of six points you are the shield, the cause of dissolution of adversity. Always stay in the hand of the Goddess, and protect me.

ॐ खेटकाय नमः

oṁ kheṭakāya namaḥ

Oṁ I bow to the Shield.

सर्वायुध महामात्र सर्वदेवारिसुदन ।
चाप मां सर्वतो रक्ष साकं सायकसत्तमैः ॥

sarvāyudha mahāmātra sarvadevārisudana
cāpa māṁ sarvato rakṣa sākaṁ sāyakasattamaiḥ

The great measurement of all warriors makes all the Gods victorious. Always protect me with the bow, with arrows ready to be hurled.

ॐ पूर्णचापाय नमः

oṁ pūrṇacāpāya namaḥ

Oṁ I bow to the bow.

पाश त्वं नागरूपोऽसि विषपूर्णो विषोदरः ।
शत्रुणां दुःसहो नित्यं नागपाश नमोऽस्तु ते ॥

pāśa tvaṁ nāgarūpo-si viṣapūrṇo viṣodaraḥ
śatruṇāṁ duḥsaho nityaṁ nāgapāśa namo-stu te

You are the bond in the form of a snake full of venom ready to strike. You always cause pain to enemies. Snake-bond, I bow to you.

ॐ नागपाशाय नमः

oṁ nāgapāśāya namaḥ

Oṁ I bow to the Snake-bond.

अङ्कुशोऽसि नमस्तुभ्यं गजानां नियमः सदा ।
लोकानां सर्वरक्षार्थं विधृतः पार्वतीकरे ॥

aṅkuśo-si namastubhyaṁ gajānāṁ niyamaḥ sadā
lokānāṁ sarvarakṣārthaṁ vidhṛtaḥ pārvatīkare
Curved Sword or prod, we bow to you. Always you discipline elephants. In order to protect the worlds, remain in Pārvatī's hands.

ॐ अङ्कुशाय नमः

oṁ aṅkuśāya namaḥ
Oṁ I bow to the Curved Sword.

हिनस्ति दैत्यतेजांसि स्वनेनापूर्य या जगत् ।
सा घण्टा पातु नो देवि पापेभ्योऽनः सुतानिव ॥

hinasti daitya tejāṁsi svanenāpūrya yā jagat
sā ghaṇṭā pātu no devi pāpebhyo-naḥ sutāniva
Oh Goddess, may the sound of your bell, which fills the perceivable world, destroying the prowess of all thoughts, protect us from evil as a Mother protects Her children.

ॐ घण्टाय नमः

oṁ ghaṇṭāya namaḥ
Oṁ I bow to the Bell.

परशो त्वं महातीक्ष्न सर्वदेवारिसूदनः ।
देवीहास्तस्थितो नित्यं शत्रुक्षय नमोऽस्तु ते ॥

paraśo tvaṁ mahātīkṣna sarvadevārisūdanaḥ
devīhāstasthito nityaṁ śatrukṣaya namo-stu te
Oh Battle Axe, you are very sharp as you defend all the Gods. Always stay in the hands of the Goddess. Destroyer of enemies, we bow to you.

ॐ परशवे नमः

oṁ paraśave namaḥ
Oṁ I bow to the Battle Axe.

ॐ ह्रीं श्रीं सर्वायुधधारिण्यै दुर्गायै नमः

oṁ hrīṁ śrīṁ sarvāyudhadhāriṇyai durgāyai namaḥ
Oṁ Māyā, Increase, I bow to Durgā, who holds all the weapons of war.

सर्वायुधानां श्रेष्ठानि यानि यानि त्रिपिष्ठपे ।
तानि तानि दधत्यै ते चण्डिकायै नमो नमः ॥

sarvāyudhānāṁ śreṣṭāni yāni yāni tripiṣṭape
tāni tāni dadhatyai te caṇḍikāyai namo namaḥ
She is the most excellent of all warriors, wherever, wherever in the three worlds. Where there exist forces of duality, we bow to You, to She Who Tears Apart Thought, we bow.

ॐ ह्रीं श्रीं सर्वायुधधारिण्यै चण्डिकायै नमः

oṁ hrīṁ śrīṁ sarvāyudhadhāriṇyai caṇḍikāyai namaḥ
Oṁ Māyā, Increase, I bow to Caṇḍikā who holds all the weapons of war.

bāhya mātrikā nyāsa

establishment of the letters in the external body

Every object in creation has a name to correspond to its form. There is a name which is agreed upon by the customs of language, what we may call an object; and there is a natural sound which is being emitted as a consequence of the vibrations which are taking place in the object itself, the movement of protons, nutrons, electrons, etc. Every manifested object of creation has a vibration, whether perceivable or not, and every vibration emits a sound whether audible to the physical organ of hearing or not. Every sound is expressible by a letter which symbolizes the sound that most closely approximates the vibration indicated, so that all the letters of the alphabets symbolize the total possibility of all vibrations which can be evolved or can be expressed the totality of creation.

This natural name is called a Bījā Mantra, often translated as Seed Mantra. These Bījās are another name for the Mātṛkās, the letters of the Saṁskṛta alphabet. In Saṁskṛta Philosophy, the microcosm is an exact replica of the macrocosm. Hence every physical body contains all the vibrations possible in the cosmos. Bāhya Mātṛkā Nyāsa means the establishment of the letters of the Saṁskṛta Alphabet within the "Outside" or the gross body of the worshiper. Bāhya Mātṛkā Nyāsa ascribes a position in each of the centers of activity for each of the letters, so that the worshiper can understand and experience the totality of creation as existing within the physical body. By using the different Mudrās described, the worshiper begins by placing the sixteen vowels in their respective positions.

Thumb 1 Pointer 2 Middle 3 Ring 4 Pinky 5

ॐ अं नमः

oṁ aṁ namaḥ R.1.4 base top of head

ॐ आं नमः

oṁ āṁ namaḥ R.1.4 base mouth

ॐ इं नमः

oṁ iṁ namaḥ R. 4 R. eye

ॐ ईं नमः

oṁ īṁ namaḥ L. 4 L. eye

ॐ उं नमः
oṁ uṁ namaḥ R. 1 R. ear

ॐ ऊं नमः
oṁ ūṁ namaḥ L. 1 L. ear

ॐ ऋं नमः
oṁ ṛṁ namaḥ R. 1.5 R. nostril

ॐ ॠं नमः
oṁ ṝṁ namaḥ L. 1.5 L. nostril

ॐ ऌं नमः
oṁ lṛṁ namaḥ R. 2.3.4 R. cheek

ॐ ॡं नमः
oṁ lṝṁ namaḥ L. 2.3.4 L. cheek

ॐ एं नमः
oṁ eṁ namaḥ R. 3 upper lip

ॐ ऐं नमः
oṁ aiṁ namaḥ R. 3 lower lip

ॐ ओं नमः
oṁ oṁ namaḥ R. 4 upper teeth

ॐ औं नमः
oṁ auṁ namaḥ R. 4 lower teeth

ॐ अं नमः
oṁ aṁ namaḥ R. 3.4 crown of head

ॐ अः नमः
oṁ aḥ namaḥ R. 3.4 mouth

ॐ कं नमः
oṁ kaṁ namaḥ L. 1.3.5 R. shoulder

ॐ खं नमः
oṁ khaṁ namaḥ L. 1.3.5 R. crook of elbow

ॐ गं नमः
oṁ gaṁ namaḥ L. 1.3.5 R. wrist

ॐ घं नमः
oṁ ghaṁ namaḥ L. 1.3.5 R. joint of hand

ॐ ङं नमः
oṁ ṅaṁ namaḥ L. 1.3.5 R. finger tips

ॐ चं नमः
oṁ caṁ namaḥ R. 1.3.5 L. shoulder

ॐ छं नमः
oṁ chaṁ namaḥ R. 1.3.5 L. crook of elbow

ॐ जं नमः
oṁ jaṁ namaḥ R. 1.3.5 L. wrist

ॐ झं नमः
oṁ jhaṁ namaḥ R. 1.3.5 L. joint of hand

ॐ ञं नमः
oṁ ñaṁ namaḥ R. 1.3.5 L. finger tips

ॐ टं नमः
oṁ ṭaṁ namaḥ L. 1.3.5 R. hip

ॐ ठं नमः
oṁ ṭhaṁ namaḥ L. 1.3.5 R. knees

ॐ डं नमः
oṁ ḍaṁ namaḥ L. 1.3.5 R. ankle

ॐ ढं नमः
oṁ ḍhaṁ namaḥ L. 1.3.5 R. joint of toes

ॐ णं नमः
oṁ ṇaṁ namaḥ L. 1.3.5 R. tip of toes

ॐ तं नमः
oṁ taṁ namaḥ R. 1.3.5 L. hip

ॐ थं नमः
oṁ thaṁ namaḥ R. 1.3.5 L. knees

ॐ दं नमः
oṁ daṁ namaḥ R. 1.3.5 L. ankle

ॐ धं नमः
oṁ dhaṁ namaḥ R. 1.3.5 L. joint of toes

ॐ नं नमः
oṁ naṁ namaḥ R. 1.3.5 L. tip of toes

ॐ पं नमः
oṁ paṁ namaḥ L. 1.4 base R. side

ॐ फं नमः
oṁ phaṁ namaḥ R. 1.4 base L. side

ॐ बं नमः
oṁ baṁ namaḥ R. 1.4 base Belly

ॐ भं नमः
oṁ bhaṁ namaḥ L. 1.4 base Back

ॐ मं नमः
oṁ maṁ namaḥ R. 1.2.3.4.5. flat Navel

ॐ यं नमः
oṁ yaṁ namaḥ R. 1.4 base Heart

ॐ रं नमः
oṁ raṁ namaḥ L. 1.4 base R. shoulder

ॐ लं नमः
oṁ laṁ namaḥ R. 1.4 base back of neck

ॐ वं नमः
oṁ vaṁ namaḥ R. 1.4 base L. shoulder

ॐ शं नमः
oṁ śaṁ namaḥ R. 1.4 L. shoulder to hand full

ॐ षं नमः
oṁ ṣaṁ namaḥ L. 1.4 R. shoulder to hand full

ॐ सं नमः

oṁ saṁ namaḥ L. 1.4 R. hip to leg full

ॐ हं नमः

oṁ haṁ namaḥ R. 1.4 L. hip to leg full

ॐ ळं नमः

oṁ ḷaṁ namaḥ L. 1.4 sternum to navel

ॐ क्षं नमः

oṁ kṣaṁ namaḥ R. 1.4 sternum to throat

ॐ ह्रीं श्रीं दुं दुर्गायै नमः

oṁ hrīṁ śrīṁ duṁ durgāyai namaḥ
Oṁ I bow to the Goddess, Durgā, the Grantor of Increase, who Removes all Difficulties.

mātṛkā nyāsa

establishment of the letters in the cakras

Following Pāṇiṇī's Grammar, which is the most authoritative on the subject, in the Bāhya Mātṛkā Nyāsa there are thirty-five consonants. Actually the number of letters varies according to different enumerations regarding differing functions, and in the Mātṛkā Nyāsa which follows, only fifty letters are to be placed. Saṁskṛt is commonly taught with fifty letters, sixteen vowels and thirty-four consonants. Occasionally it is taught with fifty-two letters, with the addition of oṁ and hrīṁ. For the purpose of these Nyāsas, we will follow the two formats presented, as the best authorities for their accuracy agree from all the versions consulted. The explanation as to why they differ in the number of letters contained, will not be addressed here. Mātṛkā Nyāsa places the Bījās or natural names inside the Cakras, which are the energy centers within the body. In this meditation we conceive that not only is all existence moving in My every movement, as in the former Nyāsa, but also that all the vibrations of the universe comprise the very essence of my being. Haṁ stands for the Prāṇātman, the second ḷaṁ, for the Jīvātman, and kṣaṁ for Paramātman. In this way, Jīva puts on, so to speak, or wears the universe as a gown. All the vibrations of existence make up the cloak which covers the ever more subtle essence of consciousness, which is the Silent Witness to the Dance of Creation.

Viśuddha (5th Cakra) 16 petals

ॐ अं नमः
oṁ aṁ namaḥ

ॐ आं नमः
oṁ āṁ namaḥ

ॐ इं नमः
oṁ iṁ namaḥ

ॐ ईं नमः
oṁ īṁ namaḥ

ॐ उं नमः
oṁ uṁ namaḥ

ॐ ऊं नमः
oṁ ūṁ namaḥ

ॐ ऋं नमः
oṁ ṛṁ namaḥ

ॐ ॠं नमः
oṁ ṝṁ namaḥ

ॐ ऌं नमः
oṁ ḷṛṁ namaḥ

ॐ ॡं नमः
oṁ ḷṝṁ namaḥ

ॐ एं नमः
oṁ eṁ namaḥ

ॐ ऐं नमः
oṁ aiṁ namaḥ

ॐ ओं नमः
oṁ oṁ namaḥ

ॐ औं नमः
oṁ auṁ namaḥ

ॐ अं नमः
oṁ aṁ namaḥ

ॐ अः नमः
oṁ aḥ namaḥ

Anahāta (4th Cakra) 12 petals

ॐ कं नमः
oṁ kaṁ namaḥ

ॐ खं नमः
oṁ khaṁ namaḥ

ॐ गं नमः
oṁ gaṁ namaḥ

ॐ घं नमः
oṁ ghaṁ namaḥ

ॐ ङं नमः
oṁ ṅaṁ namaḥ

ॐ चं नमः
oṁ caṁ namaḥ

ॐ छं नमः
oṁ chaṁ namaḥ

ॐ जं नमः
oṁ jaṁ namaḥ

ॐ झं नमः
oṁ jhaṁ namaḥ

ॐ ञं नमः
oṁ ñaṁ namaḥ

ॐ टं नमः
oṁ ṭaṁ namaḥ

ॐ ठं नमः
oṁ ṭhaṁ namaḥ

Maṇipura (3rd Cakra) 10 petals

ॐ डं नमः
oṁ ḍaṁ namaḥ

ॐ ढं नमः
oṁ ḍhaṁ namaḥ

ॐ णं नमः
oṁ ṇaṁ namaḥ

ॐ तं नमः
oṁ taṁ namaḥ

ॐ थं नमः
oṁ thaṁ namaḥ

ॐ दं नमः
oṁ daṁ namaḥ

ॐ धं नमः
oṁ dhaṁ namaḥ

ॐ नं नमः
oṁ naṁ namaḥ

ॐ पं नमः
oṁ paṁ namaḥ

ॐ फं नमः
oṁ phaṁ namaḥ

Swādiṣṭhana (2nd Cakra) 6 petals

ॐ बं नमः
oṁ baṁ namaḥ

ॐ भं नमः
oṁ bhaṁ namaḥ

ॐ मं नमः
oṁ maṁ namaḥ

ॐ यं नमः
oṁ yaṁ namaḥ

ॐ रं नमः
oṁ raṁ namaḥ

ॐ लं नमः
oṁ laṁ namaḥ

Mulādhāra (1st Cakra) 4 petals

ॐ वं नमः
oṁ vaṁ namaḥ

ॐ शं नमः
oṁ śaṁ namaḥ

ॐ षं नमः
oṁ ṣaṁ namaḥ

ॐ सं नमः
oṁ saṁ namaḥ

Āgnyā (6th Cakra) 2 petals

ॐ हं नमः
oṁ haṁ namaḥ

ॐ क्षं नमः
oṁ kṣaṁ namaḥ

ॐ ह्रीं श्रीं दुं दुर्गायै नमः

oṁ hrīṁ śrīṁ duṁ durgāyai namaḥ
Oṁ I bow to the Goddess, Durgā, the Grantor of Increase, who Removes all Difficulties.

Then perform Saṁhara Mātṛkā Nyāsa and Bāhya Mātṛkā Nyāsa by repeating the processes in reverse order from the end to the beginning.

aṅga pūjā

worship of the Divine Mother's body
Using Tattva Mudrā on both hands touch:

ॐ दुर्गायै नमः पादौ पूजयामि

oṁ durgāyai namaḥ pādau pūjayāmi feet
I bow to the Reliever of Difficulties and worship Her feet.

ॐ गिरिजायै नमः गुल्फौ पूजयामि

oṁ girijāyai namaḥ gulphau pūjayāmi ankles
I bow to the Unconquerable One from the Mountains and worship Her ankles.

ॐ अपर्णायै नमः जानुनी पूजयामि

oṁ aparṇāyai namaḥ jānunī pūjayāmi knees
I bow to the Unseverable Energy and worship Her knees.

ॐ हरिप्रियायै नमः ऊरू पूजयामि

oṁ haripriyāyai namaḥ ūrū pūjayāmi thighs
I bow to the Beloved of Consciousness and worship Her thighs.

ॐ पार्वत्यै नमः कटिं पूजयामि

oṁ pārvatyai namaḥ kaṭiṁ pūjayāmi hips
I bow to the Daughter of the Mountains and worship Her hips.

ॐ आर्यायै नमः नाभिं पूजयामि

oṁ āryāyai namaḥ nābhiṁ pūjayāmi navel
I bow to the One Purified by Knowledge and worship Her navel.

ॐ जगन्मात्रे नमः उदरं पूजयामि

oṁ jaganmātre namaḥ udaraṁ pūjayāmi stomach
I bow to the Mother of the Perceivable Universe and worship Her stomach.

ॐ मंगलायै नमः कुक्षिं पूजयामि

oṁ maṁgalāyai namaḥ kukṣiṁ pūjayāmi sternum
I bow to the Energy of Welfare and worship Her sternum.

ॐ शिवायै नमः हृदयं पूजयामि

oṁ śivāyai namaḥ hṛdayaṁ pūjayāmi heart
I bow to the Energy of Infinite Goodness and worship Her heart.

ॐ महेश्वर्यै नमः कण्ठं पूजयामि

oṁ maheśvaryai namaḥ kaṇṭhaṁ pūjayāmi throat
I bow to the Energy of the Great Seer of All and worship Her throat.

ॐ विश्ववन्द्यायै नमः स्कन्धौ पूजयामि

oṁ viśvavandyāyai namaḥ skandhau pūjayāmi shoulders
I bow to She who is Praised by the Universe and worship Her shoulders.

ॐ काल्यै नमः बाहू पूजयामि

oṁ kālyai namaḥ bāhū pūjayāmi arms
I bow to She who Takes Away Darkness and worship Her arms.

ॐ आद्यायै नमः हस्तौ पूजयामि

oṁ ādyāyai namaḥ hastau pūjayāmi hands
I bow to She who is Sacred Study and worship Her hands.

ॐ वरदायै नमः मुखं पूजयामि

oṁ varadāyai namaḥ mukhaṁ pūjayāmi mouth
I bow to She who Grants Boons and worship Her mouth.

ॐ सुवाण्यै नमः नासिकां पूजयामि

oṁ suvāṇyai namaḥ nāsikāṁ pūjayāmi nose

I bow to She of Excellent Music and worship Her nose.

ॐ कमलाक्ष्म्यै नमः नेत्रे पूजयामि

oṁ kamalākṣmyai namaḥ netre pūjayāmi three eyes

I bow to the Lotus-eyed and worship Her eyes.

ॐ अम्बिकायै नमः शिरः पूजयामि

oṁ ambikāyai namaḥ śiraḥ pūjayāmi top of head

I bow to the Mother of All and worship Her head.

ॐ देव्यै नमः सर्वाङ्ग पूजयामि

oṁ devyai namaḥ sarvāṅga pūjayāmi entire body

I bow to the Goddess and worship Her entire body.

हं रं ईं ह्रीं

haṁ raṁ īṁ hrīṁ

ॐ हकारः स्थूलदेहः स्याद्रकार सूक्ष्मदेहकः ।
ईकारः कारणात्मासौ ह्रींक्कारोऽहं तुरीयकम् ॥

oṁ hakāraḥ sthūladehaḥ syād
rakāra sūkṣmadehakaḥ
īkāraḥ kāraṇātmāsau hrīṅkāro-haṁ turīyakam

The letter Ha indicates the Gross Body; the letter Ra is the Subtle Body. The letter Ī is the Causal Body; and as the entire letter Hrīṁ, I am beyond manifestation.

pītha nyāsa

establishment of the place of internal worship
With Tattva Mudrā place on the yantra on your chest:

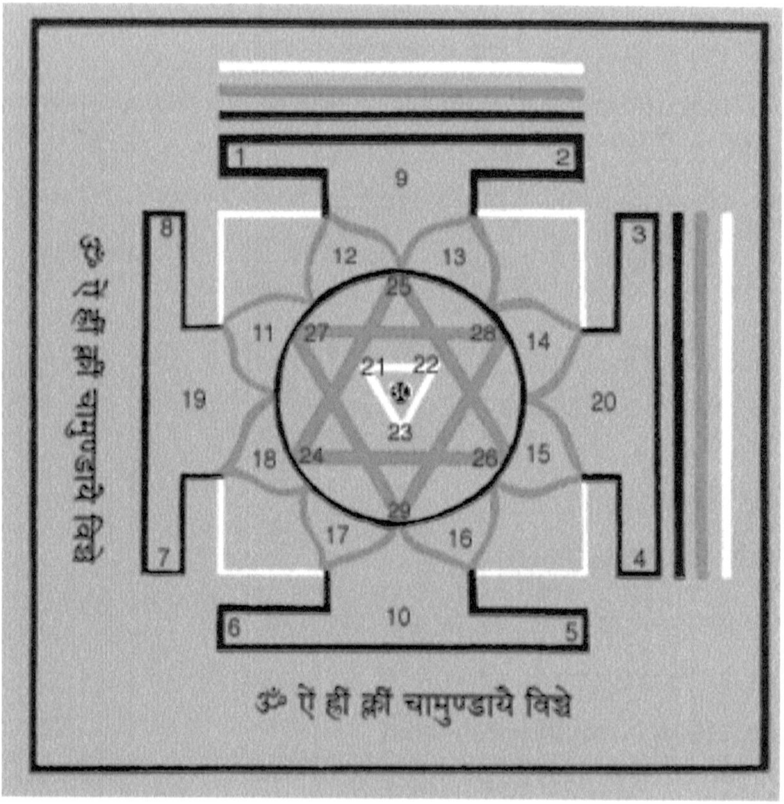

- 1 -

ॐ आधारशक्तये नमः

oṁ ādhāraśaktaye namaḥ

oṁ I bow to the primal energy which sustains existence.

- 2 -

ॐ कूर्माय नमः

oṁ kūrmāya namaḥ

oṁ I bow to the Tortoise which supports creation.

- 3 -

ॐ अनन्ताय नमः

oṁ anantāya namaḥ

oṁ I bow to Infinity (personified as a thousand hooded snake who holds aloft the worlds).

- 4 -

ॐ पृथिव्यै नमः

oṁ pṛthivyai namaḥ

oṁ I bow to the Earth.

- 5 -

ॐ क्षीरसमूद्राय नमः

oṁ kṣīrasamūdrāya namaḥ

oṁ I bow to the milk ocean, or ocean of nectar, the infinite expanse of existence from which all manifested.

- 6 -

ॐ श्वेतद्वीपाय नमः

oṁ śvetadvīpāya namaḥ

oṁ I bow to the Island of Purity, which is in the ocean.

- 7 -

ॐ मणिमन्दपाय नमः

oṁ maṇimandapāya namaḥ

oṁ I bow to the Palace of Gems, which is on the island, the home of the Divine Mother.

- 8 -

ॐ कल्पवृक्षाय नमः

oṁ kalpavṛkṣāya namaḥ

oṁ I bow to the Tree of Fulfillment, which satisfies all desires, growing in the palace courtyard.

- 9 -

ॐ मणिवेदिकायै नमः

oṁ maṇivedikāyai namaḥ

oṁ I bow to the altar containing the gems of wisdom.

- 10 -

ॐ रत्नसिंहासनाय नमः

oṁ ratnasiṁhāsanāya namaḥ
oṁ I bow to the throne of the jewel.

- 11 -

ॐ धर्माय नमः

oṁ dharmāya namaḥ
oṁ I bow to the Way of Truth and Harmony.

- 12 -

ॐ ज्ञानाय नमः

oṁ jñānāya namaḥ
oṁ I bow to Wisdom.

- 13 -

ॐ वैराग्याय नमः

oṁ vairāgyāya namaḥ
oṁ I bow to Detachment.

- 14 -

ॐ ऐश्वर्याय नमः

oṁ aiśvaryāya namaḥ
oṁ I bow to the Imperishable Qualities.

- 15 -

ॐ अधर्माय नमः

oṁ adharmāya namaḥ
oṁ I bow to Disharmony.

- 16 -

ॐ अज्ञानाय नमः

oṁ ajñānāya namaḥ
oṁ I bow to Ignorance.

- 17 -

ॐ अवैराग्याय नमः

oṁ avairāgyāya namaḥ
oṁ I bow to Attachment.

- 18 -

ॐ अनैश्वर्याय नमः

oṁ anīśvaryāya namaḥ
oṁ I bow to the Transient.

- 19 -

ॐ अनन्ताय नमः

oṁ anantāya namaḥ
oṁ I bow to the Infinite.

- 20 -

ॐ पद्माय नमः

oṁ padmāya namaḥ
oṁ I bow to the Lotus.

- 21 -

अं अर्कमण्डलाय द्वादशकलात्मने नमः

aṁ arkamaṇḍalāya dvādaśakalātmane namaḥ
"A" we bow to the twelve aspects of the realm of the sun. Tapinī, Tāpinī, Dhūmrā, Marīci, Jvālinī, Ruci, Sudhūmrā, Bhoga-dā, Viśvā, Bodhinī, Dhārinī, Kṣamā; Containing heat, Emanating heat, Smoky, Ray-producing, Burning, Lustrous, Purple or Smoky-red, Granting enjoyment, Universal, Which makes known, Productive of Consciousness, Which supports, Which forgives.

- 22 -

उं सोममण्डलाय षोडशकलात्मने नमः

uṁ somamaṇḍalāya ṣoḍaśakalātmane namaḥ
"U" I bow to the sixteen aspects of the realm of the moon. Amṛta, Prāṇada, Puṣā, Tuṣṭi, Puṣṭi, Rati, Dhṛti, Śaśinī, Candrikā, Kānti, Jyotsnā, Śrī, Prīti, Angadā, Pūrṇā, Pūrnāmṛta; Nectar, Which sustains life, Which supports, Satisfying, Nourishing, Playful, Constancy, Unfailing, Producer of Joy, Beauty enhanced by love, Light, Grantor of Prosperity, Affectionate, Purifying the body, Complete, Full of Bliss.

- 23 -

मं वह्निमण्डलाय दशकलात्मने नमः

maṁ vahnimaṇḍalāya daśakalātmane namaḥ
"M" we bow to the ten aspects of the realm of fire: Dhūmrā, Arciḥ, Jvalinī, Śūkṣmā, Jvālinī, Visphuliṅginī, Suśrī, Surūpā, Kapilā, Havya-Kavya-Vahā; Smoky Red, Flaming, Shining, Subtle,

Burning, Sparkling, Beautiful, Well-formed, Tawny, The Messenger to Gods and Ancestors.

- 24 -

ॐ सं सत्त्वाय नमः

oṁ saṁ sattvāya namaḥ

oṁ I bow to activity, execution, light, knowledge, being.

- 25 -

ॐ रं रजसे नमः

oṁ raṁ rajase namaḥ

oṁ I bow to desire, inspiration, becoming.

- 26 -

ॐ तं तमसे नमः

oṁ taṁ tamase namaḥ

oṁ I bow to wisdom, to the darkness which exposes light, to rest.

- 27 -

ॐ आं आत्मने नमः

oṁ āṁ ātmane namaḥ

oṁ I bow to the Soul.

- 28 -

ॐ अं अन्तरात्मने नमः

oṁ aṁ antarātmane namaḥ

oṁ I bow to the Innermost Soul.

- 29 -

ॐ पं परमात्मने नमः

oṁ paṁ paramātmane namaḥ

oṁ I bow to the Universal Soul, or the Consciousness which exceeds manifestation.

- 30 -

ॐ ह्रीं ज्ञानात्मने नमः

oṁ hrīṁ jñānātmane namaḥ

oṁ I bow to the Soul of Infinite Wisdom.

āvāhaṇa
invitation

अनेकरत्न संयुक्तं नानामणि गणान्वितम् ।
कार्तस्वरमयं दिव्यमासनं प्रतिगृह्यताम् ॥
ॐ ह्रीं श्रीं दुं दुर्गायै नमः आसनं समर्पयामि

anekaratna saṁyuktaṁ nānāmaṇi gaṇānvitam
kārtasvaramayaṁ divyamāsanaṁ pratigṛhyatām
oṁ hrīṁ śrīṁ duṁ durgāyai namaḥ āsanaṁ samarpayāmi

United with many gems and a multitude of various jewels, voluntarily accept my offering of a divine seat. With the offering of a seat Oṁ I bow to the Goddess, Durgā, the Grantor of Increase, who Removes all Difficulties.

establishment within

āvāhaṇi mudrā (I invite you, please come.)

ॐ ह्रीं श्रीं दुं दुर्गायै नमः इहागच्छ

oṁ hrīṁ śrīṁ duṁ durgāyai namaḥ ihāgaccha

Oṁ I bow to the Goddess, Durgā, the Grantor of Increase, who Removes all Difficulties, I invite you, please come.

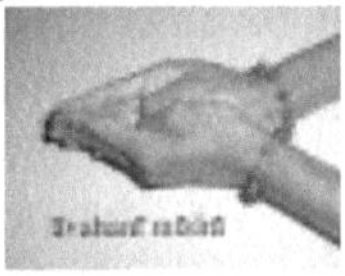

sthāpanī mudrā (I establish you within.)

इह तिष्ठ

iha tiṣṭha

I establish you within.

sannidhāpanī mudrā (I know you have many devotees who are requesting your attention, but I request that you pay special attention to me.)

इह सन्निरुध्यस्व

iha sannirudhyasva

I am binding you to remain here.

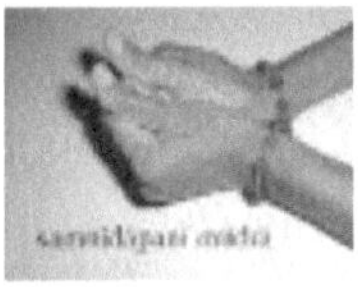

saṁrodhanī mudrā (I am sorry for any inconvenience caused.)

इह सनिहित भव

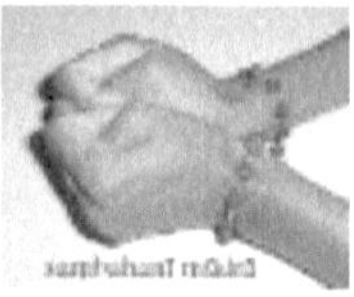

iha sanihita bhava

You bestow abundant wealth.

atmā samarpaṇa mudrā (I surrender my soul to you.)

अत्राधिष्ठानं कुरु

atrādhiṣṭhānaṁ kuru

I am depending upon you to forgive me in this matter.

prakṣan (I bow to you with devotion.)

देवि मम पूजां गृहाण

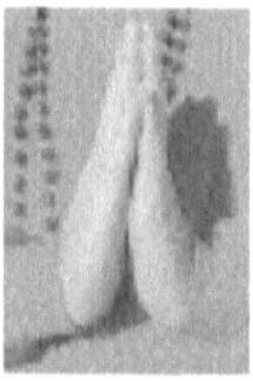

देवेशि भक्तशूल्वे परित्राण करायिते ।

यावत् त्वं पूजयिष्यामि तावत् त्वं सुस्थिरा भव ॥

devi mama pūjāṁ gṛhāṇa
deveśi bhaktaśūlave paritrāṇa karāyite
yāvat tvaṁ pūjayiṣyāmi tāvat tvaṁ susthirā bhava

Oh Goddess, please accept my worship. Oh Goddess, remove all pain from your devotees. For so long as I worship you, please remain sitting still.

prāṇa pratiṣṭhā
establishment of life

ॐ अं आं ह्रीं क्रों यं रं लं वं शं षं सं हों हं सः

oṁ aṁ āṁ hrīṁ kroṁ yaṁ raṁ laṁ vaṁ śaṁ ṣaṁ saṁ hoṁ haṁ saḥ

oṁ The Infinite Beyond Conception, Creation (the first letter), Consciousness, Māyā, the cause of the movement of the subtle body to perfection and beyond; the path of fulfillment: control, subtle illumination, one with the earth, emancipation, the soul of peace, the soul of delight, the soul of unity (all this is I), perfection, Infinite Consciousness, this is I.

ॐ ह्रीं श्रीं दुं दुर्गायै नमः प्राणा इह प्राणाः

oṁ hrīṁ śrīṁ duṁ durgāyai namaḥ prāṇā iha prāṇāḥ

Oṁ I bow to the Goddess, Durgā, the Grantor of Increase, who Removes all Difficulties. You are the life of this life!

ॐ अं आं ह्रीं क्रों यं रं लं वं शं षं सं हों हं सः

oṁ aṁ āṁ hrīṁ kroṁ yaṁ raṁ laṁ vaṁ śaṁ ṣaṁ saṁ hoṁ haṁ saḥ

oṁ The Infinite Beyond Conception, Creation (the first letter), Consciousness, Māyā, the cause of the movement of the subtle body to perfection and beyond; the path of fulfillment: control, subtle illumination, one with the earth, emancipation, the soul of peace, the soul of delight, the soul of unity (all this is I), perfection, Infinite Consciousness, this is I.

ॐ ह्रीं श्रीं दुं दुर्गायै नमः जीव इह स्थितः

oṁ hrīṁ śrīṁ duṁ durgāyai namaḥ jīva iha sthitaḥ

Oṁ I bow to the Goddess, Durgā, the Grantor of Increase, who Removes all Difficulties. You are situated in this life (or individual consciousness).

ॐ अं आं ह्रीं क्रों यं रं लं वं शं षं सं हों हं सः

oṁ aṁ āṁ hrīṁ kroṁ yaṁ raṁ laṁ vaṁ śaṁ ṣaṁ saṁ hoṁ haṁ saḥ

oṁ The Infinite Beyond Conception, Creation (the first letter), Consciousness, Māyā, the cause of the movement of the subtle body to perfection and beyond; the path of fulfillment: control, subtle illumination, one with the earth, emancipation, the soul of peace, the soul of delight, the soul of unity (all this is I), perfection, Infinite Consciousness, this is I.

ॐ ह्रीं श्रीं दुं दुर्गायै नमः सर्वेन्द्रियाणि

oṁ hrīṁ śrīṁ duṁ durgāyai namaḥ sarvendriyāṇi
Oṁ I bow to the Goddess, Durgā, the Grantor of Increase, who Removes all Difficulties. You are all these organs (of action and knowledge).

ॐ अं आं ह्रीं क्रों यं रं लं वं शं षं सं हों हं सः

oṁ aṁ āṁ hrīṁ kroṁ yaṁ raṁ laṁ vaṁ śaṁ ṣaṁ saṁ hoṁ haṁ saḥ
oṁ The Infinite Beyond Conception, Creation (the first letter), Consciousness, Māyā, the cause of the movement of the subtle body to perfection and beyond; the path of fulfillment: control, subtle illumination, one with the earth, emancipation, the soul of peace, the soul of delight, the soul of unity (all this is I), perfection, Infinite Consciousness, this is I.

ॐ ह्रीं श्रीं दुं दुर्गायै नमः वाग् मनस्त्वक्चक्षुः-श्रोत्र-घ्राण-प्राणा इहागत्य सुखं चिरं तिष्ठन्तु स्वाहा

oṁ hrīṁ śrīṁ duṁ durgāyai namaḥ vāg manastvakcakṣuḥ śrotra ghrāṇa prāṇā ihāgatya sukhaṁ ciraṁ tiṣṭhantu svāhā
Oṁ I bow to the Goddess, Durgā, the Grantor of Increase, who Removes all Difficulties. You are all these vibrations, mind, sound, eyes, ears, tongue, nose and life force. Bring forth infinite peace and establish it forever, I am One with God!

kara nyāsa
establishment in the hands

ॐ ह्रां अंगुष्ठाभ्यां नमः

oṁ hrāṁ aṅguṣṭhābhyāṁ namaḥ thumb forefinger
Oṁ hrāṁ in the thumb I bow.

ॐ ह्रीं तर्जनीभ्यां स्वाहा

oṁ hrīṁ tarjanībhyāṁ svāhā thumb forefinger
Oṁ hrīṁ in the forefinger, I am One with God!

ॐ ह्रूं मध्यमाभ्यां वषट्

oṁ hrūṁ madhyamābhyāṁ vaṣaṭ thumb middlefinger
Oṁ hrūṁ in the middle finger, Purify!

ॐ ह्रैं अनामिकाभ्यां हुं

oṁ hraiṁ anāmikābhyāṁ huṁ thumb ring finger
Oṁ hraiṁ in the ring finger, Cut the Ego!

ॐ ह्रौं कनिष्ठिकाभ्यां बौषट्

oṁ hrauṁ kaniṣṭhikābhyāṁ vauṣaṭ thumb little finger
Oṁ hrauṁ in the little finger, Ultimate Purity!

Roll hand over hand forwards while reciting karatal kar, and backwards while chanting pṛṣṭhābhyāṁ, then clap hands when chanting astrāya phaṭ.

ॐ ह्रः करतल कर पृष्ठाभ्यां अस्त्राय फट् ॥

oṁ hraḥ karatal kar pṛṣṭhābhyāṁ astrāya phaṭ
Oṁ hraḥ I bow with the weapon of Virtue.

ॐ ह्रीं श्रीं दुं दुर्गायै नमः

oṁ hrīṁ śrīṁ duṁ durgāyai namaḥ
Oṁ I bow to the Goddess, Durgā, the Grantor of Increase, who Removes all Difficulties.

aṅga nyāsa
establishment in the body
Holding tattva mudrā, touch heart.

ॐ ह्रां हृदयाय नमः

oṁ hrāṁ hṛdayāya namaḥ touch heart
Oṁ hrāṁ in the heart, I bow.

Holding tattva mudrā, touch top of head.

ॐ ह्रीं शिरसे स्वाहा

oṁ hrīṁ śirase svāhā top of head
Oṁ hrīṁ on the top of the head, I am One with God!

With thumb extended, touch back of head.

ॐ ह्रूं शिखायै वषट्

oṁ hrūṁ śikhāyai vaṣaṭ back of head
Oṁ hrūṁ on the back of the head, Purify!

Holding tattva mudrā, cross both arms.

ॐ ह्रैं कवचाय हुं

oṁ hraiṁ kavacāya huṁ cross both arms
Oṁ hraiṁ crossing both arms, Cut the Ego!

Holding tattva mudrā, touch two eyes and in between at once with three middle fingers.

ॐ ह्रौं नेत्रत्रयाय वौषट्

oṁ hrauṁ netratrayāya vauṣaṭ touch three eyes
Oṁ hrauṁ in the three eyes, Ultimate Purity!

Roll hand over hand forwards while reciting karatala kara and backwards while chanting pṛṣṭhābhyāṁ, then clap hands when chanting astrāya phaṭ.

ॐ ह्रः करतल कर पृष्ठाभ्यां अस्त्राय फट् ॥

oṁ hraḥ karatal kar pṛṣṭhābhyāṁ astrāya phaṭ
Oṁ hraḥ I bow with the weapon of Virtue.

ॐ ह्रीं श्रीं दुं दुर्गायै नमः

oṁ hrīṁ śrīṁ duṁ durgāyai namaḥ

Oṁ I bow to the Goddess, Durgā, the Grantor of Increase, who Removes all Difficulties.

japa

hold flower to your heart

ॐ अम्बे अम्बिकेऽम्बालिके न मा नयति कश्चन ।

ससस्त्यश्वकः सुभद्रिकां काम्पीलवासिनीम् ॥

oṁ ambe ambike-mbālike na mā nayati kaścana
sasastyaśvakaḥ subhadrikāṁ kāmpīlavāsinīm

Mother of the Perceivable Universe, Mother of the Conceivable Universe, Mother of the Universe of Intuitive Vision, lead me to that True Existence. As excellent crops (or grains) are harvested, so may I be taken to reside with the Infinite Consciousness.

place flower on yantra

ॐ जयन्ती मङ्गला काली भद्रकाली कपालिनी ।

दुर्गा क्षमा शिवा धात्री स्वाहा स्वधा नमोऽस्तु ते ॥

oṁ jayantī maṅgalā kālī bhadra kālī kapālinī
durgā kṣamā śivā dhātrī svāhā svadhā namo-stu te

Oṁ. She Who Conquers Over All, All-Auspicious, She Who is Beyond Time, the Excellent One Beyond Time, the Bearer of the Skulls of Impure Thought, the Reliever of Difficulties, Loving Forgiveness, Supporter of the Universe, Oblations of I am One with God, Oblations of Ancestral Praise, to You, we bow.

upasaṁhara sthāpana mudrā

दुर्गां शिवां शान्तिकरीं ब्रह्माणीं ब्रह्मणः प्रियाम् ।
सर्वलोक प्रणेत्रीञ्च प्रणमामि सदा शिवाम् ॥

durgāṁ śivāṁ śāntikarīṁ brahmāṇīṁ brahmaṇaḥ priyām
sarvaloka praṇetrīñca praṇamāmi sadā śivām

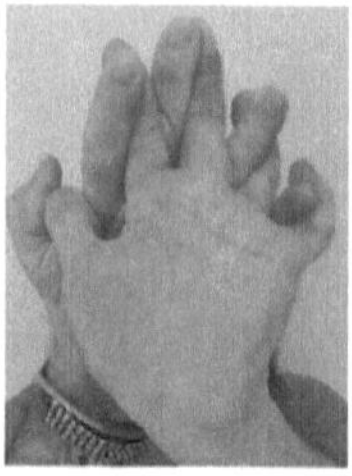

The Reliever of Difficulties, Exposer of Goodness, Cause of Peace, Infinite Consciousness, Beloved by Knowers of Consciousness; all the inhabitants of all the worlds always bow to Her, and I am bowing to Goodness Herself.

मङ्गलां शोभनां शुद्धां निष्कलां परमां कलाम् ।
विश्वेश्वरीं विश्वमातां चण्डिकां प्रणमाम्यहम् ॥

maṅgalāṁ śobhanāṁ śuddhāṁ niṣkalāṁ paramāṁ kalām
viśveśvarīṁ viśvamātāṁ caṇḍikāṁ praṇamāmyaham

Welfare, Radiant Beauty, Completely Pure, Without Limitations, the Ultimate Limitation, the Lord of the Universe, the Mother of the Universe, to you Caṇḍi, to the Energy that Tears Apart Thought, I bow in submission.

ॐ कात्यायनाय विद्महे कन्याकुमारी धीमहि ।
तन्नो दुर्गिः प्रचोदयात् ॐ ॥

oṁ kātyāyanāya vidmahe kanyākumārī dhīmahi
tanno durgiḥ pracodayāt oṁ

Oṁ We meditate on the Ever Pure One, we contemplate the Daughter Without Flaw or Imperfection. May that Goddess grant us increase.

āvāhaṇi mudrā (I invite you, please come.)

ॐ ह्रीं श्रीं दुं दुर्गायै नमः इहागच्छ

oṁ hrīṁ śrīṁ duṁ durgāyai namaḥ ihāgaccha

Oṁ I bow to the Goddess, Durgā, the Grantor of Increase, who Removes all Difficulties, I invite you, please come.

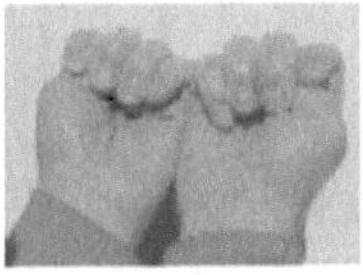

sthāpanī mudrā (I establish you within.)

इह तिष्ठ

iha tiṣṭha

I establish you within.

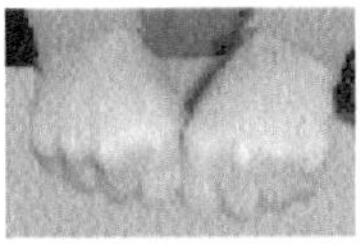

sannidhāpanī mudrā (I know you have many devotees who are requesting your attention, but I request that you pay special attention to me.)

इह सन्निदेहि

iha sannidehi

I am binding you to remain here.

saṁrodhanī mudrā (I am sorry for any inconvenience caused.)

इह सनिहित भव

iha sanihita bhava

You bestow abundant wealth.

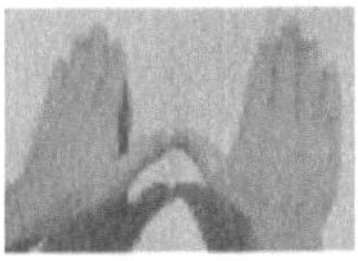

atmā samarpaṇa mudrā (I surrender my soul to you.)

अत्राधिष्ठानं कुरु

atrādhiṣṭhānaṁ kuru

I am depending upon you to forgive me in this matter.

prakṣan (I bow to you with devotion.)

देवि मम पूजां गृहाण

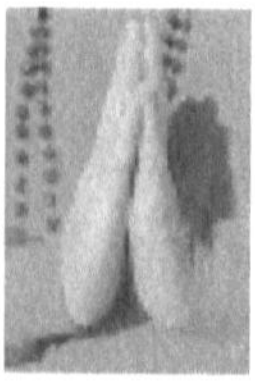

देवेशि भक्तशूल्वे परित्राण करायिते ।

यावत् त्वं पूजयिष्यामि तावत् त्वं सुस्थिरा भव ॥

devi mama pūjāṁ gṛhāṇa
deveśi bhaktaśūlave paritrāṇa karāyite
yāvat tvaṁ pūjayiṣyāmi tāvat tvaṁ susthirā bhava

Oh Goddess, please accept my worship. Oh Goddess, remove all pain from your devotees. For so long as I worship you, please remain sitting still.

pūjā naivedya
offerings of worship
invitation

आगच्छेह महादेवि ! सर्वसम्पत्प्रदायिनि ।
यावद् व्रतं समाप्येत तावत्त्वं सन्निधौ भव ॥
ॐ ह्रीं श्रीं दुं दुर्गायै नमः आवाहनं समर्पयामि

āgaccheha mahādevi ! sarvasampatpradāyini
yāvad vrataṁ samāpyeta tāvattvaṁ sannidhau bhava
oṁ hrīṁ śrīṁ duṁ durgāyai namaḥ āvāhanaṁ samarpayāmi

Please come here, oh Great Goddess, Giver of all wealth! Please remain sitting still until this vow of worship is not complete. With the offering of an invitation Oṁ I bow to the Goddess, Durgā, the Grantor of Increase, who Removes all Difficulties.

seat

अनेकरत्नसंयुक्तं नानामणिगणान्वितम् ।
कार्तस्वरमयं दिव्यमासनं प्रतिगृह्यताम् ॥
ॐ ह्रीं श्रीं दुं दुर्गायै नमः आसनं समर्पयामि

anekaratna saṁyuktaṁ nānāmaṇi gaṇānvitam
kārtasvaramayaṁ divyamāsanaṁ pratigṛhyatām
oṁ hrīṁ śrīṁ duṁ durgāyai namaḥ āsanaṁ samarpayāmi

United with many gems and a multitude of various jewels, voluntarily accept my offering of a divine seat. With the offering of a seat Oṁ I bow to the Goddess, Durgā, the Grantor of Increase, who Removes all Difficulties.

foot bath

ॐ गङ्गादिसर्वतीर्थेभ्यो मया प्रार्थनयाहृतम् ।
तोयमेतत् सुखस्पर्शं पाद्यार्थं प्रतिगृह्यताम् ॥
ॐ ह्रीं श्रीं दुं दुर्गायै नमः पाद्यं समर्पयामि

oṁ gaṅgādi sarva tīrthebhyo mayā prārthanayāhṛtam
toyametat sukha sparśaṁ pādyārthaṁ pratigṛhyatām
oṁ hrīṁ śrīṁ duṁ durgāyai namaḥ pādyaṁ samarpayāmi

The Gaṅges and other waters from all the places of pilgrimage are mingled together in this our prayer, that you please accept the comfortable touch of these waters offered to wash your lotus feet. With this offering of foot bath waters Oṁ I bow to the Goddess, Durgā, the Grantor of Increase, who Removes all Difficulties.

water for washing hands and mouth

कर्पूरेण सुगन्धेन सुरभिस्वादु शीतलम् ।
तोयमाचमनीयार्थं देवीदं प्रतिगृह्यताम् ॥
ॐ ह्रीं श्रीं दुं दुर्गायै नमः आचमनीयं समर्पयामि

karpūreṇa sugandhena surabhisvādu śītalam
toyamācamanīyārthaṁ devīdaṁ pratigṛhyatām
oṁ hrīṁ śrīṁ duṁ durgāyai namaḥ ācamanīyaṁ samarpayāmi

With camphor and excellent scent, cool with excellent taste, this water is being offered for washing, Oh Goddess, please accept. With this offering of washing waters Oṁ I bow to the Goddess, Durgā, the Grantor of Increase, who Removes all Difficulties.

arghya

निधीनां सर्वदेवानां त्वमनर्घ्यगुणा ह्यसि ।
सिंहोपरिस्थिते देवि ! गृहाणार्घ्यं नमोऽस्तु ते ॥
ॐ ह्रीं श्रीं दुं दुर्गायै नमः अर्घ्यं समर्पयामि

nidhīnāṁ sarvadevānāṁ tvamanarghyaguṇā hyasi
siṁhoparisthite devi ! gṛhāṇārghyaṁ namo-stu te
oṁ hrīṁ śrīṁ duṁ durgāyai namaḥ arghyaṁ samarpayāmi

Presented to all the Gods, you, oh Arghya, bring an abundance of pleasure. Oh Goddess who is seated upon the lion, accept this arghya. I bow to you. With this offering of arghya Oṁ I bow to the Goddess, Durgā, the Grantor of Increase, who Removes all Difficulties.

madhuparka

दधिमधुघृतसमायुक्तं पात्रयुग्मं समन्वितम् ।
मधुपर्कं गृहाण त्वं शुभदा भव शोभने ॥
ॐ ह्रीं श्रीं दुं दुर्गायै नमः मधुपर्कं समर्पयामि

dadhi madhu ghṛtasamāyuktaṁ
pātrayugmaṁ samanvitam
madhuparkaṁ gṛhāṇa tvaṁ śubhadā bhava śobhane
oṁ hrīṁ śrīṁ duṁ durgāyai namaḥ madhuparkaṁ samarpayāmi

Yogurt, honey, ghee mixed together, and blended fine in a vessel; please accept this madhuparka shining with radiant purity. With this offering of madhuparka Oṁ I bow to the Goddess, Durgā, the Grantor of Increase, who Removes all Difficulties.

milk bath

ॐ कामधेनुसमुद्भूतं सर्वेषां जीवनं परम् ।
पावनं यज्ञहेतुश्च स्नानार्थं प्रतिगृह्यताम् ॥
ॐ ह्रीं श्रीं दुं दुर्गायै नमः पयस्नानं समर्पयामि

oṁ kāmadhenu samudbhūtaṁ sarveṣāṁ jīvanaṁ param
pāvanaṁ yajña hetuśca snānārthaṁ pratigṛhyatām
oṁ hrīṁ śrīṁ duṁ durgāyai namaḥ paya snānaṁ samarpayāmi

Coming from the ocean of being, the Fulfiller of all Desires, Grantor of Supreme Bliss to all souls. For the motive of purifying or sanctifying this holy union, we request you to accept this bath. With this offering of milk for your bath Oṁ I bow to the Goddess, Durgā, the Grantor of Increase, who Removes all Difficulties.

yogurt bath

ॐ पयसस्तु समुद्भूतं मधुराम्लं शशिप्रभम् ।
दध्यानितं मया दत्तं स्नानार्थं प्रतिगृह्यताम् ॥
ॐ ह्रीं श्रीं दुं दुर्गायै नमः दधिस्नानं समर्पयामि

oṁ payasastu samudbhūtaṁ madhurāmlaṁ śaśiprabham
dadhyānitaṁ mayā dattaṁ snānārthaṁ pratigṛhyatām
oṁ hrīṁ śrīṁ duṁ durgāyai namaḥ dadhi snānaṁ samarpayāmi

Derived from milk from the ocean of being, sweet and pleasing like the glow of the moon, let these curds eternally be our ambassador, as we request you to accept this bath. With this offering of yogurt for your bath Oṁ I bow to the Goddess, Durgā, the Grantor of Increase, who Removes all Difficulties.

ghee bath

ॐ नवनीतसमुत्पन्नं सर्वसन्तोषकारकम् ।

घृतं तुभ्यं प्रदास्यामि स्नानार्थं प्रतिगृह्यताम् ॥

ॐ ह्रीं श्रीं दुं दुर्गायै नमः घृतस्नानं समर्पयामि

oṁ navanīta samutpannaṁ sarvasantoṣakārakam
ghṛtaṁ tubhyaṁ pradāsyāmi snānārthaṁ pratigṛhyatām
oṁ hrīṁ śrīṁ duṁ durgāyai namaḥ ghṛta snānaṁ samarpayāmi

Freshly prepared from the ocean of being, causing all fulfillment, we offer this delightful ghee (clarified butter) and request you to accept this bath. With this offering of ghee for your bath Oṁ I bow to the Goddess, Durgā, the Grantor of Increase, who Removes all Difficulties.

honey bath

ॐ तरुपुष्पसमुद्भूतं सुस्वादु मधुरं मधु ।

तेजोपुष्टिकरं दिव्यं स्नानार्थं प्रतिगृह्यताम् ॥

ॐ ह्रीं श्रीं दुं दुर्गायै नमः मधुस्नानं समर्पयामि

oṁ tarupuṣpa samudbhūtam susvādu madhuraṁ madhu
tejo puṣṭikaraṁ divyaṁ snānārtham pratigṛhyatām
oṁ hrīṁ śrīṁ duṁ durgāyai namaḥ madhu snānaṁ samarpayāmi

Prepared from flowers of the ocean of being, enjoyable as the sweetest of the sweet, causing the fire of divine nourishment to burn swiftly, we request you to accept this bath. With this offering of honey for your bath Oṁ I bow to the Goddess, Durgā, the Grantor of Increase, who Removes all Difficulties.

sugar bath

ॐ इक्षुसारसमुद्भूता शर्करा पुष्टिकारिका ।

मलापहारिका दिव्या स्नानार्थं प्रतिगृह्यताम् ॥

ॐ ह्रीं श्रीं दुं दुर्गायै नमः शर्करास्नानं समर्पयामि

oṁ ikṣusāra samudbhūtā śarkarā puṣṭikārikā
malāpahārikā divyā snānārthaṁ pratigṛhyatām
oṁ hrīṁ śrīṁ duṁ durgāyai namaḥ śarkarā snānaṁ samarpayāmi

From the lake of sugar-cane, from the ocean of being, which causes the nourishment of sugar to give divine protection from all impurity, we request you to accept this bath. With this offering of sugar for your bath Oṁ I bow to the Goddess, Durgā, the Grantor of Increase, who Removes all Difficulties.

five nectars bath

ॐ पयो दधि घृतं चैव मधु च शर्करायुतम् ।

पञ्चामृतं मयाऽऽनीतं स्नानार्थं प्रतिगृह्यताम् ॥

ॐ ह्रीं श्रीं दुं दुर्गायै नमः पञ्चामृतस्नानं समर्पयामि

oṁ payo dadhi ghṛtaṁ caiva madhu ca śarkarāyutam
pañcāmṛtaṁ mayā--nītaṁ snānārthaṁ pratigṛhyatām
oṁ hrīṁ śrīṁ duṁ durgāyai namaḥ pañcāmṛta snānaṁ samarpayāmi

Milk, curd, ghee and then honey and sugar mixed together; these five nectars are our ambassador, as we request you to accept this bath. With this offering of five nectars for your bath Oṁ I bow to the Goddess, Durgā, the Grantor of Increase, who Removes all Difficulties.

scented oil

ॐ नानासुगन्धिद्रव्यं च चन्दनं रजनीयुतम् ।

उद्वर्तनं मया दत्तं स्नानार्थं प्रतिगृह्यताम् ॥

ॐ ह्रीं श्रीं दुं दुर्गायै नमः उद्वर्तनस्नानं समर्पयामि

oṁ nānāsugandhidravyaṁ ca candanaṁ rajanīyutam
udvartanaṁ mayā dattaṁ snānārthaṁ pratigṛhyatām
oṁ hrīṁ śrīṁ duṁ durgāyai namaḥ udvartana snānaṁ samarpayāmi

oṁ With various beautifully smelling ingredients, as well as the scent of sandal, we offer you this scented oil, Oh Lord. With this offering of scented oil Oṁ I bow to the Goddess, Durgā, the Grantor of Increase, who Removes all Difficulties.

scent bath

गन्धद्वारां दुराधर्षां नित्यपुष्टां करीषिणीम् ।

ईश्वरीं सर्वभूतानां तामिहोपह्वये श्रियम् ॥

ॐ ह्रीं श्रीं दुं दुर्गायै नमः गन्धस्नानं समर्पयामि

gandhadvārāṁ durādharṣāṁ nityapuṣṭāṁ karīṣiṇīm
īśvarīṁ sarvabhūtānāṁ tāmihopahvaye śriyam
oṁ hrīṁ śrīṁ duṁ durgāyai namaḥ gandha snānaṁ samarpayāmi

She is the cause of the scent which is the door to religious ecstasy, unconquerable (never-failing), continually nurturing for all time. May we never tire from calling that manifestation of the Highest Respect, the Supreme Goddess of all existence. With this offering of scented bath Oṁ I bow to the Goddess, Durgā, the Grantor of Increase, who Removes all Difficulties.

water bath

ॐ गङ्गे च जमुने चैव गोदावरि सरस्वति ।

नर्मदे सिन्धु कावेरि स्नानार्थं प्रतिगृह्यताम् ॥

ॐ ह्रीं श्रीं दुं दुर्गायै नमः गङ्गास्नानं समर्पयामि

oṁ gaṅge ca jamune caiva godāvari sarasvati
narmade sindhu kāveri snānārthaṁ pratigṛhyatām
oṁ hrīṁ śrīṁ duṁ durgāyai namaḥ gaṅgā snānaṁ samarpayāmi

Please accept the waters from the Gaṅges, the Jamunā, Godāvarī, Sarasvatī, Narmadā, Sindhu and Kāverī, which have been provided for your bath. With this offering of Ganges bath waters Oṁ I bow to the Goddess, Durgā, the Grantor of Increase, who Removes all Difficulties.

cloth

ॐ शीतवातोष्णसंत्राणं लज्जायै रक्षणं परं ।

देहालंकरणं वस्त्रं अथ शान्तिं प्रयच्छ मे ॥

ॐ ह्रीं श्रीं दुं दुर्गायै नमः वस्त्रं समर्पयामि

oṁ śīta vātoṣṇa saṁ trāṇaṁ lajjāyai rakṣaṇaṁ paraṁ
dehālaṅkaraṇaṁ vastraṁ atha śāntiṁ prayaccha me
oṁ hrīṁ śrīṁ duṁ durgāyai namaḥ vastraṁ samarpayāmi

To take away the cold and the wind and to fully protect your modesty, we adorn your body with this cloth, and thereby find the greatest Peace. With this offering of wearing apparel Oṁ I bow to the Goddess, Durgā, the Grantor of Increase, who Removes all Difficulties.

sacred thread

ॐ यज्ञोपवीतं परमं पवित्रं प्रजापतेर्यत् सहजं पुरस्तात् ।

आयुष्यमग्रं प्रतिमुञ्च शुभ्रं यज्ञोपवीतं बलमस्तु तेजः ॥

oṁ yajñopavītaṁ paramaṁ pavitraṁ
prajāpateryat sahajaṁ purastāt
āyuṣyamagraṁ pratimuñca śubhraṁ
yajñopavītaṁ balamastu tejaḥ

Oṁ the sacred thread of the highest purity is given by Prajāpati, the Lord of Creation, for the greatest facility. You bring life and illuminate the greatness of liberation. Oh sacred thread, let your strength be of radiant light.

शमो दमस्तपः शौचं क्षान्तिरार्जवमेव च ।

ज्ञानं विज्ञानमास्तिक्यं ब्रह्मकर्म स्वभावजम् ॥

śamo damastapaḥ śaucaṁ kṣāntirārjavameva ca
jñānaṁ vijñānamāstikyaṁ brahmakarma svabhāvajam

Peacefulness, self-control, austerity, purity of mind and body, patience and forgiveness, sincerity and honesty, wisdom, knowledge, and self-realization, are the natural activities of a Brahmaṇa.

नवभिस्तन्तुभिर्युक्तं त्रिगुणं देवतामयं ।
उपवीतं मया दत्तं गृहाण त्वं सुरेश्वरि ॥
ॐ ह्रीं श्रीं दुं दुर्गायै नमः यज्ञोपवीतं समर्पयामि

navabhiṣṭantubhiryuktaṁ triguṇaṁ devatā mayaṁ
upavītaṁ mayā dattaṁ gṛhāṇa tvaṁ sureśvari
oṁ hrīṁ śrīṁ duṁ durgāyai namaḥ yajñopavītaṁ samarpayāmi

With nine desirable threads all united together, exemplifying the three guṇas (or three qualities of harmony of our deity), this sacred thread will be our ambassador. Oh Ruler of the Gods, please accept. With this offering of a sacred thread Oṁ I bow to the Goddess, Durgā, the Grantor of Increase, who Removes all Difficulties.

rudrākṣa

त्र्यम्बकं यजामहे सुगन्धिं पुष्टिवर्द्धनम् ।
उर्व्वारुकमिव बन्धनान्मृत्योर्म्मुक्षीयमामृतात् ॥
ॐ ह्रीं श्रीं दुं दुर्गायै नमः रुद्राक्षं समर्पयामि

tryambakaṁ yajāmahe sugandhiṁ puṣṭivarddhanam
urvvārukamiva bandhanānmṛtyormmukṣīyamāmṛtāt
oṁ hrīṁ śrīṁ duṁ durgāyai namaḥ rudrākṣaṁ samarpayāmi

We adore the Father of the three worlds, of excellent fame, Grantor of Increase. As a cucumber is released from its bondage to the stem, so may we be freed from Death to dwell in immortality. With this offering of rudrākṣa Oṁ I bow to the Goddess, Durgā, the Grantor of Increase, who Removes all Difficulties.

mālā

ॐ मां माले महामाये सर्वशक्तिस्वरूपिणि ।
चतुर्वर्गस्त्वयि न्यस्तस्तस्मान्मे सिद्धिदा भव ॥
ॐ ह्रीं श्रीं दुं दुर्गायै नमः मालां समर्पयामि

oṁ māṁ māle mahāmāye sarvaśaktisvarūpiṇi
caturvargastvayi nyastastasmānme siddhidā bhava
oṁ hrīṁ śrīṁ duṁ durgāyai namaḥ mālāṁ samarpayāmi

Oṁ my rosary, the Great Limitation of Consciousness, containing all energy within as your intrinsic nature, fulfilling the four desires of men, give us the attainment of your perfection. With this offering of a mālā Oṁ I bow to the Goddess, Durgā, the Grantor of Increase, who Removes all Difficulties.

red powder

ॐ सिन्दूरमरुणाभासं जपाकुसुमसन्निभम् ।
पूजिताऽसि मया देवि प्रसीद परमेश्वरि ॥
ॐ ह्रीं श्रीं दुं दुर्गायै नमः सिन्दूरं समर्पयामि

oṁ sindūramaruṇābhāsaṁ japākusumasannibham
pūjitā-si mayā devi prasīda parameśvari
oṁ hrīṁ śrīṁ duṁ durgāyai namaḥ sindūraṁ samarpayāmi

This red colored powder indicates Love, who drives the chariot of the Light of Wisdom, with which we are worshiping our Lord. Please be pleased, Oh Great Seer of All. With this offering of red colored powder Oṁ I bow to the Goddess, Durgā, the Grantor of Increase, who Removes all Difficulties.

kuṅkum

ॐ कुङ्कुमं कान्तिदं दिव्यं कामिनीकामसम्भवम् ।
कुङ्कुमेनाऽर्चिते देवि प्रसीद परमेश्वरि ॥
ॐ ह्रीं श्रीं दुं दुर्गायै नमः कुङ्कुमं समर्पयामि

oṁ kuṅkumaṁ kāntidaṁ divyaṁ
kāminī kāmasambhavam
kuṅkumenā-rcite devi prasīda parameśvari
oṁ hrīṁ śrīṁ duṁ durgāyai namaḥ kuṅkumaṁ samarpayāmi

You are being adorned with this divine red powder, which is made more beautiful by the love we share with you, and is so pleasing. Oh Lord, when we present this red powder be pleased, Oh Supreme Ruler of All. With this offering of red colored powder Oṁ I bow to the Goddess, Durgā, the Grantor of Increase, who Removes all Difficulties.

sandal paste

ॐ श्रीखण्डचन्दनं दिव्यं गन्धाढ्यं सुमनोहरम् ।
विलेपनं च देवेशि चन्दनं प्रतिगृह्यताम् ॥
ॐ ह्रीं श्रीं दुं दुर्गायै नमः चन्दनं समर्पयामि

oṁ śrīkhaṇḍacandanaṁ divyaṁ
gandhāḍhyaṁ sumano haram
vilepanaṁ ca deveśi candanaṁ pratigṛhyatām
oṁ hrīṁ śrīṁ duṁ durgāyai namaḥ candanaṁ samarpayāmi

You are being adorned with this beautiful divine piece of sandal wood, ground to a paste which is so pleasing. Please accept this offering of sandal paste, Oh Supreme Sovereign of all the Gods. With the offering of sandal paste Oṁ I bow to the Goddess, Durgā, the Grantor of Increase, who Removes all Difficulties.

turmeric

ॐ हरिद्रारञ्जिता देवि सुख-सौभाग्यदायिनि ।
तस्मात्त्वं पूजयाम्यत्र दुःखशान्तिं प्रयच्छ मे ॥
ॐ ह्रीं श्रीं दुं दुर्गायै नमः हरिद्रां समर्पयामि

oṁ haridrārañjitā devi sukha saubhāgyadāyini
tasmāttvaṁ pūjayāmyatra duḥkha śāntiṁ prayaccha me
oṁ hrīṁ śrīṁ duṁ durgāyai namaḥ haridrāṁ samarpayāmi

Oh Lord, you are being gratified by this turmeric, the giver of comfort and beauty. When you are worshiped like this, then you must bestow upon us the greatest peace. With the offering of turmeric Oṁ I bow to the Goddess, Durgā, the Grantor of Increase, who Removes all Difficulties.

bracelets

ॐ माणिक्यमुक्ताखण्डयुक्ते सुवर्णकारेण च संस्कृते ये ।
ते किङ्किणीभिः स्वरिते सुवर्णे
मयाऽर्पिते देवि गृहाण कङ्कणे ॥
ॐ ह्रीं श्रीं दुं दुर्गायै नमः कङ्कणे समर्पयामि

oṁ māṇikya muktā khaṇḍayukte
suvarṇakāreṇa ca saṁskṛte ye
te kiṅkiṇībhiḥ svarite suvarṇe
mayā-rpite devi gṛhāṇa kaṅkaṇe
oṁ hrīṁ śrīṁ duṁ durgāyai namaḥ kaṅkaṇe samarpayāmi

Oṁ United with gems and pearls, excellent gold and the alphabets of Saṁskṛta, this bracelet is yours and radiance I am offering. Oh Goddess, accept this bracelet. With this offering of a bracelet Oṁ I bow to the Goddess, Durgā, the Grantor of Increase, who Removes all Difficulties.

conch ornaments

ॐ शङ्खञ्च विविधं चित्रं बाहूनाञ्च विभूषणम् ।
मया निवेदितं भक्त्या गृहाण परमेश्वरि ॥
ॐ ह्रीं श्रीं दुं दुर्गायै नमः शङ्खालङ्कारं समर्पयामि

oṁ śaṅkhañca vividhaṁ citraṁ bāhūnāñca vibhūṣaṇam
mayā niveditaṁ bhaktyā gṛhāṇa parameśvari
oṁ hrīṁ śrīṁ duṁ durgāyai namaḥ śaṅkhālaṅkāraṁ samarpayāmi

I am offering you with devotion ornaments worn upon the arms made of various qualities of conch shell. Please accept them, oh Supreme Divinity. With this offering of ornaments made of conch shell Oṁ I bow to the Goddess, Durgā, the Grantor of Increase, who Removes all Difficulties.

ornaments

ॐ दिव्यरत्नसमायुक्ता वह्निभानुसमप्रभाः ।
गात्राणि शोभयिष्यन्ति अलङ्काराः सुरेश्वरि ॥
ॐ ह्रीं श्रीं दुं दुर्गायै नमः अलङ्कारान् समर्पयामि

oṁ divyaratnasamāyuktā vahnibhānusamaprabhāḥ
gātrāṇi śobhayiṣyanti alaṅkārāḥ sureśvari
oṁ hrīṁ śrīṁ duṁ durgāyai namaḥ alaṅkārān samarpayāmi

Oṁ United with divine jewels that are radiant like fire, and stones which are shining, please accept these ornaments, oh Supreme among the Gods. With this offering of ornaments Oṁ I bow to the Goddess, Durgā, the Grantor of Increase, who Removes all Difficulties.

rice

अक्षतान् निर्मलान् शुद्धान् मुक्ताफलसमन्वितान् ।
गृहाणेमान् महादेवि देहि मे निर्मलां धियम् ॥
ॐ ह्रीं श्रीं दुं दुर्गायै नमः अक्षतान् समर्पयामि

akṣatān nirmalān śuddhān muktāphalasamanvitān
gṛhāṇemān mahādevi dehi me nirmalāṁ dhiyam
oṁ hrīṁ śrīṁ duṁ durgāyai namaḥ akṣatān samarpayāmi

Oh Great Goddess, please accept these grains of rice, spotlessly clean, bestowing the fruit of liberation, and give us a spotlessly clean mind. With this offering of grains of rice Oṁ I bow to the Goddess, Durgā, the Grantor of Increase, who Removes all Difficulties.

food offering

ॐ सत्पात्रं शुद्धसुहविर्व्विविधानेकभक्षणम् ।
निवेदयामि देवेशि सर्वतृप्तिकरं परम् ॥

oṁ satpātraṁ śuddhasuhavirv vividhānekabhakṣaṇam
nivedayāmi deveśi sarvatṛptikaraṁ param

Oṁ This ever-present platter containing varieties of the purest offerings of food we are presenting to the Lord of Gods to cause all satisfaction, most excellent and transcendental.

ॐ अन्नपूर्णे सदा पूर्णे शङ्करप्राणवल्लभे ।
ज्ञानवैराग्यसिद्ध्यर्थं भिक्षां देहि नमोऽस्तु ते ॥

oṁ annapūrṇe sadā pūrṇe śaṅkara prāṇavallabhe
jñānavairāgyasiddhyarthaṁ
bhikṣāṁ dehi namo-stu te

Oṁ Goddess who is full, complete and perfect with food and grains, always full, complete and perfect, the strength of the life force of Śiva, the Cause of Peace. For the attainment of perfection in wisdom and renunciation, please give us offerings. We bow down to you.

माता च पार्वती देवी पिता देवो महेश्वरः ।
बान्धवाः शिवभक्ताश्च स्वदेशो भुवनत्रयम् ॥

mātā ca pārvatī devī pitā devo maheśvaraḥ
bāndhavāḥ śivabhaktāśca svadeśo bhuvanatrayam

Our Mother is the Goddess, Pārvatī, and our Father is the Supreme Lord, Maheśvara. The Consciousness of Infinite Goodness, Śiva, Lord of the three worlds, is being extolled by his devotees.

ॐ ह्रीं श्रीं दुं दुर्गायै नमः भोगनैवेद्यम् समर्पयामि

oṁ hrīṁ śrīṁ duṁ durgāyai namaḥ bhog-naivedyam samarpayāmi

With this presentation of food Oṁ I bow to the Goddess, Durgā, the Grantor of Increase, who Removes all Difficulties.

drinking water

ॐ समस्तदेवदेवेशि सर्वतृप्तिकरं परम् ।
अखण्डानन्दसम्पूर्णं गृहाण जलमुत्तमम् ॥
ॐ ह्रीं श्रीं दुं दुर्गायै नमः पानार्थं जलम् समर्पयामि

oṁ samasta devadeveśi sarvatṛptikaraṁ param
akhaṇḍānanda sampūrṇaṁ gṛhāṇa jalamuttamam
oṁ hrīṁ śrīṁ duṁ durgāyai namaḥ pānārthaṁ jalam samarpayāmi

Oṁ Goddess of All the Gods and the fullness of Infinite Bliss, please accept this excellent drinking water. With this offering of drinking water Oṁ I bow to the Goddess, Durgā, the Grantor of Increase, who Removes all Difficulties.

betel nuts

पूगीफलं महद्दिव्यं नागवल्ली दलैर्युतम् ।
एलादिचूर्णसंयुक्तं ताम्बूलं प्रतिगृह्यताम् ॥
ॐ ह्रीं श्रीं दुं दुर्गायै नमः ताम्बूलं समर्पयामि

pūgīphalaṁ mahaddivyaṁ nāgavallī dalairyutam
elādicūrṇasaṁyuktaṁ tāmbūlaṁ pratigṛhyatām
oṁ hrīṁ śrīṁ duṁ durgāyai namaḥ tāmbūlaṁ samarpayāmi

These betel nuts, which are great and divine, come from vines that creep like a snake. United with cardamom ground to a powder, please accept this offering of mouth-freshening betel nuts. With this offering of mouth freshening betel nuts Oṁ I bow to the Goddess, Durgā, the Grantor of Increase, who Removes all Difficulties.

dakṣiṇā

ॐ पूजाफलसमृद्ध्यर्थं तवाग्रे स्वर्णमीश्वरि ।
स्थापितं तेन मे प्रीता पूर्णान् कुरु मनोरथान् ॥

oṁ pūjāphalasmṛddhyarthaṁ tavāgre svarṇamīśvari
sthāpitaṁ tena me prītā pūrṇān kuru manorathān

Oṁ For the purpose of increasing the fruits of worship, Oh Supreme Goddess of all Wealth, we establish this offering of that which is dear to me. Bring to perfection the journey of my mind.

हिरण्यगर्भगर्भस्थं हेमबीजं विभावसोः ।
अनन्तपुण्यफलदमतः शान्तिं प्रयच्छ मे ॥

hiraṅyagarbhagarbhasthaṁ hemabījaṁ vibhāvasoḥ
anantapuṇyaphaladamataḥ śāntiṁ prayaccha me

Oh Golden Womb, in whom all wombs are situated, shining brightly with the golden seed. Give infinite merits as fruits, we are wanting for peace.

ॐ ह्रीं श्रीं दुं दुर्गायै नमः दक्षिणां समर्पयामि

oṁ hrīṁ śrīṁ duṁ durgāyai namaḥ dakṣiṇāṁ samarpayāmi

Oṁ With this offering of wealth Oṁ I bow to the Goddess, Durgā, the Grantor of Increase, who Removes all Difficulties.

umbrella

छत्रं देवि जगद्धात्रि ! घर्मवातप्रणाशनम् ।
गृहाण हे महामाये ! सौभाग्यं सर्वदा कुरु ॥
ॐ ह्रीं श्रीं दुं दुर्गायै नमः छत्रं समर्पयामि

chatraṁ devi jagaddhātri gharma vāta praṇāśanam
gṛhāṇa he mahāmāye saubhāgyaṁ sarvadā kuru
oṁ hrīṁ śrīṁ duṁ durgāyai namaḥ chatraṁ samarpayāmi

Oh Goddess, Creator of the Universe! This umbrella will protect you from heat and wind. Please accept it, oh Great Māyā, and remain always beautiful. With this offering of an umbrella Oṁ I bow to the Goddess, Durgā, the Grantor of Increase, who Removes all Difficulties.

fly whisk

चामरं हे महादेवि चमरीपुच्छनिर्मितम् ।
गृहीत्वा पापराशीनां खण्डनं सर्वदा कुरु ॥
ॐ ह्रीं श्रीं दुं दुर्गायै नमः चामरं समर्पयामि

cāmaraṁ he mahādevi camarīpucchanirmitam
gṛhītvā pāparāśīnāṁ khaṇḍanaṁ sarvadā kuru
oṁ hrīṁ śrīṁ duṁ durgāyai namaḥ cāmaraṁ samarpayāmi

Oh Great Goddess, this fly whisk is made of yak's tail. Please accept it, and always whisk away all sin. With this offering of a fly whisk Oṁ I bow to the Goddess, Durgā, the Grantor of Increase, who Removes all Difficulties.

fan

बर्हिर्बर्हकृताकारं मध्यदण्डसमन्वितम् ।

गृह्यतां व्यजनं देवि देहस्वेदापनुत्तये ॥

ॐ ह्रीं श्रीं दुं दुर्गायै नमः तालवृन्तं समर्पयामि

barhirbarhakṛtākāraṁ madhyadaṇḍa samanvitam
gṛhyatāṁ vyajanaṁ devi dehasvedāpanuttaye
oṁ hrīṁ śrīṁ duṁ durgāyai namaḥ tālavṛntaṁ samarpayāmi

It moves back and forth with equanimity and has a stick in the middle. Please accept this fan, oh Goddess, to keep the perspiration from your body. With this offering of a fan Oṁ I bow to the Goddess, Durgā, the Grantor of Increase, who Removes all Difficulties.

mirror

दर्पणं विमलं रम्यं शुद्धबिम्बप्रदायकम् ।

आत्मबिम्बप्रदर्शार्थमर्पयामि महेश्वरि ॥

ॐ ऐं ह्रीं क्लीं चामुण्डायै विच्चे दर्पणं समर्पयामि

darpaṇaṁ vimalaṁ ramyaṁ śuddhabimbapradāyakam
ātmabimbadarśanārthamarpayāmi maheśvari
oṁ aiṁ hrīṁ klīṁ cāmuṇḍāyai vicce darpaṇaṁ samarpayāmi

This beautiful mirror will give a pure reflection. In order to reflect my soul, I am offering it to you, oh Great Seer of all. With this offering of a mirror Oṁ I bow to the Goddess, Durgā, the Grantor of Increase, who Removes all Difficulties.

ārātrikam

ॐ चन्द्रादित्यौ च धरणी विद्युदग्निस्तथैव च ।

त्वमेव सर्वज्योतीषिं आरात्रिकं प्रतिगृह्यताम् ॥

ॐ ह्रीं श्रीं दुं दुर्गायै नमः आरात्रिकं समर्पयामि

oṁ candrādityau ca dharaṇī vidyudagnistathaiva ca
tvameva sarvajyotīṣiṁ ārātrikaṁ pratigṛhyatām
oṁ hrīṁ śrīṁ duṁ durgāyai namaḥ ārātrikaṁ samarpayāmi

Oṁ All knowing as the Moon, the Sun and the Divine Fire, you alone are all light, and this light we request you to accept. With this offering of light Oṁ I bow to the Goddess, Durgā, the Grantor of Increase, who Removes all Difficulties.

flower

मल्लिकादि सुगन्धीनि मालित्यादीनि वै प्रभो ।

मयाऽहृतानि पूजार्थं पुष्पाणि प्रतिगृह्यताम् ॥

ॐ ह्रीं श्रीं दुं दुर्गायै नमः पुष्पम् समर्पयामि

mallikādi sugandhīni mālityādīni vai prabho
mayā-hṛtāni pūjārthaṁ puṣpāṇi pratigṛhyatām
oṁ hrīṁ śrīṁ duṁ durgāyai namaḥ puṣpam samarpayāmi

Various flowers, such as mallikā and others of excellent scent, are being offered to you, Our Lord. All these flowers have come from the devotion of our hearts for your worship. Please accept them. With this offering of a flower Oṁ I bow to the Goddess, Durgā, the Grantor of Increase, who Removes all Difficulties.

यज्ञेन यज्ञमयजन्त देवास्तानि धर्म्माणि प्रथमान्यासन् ।

ते ह नाकं महिमानः सचन्त यत्र पूर्वे साध्याः सन्ति देवाः ॥

yajñena yajñamayajanta devāstāni dharmmāṇi prathamānyāsan
te ha nākaṁ mahimānaḥ sacanta yatra pūrve sādhyāḥ santi devāḥ

By sacrifice, the Gods gave birth to sacrifice, and the first principles of eternal Dharma were established. Those who live according to the glorious way, ultimately reach the highest abode where the Gods dwell in that ancient perfection.

ॐ राजाधिराजाय प्रसह्य साहिने नमो वयं वैश्रवणाय कुर्महि
स मे कामान् कामकामाय मह्यं कामेश्वरो वैश्रवणो ददातु ।
कुबेराय वैश्रवणाय महाराजाय नमः ॥

oṁ rājādhirājāya prasahya sāhine namo vayaṁ vaiśravaṇāya kurmahe sa me kāmān kāmakāmāya mahyaṁ kāmeśvaro vaiśravaṇo dadātu kuberāya vaiśravaṇāya mahārājāya namaḥ

Without any selfish interest we bow down to the universal being, the King of kings, the Lord of all desires, the Universal Being. May He grant to me the full and complete enjoyment of the desire of all desires: dharma (the ideal of perfection), artha (the material necessities of life), kāma (the perfection of desire) and mokṣa (self-realization).

ॐ स्वस्ति साम्राज्यं भौज्यं स्वाराज्यं वैराज्यं पारमेष्ठ्यं
राज्यं महाराज्यमाधिपत्यमयं समन्तपर्यायि स्यात् । सार्वभौमः
सार्वायुषां तदा परार्धात् पृथिव्यै समुद्रपर्यन्ताया एकराडिति
। तदप्येष श्लोकोऽभिगीतो मरुतः परिवेष्टारो मरुत्तस्या ऽवस
न् गृहे । आवीक्षितस्य कामप्रेर्विश्वेदेवाः सभासद इति ॥

oṁ svasti sāmrājyaṁ bhaujyaṁ svārājyaṁ vairājyaṁ pārameṣṭhyaṁ rājyaṁ mahārājyamādhipatyamayaṁ samantaparyāyai syāt sārvabhaumaḥ sārvāyuṣāṁ tadā parārdhāt pṛthivyai samudraparyantāyā-ekarāḍiti tadapyeṣa śloko-bhigīto marutaḥ pariveṣṭāro maruttasyā-vasan gṛhe āvīkṣitasya kāmaprerviśvedevāḥ sabhāsada iti

Oṁ Let blessings flow to all of the kingdom, His own kingdom, the universal kingdom, the kingdom of the Supreme Divinity, the great kingdom of our Lord greater than the greatest, in the equilibrium of spiritual austerities. All that lives in the heavens or on the earth or in the seas is thus united. Those spiritual aspirants who sing these verses can aspire to dwell in the home of the purified. Having no unfulfilled desires, only desiring as the Universal Gods always.

ॐ विश्वतश्चक्षुरुत विश्वतो मुखो विश्वतो बाहुरुत
विश्वतस्पात्। सम्बाहुभ्यां धमति सम्पतत् त्रैर्द्यावा
भूमिं जनयन् देव एकः ॥

oṁ viśvataścakṣuruta viśvato mukho viśvato bāhuruta viśvataspāt
sambāhubhyāṁ dhamati sampatat trairdyāvā bhūmiṁ janayan deva ekaḥ

Oṁ He who sees the universe, the mouth of the universe, the arms of the universe, the feet of the universe. He is One God, whose two arms and two wings make possible all the activities of all that lives in the heavens and on earth.

durgā pūjā
worship of durgā

durgā gāyatrī

ॐ कात्यायनाय विद्महे कन्याकुमारी धीमहि ।
तन्नो दुर्गिः प्रचोदयात् ॐ ॥

oṁ kātyāyanāya vidmahe kanyākumārī dhīmahi
tanno durgiḥ pracodayāt oṁ

Oṁ We meditate on the Ever Pure One, we contemplate the Daughter Without Flaw or Imperfection. May that Goddess grant us increase.

एते गन्धपुष्पे ॐ ह्रीं श्रीं दुं दुर्गायै नमः

ete gandhapuṣpe oṁ hrīṁ śrīṁ duṁ durgāyai namaḥ

With these scented flowers oṁ I bow to the Goddess, Durgā, the Grantor of Increase, who Removes all Difficulties.

dhyānam
meditation

ॐ जटाजूटसमायुक्तामर्द्धेन्दुकृतशेखराम् ।
लोचनत्रयसंयुक्तां पूर्णेन्दुसदृशाननाम् ॥

oṁ jaṭājūṭasamāyuktāmarddhendukṛtaśekharām
locanatrayasaṁyuktāṁ pūrṇendusadṛśānanām

Oṁ With loose-flowing tresses, poised with equanimity with the radiant half-moon upon her head, her three eyes are shining like the full moon.

तप्तकाञ्चनवर्णाभां सुप्रतिष्ठां सुलोचनाम् ।
नवयौवनसम्पन्नां सर्वाभरणभूषिताम् ॥

taptakāñcanavarṇābhāṁ supratiṣṭāṁ sulocanām
navayauvanasampannāṁ sarvābharaṇabhūṣitām

She is of the color of melted gold, of excellent birth and has beautiful eyes. She has nine manifestations, all resplendantly shining with ornaments.

सुचारुदशनां तद्वत् पीनोन्नतपयोधराम् ।
त्रिभङ्गस्थानसंस्थानां महिषासुरमर्दिनीम् ॥

sucārudaśanāṁ tadvat pīnonnatapayodharām
tribhaṅgasthānasaṁsthānāṁ mahiṣāsuramardinīm

She holds aloft ten excellent weapons in her hands, and has three beautiful folds under her breasts - the Slayer of the Great Ego.

मृणालायतसंस्पर्श दशबाहु समन्विताम् ।
त्रिशूलं दक्षिणे ध्येयं खड्गं चक्रं क्रमादधः ॥

mṛṇālāyatasaṁsparśa daśabāhu samanvitām
triśūlaṁ dakṣiṇe dhyeyaṁ khaḍgaṁ cakraṁ kramādadhaḥ

She bears the touch of death to the Ego in each of her ten arms. We meditate on the order of weapons, beginning at the upper right: trident, sword, discus,

तीक्ष्नबाणं तथा शक्तिं दक्षिणेषु विचिन्तयेत् ।
खेटकं पूर्णचापञ्च पाशमङ्कुशमेव च ॥

tīkṣnabāṇaṁ tathā śaktiṁ dakṣiṇeṣu vicintayet
kheṭakaṁ pūrṇacāpañca pāśamaṅkuśameva ca

bow and arrow, and then energy we contemplate on her right side. The shield, club, noose, curved sword, and

घण्टां वा परशु वापि वामतः सन्निवेशयेत् ।
अधस्तान्महिषं तद्वद्विशिरस्कं प्रदर्शयेत् ॥

ghaṇṭāṁ vā paraśu vāpi vāmataḥ sanniveśayet
adhastānmahiṣaṁ tadvadviśiraskaṁ pradarśayet

the bell or battle axe we contemplate on her left side. Below lies the severed head of the Great Ego in the form of a buffalo.

शिरश्छेदोद्भवं तद्वद्दानवं खड्गपाणिनम् ।
हृदि शूलेन निर्भिन्नं निर्जदन्त्रविभूषितम् ॥

śiraśchedodbhavaṁ tadvaddānavaṁ khaḍgāpāṇinam
hṛdi śūlena nirbhinnaṁ nirjadantravibhūṣitam

In place of the severed head, on his neck is the demonic image of the Great Ego with a sword in his hand. He is shown gritting his teeth from the spear that has pierced his heart.

रक्तारक्तीकृताङ्गञ्च रक्तविस्फूरितेक्षणम् ।
वेष्ठितं नागपाशेन भ्रूकुटीभीषणाननम् ॥

raktāraktīkṛtāṅgañca raktavisphūritekṣaṇam
veṣṭhitaṁ nāgapāśena bhrūkuṭībhīṣaṇānanam

Blood is flowing over his body and red is seen on all his limbs. The cobra snake in the form of a noose has wrapped itself around his brow and upper left arm.

सपाशवामहस्तेन धृतकेशन्तु दुर्गया ।
वमद्रुधिरवक्त्रञ्च देव्याः सिंहं प्रदर्शयेत् ॥

sapāśavāmahastena dhṛtakeśantu durgayā
vamadrudhiravaktrañca devyāḥ siṁhaṁ pradarśayet

On the side of the Goddess is shown the lion, Dharma, who is her conveyance and is facing the left.

देव्यास्तु दक्षिणं पादं समं सिंहोपरि स्थितम् ।
किञ्चिदूर्द्धं तथा वाममङ्गुष्ठं महिषोपरि ॥

devyāstu dakṣiṇaṁ pādaṁ samaṁ siṁhopari sthitam
kiñcidūrddhaṁ tathā vāmamaṅguṣṭhaṁ mahiṣopari

The Goddess's right foot is flatly positioned on top of the lion. Slightly elevated, only her left toe is on top of the Great Ego.

प्रसन्नवदनां देवीं सर्वकामफलप्रदां ।
स्तुयमानञ्च तद्रूपममरैः सन्निवेशयेत् ॥

prasannavadanāṁ devīṁ sarvakāmaphalapradāṁ
stuyamānañca tadrūpamamaraiḥ sanniveśayet

The Goddess is extremely pleased and grants the fruits of all desires to those who contemplate her excellent form and with one mind sing her praises:

ऊग्रचण्डा प्रचण्डा च चण्डोग्रा चण्डनायिका ।
चण्डा चण्डवती चैव चण्डरूपातिचण्डिका ॥

ūgracaṇḍā pracaṇḍā ca caṇḍogrā caṇḍanāyikā
caṇḍā caṇḍavatī caiva caṇḍarūpāticaṇḍikā

The Terrible Slayer of Passion, Whose Nature Removes Fear, She Who Slays Fear, She Who Sees Everywhere Freedom from Fear, She Who Tears Apart Fear, She Who Contains Fearlessness, The Form of the Erradicator of Fear and the Supreme She Who Tears Apart All Thoughts.

अष्टाभिः शक्तिभिस्ताभिः सततं परिवेष्ठिताम् ।
चिन्तयेज्जगतां धात्रीं धर्म्मकामार्थमोक्षदाम् ॥

aṣṭābhiḥ śaktibhistābhiḥ satataṁ pariveṣṭhitām
cintayejjagatāṁ dhātrīṁ dharmmakāmārthamokṣadām

With these eight energies always surrounding her, we think of the Creator of the Perceivable Universe, who bestows the Way of Truth and Harmony, Satiation of Desires, Material Sustenance and Liberation, otherwise known as Self-Realization.

ॐ ह्रीं श्रीं दुं दुर्गायै नमः

oṁ hrīṁ śrīṁ duṁ durgāyai namaḥ

Oṁ I bow to the Goddess, Durgā, the Grantor of Increase, who Removes all Difficulties

kara nyāsa

establishment in the hands

ॐ ह्रां अंगुष्ठाभ्यां नमः

oṁ hrāṁ aṅguṣṭhābhyāṁ namaḥ thumb forefinger

Oṁ hrāṁ in the thumb I bow.

ॐ ह्रीं तर्जनीभ्यां स्वाहा

oṁ hrīṁ tarjanībhyāṁ svāhā thumb forefinger

Oṁ hrīṁ in the forefinger, I am One with God!

ॐ ह्रूं मध्यमाभ्यां वषट्

oṁ hrūṁ madhyamābhyāṁ vaṣaṭ thumb middlefinger

Oṁ hrūṁ in the middle finger, Purify!

ॐ ह्रैं अनामिकाभ्यां हुं

oṁ hraiṁ anāmikābhyāṁ huṁ thumb ring finger

Oṁ hraiṁ in the ring finger, Cut the Ego!

ॐ ह्रौं कनिष्ठिकाभ्यां बौषट्

oṁ hrauṁ kaniṣṭhikābhyāṁ vauṣaṭ thumb little finger

Oṁ hrauṁ in the little finger, Ultimate Purity!

Roll hand over hand forwards while reciting karatal kar,
and backwards while chanting pṛṣṭhābhyāṁ,
then clap hands when chanting astrāya phaṭ.

ॐ ह्रः करतल कर पृष्ठाभ्यां अस्त्राय फट् ॥

oṁ hraḥ karatal kar pṛṣṭhābhyāṁ astrāya phaṭ

Oṁ hraḥ I bow to the Goddess Durgā, with the weapon of Virtue.

ॐ ह्रीं श्रीं दुं दुर्गायै नमः

oṁ hrīṁ śrīṁ duṁ durgāyai namaḥ

Oṁ I bow to the Goddess, Durgā, the Grantor of Increase, who Removes all Difficulties

aṅga nyāsa

establishment in the body

Holding tattva mudrā, touch heart.

ॐ ह्रां हृदयाय नमः

oṁ hrāṁ hṛdayāya namaḥ touch heart

Oṁ hrāṁ in the heart, I bow.

Holding tattva mudrā, touch top of head.

ॐ ह्रीं शिरसे स्वाहा

oṁ hrīṁ śirase svāhā top of head

Oṁ hrīṁ on the top of the head, I am One with God!

With thumb extended, touch back of head.

ॐ ह्रूं शिखायै वषट्

oṁ hrūṁ śikhāyai vaṣaṭ back of head

Oṁ hrūṁ on the back of the head, Purify!

Holding tattva mudrā, cross both arms.

ॐ ह्रैं कवचाय हुं

oṁ hraiṁ kavacāya huṁ cross both arms

Oṁ hraiṁ crossing both arms, Cut the Ego!

Holding tattva mudrā, touch two eyes and in between at once with three middle fingers.

ॐ ह्रौं नेत्रत्रयाय वौषट्

oṁ hrauṁ netratrayāya vauṣaṭ touch three eyes

Oṁ hrauṁ in the three eyes, Ultimate Purity!

Roll hand over hand forwards while reciting karatal kar,
and backwards while chanting pṛṣṭhābhyāṁ,
then clap hands when chanting astrāya phaṭ.

ॐ ह्रः करतल कर पृष्ठाभ्यां अस्त्राय फट् ॥

oṁ hraḥ karatal kar pṛṣṭhābhyāṁ astrāya phaṭ

Oṁ hraḥ I bow to the Goddess Durgā, with the weapon of Virtue.

ॐ ह्रीं श्रीं दुं दुर्गायै नमः

oṁ hrīṁ śrīṁ duṁ durgāyai namaḥ
Oṁ I bow to the Goddess Durgā, the Grantor of Increase, who Removes all Difficulties

अथ दुर्गाद्वात्रिंशन्नाममाला

atha durgā dvātriṁśannāma mālā
The Rosary of thirty-two names of Durgā

दुर्गा दुर्गार्तिशमनी दुर्गापद्विनिवारिणी ।
दुर्गमच्छेदिनी दुर्गसाधिनी दुर्गनाशिनी ॥

durgā durgārti śamanī durgā padvinivāriṇī
durgamacchedinī durga sādhinī durga nāśinī

1. The Reliever of Difficulties
2. Who Puts Difficulties at Peace
3. The Dispeller of Difficult Adversities
4. Who Cuts Down Difficulties
5. The Performer of Discipline to Expel Difficulties
6. The Destroyer of Difficulties

दुर्गतोद्धारिणी दुर्गनिहन्त्री दुर्गमापहा ।
दुर्गमज्ञानदा दुर्गदैत्यलोकदवानला ॥

durgatod dhāriṇī durga nihantrī durga māpahā
durgamajñānadā durga daityaloka davānalā

7. Who Threatens Difficulties With Her Whip
8. Who Sends Difficulties to Ruin
9. Who Measures Difficulties
10. Who Makes Difficulties Unconscious
11. Who Destroys the World of Difficult Thoughts

दुर्गमा दुर्गमालोका दुर्गमात्मस्वरूपिणी ।
दुर्गमार्गप्रदा दुर्गमविद्या दुर्गमाश्रिता ॥

durgamā durgamālokā durgamātmasvarūpiṇī
durgamārgapradā durgam avidyā durgamāśritā

12. The Mother of Difficulties
13. Who is Beyond the World of Difficulties
14. The Intrinsic Nature of the Soul of Difficulties
15. Who Searches Through Difficulties
16. The Knowledge of Difficulties
17. The Extrication From Difficulties

दुर्गमज्ञानसंस्थाना दुर्गमध्यानभासिनी ।
दुर्गमोहा दुर्गमगा दुर्गमार्थस्वरूपिणी ॥

durgam ajñāna saṁsthānā durgam adhyāna bhāsinī
durga mohā durgamagā durgamārtha svarūpiṇī

18. The Continued Existence of Difficulties
19. Whose Meditation Remains Brilliant When in Difficulties
20. Who Deludes Difficulties
21. Who Resolves Difficulties
22. Who is the Intrinsic Nature of the Object of Difficulties

दुर्गमासुरसंहन्त्री दुर्गमायुधधारिणी ।
दुर्गमाङ्गी दुर्गमता दुर्गम्या दुर्गमेश्वरी ॥

durgam āsura saṁhantrī durgam āyudha dhāriṇī
durgamāṅgī durgamatā durgamyā durgameśvarī

23. The Annihilator of the Egotism of Difficulties
24. The Bearer of the Weapon Against Difficulties
25. The Refinery of Difficulties
26. Who is Beyond Difficulties
27. This Present Difficulty
28. The Empress of Difficulties

दुर्गभीमा दुर्गभामा दुर्गभा दुर्गदारिणी ।
नामावलिमिमां यस्तु दुर्गाया मम मानवः ।

durgabhīmā durgabhāmā durgabhā durgadāriṇī
nāmāvalimimāṁ yastu durgāyā mama mānavaḥ

29. Who is Terrible to Difficulties
30. The Lady of Difficulties
31. The Illuminator of Difficulties
32. Who Cuts Off Difficulties

Whoever will recite this garland of the names of Durgā,

पठेत् सर्वभयान्मुक्तो भविष्यति न संशयः ॥

paṭhet sarva bhayān mukto bhaviṣyati na saṁśayaḥ

the Reliever of Difficulties will be freed from every type of fear without a doubt.

श्रीदुर्गाष्टोत्तरशतनामस्तोत्रम्

śrī durgāṣṭottara śatanāma stotram

The Song containing one hundred eight names
of the Respected Reliever of Difficulties

ईश्वर उवाच

īśvara uvāca

The Supreme Lord said:

शतनाम प्रवक्ष्यामि शृणुष्व कमलानने ।
यस्य प्रसादमात्रेण दुर्गा प्रीता भवेत् सती ॥

śatanāma pravakṣyāmi śṛṇuṣva kamalānane
yasya prasādamātreṇa durgā prītā bhavet satī

Oh Lotus Eyed, I elucidate the One Hundred Eight Names by means of which the Reliever of Difficulties truly becomes extremely pleased:

ॐ सती साध्वी भवप्रीता भवानी भवमोचनी ।
आर्या दुर्गा जया चाद्या त्रिनेत्रा शूलधारिणी ॥

oṁ satī sādhvī bhavaprītā bhavānī bhavamocanī
āryā durgā jayā cādyā trinetrā śūladhāriṇī

1. Embodiment of Truth
2. Embodiment of Virtue
3. Lover of the Universe
4. Embodiment of the Universe
5. Who Releases the Bonds of the Universe
6. Purified by Knowledge
7. Reliever of Difficulties
8. Victory
9. Foremost
10. Having Three Eyes
11. Bearer of the Spear

पिनाकधारिणी चित्रा चण्डघण्टा महातपाः ।
मनो बुद्धिरहंकारा चित्तरूपा चिता चितिः ॥

pinākā dhāriṇī citrā caṇḍa ghaṇṭā mahātapāḥ
mano buddhir ahaṁkārā cittarūpā citā citiḥ

12. Bearer of the Trident
13. Characterized by Diversity
14. Who Makes Beautiful Subtle Sounds
15. Who Performs the Great Discipline of Austerities
16. Mind
17. Intellect
18. Ego
19. The Form of Recollection
20. All Recollection
21. Consciousness

सर्वमन्त्रमयी सत्ता सत्यानन्द स्वरूपिणी ।
अनन्ता भाविनी भाव्या भव्याभव्या सदागतिः ॥

sarva mantra mayī sattā satyānanda svarūpiṇī
anantā bhāvinī bhāvyā bhavyā bhavyā sadāgatiḥ

22. The Essence of all Mantras
23. The Intrinsic Nature of Being
24. The Intrinsic Nature of the Bliss of Truth
25. Infinite
26. Who Brings Forth Creation
27. The Intensity of Reality
28. The Form of Welfare
29. Who Is Always the Same
30. Who Is Always in Motion

शाम्भवी देवमाता च चिन्ता रत्नप्रिया सदा ।
सर्वविद्या दक्षकन्या दक्षयज्ञविनाशिनी ॥

śāmbhavī devamātā ca cintā ratnapriyā sadā
sarvavidyā dakṣakanyā dakṣayajña vināśinī

31. Beloved by Consciousness
32. Mother of the Gods
33. Contemplation
34. Beloved Jewel

35. All Knowledge
36. Daughter of Ability
37. Destroyer of Dakṣa's Sacrifice

अपर्णानेकवर्णा च पाटला पाटलावती ।
पट्टाम्बर परीधाना कलमञ्जीररञ्जिनी ॥

aparṇānekavarṇā ca pāṭalā pāṭalāvatī
paṭṭāmbara parīdhānā kalamañjīra rañjinī

38. Without Limbs
39. Of Various Colors, Castes, Tribes
40. Of Red Hue
41. Adorned by Red Flowers
42. Adorned by Silk Garments
43. Whose Anklets Make a Beautiful Sound

अमेयविक्रमा क्रूरा सुन्दरी सुरसुन्दरी ।
वनदुर्गा च मातङ्गी मतङ्गमुनिपूजिता ॥

ameya vikramā krūrā sundarī surasundarī
vanadurgā ca mātaṅgī mataṅga muni pūjitā

44. Wielder of Infinite Strength
45. Who is Extremely Severe to Egos
46. Beautiful One
47. Beautiful One of the Gods
48. Reliever of Difficulties from the Forest
49. Embodiment of the Mother
50. Worshipped by the Greatest of Munis

ब्राह्मी माहेश्वरी चैन्द्री कौमारी वैष्णवी तथा ।
चामुण्डा चैव वाराही लक्ष्मीश्च पुरुषाकृतिः ॥

brāhmī māheśvarī caindrī kaumārī vaiṣṇavī tathā
cāmuṇḍā caiva vārāhī lakṣmīśca puruṣākṛtiḥ

51. Creative Energy
52. Energy of the Great Seer of All
53. Energy of the Rule of the Pure
54. Ever Pure One
55. Energy That Pervades All
56. Slayer of Passion and Anger

57. Most Excellent Desire of Union
58. Goddess of Wealth
59. Maker of Men

विमलोत्कर्षिणी ज्ञाना क्रिया नित्या च बुद्धिदा ।
बहुला बहुलप्रेमा सर्ववाहन वाहना ॥

vimalot karṣiṇī jñānā kriyā nityā ca buddhidā
bahulā bahulapremā sarvavāhana vāhanā

60. Spotlessly Pure
61. Eminent One
62. Embodiment of Wisdom
63. Embodiment of Action
64. Eternal
65. Bestower of Wisdom
66. Extensive
67. Extensive Love
68. Carrier of all Carriers

निशुम्भशुम्भहननी महिषासुरमर्दिनी ।
मधुकैटभहन्त्री च चण्डमुण्डविनाशिनी ॥

niśumbha śumbha hananī mahiṣāsura mardinī
madhu kaiṭabha hantrī ca caṇḍa muṇḍa vināśinī

69. Slayer of Self-Deprecation and Self-Conceit
70. Slayer of the Great Ego
71. Annihilator of Too Much and Too Little
72. Destroyer of Passion and Anger

सर्वासुरविनाशा च सर्वदानवघातिनी ।
सर्वशास्त्रमयी सत्या सर्वास्त्रधारिणी तथा ॥

sarvāsuravināśā ca sarvadānava ghātinī
sarva śāstramayī satyā sarvāstra dhāriṇī tathā

73. Destroyer of All Egotistical Thought
74. Slayer of All Duality
75. Essence of All Scriptures
76. Truth
77. Bearer of All Weapons

अनेकशस्त्रहस्ता च अनेकास्त्रस्य धारिणी ।
कुमारी चैककन्या च कैशोरी युवती यतिः ॥

aneka śastra hastā ca anekāstrasya dhāriṇī
kumārī caika kanyā ca kaiśorī yuvatī yatiḥ

78. With Numerous Weapons in Her Hands
79. Bearer of Numerous Weapons
80. Ever Pure One
81. Sole Daughter
82. Incomparable Beauty
83. Eternal Youth
84. Ascetic

अप्रौढा चैव प्रौढा च वृद्धमाता बलप्रदा ।
महोदरी मुक्तकेशी घोररूपा महाबला ॥

aprauḍhā caiva prauḍhā ca vṛddhamātā balapradā
mahodarī muktakeśī ghorarūpā mahābalā

85. Never Aging
86. Advanced in Age
87. Mother of Old Age
88. Giver of Strength
89. Great Eminence
90. With Loose Hair
91. Of Formidable Appearance
92. One Of Great Strength

अग्निज्वाला रौद्रमुखी कालरात्रिस्तपस्विनी ।
नारायणी भद्रकाली विष्णुमाया जलोदरी ॥

agnijvālā raudramukhī kālarātristapasvinī
nārāyaṇī bhadrakālī viṣṇu māyā jalodarī

93. Shining like Fire
94. Of Fearful Face
95. The Dark Night of Overcoming Egotism
96. Performer of Severe Spiritual Discipline
97. Exposer of Consciousness
98. Excellent One Beyond Time
99. Measurement of the All-Pervading Consciousness
100. Who Came from the Waters

शिवदूती कराली च अनन्ता परमेश्वरी ।
कात्यायनी च सावित्री प्रत्यक्षा ब्रह्मवादिनी ॥

śivadūtī karālī ca anantā parameśvarī
kātyāyanī ca sāvitrī pratyakṣā brahma vādinī

101. Ambassador of Consciousness
102. Formidable One
103. Infinite
104. Supreme Sovereign
105. Ever Pure One
106. Bearer of Light
107. Perception of the Gross World
108. Who Speaks of Infinite Consciousness

य इदं प्रपठेन्नित्यं दुर्गानामशताष्टकम् ।
नासाध्यं विद्यते देवि त्रिषु लोकेषु पार्वति ॥

ya idaṁ prapaṭhen nityaṁ durgā nāmaśatāṣṭakam
nāsādhyaṁ vidyate devi triṣu lokeṣu pārvati

Oh Goddess, Pārvatī, He who recites these one hundred eight names of the Reliever of Difficulties every day will find no difficulties in the three worlds.

धनं धान्यं सुतं जायां हयं हस्तिनमेव च ।
चतुर्वर्गं तथा चान्ते लभेन्मुक्तिं च शाश्वतीम् ॥

dhanaṁ dhānyaṁ sutaṁ jāyāṁ
hayaṁ hastinameva ca
caturvargaṁ tathā cānte labhenmuktiṁ ca śāśvatīm

He will find wealth, food, sons, a loving wife, horses, elephants, and the four objectives of human life will be satisfied. At the end of his earthly existence he will attain eternal liberation.

कुमारीं पूजयित्वा तु ध्यात्वा देवीं सुरेश्वरीम् ।
पूजयेत् परया भक्त्या पठेन्नामशताष्टकम् ॥

kumārīṁ pūjayitvā tu dhyātvā devīṁ sureśvarīm
pūjayet parayā bhaktyā paṭhen nāmaśatāṣṭakam

One should worship the Ever Pure One and meditate upon the female Ruler of Gods with the highest selfless devotion. Then the recitation of these one hundred eight names should be commenced.

तस्य सिद्धिर्भवेद् देवि सर्वैः सुरवरैरपि ।
राजानो दासतां यान्ति राज्यश्रियमवाप्नुयात् ॥

tasya siddhir bhaved devi sarvaiḥ suravarairapi
rājāno dāsatāṁ yānti rājya śriyamavāpnuyāt

Oh Goddess, whoever performs in this way attains the highest perfection of the Gods. Kings become his servants and he commands the wealth of kingdoms.

गोरोचनालक्तककुङ्कुमेन
सिन्धुरकर्पूरमधुत्रयेण ।
विलिख्य यन्त्रं विधिना विधिज्ञो
भवेत् सदा धारयतेपुरारिः ॥

gorocanā laktaka kuṅkumena
sindhura karpūra madhutrayeṇa
vilikhya yantraṁ vidhinā vidhijño
bhavet sadā dhārayate purāriḥ

With fragrant gum, lac, red powders, camphor, ghee, sugar and honey, one should draw the graphic representation of this truth according to the rules laid down in the scriptures. The knowledgeable one who will wear such an inscription becomes one with the Consciousness of Infinite Goodness.

भौमावास्यानिशामग्रे चन्द्रे शतभिषां गते ।
विलिख्य प्रपठेत् स्तोत्रं स भवेत् संपदां पदम् ॥

bhaumāvāsyāniśāmagre candre śata bhiṣāṁ gate
vilikhya prapaṭhet stotraṁ
sa bhavet saṁpadāṁ padam

On the evening before the New Moon Day, known as Bhaumavatī, when the celestial configuration is in the asterism known as Śatabhiśā, if one recites these mantras, he becomes the Lord of Wealth.

ॐ ह्रीं श्रीं दुं दुर्गायै नमः

oṁ hrīṁ śrīṁ duṁ durgāyai namaḥ

Oṁ I bow to the Goddess, Durgā, the Grantor of Increase, who Removes all Difficulties

॥ दुर्गा दकारादिसहस्रनामस्तोत्रम् ॥
॥ durgā dakārādisahasranāmastotram ॥
The Thousand Names of Durga which begin with the letter D

श्रीगणेशाय नमः ।

śrīgaṇeśāya namaḥ ।
I bow to the Respected Ganesh

श्रीदेव्युवाच ।

śrīdevyuvāca ।
The Respected Goddess said:

मम नामसहस्रं च शिवपूर्वविनिर्मितम् ।
तत्पठ्यतां विधानेन तदा सर्वं भविष्यति ॥ १ ॥

mama nāmasahasraṁ ca śivapūrvavinirmitam ।
tatpaṭhyatāṁ vidhānena tadā sarvaṁ bhaviṣyati ॥ 1 ॥
1. (These are) my thousand names, which are performed completely by Śiva. Who has performed the recital of this, all (good things) will come to pass in the future.

इत्युक्त्वा पार्वती देवी श्रावयामास तच्चतान् ।
तदेव नाम साहस्रं दकारादि वरानने ॥ २ ॥

ityuktvā pārvatī devī śrāvayāmāsa taccatān ।
tadeva nāma sāhasraṁ dakārādi varānane ॥ 2 ॥
2. Thus united (with her own self) Goddess Pārvatī caused him, the God, to hear that, the thousand names of the face which grants all boons, which begin with the letter D.

रोगदारिद्र्य दौर्भाग्यशोकदुःखविनाशकम् ।
सर्वासां पूजितं नाम श्रीदुर्गादेवता मता ॥

rogadāridrya daurbhāgyaśokaduḥkhavināśakam ।
sarvāsāṁ pūjitaṁ nāma śrīdurgādevatā matā ॥ 3 ॥

3. Disease, affliction, bad fortune, grief, and pain, these all are destroyed when the Respected Goddess who takes away all difficulties is worshiped with understanding.

निजबीजं भवेद् बीजं मन्त्रं कीलकमुच्यते ।
सर्वाशापूरणे देवि विनियोगः प्रकीर्त्तितः ॥ ४ ॥

nijabījaṁ bhaved bījaṁ mantraṁ kīlakamucyate |
sarvāśāpūraṇe devi viniyogaḥ prakīrttitaḥ || 4 ||

4. Her own bija (duṁ) has become the seed of the mantra with which the pin is removed. All hopes will be fulfilled by the goddess, is the application for which this is well known.

ॐ अस्य श्रीदकारादिदुर्गासिहस्रनामस्तोत्रस्य
शिव ऋषिः अनुष्टुप् छन्दः
श्रीदुर्गादिवता दुं बीजं दुं कीलकं
दुःखदारिद्र्यरोगशोकनिवृत्तिपूर्वकं
चतुर्वर्गफलप्राप्त्यर्थे पाठे विनियोगः ।

oṁ asya śrīdakārādidurgāsahasranāmastotrasya ,
śiva ṛṣiḥ , anuṣṭup chandaḥ ,
śrīdurgādevatā , duṁ bījaṁ , duṁ kīlakaṁ ,
duḥkha-dāridrya-roga-śoka-nivṛttipūrvakaṁ-
caturvargaphalaprāptyarthe pāṭhe viniyogaḥ |

Om Presenting the Respected Song of a Thousand Names of Durgā beginning with the letter D.
Śiva is the rishi
Anuṣṭup is the meter (32 syllables to the verse)
The Respected Goddess Durgā is the deity
Duṁ is the seed
Duṁ is the pin
For the complete dissolution of pain, affliction, disease, grief, and the attainment of the four objectives of human manifestation (dharma, artha, kāma, mokṣa) this recitation is being applied.

दुं दुर्गा दुर्गतिहरा दुर्गाचलनिवासिनी
दुर्गमार्गानुसञ्चारा दुर्गमार्गनिवासिनी ॥ ५ ॥
duṁ durgā durgatiharā durgācalanivāsinī
durgamārgānusañcārā durgamārganivāsinī || 5 ||

दुर्गमार्गप्रविष्ठा च दुर्गमार्गप्रवेशिनी ।
दुर्गमार्गकृतावासा दुर्गमार्गजयप्रिया ॥ ६ ॥
durgamārgapraviṣṭhā ca durgamārgapraveśinī |
durgamārgakṛtāvāsā durgamārgajayapriyā || 6 ||

दुर्गमार्गगृहीतार्चा दुर्गमार्गस्थितात्मिका ।
दुर्गमार्गस्तुतिपरा दुर्गमार्गस्मृतिपरा ॥ ७ ॥
durgamārgagṛhītārcā durgamārgasthitātmikā |
durgamārgastutiparā durgamārgasmṛtiparā || 7 ||

दुर्गमार्गसदास्थालि दुर्गमार्गरतिप्रिया ।
दुर्गमार्गस्थलस्थाना दुर्गमार्गविलासिनी ॥ ८ ॥
durgamārgasadāsthāli durgamārgaratipriyā |
durgamārgasthalasthānā durgamārgavilāsinī || 8 ||

दुर्गमार्गत्यक्तवस्त्रा दुर्गमार्गप्रवर्त्तिनी ।
दुर्गासुरनिहन्त्री च दुगासुरनिषूदिनी ॥ ९ ॥
durgamārgatyaktavastrā durgamārgapravarttinī |
durgāsuranihantrī ca dugāsuraniṣūdinī || 9 ||

दुर्गासुरहरादूती दुर्गासुरविनाशिनी ।
दुर्गासुरवधोन्मत्ता दुर्गासुरवधोत्सुका ॥ १० ॥
durgāsuraharādūtī durgāsuravināśinī |
durgāsuravadhonmattā durgāsuravadhotsukā || 10 ||

दुर्गासुरवधोत्साहा दुर्गासुरवधोद्यता ।
दुर्गासुरवधप्रेप्सु दुर्गासुरमखान्तकृत् ॥ ११ ॥
durgāsuravadhotsāhā durgāsuravadhodyatā |
durgāsuravadhaprepsu durgāsuramakhāntakṛt || 11 ||

दुर्गासुरध्वंस्सन्तोषा दुर्गदानवदारिणी ।
दुर्गविद्रावणकरी दुर्गविद्राविणी सदा ॥ १२ ॥
durgāsuradhvaṁssantoṣā durgadānavadāriṇī |
durgavidrāvaṇakarī durgavidrāviṇī sadā || 12 ||

दुर्गविक्षोभनकरी दुर्गशीर्षनिकृन्तनी ।
दुर्गविध्वंसनकरी दुर्गदैत्यनिकृन्तनी ॥ १३ ॥
durgavikṣobhanakarī durgaśīrṣanikṛntanī |
durgavidhvaṁsanakarī durgadaityanikṛntanī || 13 ||

दुर्गदैत्यप्राणहरा दुर्गदैत्यान्तकारिणी ।
दुर्गदैत्यहरत्राता दुर्गदैत्यसृगुन्मदा ॥ १४ ॥
durgadaityaprāṇaharā durgadaityāntakāriṇī |
durgadaityaharatrātā durgadaityasṛgunmadā || 14 ||

दुर्गदैत्याशनकरी दुर्गचर्माम्बरावृता ।
दुर्गयुद्धोत्सवकरी दुर्गयुद्धविशारदा ॥ १५ ॥
durgadaityāśanakarī durgacarmāmbarāvṛtā |
durgayuddhotsavakarī durgayuddhaviśāradā || 15 ||

दुर्गयुद्धासवरता दुर्गयुद्धविमर्द्दिनी ।
दुर्गयुद्धहास्यरता दुर्गयुद्धाट्टहासिनी ॥ १६ ॥
durgayuddhāsavaratā durgayuddhavimarddinī |
durgayuddhahāsyaratā durgayuddhāṭṭahāsinī || 16 ||

दुर्गयुद्धमहामत्ता दुर्गयुद्धानुसारिणी ।
दुर्गयुद्धोत्सवोत्साहा दुर्गदेशनिषेविणी ॥ १७ ॥
durgayuddhamahāmattā durgayuddhānusāriṇī |
durgayuddhotsavotsāhā durgadeśaniṣeviṇī || 17 ||

दुर्गदेशवासरता दुर्गदेशविलासिनी ।
दुर्गदेशार्च्चनरता दुर्गदेशजनप्रिया ॥ १८ ॥
durgadeśavāsaratā durgadeśavilāsinī |
durgadeśārccanaratā durgadeśajanapriyā || 18 ||

दुर्गमस्थानसंस्थाना दुर्गमध्यानसाधना ।
दुर्गमा दुर्गमध्याना दुर्गमात्मस्वरूपिणी ॥ १९ ॥
durgamasthānasaṁsthānā durgamadhyānasādhanā |
durgamā durgamadhyānā durgamātmasvarūpiṇī || 19 ||

दुर्गमागमसन्धाना दुर्गमागमसंस्तुता ।
दुर्गमागमदुर्ज्ञेया दुर्गमश्रुतिसम्मता ॥ २० ॥
durgamāgamasandhānā durgamāgamasaṁstutā |
durgamāgamadurjñeyā durgamaśrutisammatā || 20 ||

दुर्गमश्रुतिमान्याच दुर्गमश्रुतिपूजिता ।
दुर्गमश्रुतिसुप्रीता दुर्गमश्रुतिहर्षदा ॥ २१ ॥
durgamaśrutimānyāca durgamaśrutipūjitā |
durgamaśrutisuprītā durgamaśrutiharṣadā || 21 ||

दुर्गमश्रुतिसंस्थाना दुर्गमश्रुतिमानिता ।
दुर्गमाचारसन्तुष्टा दुर्गमाचारतोषिता ॥ २२ ॥
durgamaśrutisaṁsthānā durgamaśrutimānitā |
durgamācārasantuṣṭā durgamācāratoṣitā || 22 ||

दुर्गमाचारनिर्वृत्ता दुर्गमाचारपूजिता ।
दुर्गमाचारकसिता दुर्गमस्थानदायिनी ॥ २३ ॥
durgamācāranirvṛttā durgamācārapūjitā |
durgamācārakasitā durgamasthānadāyinī || 23 ||

दुर्गमप्रेमनिरता दुर्गमद्रविणप्रदा ।
दुर्गमाम्बुजमध्यस्था दुर्गमाम्बुजवासिनी ॥ २४ ॥
durgamapremaniratā durgamadraviṇapradā |
durgamāmbujamadhyasthā durgamāmbujavāsinī || 24 ||

दुर्गनाडीमार्गगती दुर्गनाडीप्रचारिणी ।
दुर्गनाडीपद्मरता दुर्गनाड्यम्बुजस्थिता ॥ २५ ॥
durganāḍīmārgagatī durganāḍīpracāriṇī |
durganāḍīpadmaratā durganāḍyambujasthitā || 25 ||

दुर्गनाडीगतायाता दुर्गनाडीकृतास्पदा ।
दुर्गनाडीरतरता दुर्गनाडीशसंस्तुता ॥ २६ ॥
durganāḍīgatāyātā durganāḍīkṛtāspadā |
durganāḍīratāratā durganāḍīśasaṁstutā || 26 ||

दुर्गनाडीश्चररता दुर्गनाडीशचुम्बिता ।
दुर्गनाडीशक्रोडस्था दुर्गनाड्युत्थितोत्सुका ॥ २७ ॥
durganāḍīścararatā durganāḍīśacumbitā |
durganāḍīśakroḍasthā durganāḍyutthitotsukā || 27 ||

दुर्गनाड्यारोहणा च दुर्गनाडीनिषेविता ।
दरीस्थाना दरीस्थानवासिनी दनुजान्तकृत् ॥ २८ ॥
durganāḍyārohaṇā ca durganāḍīniṣevitā |
darīsthānā darīsthānavāsinī danujāntakṛt || 28 ||

दरीकृततपस्या च दरीकृतहरार्च्चना ।
दरीजापितदिष्टा च दरीकृतरतिक्रिया ॥ २९ ॥
darīkṛtatapasyā ca darīkṛtaharārccanā |
darījāpitadiṣṭā ca darīkṛtaratikriyā || 29 ||

दरीकृतहरार्हा च दरीक्रीडितपुत्रिका ।
दरीसन्दर्शनरता दरीरोपितवृश्चिका ॥ ३० ॥
darīkṛtaharārhā ca darīkrīḍitaputrikā |
darīsandarśanaratā darīropitavṛścikā || 30 ||

दरीगुप्तिकौतुकाढ्या दरीभ्रमणतत्परा ।
दनुजान्तकरी दीना दनुसन्तानदारिणी ॥ ३१ ॥
darīguptikautukāḍhyā darībhramaṇatatparā |
danujāntakarī dīnā danujasantānadāriṇī || 31 ||

दनुजध्वंसिनी दूना दनुजेन्द्रविनाशिनी ।
दानवध्वंसिनीदेवी दानवानां भयङ्करी ॥ ३२ ॥
danujadhvaṁsinī dūnā danujendravināśinī |
dānavadhvaṁsinīdevī dānavānāṁ bhayaṅkarī || 32 ||

दानवी दानवाराध्या दानवेन्द्रवरप्रदा ।
दानवेन्द्रनिहन्त्री च दानवद्वेषिणी सती ॥ ३३ ॥
dānavī dānavārādhyā dānavendravarapradā |
dānavendranihantrī ca dānavadveṣiṇī satī || 33 ||

दानवारिप्रेमरता दानवारिप्रपूजिता ।
दानवारिकृतार्च्चा च दानवारिविभूतिदा ॥ ३४ ॥
dānavāripremaratā dānavāriprapūjitā |
dānavārikṛtārccā ca dānavārivibhūtidā || 34 ||

दानवारिमहानन्दा दानवारिरतिप्रिया ।
दानवारिदानरता दानवारिकृतास्पदा ॥ ३५ ॥
dānavārimahānandā dānavāriratipriyā |
dānavāridānaratā dānavārikṛtāspadā || 35 ||

दानवारिस्तुतिरता दानवारिस्मृतिप्रिया ।
दानवार्याहाररता दानवारिप्रबोधिनी ॥ ३६ ॥
dānavāristutiratā dānavārismṛtipriyā |
dānavāryāhāraratā dānavāriprabodhinī || 36 ||

दानवारिधृतप्रेमा दुःखशोकविमोचिनी ।
दुःखहन्त्री दुःखदात्री दुःखनिर्मूलकारिणी ॥ ३७ ॥
dānavāridhṛtapremā duḥkhaśokavimocinī |
duḥkhahantrī duḥkhadātrī duḥkhanirmūlakāriṇī || 37 ||

दुःखनिर्मूलनकरी दुःखदारिद्र्यनाशिनी ।
दुःखहरा दुःखनाशा दुःखग्रामा दुरासदा ॥ ३८ ॥
duḥkhanirmūlanakarī duḥkhadāridryanāśinī |
duḥkhaharā duḥkhanāśā duḥkhagrāmā durāsadā || 38 ||

दुःखहीना दुःखधारा द्रविणाचारदायिनी ।
द्रविणोत्सर्गसन्तुष्टा द्रविणत्यागतोषिका ॥ ३९ ॥
duḥkhahīnā duḥkhadhārā draviṇācāradāyinī |
draviṇotsargasantuṣṭā draviṇatyāgatoṣikā || 39 ||

द्रविणस्पर्शसन्तुष्टा द्रविणस्पर्शमानदा ।
द्रविणस्पर्शहर्षाढ्या द्रविणस्पर्शतुष्टिदा ॥ ४० ॥
draviṇasparśasantuṣṭā draviṇasparśamānadā |
draviṇasparśaharṣāḍhyā draviṇasparśatuṣṭidā || 40 ||

द्रविणस्पर्शनकरी द्रविणस्पर्शनातुरा ।
द्रविणस्पर्शनोत्साहा द्रविणस्पर्शसाधिता ॥ ४१ ॥
draviṇasparśanakarī draviṇasparśanāturā |
draviṇasparśanotsāhā draviṇasparśasādhitā || 41 ||

द्रविणस्पर्शनमता द्रविणस्पर्शपुत्रिका ।
द्रविणस्पर्शरक्षिणी द्रविणस्तोमदायिनी ॥ ४२ ॥
draviṇasparśanamatā draviṇasparśaputrikā |
draviṇasparśarakṣiṇī draviṇastomadāyinī || 42 ||

द्रविणाकर्षणकरी द्रविणौघविसर्जनी ।
द्रविणचलदानाढ्या द्रविणाचलवासिनी ॥ ४३ ॥
draviṇākarṣaṇakarī draviṇaughavisarjanī |
draviṇacaladānāḍhyā draviṇācalavāsinī || 43 ||

दीनमाता दीनबन्धु दीनविघ्नविनाशिनी ।
दीनसेव्या दीनसिद्धा दीनसाद्ध्या दिगम्बरी ॥ ४४ ॥
dīnamātā dīnabandhu dīnavighnavināśinī |
dīnasevyā dīnasiddhā dīnasāddhyā digambarī || 44 ||

दीनगेहकृतानन्दा दीनगेहविलासिनी ।
दीनभावप्रेमरता दीनभावविनोदिनी ॥ ४५ ॥
dīnagehakṛtānandā dīnagehavilāsinī |
dīnabhāvapremaratā dīnabhāvavinodinī || 45 ||

दीनमानवचेतःस्था दीनमानवहर्षदा ।
दीनदैन्यनिघातेच्छु दीनद्रविणदायिनी ॥ ४६ ॥
dīnamānavacetaḥsthā dīnamānavaharṣadā |
dīnadainyanighātecchu dīnadraviṇadāyinī || 46 ||

दीनसाधनसन्तुष्टा दीनदर्शनदायिनी ।
दीनपुत्रादिदात्रि च दीनसम्पद्विधायिनी ॥ ४७ ॥
dīnasādhanasantuṣṭā dīnadarśanadāyinī |
dīnaputrādidātri ca dīnasampadvidhāyinī || 47 ||

दत्तात्रेयध्यानरता दत्तात्रेयप्रपूजिता ।
दत्तात्रेयर्षिसंसिद्धा दत्तात्रेयविभाविता ॥ ४८ ॥
dattātreyadhyānaratā dattātreyaprapūjitā |
dattātreyarṣisaṁsiddhā dattātreyavibhāvitā || 48 ||

दत्तात्रेयकृतार्हा च दत्तात्रेयप्रसाधिता ।
दत्तात्रेयहर्षदात्री दत्तात्रेयसुखप्रदा ॥ ४९ ॥
dattātreyakṛtārhā ca dattātreyaprasādhitā |
dattātreyaharṣadātrī dattātreyasukhapradā || 49 ||

दत्तात्रेयस्तुता चैव दत्तात्रेयनुतासदा ।
दत्तात्रेयप्रेमरता दत्तात्रेयानुमानिता ॥ ५० ॥
dattātreyastutā caiva dattātreyanutāsadā |
dattātreyapremaratā dattātreyānumānitā || 50 ||

दत्तात्रेयसमुद्गीता दत्तात्रेयकुटुम्बिनी ।
दत्तात्रेयप्राणतुल्या दत्तात्रेयशरीरिणी ॥ ५१ ॥
dattātreyasamudgītā dattātreyakuṭumbinī |
dattātreyaprāṇatulyā dattātreyaśarīriṇī || 51 ||

दत्तात्रेयकृतानन्दा दत्तात्रेयांशसम्भवा ।
दत्तात्रेयविभूतिस्था दत्तात्रेयनुसारिणी ॥ ५२ ॥
dattātreyakṛtānandā dattātreyāṁśasambhavā |
dattātreyavibhūtisthā dattātreyanusāriṇī || 52 ||

दत्तात्रेयगीतिरता दत्तात्रेयधनप्रदा ।
दत्तात्रेयदुःखहरा दत्तात्रेयवरप्रदा ॥ ५३ ॥
dattātreyagītiratā dattātreyadhanapradā |
dattātreyaduḥkhaharā dattātreyavarapradā || 53 ||

दत्तात्रेयज्ञानदात्री दत्तात्रेयभयापहा ।
देवकन्या देवमान्या देवदुःखविनाशिनी ॥ ५४ ॥
dattātreyajñānadātrī dattātreyabhayāpahā |
devakanyā devamānyā devaduḥkhavināśinī || 54 ||

देवसिद्धा देवपूज्या देवेज्या देववन्दिता ।
देवमान्या देवधन्या देवविघ्नविनाशिनी ॥ ५५ ॥
devasiddhā devapūjyā devejyā devavanditā |
devamānyā devadhanyā devavighnavināśinī || 55 ||

देवरम्या देवरता देवकौतुकतत्परा ।
देवक्रीडा देवव्रीडा देववैरिविनाशिनी ॥ ५६ ॥
devaramyā devaratā devakautukatatparā |
devakrīḍā devavrīḍā devavairivināśinī || 56 ||

देवकामा देवरामा देवद्विष्टविनाशिनी ।
देवदेवप्रिया देवी देवदानववन्दिता ॥ ५७ ॥
devakāmā devarāmā devadviṣṭavināśinī |
devadevapriyā devī devadānavavanditā || 57 ||

देवदेवरतानन्दा देवदेववरोत्सुका ।
देवदेवप्रेमरता देवदेवप्रियंवदा ॥ ५८ ॥
devadevaratānandā devadevavarotsukā |
devadevapremaratā devadevapriyaṁvadā || 58 ||

देवदेवप्राणतुल्या देवदेवनितम्बिनी ।
देवदेवहृतमना देवदेवसुखावहा ॥ ५९ ॥
devadevaprāṇatulyā devadevanitambinī |
devadevahṛtamanā devadevasukhāvahā || 59 ||

देवदेवक्रोडरता देवदेवसुखप्रदा ।
देवदेवमहानन्दा देवदेवप्रचुम्बिता ॥ ६० ॥
devadevakroḍaratā devadevasukhapradā |
devadevamahānandā devadevapracumbitā || 60 ||

देवदेवोपभुक्ताच देवदेवानुसेविता ।
देवदेवगतप्राणा देवदेवगतात्मिका ॥ ६१ ॥
devadevopabhuktāca devadevānusevitā |
devadevagataprāṇā devadevagatātmikā || 61 ||

देवदेवहर्षदात्री देवदेवसुखप्रदा ।
देवदेवमहानन्दा देवदेवविलासिनी ॥ ६२ ॥
devadevaharṣadātrī devadevasukhapradā |
devadevamahānandā devadevavilāsinī || 62 ||

देवदेवधर्मपत्नी देवदेवमनोगता ।
देवदेववधूर्देव देवदेवार्चनप्रिया ॥ ६३ ॥
devadevadharmapatnī devadevamanogatā |
devadevavadhūrdeva devadevārcanapriyā || 63 ||

देवदेवाङ्गनिलया देवदेवाङ्गशायिनी ।
देवदेवाङ्गसुखिनी देवदेवाङ्गवासिनी ॥ ६४ ॥
devadevāṅganilayā devadevāṅgaśāyinī |
devadevāṅgasukhinī devadevāṅgavāsinī || 64 ||

देवदेवाङ्गभूषा च देवदेवाङ्गभूषणा ।
देवदेवप्रियकरी देवदेवाप्रियान्तकृत् ॥ ६५ ॥

devadevāṅgabhūṣā ca devadevāṅgabhūṣaṇā |
devadevapriyakarī devadevāpriyāntakṛt || 65 ||

देवदेवप्रियप्राणा देवदेवप्रियात्मिका ।
देवदेवार्चकप्राणा देवदेवार्चकप्रिया ॥ ६६ ॥

devadevapriyaprāṇā devadevapriyātmikā |
devadevārcakaprāṇā devadevārcakapriyā || 66 ||

देवदेवार्चकोत्साहा देवदेवार्चकप्रिया ।
देवदेवार्चकाविघ्ना देवदेवप्रसूरपि ॥ ६७ ॥

devadevārcakotsāhā devadevārcakapriyā |
devadevārcakāvighnā devadevaprasūrapi || 67 ||

देवदेवस्यजननी देवदेवविधायिनी ।
देवदेवस्यरमणी देवदेवहृदाश्रया ॥ ६८ ॥

devadevasyajananī devadevavidhāyinī |
devadevasyaramaṇī devadevahṛdāśrayā || 68 ||

देवदेवेष्टदेवा च देवतापसपातिनी ।
देवताभावसन्तुष्टा देवताभावतोषिता ॥ ६९ ॥

devadeveṣṭadevā ca devatāpasapātinī |
devatābhāvasantuṣṭā devatābhāvatoṣitā || 69 ||

देवताभाववरदा देवताभावसिद्धिदा ।
देवताभावसंसिद्धा देवताभावसम्भवा ॥ ७० ॥

devatābhāvavaradā devatābhāvasiddhidā |
devatābhāvasaṁsiddhā devatābhāvasambhavā || 70 ||

देवताभावसुखिनी देवताभाववन्दिता ।
देवताभावसुप्रीता देवताभावहर्षदा ॥ ७१ ॥

devatābhāvasukhinī devatābhāvavanditā |
devatābhāvasuprītā devatābhāvaharṣadā || 71 ||

देवताविघ्नहन्त्री च देवताद्विष्टनाशिनी ।
देवतापूजितपदा देवताप्रेमतोषिता ॥ ७२ ॥

devatāvighnahantrī ca devatādviṣṭanāśinī |
devatāpūjitapadā devatāprematoṣitā || 72 ||

देवतागारनिलया देवतासौख्यदायिनी ।
देवतानिजभावा च देवताहृतमानसा ॥ ७३ ॥

devatāgāranilayā devatāsaukhyadāyinī |
devatānijabhāvā ca devatāhṛtamānasā || 73 ||

देवताकृतपादार्चा देवताहृतभक्तिका ।
देवतागर्वमध्यस्था देवतादेवतादनुः ॥ ७४ ॥

devatākṛtapādārcā devatāhṛtabhaktikā |
devatāgarvamadhyasthā devatādevatādanuḥ || 74 ||

दुं दुर्गायै नमो नाम्नी दुं फट् मन्त्रस्वरूपिणी ।
दुं नमो मन्त्ररूपा च दुं नमो मूर्त्तिकात्मिका ॥ ७५ ॥

duṁ durgāyai namo nāmnī duṁ phaṭmantrasvarūpiṇī |
duṁ namo mantrarūpā ca duṁ namomūrttikātmikā || 75 ||

दूरदर्शीप्रिया दुष्टादुष्टभूतनिषेविता ।
दूरदर्शीप्रेमरता दूरदर्शीप्रियंवदा ॥ ७६ ॥

dūradarśīpriyā duṣṭāduṣṭabhūtaniṣevitā |
dūradarśīpremaratā dūradarśīpriyaṁvadā || 76 ||

दूरदर्शीसिद्धिदात्री दूरदर्शीप्रतोषिता ।
दूरदर्शीकण्ठसंस्था दूरदर्शीप्रहर्षिता ॥ ७७ ॥
dūradarśīsiddhidātrī dūradarśīpratoṣitā |
dūradarśīkaṇṭhasaṁsthā dūradarśīpraharṣitā || 77 ||

दूरदर्शीगृहीतार्चा दूरदर्शीप्रतर्पिता ।
दूरदर्शीप्राणतुल्या दूरदर्शीसुखप्रदा ॥ ७८ ॥
dūradarśīgṛhītārcā dūradarśīpratarpitā |
dūradarśīprāṇatulyā dūradarśīsukhapradā || 78 ||

दूरदर्शीभ्रान्तिहरा दूरदर्शीहृदास्पदा ।
दूरदर्श्यरिविद्भावा दीर्घदर्शिप्रमोदिनी ॥ ७९ ॥
dūradarśībhrāntiharā dūradarśīhṛdāspadā |
dūradarśyarividbhāvā dīrghadarśipramodinī || 79 ||

दीर्घदर्शीप्राणतुल्या दीर्घदर्शीवरप्रदा ।
दीर्घदर्शीहर्षदात्रि दीर्घदर्शीप्रहर्षिता ॥ ८० ॥
dīrghadarśīprāṇatulyā dīrghadarśīvarapradā |
dīrghadarśīharṣadātri dīrghadarśīpraharṣitā || 80 ||

दीर्घदर्शीमहानन्दा दीर्घदर्शीगृहालया ।
दीर्घदर्शीगृहीतार्चा दीर्घदर्शीहृतार्हणा ॥ ८१ ॥
dīrghadarśīmahānandā dīrghadarśīgṛhālayā |
dīrghadarśīgṛhītārcā dīrghadarśīhṛtārhaṇā || 81 ||

दया दानवती दात्री दयालुर्दीनवत्सला ।
दयाद्र्रा च दयाशीला दयाढ्या च दयात्मिका ॥ ८२ ॥
dayā dānavatī dātrī dayālurdīnavatsalā |
dayārdrā ca dayāśīlā dayāḍhyā ca dayātmikā || 82 ||

दयाम्बुधिर्दयासारा दयासागरपारगा ।
दयासिन्धुर्दयाभारा दयावत्करुणाकरी ॥ ८३ ॥
dayāmbudhirdayāsārā dayāsāgarapāragā |
dayāsindhurdayābhārā dayāvatkaruṇākarī || 83 ||

दयावद्वत्सला देवी दयादानरता सदा ।
दयावत्भक्तिसुखिनी दयावत्परितोषिता ॥ ८४ ॥
dayāvadvatsalā devī dayādānaratā sadā |
dayāvatbhaktisukhinī dayāvatparitoṣitā || 84 ||

दयावत्स्नेहनिरता दयावत्प्रतिपादिका ।
दयावत्त्राणकर्त्री च दयावन्मुक्तिदायिनी ॥ ८५ ॥
dayāvatsnehaniratā dayāvatpratipādikā |
dayāvattrāṇakartrī ca dayāvanmuktidāyinī || 85 ||

दयावद्भावसन्तुष्टा दयावत्परितोषिता ।
दयावत्तारणपरा दयावत् सिद्धिदायिनी ॥ ८६ ॥
dayāvadbhāvasantuṣṭā dayāvatparitoṣitā |
dayāvattāraṇaparā dayāvat siddhidāyinī || 86 ||

दयावत्पुत्रवद्भावा दयावत्पुत्ररूपिणी ।
दयावद्देहनिलया दयाबन्धु दयाश्रया ॥ ८७ ॥
dayāvatputravadbhāvā dayāvatputrarūpiṇī |
dayāvaddehanilayā dayābandhu dayāśrayā || 87 ||

दयालुवात्सल्यकरी दयालुसिद्धिदायिनी ।
दयालुशरणासक्ता दयालुदेहमन्दिरा ॥ ८८ ॥
dayāluvātsalyakarī dayālusiddhidāyinī |
dayāluśaraṇāsaktā dayāludehamandirā || 88 ||

दयालुभक्तिभावस्था दयालुप्राणरूपिणी ।
दयालुसुखदादम्भा दयालुप्रेमवर्षिणी ॥ ८९ ॥
dayālubhaktibhāvasthā dayālupraṇarūpiṇī |
dayālusukhadādambhā dayālupremavarṣiṇī || 89 ||

दयालुवशगा दीर्घा दीर्घाङ्गी दीर्घलोचना ।
दीर्घनेत्रा दीर्घचक्षु दीर्घबाहु लतात्मिका ॥ ९० ॥
dayāluvaśagā dīrghā dīrghāṅgī dīrghalocanā |
dīrghanetrā dīrghacakṣu dīrghabāhu latātmikā || 90 ||

दीर्घकेशी दीर्घमुखी दीर्घघोणा च दारुणा ।
दारुणासुरहन्त्री च दारुणासुरदारिणी ॥ ९१ ॥
dīrghakeśī dīrghamukhī dīrghaghoṇā ca dāruṇā |
dāruṇāsurahantrī ca dāruṇāsuradāriṇī || 91 ||

दारुणाहवकर्त्री च दारुणाहवहर्षिता ।
दारुणाहवहोमाढ्या दारुणाचलनाशिनी ॥ ९२ ॥
dāruṇāhavakartrī ca dāruṇāhavaharṣitā |
dāruṇāhavahomāḍhyā dāruṇācalanāśinī || 92 ||

दारुणाचारनिरता दारुणोत्सवहर्षिता ।
दारुणोद्यतरूपा च दारुणारीनिवारिणी ॥ ९३ ॥
dāruṇācāraniratā dāruṇotsavaharṣitā |
dāruṇodyatarūpā ca dāruṇārīnivāriṇī || 93 ||

दारुणेक्षणसंयुक्ता दोश्चतुष्कविराजिता ।
दशदोष्का दशभुजा दशबाहुविराजिता ॥ ९४ ॥
dāruṇekṣaṇasaṁyuktā doścatuṣkavirājitā |
daśadoṣkā daśabhujā daśabāhuvirājitā || 94 ||

दशास्त्रधारिणी देवी दशदिक्ख्यातविक्रमा ।
दशरथार्चितपदा दाशरथिप्रिया सदा ॥ ९५ ॥
daśāstradhāriṇī devī daśadikkhyātavikramā |
daśarathārcitapadā dāśarathipriyā sadā || 95 ||

दाशरथिप्रेमतुष्टा दाशरथिरतिप्रिया ।
दाशरथिप्रियकरी दाशरथिप्रियंवदा ॥ ९६ ॥
dāśarathiprematuṣṭā dāśarathiratipriyā |
dāśarathipriyakarī dāśarathipriyaṁvadā || 96 ||

दाशरथीष्टसन्दात्री दाशरथीष्टदेवता ।
दाशरथिद्वेषिनाशा दाशरथ्यानुकूल्यदा ॥ ९७ ॥
dāśarathīṣṭasandātrī dāśarathīṣṭadevatā |
dāśarathidveṣināśā dāśarathyānukūlyadā || 97 ||

दाशरथिप्रियतमा दाशरथिप्रपूजिता ।
दशाननारिसम्पूज्या दशाननारिदेवता ॥ ९८ ॥
dāśarathipriyatamā dāśarathiprapūjitā |
daśānanārisampūjyā daśānanāridevatā || 98 ||

दशाननारिप्रमदा दशाननारिजन्मभूः ।
दशाननारिरतिदा दशाननारिसेविता ॥ ९९ ॥
daśānanāripramadā daśānanārijanmabhūḥ |
daśānanāriratidā daśānanārisevitā || 99 ||

दशाननारिसुखदा दशाननारिवैरिहृत् ।
दशाननारीष्टदेवी दशग्रीवारिवन्दिता ॥ १०० ॥
daśānanārisukhadā daśānanārivairihṛt |
daśānanārīṣṭadevī daśagrīvārivanditā || 100 ||

दशग्रीवारिजननी दशग्रीवारिभाविनी ।
दशग्रीवारिसहिता दशग्रीवसभाजिता ॥ १०१ ॥
daśagrīvārijananī daśagrīvāribhāvinī |
daśagrīvārisahitā daśagrīvasabhājitā || 101 ||

दशग्रीवारिरमणी दशग्रीववधूरपी ।
दशग्रीवनाशकर्त्री दशग्रीववरप्रदा ॥ १०२ ॥
daśagrīvāriramaṇī daśagrīvavadhūrapī |
daśagrīvanāśakartrī daśagrīvavarapradā || 102 ||

दशग्रीवपुरस्था च दशग्रीववधोत्सुका ।
दशग्रीवप्रीतिदात्री दशग्रीवविनाशिनी ॥ १०३ ॥
daśagrīvapurasthā ca daśagrīvavadhotsukā |
daśagrīvaprītidātrī daśagrīvavināśinī || 103 ||

दशग्रीवहवकरी दशग्रीवानपायिनी ।
दशग्रीवप्रियावन्द्या दशग्रीवाहृता तथा ॥ १०४ ॥
daśagrīvahavakarī daśagrīvānapāyinī |
daśagrīvapriyāvandyā daśagrīvāhṛtā tathā || 104 ||

दशग्रीवाहितकरी दशग्रीवेश्वरप्रिया ।
दशग्रीवेश्वरप्राणा दशग्रीववरप्रदा ॥ १०५ ॥
daśagrīvāhitakarī daśagrīveśvarapriyā |
daśagrīveśvaraprāṇā daśagrīvavarapradā || 105 ||

दशग्रीवेश्वररता दशवर्षीयकन्यका ।
दशवर्षीयबाला च दशवर्षीयवासिनी ॥ १०६ ॥
daśagrīveśvararatā daśavarṣīyakanyakā |
daśavarṣīyabālā ca daśavarṣīyavāsinī || 106 ||

दशपापहरा दम्या दशहस्तविभूषिता ।
दशशस्त्रलसद्दोष्का दशदिक्पालवन्दिता ॥ १०७ ॥
daśapāpaharā damyā daśahastavibhūṣitā |
daśaśastralasaddoṣkā daśadikpālavanditā || 107 ||

दशावताररूपा च दशावताररूपिणी ।
दशविद्याभिन्नदेवी दशप्राणस्वरूपिणी ॥ १०८ ॥
daśāvatārarūpā ca daśāvatārarūpiṇī |
daśavidyābhinnadevī daśaprāṇasvarūpiṇī || 108 ||

दशविद्यास्वरूपा च दशविद्यामयी तथा ।
दृक्स्वरूपा दृक्प्रदात्री दृग्रूपा दृक्प्रकाशिनी ॥ १०९ ॥
daśavidyāsvarūpā ca daśavidyāmayī tathā |
dṛksvarūpā dṛkpradātrī dṛgrūpā dṛkprakāśinī || 109 ||

दिगन्तरा दिगन्तःस्था दिगम्बरविलासिनी ।
दिगम्बरसमाजस्था दिगम्बरप्रपूजिता ॥ ११० ॥
digantarā digantaḥsthā digambaravilāsinī |
digambarasamājasthā digambaraprapūjitā || 110 ||

दिगम्बरसहचरी दिगम्बरकृतास्पदा ।
दिगम्बरहृताचित्ता दिगम्बरकथाप्रिया ॥ १११ ॥
digambarasahacarī digambarakṛtāspadā |
digambarahṛtācittā digambarakathāpriyā || 111 ||

दिगम्बरगुणरता दिगम्बरस्वरूपिणी ।
दिगम्बरशिरोधार्या दिगम्बरहृताश्रया ॥ ११२ ॥
digambaraguṇaratā digambarasvarūpiṇī |
digambaraśirodhāryā digambarahṛtāśrayā || 112 ||

दिगम्बरप्रेमरता दिगम्बररतातुरा ।
दिगम्बरीस्वरूपा च दिगम्बरीगणार्चिता ॥ ११३ ॥

digambarapremaratā digambararatāturā |
digambarīsvarūpā ca digambarīgaṇārcitā || 113 ||

दिगम्बरीगणप्राणा दिगम्बरीगणप्रिया ।
दिगम्बरीगणाराध्या दिगम्बरगणेश्वरी ॥ ११४ ॥

digambarīgaṇaprāṇā digambarīgaṇapriyā |
digambarīgaṇārādhyā digambaragaṇeśvarī || 114 ||

दिगम्बरगणस्पर्शा मदिरापानविह्वला ।
दिगम्बरीकोटिवृता दिगम्बरीगणावृता ॥ ११५ ॥

digambaragaṇasparśā madirāpānavihvalā |
digambarīkoṭivṛtā digambarīgaṇāvṛtā || 115 ||

दुरन्ता दुष्कृतिहरा दुर्ध्येया दुरतिक्रमा ।
दुरन्तदानवद्वेष्टी दुरन्तदनुजान्तकृत् ॥ ११६ ॥

durantā duṣkṛtiharā durdhyeyā duratikramā |
durantadānavadveṣṭī durantadanujāntakṛt || 116 ||

दुरन्तपापहन्त्री च दस्रनिस्तारकारिणी ।
दस्रमानससंस्थाना दस्रज्ञानविवर्द्धिनी ॥ ११७ ॥

durantapāpahantrī ca dasranistārakāriṇī |
dasramānasasaṁsthānā dasrajñānavivarddhinī || 117 ||

दस्रसम्भोगजननी दस्रसम्भोगदायिनी ।
दस्रसम्भोगभवना दस्रविद्याविधायिनी ॥ ११८ ॥

dasrasambhogajananī dasrasambhogadāyinī |
dasrasambhogabhavanā dasravidyāvidhāyinī || 118 ||

दस्रोद्वेगहरा दस्रजननी दस्रसुन्दरी ।
दस्रभक्तविधाज्ञाना दस्रद्विष्टविनाशिनी ॥ ११९ ॥
dasrodvegaharā dasrajananī dasrasundarī |
dasrabhaktavidhājñānā dasradviṣṭavināśinī || 119 ||

दस्रापकारदमनी दस्रसिद्धिविधायिनी ।
दस्रताराराधिता च दस्र मातृप्रपूजिता ॥ १२० ॥
dasrāpakāradamanī dasrasiddhividhāyinī |
dasratārārādhitā ca dasra mātṛprapūjitā || 120 ||

दस्रदैन्यहरा चैव दस्रतातनिषेविता ।
दस्रपितृशतज्योति दस्रकौशलदायिनी ॥ १२१ ॥
dasradainyaharā caiva dasratātaniṣevitā |
dasrapitṛśatajyoti dasrakauśaladāyinī || 121 ||

दशशीर्षारिसहिता दशशीर्षारिकामिनी ।
दशशीर्षपुरी देवी दशशीर्षसभाजिता ॥ १२२ ॥
daśaśīrṣārisahitā daśaśīrṣārikāminī |
daśaśīrṣapurī devī daśaśīrṣasabhājitā || 122 ||

दशशीर्षारिसुप्रीता दशशीर्षवधूप्रिया ।
दशशीर्षशिरश्छेत्री दशशीर्षनितम्बिनी ॥ १२३ ॥
daśaśīrṣārisuprītā daśaśīrṣavadhūpriyā |
daśaśīrṣaśiraśchetrī daśaśīrṣanitambinī || 123 ||

दशशीर्षहरप्राणा दशशीर्षहरात्मिका ।
दशशीर्षहराराध्या दशशीर्षारिवन्दिता ॥ १२४ ॥
daśaśīrṣaharaprāṇā daśaśīrṣaharātmikā |
daśaśīrṣaharārādhyā daśaśīrṣārivanditā || 124 ||

दशशीर्षारिसुखदा दशशीर्षकपालिनी ।
दशशीर्षज्ञानदात्री दशशीर्षारिदेहिता ॥ १२५ ॥
daśaśīrṣārisukhadā daśaśīrṣakapālinī |
daśaśīrṣajñānadātrī daśaśīrṣāridehitā || 125 ||

दशशीर्षवधोपात्त श्रीरामचन्द्ररूपता ।
दशशीर्षराष्ट्रदेवी दशशीर्षारिसारिणी ॥ १२६ ॥
daśaśīrṣavadhopātta śrīrāmacandrarūpatā |
daśaśīrṣarāṣṭradevī daśaśīrṣārisāriṇī || 126 ||

दशशीर्षभ्रातृतुष्टा दशशीर्षवधूप्रिया ।
दशशीर्षवधूप्राणा दशशीर्षवधूरता ॥ १२७ ॥
daśaśīrṣabhrātṛtuṣṭā daśaśīrṣavadhūpriyā |
daśaśīrṣavadhūprāṇā daśaśīrṣavadhūratā || 127 ||

दैत्यगुरुरतासाध्वी दैत्यगुरुप्रपूजिता ।
दैत्यगुरूपदेष्टी च दैत्यगुरुनिषेविता ॥ १२८ ॥
daityagururatāsādhvī daityaguruprapūjitā |
daityagurūpadeṣṭī ca daityaguruniṣevitā || 128 ||

दैत्यगुरुगतप्राणा दैत्यगुर्तापनाशिनी ।
दुरन्तदुःखशमनि दुरन्तदमनीतमी ॥ १२९ ॥
daityagurugataprāṇā daityagurtāpanāśinī |
durantaduḥkhaśamani durantadamanītamī || 129 ||

दुरन्तशोकशमनी दुरन्तरोगनाशिनी ।
दुरन्तवैरिदमनी दुरन्तदैत्यनाशिनी ॥ १३० ॥
durantaśokaśamanī durantaroganāśinī |
durantavairidamanī durantadaityanāśinī || 130 ||

दुरन्तकलुषघ्नी च दुष्कृतिस्तोमनाशिनी ।
दुराशया दुराधारा दुर्ज्जया दुष्टकामिनी ॥ १३१ ॥
durantakaluṣaghnī ca duṣkṛtistomanāśinī |
durāśayā durādhārā durjjayā duṣṭakāminī || 131 ||

दर्शनीया च दृश्या चादृश्याच दृष्टिगोचरा ।
दूतीयागप्रिया दूती दूतीयागकरप्रिया ॥ १३२ ॥
darśanīyā ca dṛśyā cādṛśyāca dṛṣṭigocarā |
dūtīyāgapriyā dūtī dūtīyāgakarapriyā || 132 ||

दूतीयागकरानन्दा दूतीयागसुखप्रदा ।
दूतीयागकरायाता दूतीयागप्रमोदिनी ॥ १३३ ॥
dūtīyāgakarānandā dūtīyāgasukhapradā |
dūtīyāgakarāyātā dūtīyāgapramodinī || 133 ||

दुर्वासःपूजिता चैव दुर्वासोमुनिभाविता ।
दुर्वासोऽर्चितपादा च दुर्वासोमुनिभाविता ॥ १३४ ॥
durvāsaḥpūjitā caiva durvāsomunibhāvitā |
durvāso-rcitapādā ca durvāsomunibhāvitā || 134 ||

दुर्वासोमुनिवन्द्या च दुर्वासोमुनिदेवता ।
दुर्वासोमुनिमाता च दुर्वासोमुनिसिद्धिदा ॥ १३५ ॥
durvāsomunivandyā ca durvāsomunidevatā |
durvāsomunimātā ca durvāsomunisiddhidā || 135 ||

दुर्वासोमुनिभावस्था दुर्वासोमुनिसेविता ।
दुर्वासोमुनिचित्तस्था दुर्वासोमुनिमण्डिता ॥ १३६ ॥
durvāsomunibhāvasthā durvāsomunisevitā |
durvāsomunicittasthā durvāsomunimaṇḍitā || 136 ||

दुर्वासोमुनिसञ्चारा दुर्वासोहृदयङ्गमा ।
दुर्वासोहृदयाराध्या दुर्वासोहृत्सरोजगा ॥ १३७ ॥
durvāsomunisañcārā durvāsohṛdayaṅgamā |
durvāsohṛdayārādhyā durvāsohṛtsarojagā || 137 ||

दुर्वासस्तापसाराध्या दुर्वासस्तापसाश्रया ।
दुर्वासस्तापसरता दुर्वासस्तापसेश्वरी ॥ १३८ ॥
durvāsastāpasārādhyā durvāsastāpasāśrayā |
durvāsastāpasaratā durvāsastāpaseśvarī || 138 ||

दुर्वासोमुनिकन्या च दुर्वासोत्भूतसिद्धिदा ।
दरराात्री दरहरा दरयुक्ता दरापहा ॥ १३९ ॥
durvāsomunikanyā ca durvāsotbhūtasiddhidā |
dararātrī daraharā darayuktā darāpahā || 139 ||

दरघ्नी दरहन्त्री च दरयुक्ता दराश्रया ॥ १४० ॥
daraghnī darahantrī ca darayuktā darāśrayā || 140 ||

दरस्मेरा दरापाङ्गी दयादात्री दयाश्रमा ।
दस्रपूज्या दस्रमाता दस्रदेवी दुरोन्मदा ॥ १४१ ॥
darasmerā darāpāṅgī dayādātrī dayāśramā |
dasrapūjyā dasramātā dasradevī duronmadā || 141 ||

दस्रसिद्धा दस्रसंस्था दस्रातापविमोचिनी ।
दस्रक्षोभहरा नित्या दस्रलोकगतात्मिका ॥ १४२ ॥
dasrasiddhā dasrasaṁsthā dasrātāpavimocinī |
dasrakṣobhaharā nityā dasralokagatātmikā || 142 ||

दैत्यगुर्वङ्गनावन्द्या दैत्यगुर्वङ्गनाप्रिया ।
दैत्यगुर्वङ्गनासिद्धा दैत्यगुर्वङ्गनोत्सुका ॥ १४३ ॥
daityagurvaṅganāvandyā daityagurvaṅganāpriyā |
daityagurvaṅganāsiddhā daityagurvaṅganotsukā || 143 ||

दैत्यगुरुप्रियतमा दैत्यगुरुनिषेविता ।
देवगुरुप्रसूरूपा देवगुरुकृतार्हणा ॥ १४४ ॥
daityagurupriyatamā daityaguruniṣevitā |
devaguruprasūrūpā devagurukṛtārhaṇā || 144 ||

देवगुरुप्रेमयुता देवगुर्वनुमानिता ।
देवगुरुप्रभावज्ञा देवगुरुसुखप्रदा ॥ १४५ ॥
devagurupremayutā devagurvanumānitā |
devaguruprabhāvajñā devagurusukhapradā || 145 ||

देवगुरुज्ञानदात्री देवगुरुप्रमोदिनी ।
दैत्यस्त्रीगणसम्पूज्या दैत्यस्त्रीगणपूजिता ॥ १४६ ॥
devagurujñānadātrī devagurupramodinī |
daityastrīgaṇasampūjyā daityastrīgaṇapūjitā || 146 ||

दैत्यस्त्रीगणरूपा च दैत्यस्त्रीचित्तहारिणी ।
देवस्त्रीगणपूज्या च देवस्त्रीगणवन्दिता ॥ १४७ ॥
daityastrīgaṇarūpā ca daityastrīcittahāriṇī |
devastrīgaṇapūjyā ca devastrīgaṇavanditā || 147 ||

देवस्त्रीगणचित्तस्था देवस्त्रीगणभूषिता ।
देवस्त्रीगणसंसिद्धा देवस्त्रीगणतोषिता ॥ १४८ ॥
devastrīgaṇacittasthā devastrīgaṇabhūṣitā |
devastrīgaṇasaṁsiddhā devastrīgaṇatoṣitā || 148 ||

देवस्त्रीगणहस्तस्थचारुचामरबीजिता ।
देवस्त्रीगणहस्तस्थचारुगन्धविलेपिता ॥ १४९ ॥

devastrīgaṇahastastha-cārucāmara-bījitā |
devastrīgaṇahastastha-cārugandha-vilepitā || 149 ||

देवाङ्गनाधृतादर्श दृष्ट्यर्त्थमुखचन्द्रमा ।
देवाङ्गनोत्सृष्ट नागवल्लीदल कृतोत्सुका ॥ १५० ॥

devāṅganādhṛtādarśa dṛṣṭyartthamukhacandramā |
devāṅganotsṛṣṭa nāgavallīdala kṛtotsukā || 150 ||

देवस्त्रीगणहस्तस्थ दीपमालाविलोकना ।
देवस्त्रीगणहस्तस्थ धूपघ्राण विनोदिनी ॥ १५१ ॥

devastrīgaṇahastastha dīpamālāvilokanā |
devastrīgaṇahastastha dhūpaghrāṇa vinodinī || 151 ||

देवनारीकरगत वासकासवपायिनी ।
देवनारीकङ्कतिका कृत्तकेश निमार्जना ॥ १५२ ॥

devanārīkaragata vāsakāsavapāyinī |
devanārīkaṅkatikā kṛttakeśa nimārjanā || 152 ||

देवनारीरुष्ट्यगात्रा देवनारि कृतोत्सुका ।
देवनारीविरचिता पुष्पमाला विराजिता ॥ १५३ ॥

devanārīruṣṭyagātrā devanāri kṛtotsukā |
devanārīviracitā puṣpamālā virājitā || 153 ||

देवनारीविचित्राङ्गी देवस्त्रीदत्तभोजना ।
देवस्त्रीगणगीता च देवस्त्रीगीतनोत्सुका ॥ १५४ ॥

devanārīvicitrāṅgī devastrīdattabhojanā |
devastrīgaṇagītā ca devastrīgītanotsukā || 154 ||

देवस्त्रीनृत्यसुखिनी देवस्त्रीनृत्यदर्शिनी ।
देवस्त्रीयोजितलसद्रत्नपादुपदाम्बुजा ॥ १५५ ॥
devastrīnṛtyasukhinī devastrīnṛtyadarśinī |
devastrīyojitalasadratnapādupadāmbujā || 155 ||

देवस्त्रीगणविस्तीर्ण चारुतल्पनिषेदुषी ।
देवनारीचारुकरा कलिताङ्घ्र्यादिदेहिका ॥ १५६ ॥
devastrīgaṇavistīrṇa cārutalpaniṣeduṣī |
devanārīcārukarā kalitāṅghryādidehikā || 156 ||

देवनारीकरव्यग्रतालवृत्तमरुत्सुखा ।
देवनारीवेणुवीणानादसोत्कण्ठमानसा ॥ १५७ ॥
devanārīkaravyagra-tālavṛtta-marutsukhā |
devanārīveṇuvīṇā-nādasotkaṇṭhamānasā || 157 ||

देवकोटिस्तुतिनुता देवकोटिकृतार्हणा ।
देवकोटिगीतगुणा देवकोटिकृतस्तुतिः ॥ १५८ ॥
devakoṭistutinutā devakoṭikṛtārhaṇā |
devakoṭigītaguṇā devakoṭikṛtastutiḥ || 158 ||

दन्तदृष्ट्योद्वेगफला देवकोलाहलाकुला ।
द्वेषरागपरित्यक्ता द्वेषरागविवर्जिता ॥ १५९ ॥
dantadṛṣṭyodvegaphalā devakolāhalākulā |
dveṣarāgaparityaktā dveṣarāgavivarjitā || 159 ||

दामपूज्या दामभूषा दामोदरविलासिनी ।
दामोदरप्रेमरता दामोदरभगिन्यपि ॥ १६० ॥
dāmapūjyā dāmabhūṣā dāmodaravilāsinī |
dāmodarapremaratā dāmodarabhaginyapi || 160 ||

दामोदरप्रसूर्दामोदरपत्नी पतिव्रता ।
दामोदराभिन्नदेहा दामोदररतिप्रिया ॥ १६१ ॥
dāmodara-prasūrdāmodarapatnī pativratā |
dāmodarābhinnadehā dāmodararatipriyā || 161 ||

दामोदराभिन्नतनुर्दामोदरकृतास्पदा ।
दामोदरकृतप्राणा दामोदरगतात्मिका ॥ १६२ ॥
dāmodarābhinnatanurdāmodarakṛtāspadā |
dāmodarakṛtaprāṇā dāmodaragatātmikā || 162 ||

दामोदरकौतुकाढ्या दामोदरकलाकला ।
दामोदरालिङ्गिताङ्गी दामोदरकुतूहला ॥ १६३ ॥
dāmodarakautukāḍhyā dāmodarakalākalā |
dāmodarāliṅgitāṅgī dāmodarakutūhalā || 163 ||

दामोदरकृताह्लादा दामोदरसुचुम्बिता ।
दामोदरसुताकृष्टा दामोदरसुखप्रदा ॥ १६४ ॥
dāmodarakṛtāhlādā dāmodarasucumbitā |
dāmodarasutākṛṣṭā dāmodarasukhapradā || 164 ||

दामोदरसहाढ्या च दामोदरसहायिनी ।
दामोदरगुणज्ञा च दामोदरवरप्रदा ॥ १६५ ॥
dāmodarasahāḍhyā ca dāmodarasahāyinī |
dāmodaraguṇajñā ca dāmodaravarapradā || 165 ||

दामोदरानुकूला च दामोदरनितम्बिनी ।
दामोदरजलक्रीडाकुशलादर्शनप्रिया ॥ १६६ ॥
dāmodarānukūlā ca dāmodaranitambinī |
dāmodarajalakrīḍā-kuśalādarśanapriyā || 166 ||

दामोदराबलक्रीडात्यक्तस्वजनसौहृदा ।
दामोदरलसद्रास केलीकौतुकिनी तथा ॥ १६७ ॥
dāmodarābalakrīḍā-tyaktasvajanasauhṛdā |
dāmodaralasadrāsa kelīkautukinī tathā || 167 ||

दामोदरभ्रातृका च दामोदरपरायणा ।
दामोदरधरा दामोदरवैरिविनाशिनी ॥ १६८ ॥
dāmodarabhrātṛkā ca dāmodaraparāyaṇā |
dāmodaradharā dāmodaravairi-vināśinī || 168 ||

दामोदरोपजाया च दामोदरनिमन्त्रिता ।
दामोदरपराभूता दामोदरपराजिता ॥ १६९ ॥
dāmodaropajāyā ca dāmodaranimantritā |
dāmodaraparābhūtā dāmodaraparājitā || 169 ||

दामोदरसमाक्रान्ता दामोदरहताशुभा ।
दामोदरोत्सवरता दामोदरोत्सवावहा ॥ १७० ॥
dāmodarasamākrāntā dāmodarahatāśubhā |
dāmodarotsavaratā dāmodarotsavāvahā || 170 ||

दामोदरस्तन्यदात्री दामोदरगवेषिता ।
दमयन्तीसिद्धिदात्री दमयन्तीप्रसाधिता ॥ १७१ ॥
dāmodarastanyadātrī dāmodaragaveṣitā |
damayantī-siddhidātrī damayantīprasādhitā || 171 ||

दमयन्तीष्टदेवी च दमयन्तीस्वरूपिणी ।
दमयन्तीकृतार्चा च दमनर्षिविभाविता ॥ १७२ ॥
damayantīṣṭadevī ca damayantīsvarūpiṇī |
damayantīkṛtārcā ca damanarṣivibhāvitā || 172 ||

दमनर्षिप्राणतुल्या दमनर्षिस्वरूपिणी ।
दमनर्षिस्वरूपा च दम्भपूरितविग्रहा ॥ १७३ ॥
damanarṣiprāṇatulyā damanarṣisvarūpiṇī |
damanarṣisvarūpā ca dambhapūritavigrahā || 173 ||

दम्भहन्त्री दम्भदात्री दम्भलोकविमोहिनी ।
दम्भशीला दम्भहरा दम्भवत्परिमर्दिनी ॥ १७४ ॥
dambhahantrī dambhadātrī dambhalokavimohinī |
dambhaśīlā dambhaharā dambhavatparimardinī || 174 ||

दम्भरूपा दम्भकरी दम्भसन्तानदारिणी ।
दत्तमोक्षा दत्तघना दत्तरोग्याथ दाम्भिका ॥ १७५ ॥
dambharūpā dambhakarī dambhasantānadāriṇī |
dattamokṣā dattaghanā dattarogyātha dāmbhikā || 175 ||

दत्तपुत्रा दत्तदारा दत्तहारा च दारिका ।
दत्तभोगा दत्तशोका दत्तहस्त्यादिवाहना ॥ १७६ ॥
dattaputrā dattadārā dattahārā ca dārikā |
dattabhogā dattaśokā dattahastyādivāhanā || 176 ||

दत्तमति दत्तभार्या दत्तशास्त्रावबोधिका ।
दत्तपाना दत्तदाना दत्तदारिद्रनाशिनि ॥ १७७ ॥
dattamati dattabhāryā dattaśāstrāvabodhikā |
dattapānā dattadānā dattadāridranāśini || 177 ||

दत्तसौधावनीवासा दत्तस्वर्गा च दासदा ।
दास्यतुष्टा दास्यहरा दासदासीशतप्रदा ॥ १७८ ॥
dattasaudhāvanīvāsā dattasvargā ca dāsadā |
dāsyatuṣṭā dāsyaharā dāsadāsīśatapradā || 178 ||

दाररूपा दारवासा दारवासिहृदास्पदा ।
दारवासिजनाराध्या दारवासिजनप्रिया ॥ १७९ ॥
dārarūpā dāravāsā dāravāsihṛdāspadā |
dāravāsijanārādhyā dāravāsijanapriyā || 179 ||

दारवासि विनिर्नीता दारवासिसमर्चिता ।
दारवास्याहृतप्राणा दारवास्यारिनाशिनी ॥ १८० ॥
dāravāsi vinirnītā dāravāsisamarcitā |
dāravāsyāhṛtaprāṇā dāravāsyārināśinī || 180 ||

दारवासिविघ्नहरा दारवासिविमुक्तिदा ।
दाराग्निरूपिणि दारा दारकार्य विनाशिनी ॥ १८१ ॥
dāravāsivighnaharā dāravāsivimuktidā |
dārāgnirūpiṇi dārā dārakārya vināśinī || 181 ||

दम्पती दम्पतीष्टा च दम्पतीप्राणरूपिका ।
दम्पतिस्नेहनिरता दाम्पत्यसाधनप्रिया ॥ १८२ ॥
dampatī dampatīṣṭā ca dampatīprāṇarūpikā |
dampatisnehaniratā dāmpatyasādhanapriyā || 182 ||

दाम्पत्यसुखसेना च दाम्पत्यसुखदायिनी ।
दम्पत्याचारनिरता दम्पत्यामोदमोदिता ॥ १८३ ॥
dāmpatyasukhasenā ca dāmpatyasukhadāyinī |
dampatyācāraniratā dampatyāmodamoditā || 183 ||

दम्पत्यामोदसुखिनि दाम्पत्याह्लादकारिणी ।
दम्पतीष्टपादपद्मा दाम्पत्यप्रेमरूपिणी ॥ १८४ ॥
dampatyāmodasukhini dāmpatyāhlādakāriṇī |
dampatīṣṭapādapadmā dāmpatyapremarūpiṇī || 184 ||

दाम्पत्यभोगभवना दाडिमीफलभोजिनी ।
दाडिमीफलसन्तुष्टा दाडिमीफलमानसा ॥ १८५ ॥
**dāmpatyabhogabhavanā dāḍimīphalabhojinī |
dāḍimīphalasantuṣṭā dāḍimīphalamānasā || 185 ||**

दाडिमीवृक्षसंस्थाना दाडिमीवृक्षवासिनी ।
दाडिमीवृक्षरूपाच दाडिमीवनवासिनी ॥ १८६ ॥
**dāḍimīvṛkṣasaṁsthānā dāḍimīvṛkṣavāsinī |
dāḍimīvṛkṣarūpāca dāḍimīvanavāsinī || 186 ||**

दाडिमीफलसाम्योरु पयोधरविवर्जिता ।
दक्षिणा दक्षिणारूपा दक्षिणारूपधारिणी ॥ १८७ ॥
**dāḍimīphalasāmyoru payodharavivarjitā |
dakṣiṇā dakṣiṇārūpā dakṣiṇārūpadhāriṇī || 187 ||**

दक्षकन्या दक्षपुत्री दक्षमाता च दक्षसूः ।
दक्षगोत्रा दक्षसुता दक्षयज्ञविनाशिनी ॥ १८८ ॥
**dakṣakanyā dakṣaputrī dakṣamātā ca dakṣasūḥ |
dakṣagotrā dakṣasutā dakṣayajñavināśinī || 188 ||**

दक्षयज्ञनाशकर्त्री दक्षयज्ञान्तकारिणी ।
दक्षप्रसूतिर्दक्षेज्या दक्षवंशैकपावनी ॥ १८९ ॥
**dakṣayajñanāśakartrī dakṣayajñāntakāriṇī |
dakṣaprasūtirdakṣejyā dakṣavaṁśaikapāvanī || 189 ||**

दक्षात्मजा दक्षसूनुर्दक्षजा दक्षजातिका ।
दक्षजन्मा दक्षजनुर्दक्षदेहसमुद्भवा ॥ १९० ॥
**dakṣātmajā dakṣasūnurdakṣajā dakṣajātikā |
dakṣajanmā dakṣajanurdakṣadehasamudbhavā || 190 ||**

दक्षजनिर्दक्षयागध्वंसिनि दक्षकन्यका ।
दक्षिणाचारनिरता दक्षिणाचारतुष्टिदा ॥ १९१ ॥
dakṣajanirdakṣayāgadhvaṁsini dakṣakanyakā |
dakṣiṇācāraniratā dakṣiṇācāratuṣṭidā || 191 ||

दक्षिणाचारसंसिद्धा दक्षिणाचारभाविता ।
दक्षिणाचारसुखिनी दक्षिणाचारसाधिता ॥ १९२ ॥
dakṣiṇācārasaṁsiddhā dakṣiṇācārabhāvitā |
dakṣiṇācārasukhinī dakṣiṇācārasādhitā || 192 ||

दक्षिणाचारमोक्षाप्ति दक्षिणाचारवन्दिता ।
दक्षिणाचारशरणा दक्षिणाचारहर्षिता ॥ १९३ ॥
dakṣiṇācāramokṣāpti dakṣiṇācāravanditā |
dakṣiṇācāraśaraṇā dakṣiṇācāraharṣitā || 193 ||

द्वारपालप्रिया द्वारवासिनी द्वारसंस्थिता ।
द्वाररूपा द्वारसंस्था द्वारदेशनिवासिनी ॥ १९४ ॥
dvārapālapriyā dvāravāsinī dvārasaṁsthitā |
dvārarūpā dvārasaṁsthā dvāradeśanivāsinī || 194 ||

द्वारकरी द्वारधात्री दोषमात्रविवर्जिता ।
दोषकरा दोषहरा दोषराशिविनाशिनी ॥ १९५ ॥
dvārakarī dvāradhātrī doṣamātravivarjitā |
doṣakarā doṣaharā doṣarāśivināśinī || 195 ||

दोषाकरविभूषाढ्या दोषाकरकपालिनी ।
दोषाकरसहस्राभा दोशाकरसमानना ॥ १९६ ॥
doṣākaravibhūṣāḍhyā doṣākarakapālinī |
doṣākarasahasrābhā dośākarasamānanā || 196 ||

दोषाकरमुखीदिव्या दोषाकरकराग्रजा ।
दोषाकरसमज्योति दोषाकरसुशीतला ॥ १९७ ॥
doṣākaramukhīdivyā doṣākarakarāgrajā |
doṣākarasamajyoti doṣākarasuśītalā || 197 ||

दोषाकरश्रेणी दोषसदृशापाङ्गवीक्षणा ।
दोषाकरेष्टदेवी च दोषाकरनिषेविता ॥ १९८ ॥
doṣākaraśreṇī doṣasadṛśāpāṅgavīkṣaṇā |
doṣākareṣṭadevī ca doṣākaraniṣevitā || 198 ||

दोषाकरप्राणरूपा दोषाकरमरीचिका ।
दोषाकरोल्लसद्भाला दोशाकरसुहर्षिणी ॥ १९९ ॥
doṣākaraprāṇarūpā doṣākaramarīcikā |
doṣākarollasadbhālā dośākarasuharṣiṇī || 199 ||

दोषाकरशिरोभूषा दोषाकरवधूप्रिया ।
दोषाकरवधूप्राणा दोषाकरवधूर्मता ॥ २०० ॥
doṣākaraśirobhūṣā doṣākaravadhūpriyā |
doṣākaravadhūprāṇā doṣākaravadhūrmatā || 200 ||

दोषाकरवधूप्रीता दोषाकरवधूरपि ।
दोषापूज्या तथा दोषापूजिता दोषहारिणी ॥ २०१ ॥
doṣākaravadhūprītā doṣākaravadhūrapi |
doṣāpūjyā tathā doṣāpūjitā doṣahāriṇī || 201 ||

दोषाजापमहानन्दा दोषाजापपरायणा ।
दोषापुरश्चाररता दोषापूजकपुत्रिणी ॥ २०२ ॥
doṣājāpamahānandā doṣājāpaparāyaṇā |
doṣāpuraścāraratā doṣāpūjakaputriṇī || 202 ||

दोषापूजकवात्सल्यकारिणी जगदम्बिका ।
दोषापूजकवैरिघ्नि दोषापूजकविघ्नहृत् ॥ २०३ ॥
doṣāpūjaka-vātsalyakāriṇī jagadambikā |
doṣāpūjakavairighni doṣāpūjakavighnahṛt || 203 ||

दोषापूजकसन्तुष्टा दोषापूजकमुक्तिदा ।
दमप्रसूनसम्पूज्या दमपुष्पप्रिया सदा ॥ २०४ ॥
doṣāpūjakasantuṣṭā doṣāpūjakamuktidā |
damaprasūnasampūjyā damapuṣpapriyā sadā || 204 ||

दुर्योधनपूज्या च दुःशासनसमर्चिता ।
दण्डपाणिप्रिया दण्डपाणिमाता दयानिधिः ॥ २०५ ॥
duryodhanapūjyā ca duḥśāsanasamarcitā |
daṇḍapāṇipriyā daṇḍapāṇimātā dayānidhiḥ || 205 ||

दण्डपाणिसमाराध्या दण्डपाणिप्रपूजिता ।
दण्डपाणिगृहासक्ता दण्डपाणिप्रियंवदा ॥ २०६ ॥
daṇḍapāṇisamārādhyā daṇḍapāṇiprapūjitā |
daṇḍapāṇigṛhāsaktā daṇḍapāṇipriyaṁvadā || 206 ||

दण्डपाणिप्रियतमा दण्डपाणिमनोहरा ।
दण्डपाणिहृतप्राणा दण्डपाणिसुसिद्धिदा ॥ २०७ ॥
daṇḍapāṇipriyatamā daṇḍapāṇimanoharā |
daṇḍapāṇihṛtaprāṇā daṇḍapāṇisusiddhidā || 207 ||

दण्डपाणिपरामृष्टा दण्डपाणिप्रहर्षिता ।
दण्डपाणिविघ्नहरा दण्डपाणिशिरोधृता ॥ २०८ ॥
daṇḍapāṇiparāmṛṣṭā daṇḍapāṇipraharṣitā |
daṇḍapāṇivighnaharā daṇḍapāṇiśirodhṛtā || 208 ||

दण्डपाणिप्राप्तचर्चा दण्डपाण्युन्मुखी सदा ।
दण्डपाणिप्राप्तपदा दण्डपाणिवरोन्मुखी ॥ २०९ ॥
daṇḍapāṇiprāptacarcā daṇḍapāṇyunmukhī sadā |
daṇḍapāṇiprāptapadā daṇḍapāṇivaronmukhī || 209 ||

दण्डहस्ता दण्डपाणिर्दण्डबाहुर्दरान्तकृत् ।
दण्डदोष्का दण्डकरा दण्डचित्तकृतास्पदा ॥ २१० ॥
daṇḍahastā daṇḍapāṇirdaṇḍabāhurdarāntakṛt |
daṇḍadoṣkā daṇḍakarā daṇḍacittakṛtāspadā || 210 ||

दण्डविद्या दण्डिमाता दण्डिखण्डकनाशिनी ।
दण्डिप्रिया दण्डिपूज्या दण्डिसन्तोषदायिनी ॥ २११ ॥
daṇḍavidyā daṇḍimātā daṇḍikhaṇḍakanāśinī |
daṇḍipriyā daṇḍipūjyā daṇḍisantoṣadāyinī || 211 ||

दस्युपूज्या दस्युरता दस्युद्रविणदायिनी ।
दस्युवर्गकृतार्हा च दस्युवर्गविनाशिनी ॥ २१२ ॥
dasyupūjyā dasyuratā dasyudraviṇadāyinī |
dasyuvargakṛtārhā ca dasyuvargavināśinī || 212 ||

दस्युनिर्नाशिनि दस्युकुलनिर्नाशिनी तथा ।
दस्युप्रियकरी दस्युनृत्यदर्शनतत्परा ॥ २१३ ॥
dasyunirnāśini dasyukulanirnāśinī tathā |
dasyupriyakarī dasyunṛtyadarśanatatparā || 213 ||

दुष्टदण्डकरी दुष्टवर्गविद्राविणी तथा ।
दुष्टवर्गनिग्रहार्हा दूषकप्राणनाशिनी ॥ २१४ ॥
duṣṭadaṇḍakarī duṣṭavargavidrāviṇī tathā |
duṣṭavarganigrahārhā dūṣakaprāṇanāśinī || 214 ||

दुषकोत्तापजननी दूषकारिष्टकारिणी ।
दूषकद्वेषणकरी दाहिका दहनात्मिका ॥ २१५ ॥
duṣakottāpajananī dūṣakāriṣṭakāriṇī |
dūṣakadveṣaṇakarī dāhikā dahanātmikā || 215 ||

दारकारी निहन्त्री च दारुकेश्वरपूजिता ।
दारुकेश्वरमाता च दारुकेश्वरवन्दिता ॥ २१६ ॥
dārakārī nihantrī ca dārukeśvarapūjitā |
dārukeśvaramātā ca dārukeśvaravanditā || 216 ||

दर्भहस्ता दर्भयूता दर्भकर्मविवर्जिता ।
दर्भमयि दर्भतनुर्दर्भसर्वस्वरूपिणी ॥ २१७ ॥
darbhahastā darbhayūtā darbhakarmavivarjitā |
darbhamayi darbhatanurdarbhasarvasvarūpiṇī || 217 ||

दर्भकर्माचाररता दर्भहस्तकृतार्हणा ।
दर्भानुकूला दार्भर्या दर्वीपात्रानुदामिनी ॥ २१८ ॥
darbhakarmācārarata darbhahastakṛtārhaṇā |
darbhānukūlā dārbharyā darvīpātrānudāminī || 218 ||

दमघोषप्रपूज्या च दमघोषवरप्रदा ।
दमघोषसमाराध्या दावाग्निरूपिणी तथा ॥ २१९ ॥
damaghoṣaprapūjyā ca damaghoṣavarapradā |
damaghoṣasamārādhyā dāvāgnirūpiṇī tathā || 219 ||

दावाग्निरूपा दावाग्निनिर्नाशितमहाबला ।
दन्तदंष्ट्रासुरकला दन्तचर्चितहस्तिका ॥ २२० ॥
dāvāgnirūpā dāvāgninirnāśitamahābalā |
dantadaṁṣṭrāsurakalā dantacarcitahastikā || 220 ||

दन्तदंष्ट्रस्यन्दना च दन्तनिर्नाशितासुरा ।
दधिपूज्या दधिप्रीता दधीचिवरदायिनी ॥ २२१ ॥
dantadaṁṣṭrasyandanā ca dantanirnāśitāsurā |
dadhipūjyā dadhiprītā dadhīcivaradāyinī || 221 ||

दधीचीष्टदेवता च दधीचिमोक्षदायिनी ।
दधीचिदैन्यहन्त्री च दधीचिदरदारिणी ॥ २२२ ॥
dadhīcīṣṭadevatā ca dadhīcimokṣadāyinī |
dadhīcidainyahantrī ca dadhīcidaradāriṇī || 222 ||

दधीचिभक्तिसुखिनि दधीचिमुनिसेविता ।
दधीचिज्ञानदात्रि च दधीचिगुणदायिनी ॥ २२३ ॥
dadhīcibhaktisukhini dadhīcimunisevitā |
dadhīcijñānadātri ca dadhīciguṇadāyinī || 223 ||

दधीचिकुलसम्भूषा दधीचिभुक्तिमुक्तिदा ।
दधीचिकुलदेवी च दधीचिकुलदेवता ॥ २२४ ॥
dadhīcikulasambhūṣā dadhīcibhuktimuktidā |
dadhīcikuladevī ca dadhīcikuladevatā || 224 ||

दधीचिकुलगम्या च दधीचिकुलपूजिता ।
दधीचिसुखदात्री च दधीचिदीनहारिणी ॥ २२५ ॥
dadhīcikulagamyā ca dadhīcikulapūjitā |
dadhīcisukhadātrī ca dadhīcidīnahāriṇī || 225 ||

दधीचिदुःखहन्त्री च दधीचिकुलसुन्दरी ।
दधीचिकुलसम्भूता दधीचिकुलपालिनी ॥ २२६ ॥
dadhīciduḥkhahantrī ca dadhīcikulasundarī |
dadhīcikulasambhūtā dadhīcikulapālinī || 226 ||

दधीचिदानगम्या च दधीचिदानमानिनी ।
दधीचिदानसन्तुष्टा दधीचिदानदेवता ॥ २२७ ॥
dadhīcidānagamyā ca dadhīcidānamāninī |
dadhīcidānasantuṣṭā dadhīcidānadevatā || 227 ||

दधीचिजयसम्प्रीता दधीचिजपमानसा ।
दधीचिजपपूजाढ्या दधीचिजपमालिका ॥ २२८ ॥
dadhīcijayasamprītā dadhīcijapamānasā |
dadhīcijapapūjāḍhyā dadhīcijapamālikā || 228 ||

दधीचिजपसन्तुष्टा दधीचिजपतोषिणी ।
दधीचितापसाराध्या दधीचिशुभदायिनी ॥ २२९ ॥
dadhīcijapasantuṣṭā dadhīcijapatoṣiṇī |
dadhīcitāpasārādhyā dadhīciśubhadāyinī || 229 ||

दूर्वा दूर्वादलश्यामा दूर्वादलसमद्युतिः ।
नाम्नां सहस्रं दुर्गाया दादीनामिति कीर्तितम् ॥ २३० ॥
dūrvā dūrvādalaśyāmā dūrvādalasamadyutiḥ |
nāmnāṁ sahasraṁ durgāyā dādīnāmiti kīrtitam || 230 ||
230. (Second line) These are the thousand names of Durga which are famous because they start with the letter D, etc.

यः पठेत् साधकाधीशः सर्वसिद्धिर्लभेत्तु सः ।
प्रातर्मध्याह्नकाले च सन्ध्यायां नियतः शुचिः ॥ २३१ ॥
yaḥ paṭhet sādhakādhīśaḥ sarvasiddhirlabhettu saḥ |
prātarmadhyāhnakāle ca
sandhyāyāṁ niyataḥ śuciḥ || 231 ||
231. Whatever sadhu will recite (these) will become a master, and he or she will attain all perfection. In the early morning or mid-day times, and at the times of prayer (in the evening), a pure person,

तथाऽर्द्धरात्रसमये स महेश इवाऽपरः ।
शक्तियुक्तो महारात्रौ महावीरः प्रपूजयेत् ॥ २३२ ॥

tathā-rddharātrasamaye sa maheśa ivā-paraḥ |
śaktiyukto mahārātrau mahāvīraḥ prapūjayet || 232 ||

232. and then, at the time of the middle of the night, he or she becomes even greater than the supreme lord. United with energy in the great night, the great warrior who worships,

महादेवीमकाराद्यै पञ्चभिर्द्रव्यसत्तमैः ।
तत्पठेत् स्तुतिमिमां यः स च सिद्धिस्वरूपधृक् ॥ २३३ ॥

mahādevīmakārādyai pañcabhirdravyasattamaiḥ |
tatpaṭhet stutimimāṁ yaḥ
sa ca siddhisvarūpadhṛk || 233 ||

233. makes pleasing offerings to the great goddess with five kinds of auspicious articles, and reads this song of mine, he or she will take the form of perfection.

देवालये श्मशाने च गङ्गातीरे निजे गृहे ।
वाराङ्गनागृहे चैव श्रीगुरोः सन्निधावपि ॥ २३४ ॥

devālaye śmaśāne ca gaṅgātīre nije gṛhe |
vārāṅganāgṛhe caiva śrīguroḥ sannidhāvapi || 234 ||

234. In a temple of the gods, in the cremation grounds, on the banks of the Gaṅgā, or in his own house, and even in the house or situated near the respected guru,

पर्वते प्रान्तरे घोरे स्तोत्रमेतत् सदा पठेत् ।
दुर्गानामसहस्रं हि दुर्गा पश्यति चक्षुषा ॥ २३५ ॥

parvate prāntare ghore stotrametat sadā paṭhet |
durgānāmasahasraṁ hi durgā paśyati cakṣuṣā || 235 ||

235. on a mountain, or in a fearful forest, who will always recite this song of mine, these thousand names of Durgā, will actually see Durgā with his or her own eyes.

शतावर्त्तनमेतस्य पुरश्चरणमुच्यते ।
स्तुतिसारो निगदितः किं भूयः श्रोतुमिच्छसिः ॥ २३६ ॥

śatāvarttanametasya puraścaraṇamucyate |
stutisāro nigaditaḥ kiṁ bhūyaḥ śrotumicchasiḥ || 236 ||

236. One hundred times is required for the puraścaraṇa (completed offering in the homa fire) the song of this name is to be recited. About what else do you desire to hear?

॥ इति श्रीकुलार्णवे दकारादि दुर्गासहस्रनामस्तोत्रं सम्पूर्णम् ॥

|| iti śrīkulārṇave dakārādi durgāsahasranāmastotraṁ sampūrṇam ||

Thus ends the Song of a Thousand Names of Durgā beginning with the letter D from the Respected Kulārṇava Tantra

-१-

ॐ दुं दुर्गायै स्वाहा

oṁ duṁ durgāyai svāhā

1. To the Reliever of difficulties

-२-

ॐ दुर्गतिहरायै स्वाहा

oṁ durgatiharāyai svāhā

2. To she who takes away all difficulties

-३-

ॐ दुर्गाचलनिवासिन्यै स्वाहा

oṁ durgācalanivāsinyai svāhā

3. To she who resides in the mountains of difficulties

-४-

ॐ दुर्गमार्गानुसञ्चारायै स्वाहा

oṁ durgamārgānusañcārāyai svāhā

4. To she who moves along the path which searches through difficulties

-५-

ॐ दुर्गमार्गनिवासिन्यै स्वाहा

oṁ durgamārganivāsinyai svāhā

5. To she who resides on the path beyond difficulties

-६-

ॐ दुर्गमार्गप्रविष्ठायै स्वाहा

oṁ durgamārgapraviṣṭhāyai svāhā

6. To she who answers the path beyond difficulties

-७-

ॐ दुर्गमार्गप्रवेशिन्यै स्वाहा

oṁ durgamārgapraveśinyai svāhā

7. To she who enters the path beyond difficulties

-८-

ॐ दुर्गमार्गकृतावासायै स्वाहा

oṁ durgamārgakṛtāvāsāyai svāhā

8. To she who resides in the path of actions which take us beyond difficulties

-९-

ॐ दुर्गमार्गजयप्रियायै स्वाहा

oṁ durgamārgajayapriyāyai svāhā

9. To she who loves the path which is victorious over difficulties

-१०-

ॐ दुर्गमार्गगृहीतार्चायै स्वाहा

oṁ durgamārgagṛhītārcāyai svāhā

10. To she who is the teacher of the path which leads to the house beyond difficulties

-११-

ॐ दुर्गमार्गस्थितात्मिकायै स्वाहा

oṁ durgamārgasthitātmikāyai svāhā

11. To she who is situated in the soul of the path which leads beyond difficulties

-१२-

ॐ दुर्गमार्गस्तुतिपरायै स्वाहा

oṁ durgamārgastutiparāyai svāhā

12. To she who is beyond the song of praise of the path which takes us beyond difficulties

-१३-

ॐ दुर्गमार्गस्मृतिपरायै स्वाहा

oṁ durgamārgasmṛtiparāyai svāhā

13. To she who is beyond the remembrance of the path which takes us beyond difficulties

-१४-

ॐ दुर्गमार्गसदास्थाल्यै स्वाहा

oṁ durgamārgasadāsthālyai svāhā

14. To she who is always situated in the path which takes us beyond difficulties

-१५-

ॐ दुर्गमार्गरतिप्रियायै स्वाहा

oṁ durgamārgaratipriyāyai svāhā

15. To she who is beloved of the wonderful path which takes us beyond difficulties

-१६-

ॐ दुर्गमार्गस्थलस्थानायै स्वाहा

oṁ durgamārgasthalasthānāyai svāhā

16. To she who is situated in the path which takes us beyond difficulties

-१७-

ॐ दुर्गमार्गविलासिन्यै स्वाहा

oṁ durgamārgavilāsinyai svāhā

17. To she who desires the path which takes us beyond difficulties

-१८-

ॐ दुर्गमार्गत्यक्तवस्त्रायै स्वाहा

oṁ durgamārgatyaktavastrāyai svāhā

18. To she who is the individual clothed in the path which takes us beyond difficulties

-१९-

ॐ दुर्गमार्गप्रवर्त्तिन्यै स्वाहा

oṁ durgamārgapravarttinyai svāhā

19. To she who chooses the path which takes us beyond difficulties

-२०-

ॐ दुर्गासुरनिहन्त्र्यै स्वाहा

oṁ durgāsuranihantryai svāhā

20. To she who slays the duality beyond difficulties

-२१-

ॐ दुगासुरनिषूदिन्यै स्वाहा

oṁ dugāsuraniṣūdinyai svāhā

21. To she who purifies the duality beyond difficulties

-२२-

ॐ दुर्गासुरहरायै स्वाहा

oṁ durgāsuraharāyai svāhā

22. To she takes away the duality beyond difficulties

-२३-

ॐ दूत्यै स्वाहा

oṁ dūtyai svāhā

23. To she who is the ambassador

-२४-

ॐ दुर्गासुरविनाशिन्यै स्वाहा

oṁ durgāsuravināśinyai svāhā

24. To she who is the destroyer of all difficulties

-२५-

ॐ दुर्गासुरवधोन्मत्तायै स्वाहा

oṁ durgāsuravadhonmattāyai svāhā

25. To she who goes crazy for the death of duality

-२६-

ॐ दुर्गासुरवधोत्सुकायै स्वाहा

oṁ durgāsuravadhotsukāyai svāhā

26. To she who is enthusiastic about the death of duality

-२७-

ॐ दुर्गासुरवधोत्साहायै स्वाहा

oṁ durgāsuravadhotsāhāyai svāhā

27. To she who is excited about the death of duality

-२८-

ॐ दुर्गासुरवधोद्यतायै स्वाहा

oṁ durgāsuravadhodyatāyai svāhā

28. To she who is uplifted by the death of duality

-२९-

ॐ दुर्गासुरवधप्रेप्स्वे स्वाहा

oṁ durgāsuravadhaprepsve svāhā

29. To she who is questioned by the death of duality

-३०-

ॐ दुर्गासुरमखान्तकृते स्वाहा

oṁ durgāsuramakhāntakṛte svāhā

30. To she who is made alone by the death of duality

-३१-

ॐ दुर्गासुरध्वंस्सन्तोषायै स्वाहा

oṁ durgāsuradhvaṁssantoṣāyai svāhā

31. To she who is satisfied by the death of duality

-३२-

ॐ दुर्गदानवदारिण्यै स्वाहा

oṁ durgadānavadāriṇyai svāhā

32. To she who supports the freedom from duality

-३३-

ॐ दुर्गविद्रावणकर्यै स्वाहा

oṁ durgavidrāvaṇakaryai svāhā

33. To she who renews with the removal of difficulties

-३४-

ॐ दुर्गविद्राविण्यै स्वाहा

oṁ durgavidrāviṇyai svāhā

34. To she who is renewed by the removal of difficulties

-३५-

ॐ दुर्गविक्षोभनकर्यै स्वाहा

oṁ durgavikṣobhanakaryai svāhā

35. To she who causes us to be tossed about when removing difficulties

-३६-

ॐ दुर्गशीर्षनिकृन्तन्यै स्वाहा

oṁ durgaśīrṣanikṛntanyai svāhā

36. To she who causes the heads to be chopped off from difficulties

-३७-

ॐ दुर्गविध्वंसनकर्यै स्वाहा

oṁ durgavidhvaṁsanakaryai svāhā

37. To she who causes the destruction of difficulties

-३८-

ॐ दुर्गदैत्यनिकृन्तन्यै स्वाहा

oṁ durgadaityanikṛntanyai svāhā

38. To she who tosses about the duality of difficulties

-३९-

ॐ दुर्गदैत्यप्राणहरायै स्वाहा

oṁ durgadaityaprāṇaharāyai svāhā

39. To she who takes away the life force from the duality of difficulties

-४०-

ॐ दुर्गदैत्यान्तकारिण्यै स्वाहा

oṁ durgadaityāntakāriṇyai svāhā

40. To she who is the cause of the end of the duality of difficulties

-४१-

ॐ दुर्गदैत्यहरत्रातायै स्वाहा

oṁ durgadaityaharatrātāyai svāhā

41. To she who takes away the dualities of the difficulties of the three worlds

-४२-

ॐ दुर्गदैत्यसृगुन्मदायै स्वाहा

oṁ durgadaityasṛgunmadāyai svāhā

42. To she who extricates from the qualities of the dualities of difficulties

-४३-

ॐ दुर्गदैत्याशनकर्यै स्वाहा

oṁ durgadaityāśanakaryai svāhā

43. To she who is the cause of the establishment of the dualities of difficulties

-४४-

ॐ दुर्गचर्माम्बरावृतायै स्वाहा

oṁ durgacarmāmbarāvṛtāyai svāhā

44. To she who changes the appearance of difficulties

-४५-

ॐ दुर्गयुद्धोत्सवकर्यै स्वाहा

oṁ durgayuddhotsavakaryai svāhā

45. To she who is the cause of the festival of war with difficulties

-४६-

ॐ दुर्गयुद्धविशारदायै स्वाहा

oṁ durgayuddhaviśāradāyai svāhā

46. To she who gives knowledge of the war with difficulties

-४७-

ॐ दुर्गयुद्धासवरतायै स्वाहा

oṁ durgayuddhāsavaratāyai svāhā
47. To she who is the ultimate commander of the warriors against difficulties

-४८-

ॐ दुर्गयुद्धविमर्द्दिन्यै स्वाहा

oṁ durgayuddhavimarddinyai svāhā
48. To she who slays the warriors who create difficulties

-४९-

ॐ दुर्गयुद्धहास्यरतायै स्वाहा

oṁ durgayuddhahāsyaratāyai svāhā
49. To she who emits laughter at warriors who create difficulties

-५०-

ॐ दुर्गयुद्धाट्टहासिन्यै स्वाहा

oṁ durgayuddhāṭṭahāsinyai svāhā
50. To she who laughs at warriors who create difficulties

-५१-

ॐ दुर्गयुद्धमहामत्तायै स्वाहा

oṁ durgayuddhamahāmattāyai svāhā
51. To she who is the great mind of warriors who create difficulties

-५२-

ॐ दुर्गयुद्धानुसारिण्यै स्वाहा

oṁ durgayuddhānusāriṇyai svāhā
52. To she who wages war to protect the innocence of those in difficulties

-५३-

ॐ दुर्गयुद्धोत्सवोत्साहायै स्वाहा

oṁ durgayuddhotsavotsāhāyai svāhā

53. To she who is enthusiastic in the festival of war against difficulties

-५४-

ॐ दुर्गदेशनिषेविण्यै स्वाहा

oṁ durgadeśaniṣeviṇyai svāhā

54. To she who is the unending location of difficulties

-५५-

ॐ दुर्गदेशवासरतायै स्वाहा

oṁ durgadeśavāsaratāyai svāhā

55. To she who controls the location of difficulties

-५६-

ॐ दुर्गदेशविलासिन्यै स्वाहा

oṁ durgadeśavilāsinyai svāhā

56. To she who resides in the location of difficulties

-५७-

ॐ दुर्गदेशार्च्चनरतायै स्वाहा

oṁ durgadeśārccanaratāyai svāhā

57. To she who offers in the location of difficulties

-५८-

ॐ दुर्गदेशजनप्रियायै स्वाहा

oṁ durgadeśajanapriyāyai svāhā

58. To she who is beloved by the people in the location of difficulties

-५९-

ॐ दुर्गमस्थानसंस्थानायै स्वाहा

oṁ durgamasthānasaṁsthānāyai svāhā

59. To she who is situated in the location of difficulties

-६०-

ॐ दुर्गमध्यानसाधनायै स्वाहा

oṁ durgamadhyānasādhanāyai svāhā

60. To she who is searched for in the midst of difficulties

-६१-

ॐ दुर्गमायै स्वाहा

oṁ durgamāyai svāhā

61. To she who is the mother of difficulties

-६२-

ॐ दुर्गमध्यानायै स्वाहा

oṁ durgamadhyānāyai svāhā

62. To she who is in the midst of difficulties

-६३-

ॐ दुर्गमात्मस्वरूपिण्यै स्वाहा

oṁ durgamātmasvarūpiṇyai svāhā

63. To she who is the intrinsic nature of the soul difficulties

-६४-

ॐ दुर्गमागमसन्धानायै स्वाहा

oṁ durgamāgamasandhānāyai svāhā

64. To see who searches for the arrival of difficulties

-६५-

ॐ दुर्गमागमसंस्तुतायै स्वाहा

oṁ durgamāgamasaṁstutāyai svāhā

65. To she whose praise is sung upon the arrival of difficulties

-६६-

ॐ दुर्गमागमदुर्ज्ञेयायै स्वाहा

oṁ durgamāgamadurjñeyāyai svāhā

66. To she who is the corrupted knowledge upon the arrival of difficulties

-६७-

ॐ दुर्गमश्रुतिसम्मतायै स्वाहा

oṁ durgamaśrutisammatāyai svāhā

67. To she who gives full mind to the news of difficulties

-६८-

ॐ दुर्गमश्रुतिमान्याचयै स्वाहा

oṁ durgamaśrutimānyācayai svāhā

68. To she who contemplates the news of difficulties

-६९-

ॐ दुर्गमश्रुतिपूजितायै स्वाहा

oṁ durgamaśrutipūjitāyai svāhā

69. To she who is worshiped with the news of difficulties

-७०-

ॐ दुर्गमश्रुतिसुप्रीतायै स्वाहा

oṁ durgamaśrutisuprītāyai svāhā

70. To she who is beloved with the news of difficulties

-७१-

ॐ दुर्गमश्रुतिहर्षदायै स्वाहा

oṁ durgamaśrutiharṣadāyai svāhā

71. To she who is delighted with the news of difficulties

-७२-

ॐ दुर्गमश्रुतिसंस्थानायै स्वाहा

oṁ durgamaśrutisaṁsthānāyai svāhā

72. To she who is established in the news of difficulties

-७३-

ॐ दुर्गमश्रुतिमानितायै स्वाहा

oṁ durgamaśrutimānitāyai svāhā

73. To she who is contemplated with the news of difficulties

-७४-

ॐ दुर्गमाचारसन्तुष्टायै स्वाहा

oṁ durgamācārasantuṣṭāyai svāhā

74. To she who is satisfied with the immobilization of difficulties

-७५-

ॐ दुर्गमाचारतोषितायै स्वाहा

oṁ durgamācāratoṣitāyai svāhā

75. To she who is delighted by the immobilization of difficulties

-७६-

ॐ दुर्गमाचारनिर्वृत्तायै स्वाहा

oṁ durgamācāranirvṛttāyai svāhā

76. To she who does not change with the immobilization of difficulties

-७७-

ॐ दुर्गमाचारपूजितायै स्वाहा

oṁ durgamācārapūjitāyai svāhā

77. To she who is worshiped with the immobilization of difficulties

-७८-

ॐ दुर्गमाचारकसितायै स्वाहा

oṁ durgamācārakasitāyai svāhā

78. To she who controls the immobilization of difficulties

-७९-

ॐ दुर्गमस्थानदायिन्यै स्वाहा

oṁ durgamasthānadāyinyai svāhā

79. To she who gives the location of difficulties

-८०-

ॐ दुर्गमप्रेमनिरतायै स्वाहा

oṁ durgamapremaniratāyai svāhā

80. To she who offers love to difficulties

-८१-

ॐ दुर्गमद्रविणप्रदायै स्वाहा

oṁ durgamadraviṇapradāyai svāhā

81. To she who gives the essence of difficulties

-८२-

ॐ दुर्गमाम्बुजमध्यस्थायै स्वाहा

oṁ durgamāmbujamadhyasthāyai svāhā

82. To she who is situated in the midst of the lotus of difficulties

-८३-

ॐ दुर्गमाम्बुजवासिन्यै स्वाहा

oṁ durgamāmbujavāsinyai svāhā

83. To she who resides within the lotus of difficulties

-८४-

ॐ दुर्गनाडीमार्गगत्यै स्वाहा

oṁ durganāḍīmārgagatyai svāhā

84. To she who travels by the boulevards and lanes of difficulties

-८५-

ॐ दुर्गनाडीप्रचारिण्यै स्वाहा

oṁ durganāḍīpracāriṇyai svāhā

85. To she who makes known the paths of difficulties

-८६-

ॐ दुर्गनाडीपद्मरतायै स्वाहा

oṁ durganāḍīpadmaratāyai svāhā

86. To she who is the lotus at the end of the path of difficulties

-८७-

ॐ दुर्गनाड्यम्बुजस्थितायै स्वाहा

oṁ durganāḍyambujasthitāyai svāhā

87. To she who situated in the lotus on the path of difficulties

-८८-

ॐ दुर्गनाडीगतायातायै स्वाहा

oṁ durganāḍīgatāyātāyai svāhā

88. To she who makes efforts to travel the paths of difficulties

-८९-

ॐ दुर्गनाडिकृतास्पदायै स्वाहा

oṁ durganāḍikṛtāspadāyai svāhā

89. To she who walks along the paths of difficulties

-९०-

ॐ दुर्गनाडीरतरतायै स्वाहा

oṁ durganāḍīrataratāyai svāhā

90. To she who is the ultimate end of the path of difficulties

-९१-

ॐ दुर्गनाडीशसंस्तुतायै स्वाहा

oṁ durganāḍīśasaṁstutāyai svāhā

91. To she whose praise is sung as the path of difficulties

-९२-

ॐ दुर्गनाडीश्चररतायै स्वाहा

oṁ durganāḍīścararatāyai svāhā

92. To she who moves to the end of the path of difficulties

-९३-

ॐ दुर्गनाडीशचुम्बितायै स्वाहा

oṁ durganāḍīśacumbitāyai svāhā

93. To she who gives birth to the truth of the path of difficulties

-९४-

ॐ दुर्गनाडीशक्रोडस्थायै स्वाहा

oṁ durganāḍīśakroḍasthāyai svāhā

94. To she who is situated in anger along the path of difficulties

-९५-

ॐ दुर्गनाड्युत्थितोत्सुकायै स्वाहा

oṁ durganāḍyutthitotsukāyai svāhā
95. To she gives comfort along the path of difficulties

-९६-

ॐ दुर्गनाड्यारोहणायै स्वाहा

oṁ durganāḍyārohaṇāyai svāhā
96. To she who descends from the mountain paths of difficulties

-९७-

ॐ दुर्गनाडीनिषेवितायै स्वाहा

oṁ durganāḍīniṣevitāyai svāhā
97. To she who inhabits the paths of difficulties

-९८-

ॐ दरीस्थानायै स्वाहा

oṁ darīsthānāyai svāhā
98. To she who resides in caves

-९९-

ॐ दरीस्थानवासिन्यै स्वाहा

oṁ darīsthānavāsinyai svāhā
99. To she who is the resident situated in caves

-१००-

ॐ दनुजान्तकृते स्वाहा

oṁ danujāntakṛte svāhā
100. To she who causes the end to Danu, the Mother of the dānavas

-१०१-

ॐ दरीकृततपस्यायै स्वाहा

oṁ darīkṛtatapasyāyai svāhā
101. To she who performs tapasya in caves

-१०२-

ॐ दरीकृतहरार्च्चनायै स्वाहा

oṁ darīkṛtaharārccanāyai svāhā
102. To she who offers to Shiva in caves

-१०३-

ॐ दरीजापितदिष्टायै स्वाहा

oṁ darījāpitadiṣṭāyai svāhā
103. To she who makes constant recitation of mantras for her beloved in caves

-१०४-

ॐ दरीकृतरतिक्रियायै स्वाहा

oṁ darīkṛtaratikriyāyai svāhā
104. To she who makes love with her beloved in caves

-१०५-

ॐ दरीकृतहरार्हायै स्वाहा

oṁ darīkṛtaharārhāyai svāhā
105. To she who feeds her beloved in caves

-१०६-

ॐ दरीक्रीडितपुत्रिकायै स्वाहा

oṁ darīkrīḍitaputrikāyai svāhā
106. To she who nurtures her daughter in caves

-१०७-

ॐ दरीसन्दर्शनरतायै स्वाहा

oṁ darīsandarśanaratāyai svāhā
107. To she who is the ultimate vision in caves

-१०८-

ॐ दरीरोपितवृश्चिकायै स्वाहा

oṁ darīropitavṛścikāyai svāhā
108. To she who dwells in the cave targeted by scorpions

-१०९-

ॐ दरीगुप्तिकौतुकाढ्यायै स्वाहा

oṁ darīguptikautukāḍhyāyai svāhā
109. To she who rides upon the unseen animals in the cave

-११०-

ॐ दरीभ्रमणतत्परायै स्वाहा

oṁ darībhramaṇatatparāyai svāhā
110. To she who is above all who move in the cave

-१११-

ॐ दनुजान्तकर्यै स्वाहा

oṁ danujāntakaryai svāhā
111. To she who is cause and effect of the end of Danu, the mother of the dānavas

-११२-

ॐ दीनायै स्वाहा

oṁ dīnāyai svāhā
112. To she who is with the lowly

-११३-

ॐ दनुजसन्तानदारिण्यै स्वाहा

oṁ danujasantānadāriṇyai svāhā
113. To she who supports the children of Danu

-११४-

ॐ दनुजध्वंसिन्यै स्वाहा

oṁ danujadhvaṁsinyai svāhā
114. To she who destroys those born of Danu

-११५-

ॐ दूतायै स्वाहा

oṁ dūtāyai svāhā
115. To she who sends ambassadors

-११६-

ॐ दनुजेन्द्रविनाशिन्यै स्वाहा

oṁ danujendravināśinyai svāhā
116. To she who destroys the leader of those born of Danu

-११७-

ॐ दानवध्वंसिन्यै स्वाहा

oṁ dānavadhvaṁsinyai svāhā
117. To she who destroys the dānavas

-११८-

ॐ देव्यै स्वाहा

oṁ devyai svāhā
118. To she who is the goddess

-११९-

ॐ दानवानां भयङ्कर्यै स्वाहा

oṁ dānavānāṁ bhayaṅkaryai svāhā
119. To she who causes fear in the dānavas

-१२०-

ॐ दानव्यै स्वाहा

oṁ dānavyai svāhā
120. To she who is a dānava

-१२१-

ॐ दानवाराध्यायै स्वाहा

oṁ dānavārādhyāyai svāhā
121. To she who pleases the dānavas

-१२२-

ॐ दानवेन्द्रवरप्रदायै स्वाहा

oṁ dānavendravarapradāyai svāhā
122. To she who gives a boon to the leader of the dānavas

-१२३-

ॐ दानवेन्द्रनिहन्त्र्यै स्वाहा

oṁ dānavendranihantryai svāhā

123. To she who slays the leader of the dānavas

-१२४-

ॐ दानवद्वेषिणी सत्यै स्वाहा

oṁ dānavadveṣiṇī satyai svāhā

124. To she who is the true embodiment of the enemies of the dānavas

-१२५-

ॐ दानवारिप्रेमरतायै स्वाहा

oṁ dānavāripremaratāyai svāhā

125. To she who is the ultimate love of the enemies of the dānavas

-१२६-

ॐ दानवारिप्रपूजितायै स्वाहा

oṁ dānavāriprapūjitāyai svāhā

126. To she who is worshiped by the enemies of the dānavas

-१२७-

ॐ दानवारिकृतार्च्चायै स्वाहा

oṁ dānavārikṛtārccāyai svāhā

127. To she who is the teacher of the enemies of the dānavas

-१२८-

ॐ दानवारिविभूतिदायै स्वाहा

oṁ dānavārivibhūtidāyai svāhā

128. To she gives blessings of purity to the enemies of the dānavas

-१२९-

ॐ दानवारिमहानन्दायै स्वाहा

oṁ dānavārimahānandāyai svāhā

129. To she who is the great bliss of the enemies of the dānavas

-१३०-

ॐ दानवारिरतिप्रियायै स्वाहा

oṁ dānavāriratipriyāyai svāhā

130. To she who enjoys the amorous affection of the enemies of the dānavas

-१३१-

ॐ दानवारिदानरतायै स्वाहा

oṁ dānavāridānaratāyai svāhā

131. To she who gives the ultimate gift to the enemies of the dānavas

-१३२-

ॐ दानवारिकृतास्पदायै स्वाहा

oṁ dānavārikṛtāspadāyai svāhā

132. To she who walks with the enemies of the dānavas

-१३३-

ॐ दानवारिस्तुतिरतायै स्वाहा

oṁ dānavāristutiratāyai svāhā

133. To she who is the ultimate song of the enemies of the dānavas

-१३४-

ॐ दानवारिस्मृतिप्रियायै स्वाहा

oṁ dānavārismṛtipriyāyai svāhā

134. To she who is enjoyed in the memories of the enemies of the dānavas

-१३५-

ॐ दानवार्याहाररतायै स्वाहा

oṁ dānavāryāhāraratāyai svāhā

135. To she who is the ultimate food of the enemies of the dānavas

-१३६-

ॐ दानवारिप्रबोधिन्यै स्वाहा

oṁ dānavāriprabodhinyai svāhā
136. To she who is the ultimate knowledge of the enemies of the dānavas

-१३७-

ॐ दानवारिधृतप्रेमायै स्वाहा

oṁ dānavāridhṛtapremāyai svāhā
137. To she who supports the love of the enemies of the dānavas

-१३८-

ॐ दुःखशोकविमोचिन्यै स्वाहा

oṁ duḥkhaśokavimocinyai svāhā
138. To she who removes pain and grief

-१३९-

ॐ दुःखहन्त्र्यै स्वाहा

oṁ duḥkhahantryai svāhā
139. To she takes away pain

-१४०-

ॐ दुःखदात्र्यै स्वाहा

oṁ duḥkhadātryai svāhā
140. To she who gives pain

-१४१-

ॐ दुःखनिर्मूलकारिण्यै स्वाहा

oṁ duḥkhanirmūlakāriṇyai svāhā
141. To she who is the root cause of pain

-१४२-

ॐ दुःखनिर्म्मूलनकर्यै स्वाहा

oṁ duḥkhanirmmūlanakaryai svāhā
142. To she who is the cause of the root of pain

-१४३-

ॐ दुःखदारिद्र्यनाशिन्यै स्वाहा

oṁ duḥkhadāridryanāśinyai svāhā

143. To she destroys pain and affliction

-१४४-

ॐ दुःखहरायै स्वाहा

oṁ duḥkhaharāyai svāhā

144. To she who takes away pain

-१४५-

ॐ दुःखनाशायै स्वाहा

oṁ duḥkhanāśāyai svāhā

145. To she who destroys pain

-१४६-

ॐ दुःखग्रामायै स्वाहा

oṁ duḥkhagrāmāyai svāhā

146. To she who moves with pain

-१४७-

ॐ दुरासदायै स्वाहा

oṁ durāsadāyai svāhā

147. To she who will not accept evil

-१४८-

ॐ दुःखहीनायै स्वाहा

oṁ duḥkhahīnāyai svāhā

148. To she who has no pain

-१४९-

ॐ दुःखधारायै स्वाहा

oṁ duḥkhadhārāyai svāhā

149. To she who supports us while in pain

-१५०-

ॐ द्रविणाचारदायिन्यै स्वाहा

oṁ draviṇācāradāyinyai svāhā

150. To she who gives the behavior of unity of our family

-१५१-

ॐ द्रविणोत्सर्गसन्तुष्टायै स्वाहा

oṁ draviṇotsargasantuṣṭāyai svāhā

151. To she who gives upliftment for the unity of our family

-१५२-

ॐ द्रविणत्यागतोषिकायै स्वाहा

oṁ draviṇatyāgatoṣikāyai svāhā

152. To she who renounces attachment with joy for the unity of our family

-१५३-

ॐ द्रविणस्पर्शसन्तुष्टायै स्वाहा

oṁ draviṇasparśasantuṣṭāyai svāhā

153. To she who touches with great satisfaction for the unity of our family

-१५४-

ॐ द्रविणस्पर्शमानदायै स्वाहा

oṁ draviṇasparśamānadāyai svāhā

154. To she gives the subtle understanding to those who touch for the unity of our family

-१५५-

ॐ द्रविणस्पर्शहर्षाढ्यायै स्वाहा

oṁ draviṇasparśaharṣāḍhyāyai svāhā

155. To she is filled with delight for those who touch for the unity of our family

-१५६-

ॐ द्रविणस्पर्शतुष्टिदायै स्वाहा

oṁ draviṇasparśatuṣṭidāyai svāhā

156. To she who gives satisfaction to those who touch for the unity of our family

-१५७-

ॐ द्रविणस्पर्शनकर्यै स्वाहा

oṁ draviṇasparśanakaryai svāhā

157. To she who is the cause of touching for the unity of our family

-१५८-

ॐ द्रविणस्पर्शनातुरायै स्वाहा

oṁ draviṇasparśanāturāyai svāhā

158. To she who has no end to touching for the unity of our family

-१५९-

ॐ द्रविणस्पर्शनोत्साहायै स्वाहा

oṁ draviṇasparśanotsāhāyai svāhā

159. To she who is enthusiastic for touching for the unity of our family

-१६०-

ॐ द्रविणस्पर्शसाधितायै स्वाहा

oṁ draviṇasparśasādhitāyai svāhā

160. To she who is excessive in touching for the unity of our family

-१६१-

ॐ द्रविणस्पर्शनमतायै स्वाहा

oṁ draviṇasparśanamatāyai svāhā

161. To she who offers respect by touching for the unity of our family

-१६२-

ॐ द्रविणस्पर्शपुत्रिकायै स्वाहा

oṁ draviṇasparśaputrikāyai svāhā

162. To she who is the daughter who touches for the unity of the family

-१६३-

ॐ द्रविणस्पर्शरक्षिण्यै स्वाहा

oṁ draviṇasparśarakṣiṇyai svāhā

163. To she protects touching for the unity of the family

-१६४-

ॐ द्रविणस्तोमदायिन्यै स्वाहा

oṁ draviṇastomadāyinyai svāhā

164. To she gives forth hymns regarding the unity of the family

-१६५-

ॐ द्रविणाकर्षणकर्यै स्वाहा

oṁ draviṇākarṣaṇakaryai svāhā

165. To she who is the cause of attraction to the unity of the family

-१६६-

ॐ द्रविणौघविसर्जन्यै स्वाहा

oṁ draviṇaughavisarjanyai svāhā

166. To she who is the ultimate culmination of the unity of the family

-१६७-

ॐ द्रविणचलदानाढ्यायै स्वाहा

oṁ draviṇacaladānāḍhyāyai svāhā

167. To she who scales heights for the unity of the family

-१६८-

ॐ द्रविणाचलवासिन्यै स्वाहा

oṁ draviṇācalavāsinyai svāhā
168. To she who resides upon the mountains for the unity of the family

-१६९-

ॐ दीनमातायै स्वाहा

oṁ dīnamātāyai svāhā
169. To she who is the mother of the lowly

-१७०-

ॐ दीनबन्धवे स्वाहा

oṁ dīnabandhave svāhā
170. To she who is the friend of the lowly

-१७१-

ॐ दीनविघ्नविनाशिन्यै स्वाहा

oṁ dīnavighnavināśinyai svāhā
171. To she who destroys the obstacles of the lowly

-१७२-

ॐ दीनसेव्यायै स्वाहा

oṁ dīnasevyāyai svāhā
172. To she who serves the lowly

-१७३-

ॐ दीनसिद्धायै स्वाहा

oṁ dīnasiddhāyai svāhā
173. To she who is the perfection of the lowly

-१७४-

ॐ दीनसाद्ध्यायै स्वाहा

oṁ dīnasāddhyāyai svāhā
174. To she who is the true contemplation of the lowly

-१७५-

ॐ दिगम्बर्यै स्वाहा

oṁ digambaryai svāhā
175. To she who is clothed in space

-१७६-

ॐ दीनगेहकृतानन्दायै स्वाहा

oṁ dīnagehakṛtānandāyai svāhā
176. To she who gives bliss to those who lead the householders' life of the lowly

-१७७-

ॐ दीनगेहविलासिन्यै स्वाहा

oṁ dīnagehavilāsinyai svāhā
177. To she who dwells in the householders' life of the lowly

-१७८-

ॐ दीनभावप्रेमरतायै स्वाहा

oṁ dīnabhāvapremaratāyai svāhā
178. To she who is the ultimate attitude of love of the lowly

-१७९-

ॐ दीनभावविनोदिन्यै स्वाहा

oṁ dīnabhāvavinodinyai svāhā
179. To she is the attitude of a fun joke of the lowly

-१८०-

ॐ दीनमानवचेतःस्थायै स्वाहा

oṁ dīnamānavacetaḥsthāyai svāhā
180. To she who is established in the thoughts and consciousness of the lowly

-१८१-

ॐ दीनमानवहर्षदायै स्वाहा

oṁ dīnamānavaharṣadāyai svāhā
181. To she who gives gladness to the thoughts of the lowly

-१८२-

ॐ दीनदैन्यनिघातेच्छवे स्वाहा

oṁ dīnadainyanighātecchave svāhā
182. To she destroys the duality of the lowly

-१८३-

ॐ दीनद्रविणदायिन्यै स्वाहा

oṁ dīnadraviṇadāyinyai svāhā
183. To she gives the unity of the family to the lowly

-१८४-

ॐ दीनसाधनसन्तुष्टायै स्वाहा

oṁ dīnasādhanasantuṣṭāyai svāhā
184. To she who is satisfied with the discipline of the lowly

-१८५-

ॐ दीनदर्शनदायिन्यै स्वाहा

oṁ dīnadarśanadāyinyai svāhā
185. To she who gives intuitive vision to the lowly

-१८६-

ॐ दीनपुत्रादिदात्र्यै स्वाहा

oṁ dīnaputrādidātryai svāhā
186. To she who is the giver of sons and daughters to the lowly

-१८७-

ॐ दीनसम्पद्विधायिन्यै स्वाहा

oṁ dīnasampadvidhāyinyai svāhā
187. To she who supports the benefit of the lowly

-१८८-

ॐ दत्तात्रेयध्यानरतायै स्वाहा

oṁ dattātreyadhyānaratāyai svāhā
188. To she who is the ultimate meditation of the Ambassador of the three, Dattātreya

-१८९-

ॐ दत्तात्रेयप्रपूजितायै स्वाहा

oṁ dattātreyaprapūjitāyai svāhā
189. To she who is worshiped by the Ambassador of the three, Dattātreya

-१९०-

ॐ दत्तात्रेयर्षिसंसिद्धायै स्वाहा

oṁ dattātreyarṣisaṁsiddhāyai svāhā
190. To she who gives complete perfection to the followers of the Ambassador of the three, Dattātreya

-१९१-

ॐ दत्तात्रेयविभावितायै स्वाहा

oṁ dattātreyavibhāvitāyai svāhā
191. To she who maintains the attitude of the Ambassador of the three, Dattātreya

-१९२-

ॐ दत्तात्रेयकृतार्हायै स्वाहा

oṁ dattātreyakṛtārhāyai svāhā
192. To she who is praised by the Ambassador of the three, Dattātreya

-१९३-

ॐ दत्तात्रेयप्रसाधितायै स्वाहा

oṁ dattātreyaprasādhitāyai svāhā
193. To she who is the consecrated offering of the Ambassador of the three, Dattātreya

-१९४-

ॐ दत्तात्रेयहर्षदात्र्यै स्वाहा

oṁ dattātreyaharṣadātryai svāhā
194. To she who gives delight to the Ambassador of the three, Dattātreya

-१९५-

ॐ दत्तात्रेयसुखप्रदायै स्वाहा

oṁ dattātreyasukhapradāyai svāhā

195. To she who bestows comfort upon the Ambassador of the three, Dattātreya

-१९६-

ॐ दत्तात्रेयस्तुतायै स्वाहा

oṁ dattātreyastutāyai svāhā

196. To she whose praise is sung by the Ambassador of the three, Dattātreya

-१९७-

ॐ दत्तात्रेयनुतासदायै स्वाहा

oṁ dattātreyanutāsadāyai svāhā

197. To she who joins the smallest particles of the family of the Ambassador of the three, Dattātreya

-१९८-

ॐ दत्तात्रेयप्रेमरतायै स्वाहा

oṁ dattātreyapremaratāyai svāhā

198. To she who is the ultimate love of the Ambassador of the three, Dattātreya

-१९९-

ॐ दत्तात्रेयानुमानितायै स्वाहा

oṁ dattātreyānumānitāyai svāhā

199. To she who is the opinion of the Ambassador of the three, Dattātreya

-२००-

ॐ दत्तात्रेयसमुद्गीतायै स्वाहा

oṁ dattātreyasamudgītāyai svāhā

200. To she who is the delightful song of the Ambassador of the three, Dattātreya

-२०१-

ॐ दत्तात्रेयकुटुम्बिन्यै स्वाहा

oṁ dattātreyakuṭumbinyai svāhā
201. To she who is the family of the Ambassador of the three, Dattātreya

-२०२-

ॐ दत्तात्रेयप्राणतुल्यायै स्वाहा

oṁ dattātreyaprāṇatulyāyai svāhā
202. To she who is equal to the life force of the Ambassador of the three, Dattātreya

-२०३-

ॐ दत्तात्रेयशरीरिण्यै स्वाहा

oṁ dattātreyaśarīriṇyai svāhā
203. To she who is the embodiment of the Ambassador of the three, Dattātreya

-२०४-

ॐ दत्तात्रेयकृतानन्दायै स्वाहा

oṁ dattātreyakṛtānandāyai svāhā
204. To she gives bliss to those who act like the Ambassador of the three, Dattātreya

-२०५-

ॐ दत्तात्रेयांशसम्भवायै स्वाहा

oṁ dattātreyāṁśasambhavāyai svāhā
205. To she who gives existence to the descendants of the Ambassador of the three, Dattātreya

-२०६-

ॐ दत्तात्रेयविभूतिस्थायै स्वाहा

oṁ dattātreyavibhūtisthāyai svāhā
206. To she who is established in the consecrated offering of the Ambassador of the three, Dattātreya

-२०७-

ॐ दत्तात्रेयनुसारिण्यै स्वाहा

oṁ dattātreyanusāriṇyai svāhā
207. To she is followed by the Ambassador of the three, Dattātreya

-२०८-

ॐ दत्तात्रेयगीतिरतायै स्वाहा

oṁ dattātreyagītiratāyai svāhā
208. To she is always the ultimate song of the Ambassador of the three, Dattātreya

-२०९-

ॐ दत्तात्रेयधनप्रदायै स्वाहा

oṁ dattātreyadhanapradāyai svāhā
209. To she who bestows wealth upon the Ambassador of the three, Dattātreya

-२१०-

ॐ दत्तात्रेयदुःखहरायै स्वाहा

oṁ dattātreyaduḥkhaharāyai svāhā
210. To she takes away the pain from the Ambassador of the three, Dattātreya

-२११-

ॐ दत्तात्रेयवरप्रदायै स्वाहा

oṁ dattātreyavarapradāyai svāhā
211. To she who grants the boon of the Ambassador of the three, Dattātreya

-२१२-

ॐ दत्तात्रेयज्ञानदात्र्यै स्वाहा

oṁ dattātreyajñānadātryai svāhā
212. To she gives wisdom to the Ambassador of the three, Dattātreya

-२१३-

ॐ दत्तात्रेयभयापहायै स्वाहा

oṁ dattātreyabhayāpahāyai svāhā
213. To she who destroys the pain of the Ambassador of the three, Dattātreya

-२१४-

ॐ देवकन्यायै स्वाहा

oṁ devakanyāyai svāhā
214. To she is the daughter of the gods

-२१५-

ॐ देवमान्यायै स्वाहा

oṁ devamānyāyai svāhā
215. To she who is the thoughts of the gods

-२१६-

ॐ देवदुःखविनाशिन्यै स्वाहा

oṁ devaduḥkhavināśinyai svāhā
216. To she who destroys the pain of the gods

-२१७-

ॐ देवसिद्धायै स्वाहा

oṁ devasiddhāyai svāhā
217. To she who is the perfection of the gods

-२१८-

ॐ देवपूज्यायै स्वाहा

oṁ devapūjyāyai svāhā
218. To she who is worshiped by the gods

-२१९-

ॐ देवेज्यायै स्वाहा

oṁ devejyāyai svāhā
219. To she who is offered oblations by the gods

-२२०-

ॐ देववन्दितायै स्वाहा

oṁ devavanditāyai svāhā
220. To she who is praised by the gods

-२२१-

ॐ देवमान्यायै स्वाहा

oṁ devamānyāyai svāhā
221. To she who is obeyed by the gods

-२२२-

ॐ देवधन्यायै स्वाहा

oṁ devadhanyāyai svāhā
222. To she who is the wealth of the gods

-२२३-

ॐ देवविघ्नविनाशिन्यै स्वाहा

oṁ devavighnavināśinyai svāhā
223. To she who destroys the obstacles of the gods

-२२४-

ॐ देवरम्यायै स्वाहा

oṁ devaramyāyai svāhā
224. To she is beautiful among the gods

-२२५-

ॐ देवरतायै स्वाहा

oṁ devaratāyai svāhā
225. To she who is ultimate among the gods

-२२६-

ॐ देवकौतुकतत्परायै स्वाहा

oṁ devakautukatatparāyai svāhā
226. To she who is celebrated as supreme among the gods

-२२७-

ॐ देवक्रीडायै स्वाहा

oṁ devakrīḍāyai svāhā
227. To she who plays with the gods

-२२८-

ॐ देवव्रीडायै स्वाहा

oṁ devavrīḍāyai svāhā
228. To she who is modest before the gods

-२२९-

ॐ देववैरिविनाशिन्यै स्वाहा

oṁ devavairivināśinyai svāhā
229. To she who destroys the enemies of the gods

-२३०-

ॐ देवकामायै स्वाहा

oṁ devakāmāyai svāhā
230. To she who is desired by the gods

-२३१-

ॐ देवरामायै स्वाहा

oṁ devarāmāyai svāhā
231. To she who is beloved by the gods

-२३२-

ॐ देवद्विष्टविनाशिन्यै स्वाहा

oṁ devadviṣṭavināśinyai svāhā
232. To she who destroys the duality of the gods

-२३३-

ॐ देवदेवप्रियायै स्वाहा

oṁ devadevapriyāyai svāhā
233. To she who is the beloved of the god of gods

-२३४-

ॐ देव्यै स्वाहा

oṁ devyai svāhā
234. To she who is the goddess

-२३५-

ॐ देवदानववन्दितायै स्वाहा

oṁ devadānavavanditāyai svāhā
235. To she who is praised by both the gods and the dānavas

-२३६-

ॐ देवदेवरतानन्दायै स्वाहा

oṁ devadevaratānandāyai svāhā
236. To she who gives bliss to the god of gods

-२३७-

ॐ देवदेववरोत्सुकायै स्वाहा

oṁ devadevavarotsukāyai svāhā
237. To she who gives the blessing of happiness to the god of gods

-२३८-

ॐ देवदेवप्रेमरतायै स्वाहा

oṁ devadevapremaratāyai svāhā
238. To she who is the ultimate love of the god of gods

-२३९-

ॐ देवदेवप्रियंवदायै स्वाहा

oṁ devadevapriyaṁvadāyai svāhā
239. To she who speaks pleasantly to the god of gods

-२४०-

ॐ देवदेवप्राणतुल्यायै स्वाहा

oṁ devadevaprāṇatulyāyai svāhā
240. To she who is equal to the life force of the god of gods

-२४१-

ॐ देवदेवनितम्बिन्यै स्वाहा

oṁ devadevanitambinyai svāhā

241. To she whose beautiful hips and buttocks are loved by the god of gods

-२४२-

ॐ देवदेवहृतमनायै स्वाहा

oṁ devadevahṛtamanāyai svāhā

242. To she whose delightful thoughts gladden the god of gods

-२४३-

ॐ देवदेवसुखावहायै स्वाहा

oṁ devadevasukhāvahāyai svāhā

243. To she who conveys comfort and happiness to the god of gods

-२४४-

ॐ देवदेवक्रोडरतायै स्वाहा

oṁ devadevakroḍaratāyai svāhā

244. To she who is the ultimate anger of the god of gods

-२४५-

ॐ देवदेवसुखप्रदायै स्वाहा

oṁ devadevasukhapradāyai svāhā

245. To she who bestows happiness upon the god of gods

-२४६-

ॐ देवदेवमहानन्दायै स्वाहा

oṁ devadevamahānandāyai svāhā

246. To she who is the great bliss of the god of gods

-२४७-

ॐ देवदेवप्रचुम्बितायै स्वाहा

oṁ devadevapracumbitāyai svāhā

247. To she who is the inspiration of the god of gods

-२४८-

ॐ देवदेवोपभुक्ताचयै स्वाहा

oṁ devadevopabhuktācayai svāhā
248. To she who grants enjoyment to the god of gods

-२४९-

ॐ देवदेवानुसेवितायै स्वाहा

oṁ devadevānusevitāyai svāhā
249. To she who serves meticulously the god of gods

-२५०-

ॐ देवदेवगतप्राणायै स्वाहा

oṁ devadevagataprāṇāyai svāhā
250. To she who is the repose of the life force is the god of gods

-२५१-

ॐ देवदेवगतात्मिकायै स्वाहा

oṁ devadevagatātmikāyai svāhā
251. To she who is the foundation of the intrinsic nature of the soul of the god of gods

-२५२-

ॐ देवदेवहर्षदात्र्यै स्वाहा

oṁ devadevaharṣadātryai svāhā
252. To she who gives happiness to the god of gods

-२५३-

ॐ देवदेवसुखप्रदायै स्वाहा

oṁ devadevasukhapradāyai svāhā
253. To she who bestows happiness upon the god of gods

-२५४-

ॐ देवदेवमहानन्दायै स्वाहा

oṁ devadevamahānandāyai svāhā
254. To she who is the great bliss of the god of gods

-२५५-

ॐ देवदेवविलासिन्यै स्वाहा

oṁ devadevavilāsinyai svāhā

255. To she who resides with the god of gods

-२५६-

ॐ देवदेवधर्मपत्न्यै स्वाहा

oṁ devadevadharmapatnyai svāhā

256. To she who is the wife in dharma the god of gods

-२५७-

ॐ देवदेवमनोगतायै स्वाहा

oṁ devadevamanogatāyai svāhā

257. To she who is the foundation of the thoughts of the god of gods

-२५८-

ॐ देवदेववधूर्देवयै स्वाहा

oṁ devadevavadhūrdevayai svāhā

258. To she who is the divine consort of the god of gods

-२५९-

ॐ देवदेवार्चनप्रियायै स्वाहा

oṁ devadevārcanapriyāyai svāhā

259. To she who loves to offer to the god of gods

-२६०-

ॐ देवदेवाङ्गनिलयायै स्वाहा

oṁ devadevāṅganilayāyai svāhā

260. To she who resides in every limb of the god of gods

-२६१-

ॐ देवदेवाङ्गशायिन्यै स्वाहा

oṁ devadevāṅgaśāyinyai svāhā

261. To she who rests in every limb of the god of gods

-२६२-

ॐ देवदेवाङ्गसुखिन्यै स्वाहा

oṁ devadevāṅgasukhinyai svāhā

262. To she who is comfortable or happy in every limb of the god of gods

-२६३-

ॐ देवदेवाङ्गवासिन्यै स्वाहा

oṁ devadevāṅgavāsinyai svāhā

263. To she who dwells in every limb of the god of gods

-२६४-

ॐ देवदेवाङ्गभूषायै स्वाहा

oṁ devadevāṅgabhūṣāyai svāhā

264. To she who shines in every limb of the god of gods

-२६५-

ॐ देवदेवाङ्गभूषणायै स्वाहा

oṁ devadevāṅgabhūṣaṇāyai svāhā

265. To she who causes the shining of every limb of the god of gods

-२६६-

ॐ देवदेवप्रियकर्यै स्वाहा

oṁ devadevapriyakaryai svāhā

266. To she who is the cause of love of the god of gods

-२६७-

ॐ देवदेवाप्रियान्तकृते स्वाहा

oṁ devadevāpriyāntakṛte svāhā

267. To she who is the cause of the ultimate love of the god of gods

-२६८-

ॐ देवदेवप्रियप्राणायै स्वाहा

oṁ devadevapriyaprāṇāyai svāhā

268. To she who is the life force of the love of the god of gods

-२६९-

ॐ देवदेवप्रियात्मिकायै स्वाहा

oṁ devadevapriyātmikāyai svāhā

269. To she who is the intrinsic nature of the beloved soul of the god of gods

-२७०-

ॐ देवदेवार्चकप्राणायै स्वाहा

oṁ devadevārcakaprāṇāyai svāhā

270. To she who is the life force of the worshiper of the god of gods

-२७१-

ॐ देवदेवार्चकप्रियायै स्वाहा

oṁ devadevārcakapriyāyai svāhā

271. To she who is the beloved of the worshiper of the god of gods

-२७२-

ॐ देवदेवार्चकोत्साहायै स्वाहा

oṁ devadevārcakotsāhāyai svāhā

272. To she who is the enthusiasm of the worshiper of the god of gods

-२७३-

ॐ देवदेवार्चकप्रियायै स्वाहा

oṁ devadevārcakapriyāyai svāhā

273. To she who is the beloved of the worshiper of the god of gods

-२७४-

ॐ देवदेवार्चकाविघ्नायै स्वाहा

oṁ devadevārcakāvighnāyai svāhā

274. To she who removes all obstacles from the worshiper of the god of gods

-२७५-

ॐ देवदेवप्रस्वे स्वाहा

oṁ devadevaprasve svāhā
275. To she who is pleasant or agreeable to the god of gods

-२७६-

ॐ देवदेवस्य जनन्यै स्वाहा

oṁ devadevasya jananyai svāhā
276. To she who is the mother of the god of gods

-२७७-

ॐ देवदेवविधायिन्यै स्वाहा

oṁ devadevavidhāyinyai svāhā
277. To she who is the divisions or individual aspects of the god of gods

-२७८-

ॐ देवदेवस्यरमण्यै स्वाहा

oṁ devadevasyaramaṇyai svāhā
278. To she who is the beautiful one of the god of gods

-२७९-

ॐ देवदेवहृदाश्रयायै स्वाहा

oṁ devadevahṛdāśrayāyai svāhā
279. To she who takes refuge in the heart of the god of gods

-२८०-

ॐ देवदेवेष्टदेवायै स्वाहा

oṁ devadeveṣṭadevāyai svāhā
280. To she who is the chosen goddess to be worshiped by the god of gods

-२८१-

ॐ देवतापसपातिन्यै स्वाहा

oṁ devatāpasapātinyai svāhā
281. To she who rules over the austerities of the gods

-२८२-

ॐ देवताभावसन्तुष्टायै स्वाहा

oṁ devatābhāvasantuṣṭāyai svāhā

282. To she who is the attitude of satisfaction within the gods

-२८३-

ॐ देवताभावतोषितायै स्वाहा

oṁ devatābhāvatoṣitāyai svāhā

283. To she who gives the attitude of satisfaction to the gods

-२८४-

ॐ देवताभाववरदायै स्वाहा

oṁ devatābhāvavaradāyai svāhā

284. To she who gives the boon of positive attitude to the gods

-२८५-

ॐ देवताभावसिद्धिदायै स्वाहा

oṁ devatābhāvasiddhidāyai svāhā

285. To she who gives the attitude of perfection to the gods

-२८६-

ॐ देवताभावसंसिद्धायै स्वाहा

oṁ devatābhāvasaṁsiddhāyai svāhā

286. To she who gives the attitude of all perfection to the gods

-२८७-

ॐ देवताभावसम्भवायै स्वाहा

oṁ devatābhāvasambhavāyai svāhā

287. To she gives birth to the attitude of agreement among to the gods

-२८८-

ॐ देवताभावसुखिन्यै स्वाहा

oṁ devatābhāvasukhinyai svāhā

288. To she who is the attitude of happiness among the gods

-२८९-

ॐ देवताभाववन्दितायै स्वाहा

oṁ devatābhāvavanditāyai svāhā

289. To she who is the attitude of praise among the gods

-२९०-

ॐ देवताभावसुप्रीतायै स्वाहा

oṁ devatābhāvasuprītāyai svāhā

290. To she who is the attitude of excellent love among the gods

-२९१-

ॐ देवताभावहर्षदायै स्वाहा

oṁ devatābhāvaharṣadāyai svāhā

291. To she who gives the attitude of joy among the gods

-२९२-

ॐ देवताविघ्नहन्त्र्यै स्वाहा

oṁ devatāvighnahantryai svāhā

292. To she removes all obstacles from the gods

-२९३-

ॐ देवताद्विष्टनाशिन्यै स्वाहा

oṁ devatādviṣṭanāśinyai svāhā

293. To she who destroys duality from the gods

-२९४-

ॐ देवतापूजितपदायै स्वाहा

oṁ devatāpūjitapadāyai svāhā

294. To she who gives worship to the gods

-२९५-

ॐ देवताप्रेमतोषितायै स्वाहा

oṁ devatāprematoṣitāyai svāhā

295. To she who is satisfied with love for the gods

-२९६-

ॐ देवतागारनिलयायै स्वाहा

oṁ devatāgāranilayāyai svāhā

296. To she who removes the poison from the gods

-२९७-

ॐ देवतासौख्यदायिन्यै स्वाहा

oṁ devatāsaukhyadāyinyai svāhā

297. To she who gives comfort to the gods

-२९८-

ॐ देवतानिजभावायै स्वाहा

oṁ devatānijabhāvāyai svāhā

298. To she who is the intrinsic attitude of the gods

-२९९-

ॐ देवताहृतमानसायै स्वाहा

oṁ devatāhṛtamānasāyai svāhā

299. To she who is the delightful thoughts of the gods

-३००-

ॐ देवताकृतपादार्चायै स्वाहा

oṁ devatākṛtapādārcāyai svāhā

300. To she who makes offerings to the gods

-३०१-

ॐ देवताहृतभक्तिकायै स्वाहा

oṁ devatāhṛtabhaktikāyai svāhā

301. To she who is delighted with those who offer devotion to gods

-३०२-

ॐ देवतागर्वमध्यस्थायै स्वाहा

oṁ devatāgarvamadhyasthāyai svāhā

302. To she who resides in the midst of the pride of the gods

-३०३-

ॐ देवतायै स्वाहा

oṁ devatāyai svāhā
303. To she who is all of the gods

-३०४-

ॐ देवतायै स्वाहा

oṁ devatāyai svāhā
304. To she who is all of the gods

-३०५-

ॐ दनवे स्वाहा

oṁ danave svāhā
305. To she who is the mother of the dānavas

-३०६-

ॐ दुंदुर्गायैनमोनाम्न्यै स्वाहा

oṁ duṁdurgāyainamonāmnyai svāhā
306. To she who is the name to which we bow dum - to Durga

-३०७-

ॐ दुं फट्मन्त्रस्वरूपिण्यै स्वाहा

oṁ duṁ phaṭmantrasvarūpiṇyai svāhā
307. To she who is the intrinsic nature of the mantras dum and phat - purify

-३०८-

ॐ दुं नमोमन्त्ररूपायै स्वाहा

oṁ duṁ namomantrarūpāyai svāhā
308. To she who is the form of the mantra dum - I bow

-३०९-

ॐ दुंनमोमूर्त्तिकात्मिकायै स्वाहा

oṁ duṁnamomūrttikātmikāyai svāhā
309. To she who is the intrinsic nature of the image of worship dum - I bow

-३१०-

ॐ दूरदर्शीप्रियायै स्वाहा

oṁ dūradarśīpriyāyai svāhā
310. To she loves extended vision

-३११-

ॐ दुष्टायै स्वाहा

oṁ duṣṭāyai svāhā
311. To she who is with the wicked

-३१२-

ॐ दुष्टभूतनिषेवितायै स्वाहा

oṁ duṣṭabhūtaniṣevitāyai svāhā
312. To she who is served by the elements of wickedness

-३१३-

ॐ दूरदर्शीप्रेमरतायै स्वाहा

oṁ dūradarśīpremaratāyai svāhā
313. To she is the ultimate love of those with extended vision

-३१४-

ॐ दूरदर्शीप्रियंवदायै स्वाहा

oṁ dūradarśīpriyaṁvadāyai svāhā
314. To she who speaks the beloved words of those with extended vision

-३१५-

ॐ दूरदर्शीसिद्धिदात्र्यै स्वाहा

oṁ dūradarśīsiddhidātryai svāhā
315. To she who gives perfection to those with extended vision

-३१६-

ॐ दूरदर्शीप्रतोषितायै स्वाहा

oṁ dūradarśīpratoṣitāyai svāhā
316. To she who gives satisfaction to those with extended vision

-३१७-

ॐ दूरदर्शीकण्ठसंस्थायै स्वाहा

oṁ dūradarśīkaṇṭhasaṁsthāyai svāhā

317. To she who resides in the throat of those with extended vision

-३१८-

ॐ दूरदर्शीप्रहर्षितायै स्वाहा

oṁ dūradarśīpraharṣitāyai svāhā

318. To she who gives gladness to those with extended vision

-३१९-

ॐ दूरदर्शीगृहीतार्चायै स्वाहा

oṁ dūradarśīgṛhītārcāyai svāhā

319. To she who offers in the homes of those with extended vision

-३२०-

ॐ दूरदर्शीप्रतर्पितायै स्वाहा

oṁ dūradarśīpratarpitāyai svāhā

320. To she who is the ancestral offering made by those with extended vision

-३२१-

ॐ दूरदर्शीप्राणतुल्यायै स्वाहा

oṁ dūradarśīprāṇatulyāyai svāhā

321. To she who is equal to the life force of those with extended vision

-३२२-

ॐ दूरदर्शीसुखप्रदायै स्वाहा

oṁ dūradarśīsukhapradāyai svāhā

322. To she who bestows happiness upon those with extended vision

-३२३-

ॐ दूरदर्शीभ्रान्तिहरायै स्वाहा

oṁ dūradarśībhrāntiharāyai svāhā

323. To she who takes away the confusion from those with extended vision

-३२४-

ॐ दूरदर्शीहृदास्पदायै स्वाहा

oṁ dūradarśīhṛdāspadāyai svāhā

324. To she who moves in the heart of those with extended vision

-३२५-

ॐ दूरदर्श्यरिविद्भावायै स्वाहा

oṁ dūradarśyarividbhāvāyai svāhā

325. To she who destroys the attitude of enmity with those of extended vision

-३२६-

ॐ दीर्घदर्शिप्रमोदिन्यै स्वाहा

oṁ dīrghadarśipramodinyai svāhā

326. To she who gives delight to those who have intuitive vision

-३२७-

ॐ दीर्घदर्शीप्राणतुल्यायै स्वाहा

oṁ dīrghadarśīprāṇatulyāyai svāhā

327. To she who is equal to the life force of those with intuitive vision

-३२८-

ॐ दीर्घदर्शीवरप्रदायै स्वाहा

oṁ dīrghadarśīvarapradāyai svāhā

328. To she who gives the boon to those with intuitive vision

-३२९-

ॐ दीर्घदर्शीहर्षदात्र्यै स्वाहा

oṁ dīrghadarśīharṣadātryai svāhā
329. To she who gives gladness to those with intuitive vision

-३३०-

ॐ दीर्घदर्शीप्रहर्षितायै स्वाहा

oṁ dīrghadarśīpraharṣitāyai svāhā
330. To see who gives joy to those with intuitive vision

-३३१-

ॐ दीर्घदर्शीमहानन्दायै स्वाहा

oṁ dīrghadarśīmahānandāyai svāhā
331. To see who is the great bliss of those with intuitive vision

-३३२-

ॐ दीर्घदर्शीगृहालयायै स्वाहा

oṁ dīrghadarśīgṛhālayāyai svāhā
332. To she who resides in the homes of those with intuitive vision

-३३३-

ॐ दीर्घदर्शीगृहीतार्चायै स्वाहा

oṁ dīrghadarśīgṛhītārcāyai svāhā
333. To she who offers in the homes of those with intuitive vision

-३३४-

ॐ दीर्घदर्शीहृतार्हणायै स्वाहा

oṁ dīrghadarśīhṛtārhaṇāyai svāhā
334. To she who is the illumination in the hearts of those with intuitive vision

-३३५-

ॐ दयायै स्वाहा

oṁ dayāyai svāhā
335. To she who gives compassion

-३३६-

ॐ दानवत्यै स्वाहा

oṁ dānavatyai svāhā
336. To she who is the spirit of the dānavas

-३३७-

ॐ दात्र्यै स्वाहा

oṁ dātryai svāhā
337. To she who is the giver

-३३८-

ॐ दयालवे स्वाहा

oṁ dayālave svāhā
338. To she who is the repository of compassion

-३३९-

ॐ दीनवत्सलायै स्वाहा

oṁ dīnavatsalāyai svāhā
339. To she who is the affectionate child of the lowly

-३४०-

ॐ दयाद्रायै स्वाहा

oṁ dayārdrāyai svāhā
340. To she who bestows compassion

-३४१-

ॐ दयाशीलायै स्वाहा

oṁ dayāśīlāyai svāhā
341. To she who is fixed in compassion

-३४२-

ॐ दयाढ्यायै स्वाहा

oṁ dayāḍhyāyai svāhā
342. To she who rides upon compassion

-३४३-

ॐ दयात्मिकायै स्वाहा

oṁ dayātmikāyai svāhā

343. To she who is the intrinsic nature of the soul of compassion

-३४४-

ॐ दयायै स्वाहा

oṁ dayāyai svāhā

344. To she who is compassion

-३४५-

ॐ दानवत्यै स्वाहा

oṁ dānavatyai svāhā

345. To she who is the spirit of the dānavas

-३४६-

ॐ दात्र्यै स्वाहा

oṁ dātryai svāhā

346. To she who is the giver

-३४७-

ॐ दयाल्वे स्वाहा

oṁ dayālave svāhā

347. To she who is the repository of compassion

-३४८-

ॐ दीनवत्सलायै स्वाहा

oṁ dīnavatsalāyai svāhā

348. To she who is the affectionate child of the lowly

-३४९-

ॐ दयाद्रायै स्वाहा

oṁ dayārdrāyai svāhā

349. To she who bestows compassion

-३५०-

ॐ दयाशीलायै स्वाहा

oṁ dayāśīlāyai svāhā
350. To she who is fixed in compassion

-३५१-

ॐ दयाढ्यायै स्वाहा

oṁ dayāḍhyāyai svāhā
351. To she who rides upon compassion

-३५२-

ॐ दयात्मिकायै स्वाहा

oṁ dayātmikāyai svāhā
352. To she who is the intrinsic nature of the soul of compassion

-३५३-

ॐ दयाम्बुधये स्वाहा

oṁ dayāmbudhaye svāhā
353. To she who is the intelligence of compassion

-३५४-

ॐ दयासारायै स्वाहा

oṁ dayāsārāyai svāhā
354. To she who is the ocean of compassion

-३५५-

ॐ दयासागरपारगायै स्वाहा

oṁ dayāsāgarapāragāyai svāhā
355. To she is a part of the ocean of compassion

-३५६-

ॐ दयासिन्धवे स्वाहा

oṁ dayāsindhave svāhā
356. To she who is within the ocean of compassion

-३५७-

ॐ दयाभारायै स्वाहा

oṁ dayābhārāyai svāhā
357. To she who has the obligation of compassion

-३५८-

ॐ दयावत्करुणाकर्यै स्वाहा

oṁ dayāvatkaruṇākaryai svāhā
358. To she who is the cause and effect of giving compassion

-३५९-

ॐ दयावद्वत्सलायै स्वाहा

oṁ dayāvadvatsalāyai svāhā
359. To she who is the affectionate child of compassion

-३६०-

ॐ देव्यै स्वाहा

oṁ devyai svāhā
360. To she who is the goddess

-३६१-

ॐ दयायै स्वाहा

oṁ dayāyai svāhā
361. To she who is compassion

-३६२-

ॐ दानरतायै स्वाहा

oṁ dānaratāyai svāhā
362. To she who is the ultimate among the dānavas

-३६३-

ॐ दयावद्भक्तिसुखिन्यै स्वाहा

oṁ dayāvadbhaktisukhinyai svāhā
363. To she who is the happiness of devotees who give compassion

-३६४-

ॐ दयावत्परितोषितायै स्वाहा

oṁ dayāvatparitoṣitāyai svāhā
364. To she who is the satisfaction of those who give compassion

-३६५-

ॐ दयावत्स्नेहनिरतायै स्वाहा

oṁ dayāvatsnehaniratāyai svāhā
365. To she who is the ultimate affection for those who give compassion

-३६६-

ॐ दयावत्प्रतिपादिकायै स्वाहा

oṁ dayāvatpratipādikāyai svāhā
366. To she who walks every step with those who give compassion

-३६७-

ॐ दयावत्त्राणकर्त्र्यै स्वाहा

oṁ dayāvattrāṇakartryai svāhā
367. To she who gives protection to those who give compassion

-३६८-

ॐ दयावन्मुक्तिदायिन्यै स्वाहा

oṁ dayāvanmuktidāyinyai svāhā
368. To she who gives liberation to those who give compassion

-३६९-

ॐ दयावद्भावसन्तुष्टायै स्वाहा

oṁ dayāvadbhāvasantuṣṭāyai svāhā
369. To she who gives the attitude of complete satisfaction to those who give compassion

-३७०-

ॐ दयावत्परितोषितायै स्वाहा

oṁ dayāvatparitoṣitāyai svāhā

370. To she who gives satisfaction to those who give compassion

-३७१-

ॐ दयावत्तारणपरायै स्वाहा

oṁ dayāvattāraṇaparāyai svāhā

371. To she who takes across to the highest goal those who give compassion

-३७२-

ॐ दयावत्सिद्धिदायिन्यै स्वाहा

oṁ dayāvatsiddhidāyinyai svāhā

372. To she who gives perfection to those who give compassion

-३७३-

ॐ दयावत्पुत्रवद्भावायै स्वाहा

oṁ dayāvatputravadbhāvāyai svāhā

373. To she who has the attitude of a son's wife for those who give compassion

-३७४-

ॐ दयावत्पुत्ररूपिण्यै स्वाहा

oṁ dayāvatputrarūpiṇyai svāhā

374. To she who is the intrinsic nature of the form of a child for those who give compassion

-३७५-

ॐ दयावद्देहनिलयायै स्वाहा

oṁ dayāvaddehanilayāyai svāhā

375. To she who resides within the body of those who give compassion

-३७६-

ॐ दयाबन्धवे स्वाहा

oṁ dayābandhave svāhā
376. To she who is in the family of those who give compassion

-३७७-

ॐ दयाश्रयायै स्वाहा

oṁ dayāśrayāyai svāhā
377. To she who takes refuge in compassion

-३७८-

ॐ दयालुवात्सल्यकर्यै स्वाहा

oṁ dayāluvātsalyakaryai svāhā
378. To she who causes the attitude of an affectionate child in those who are compassionate

-३७९-

ॐ दयालुसिद्धिदायिन्यै स्वाहा

oṁ dayālusiddhidāyinyai svāhā
379. To she who gives perfection to those who are compassionate

-३८०-

ॐ दयालुशरणासक्तायै स्वाहा

oṁ dayāluśaraṇāsaktāyai svāhā
380. To she who empowers to take refuge with the compassionate

-३८१-

ॐ दयालुदेहमन्दिरायै स्वाहा

oṁ dayāludehamandirāyai svāhā
381. To she whose temple is within the bodies of those who are compassionate

-३८२-

ॐ दयालुभक्तिभावस्थायै स्वाहा

oṁ dayālubhaktibhāvasthāyai svāhā

382. To she who resides within the attitude of devotion of those who are compassionate

-३८३-

ॐ दयालुप्राणरूपिण्यै स्वाहा

oṁ dayāluprāṇarūpiṇyai svāhā

383. To she who is the intrinsic nature of the form of the life force of those who are compassionate

-३८४-

ॐ दयालुसुखदायै

oṁ dayālusukhadāyai

384. To she gives happiness to those who are compassionate

-३८५-

ॐ दम्भायै स्वाहा

om dambhāyai svāhā

385. To she who resides in deceit

-३८६-

ॐ दयालुप्रेमवर्षिण्यै स्वाहा

oṁ dayālupremavarṣiṇyai svāhā

386. To she who causes a rain of love upon those who are compassionate

-३८७-

ॐ दयालुवशगायै स्वाहा

oṁ dayāluvaśagāyai svāhā

387. To she who moves to embrace those who are compassionate

-३८८-

ॐ दीर्घायै स्वाहा

oṁ dīrghāyai svāhā
388. To she who is expansive

-३८९-

ॐ दीर्घाङ्ग्यै स्वाहा

oṁ dīrghāṅgyai svāhā
389. To she who has expansive limbs

-३९०-

ॐ दीर्घलोचनायै स्वाहा

oṁ dīrghalocanāyai svāhā
390. To she who has expansive eyes

-३९१-

ॐ दीर्घनेत्रायै स्वाहा

oṁ dīrghanetrāyai svāhā
391. To she who has expansive eyes

-३९२-

ॐ दीर्घचक्षे स्वाहा

oṁ dīrghacakṣe svāhā
392. To she who has expansive eyes

-३९३-

ॐ दीर्घबाहुलतात्मिकायै स्वाहा

oṁ dīrghabāhulatātmikāyai svāhā
393. To she who is the intrinsic nature of the soul who has expansive arms

-३९४-

ॐ दीर्घकेश्यै स्वाहा

oṁ dīrghakeśyai svāhā
394. To she who has expansive hair

-३९५-

ॐ दीर्घमुख्यै स्वाहा

oṁ dīrghamukhyai svāhā
395. To she who has an expansive mouth

-३९६-

ॐ दीर्घघोणायै स्वाहा

oṁ dīrghaghoṇāyai svāhā
396. To she who has an expansive nose

-३९७-

ॐ दारुणायै स्वाहा

oṁ dāruṇāyai svāhā
397. To she who is excellent

-३९८-

ॐ दारुणासुरहन्त्र्यै स्वाहा

oṁ dāruṇāsurahantryai svāhā
398. To she who is excellent at destroying asuras

-३९९-

ॐ दारुणासुरदारिण्यै स्वाहा

oṁ dāruṇāsuradāriṇyai svāhā
399. To she who is the excellent enemy of asuras

-४००-

ॐ दारुणाहवकर्त्र्यै स्वाहा

oṁ dāruṇāhavakartryai svāhā
400. To she who makes the offering of excellence

-४०१-

ॐ दारुणाहवहर्षितायै स्वाहा

oṁ dāruṇāhavaharṣitāyai svāhā
401. To she who is delighted by the offering of excellence

-४०२-

ॐ दारुणाहवहोमाढ्यायै स्वाहा

oṁ dāruṇāhavahomāḍhyāyai svāhā

402. To she who rides upon the fire ceremony offered with excellence

-४०३-

ॐ दारुणाचलनाशिन्यै स्वाहा

oṁ dāruṇācalanāśinyai svāhā

403. To she who destroys the inability to move towards excellence

-४०४-

ॐ दारुणाचारनिरतायै स्वाहा

oṁ dāruṇācāraniratāyai svāhā

404. To she who is the ultimate who moves towards excellence

-४०५-

ॐ दारुणोत्सवहर्षितायै स्वाहा

oṁ dāruṇotsavaharṣitāyai svāhā

405. To she who is delighted at the festival of excellence

-४०६-

ॐ दारुणोद्यतरूपायै स्वाहा

oṁ dāruṇodyatarūpāyai svāhā

406. To she who is the form of the highest excellence

-४०७-

ॐ दारुणारीनिवारिण्यै स्वाहा

oṁ dāruṇārīnivāriṇyai svāhā

407. To she who destroys the enemies to excellence

-४०८-

ॐ दारुणेक्षणसंयुक्तायै स्वाहा

oṁ dāruṇekṣaṇasaṁyuktāyai svāhā

408. To she who unites with excellence in but a moment

-४०९-

ॐ दोश्चतुष्कविराजितायै स्वाहा

oṁ doścatuṣkavirājitāyai svāhā

409. To she who resides within the four angles

-४१०-

ॐ दशदोष्कायै स्वाहा

oṁ daśadoṣkāyai svāhā

410. To she embodies ten angles

-४११-

ॐ दशभुजायै स्वाहा

oṁ daśabhujāyai svāhā

411. To she who has ten arms

-४१२-

ॐ दशबाहुविराजितायै स्वाहा

oṁ daśabāhuvirājitāyai svāhā

412. To she who resides with the ten-armed one

-४१३-

ॐ दशास्त्रधारिण्यै स्वाहा

oṁ daśāstradhāriṇyai svāhā

413. To she who holds ten weapons

-४१४-

ॐ देव्यै स्वाहा

oṁ devyai svāhā

414. To she who is the goddess

-४१५-

ॐ दशदिक्ख्यातविक्रमायै स्वाहा

oṁ daśadikkhyātavikramāyai svāhā

415. To she who divides the ten directions

-४१६-

ॐ दशरथार्चितपदायै स्वाहा

oṁ daśarathārcitapadāyai svāhā
416. To she who moves to make offerings to the one of ten chariots, (Daśarath, father of Rāma, moved so quickly in his chariot in the war between the gods and asuras, that he seemed to come from every direction, and so was given the name Daśarath-who comes from the ten directions, or who drives ten chariots.)

-४१७-

ॐ दाशरथिप्रियायै स्वाहा

oṁ dāśarathipriyāyai svāhā
417. To she who is the beloved of Daśarath

-४१८-

ॐ दाशरथिप्रेमतुष्टायै स्वाहा

oṁ dāśarathiprematuṣṭāyai svāhā
418. To she who is satisfied with the love of Daśarath

-४१९-

ॐ दाशरथिरतिप्रियायै स्वाहा

oṁ dāśarathiratipriyāyai svāhā
419. To she who loves the affection of Daśarath

-४२०-

ॐ दाशरथिप्रियकर्यै स्वाहा

oṁ dāśarathipriyakaryai svāhā
420. To she who causes the love of Daśarath

-४२१-

ॐ दाशरथिप्रियंवदायै स्वाहा

oṁ dāśarathipriyaṁvadāyai svāhā
421. To she who speaks of the love of Daśarath

-४२२-

ॐ दाशरथीष्टसन्दात्र्यै स्वाहा

oṁ dāśarathīṣṭasandātryai svāhā
422. To she who binds the chosen form of worship of Daśarath

-४२३-

ॐ दाशरथीष्टदेवतायै स्वाहा

oṁ dāśarathīṣṭadevatāyai svāhā
423. To she who is the goddess in the chosen form of worship of Daśarath

-४२४-

ॐ दाशरथिद्वेषिनाशायै स्वाहा

oṁ dāśarathidveṣināśāyai svāhā
424. To she who destroys all enmity with Daśarath

-४२५-

ॐ दाशरथ्यानुकूल्यदायै स्वाहा

oṁ dāśarathyānukūlyadāyai svāhā
425. To she who gives agreement to the followers of Daśarath

-४२६-

ॐ दाशरथिप्रियतमायै स्वाहा

oṁ dāśarathipriyatamāyai svāhā
426. To she who is the beloved of Daśarath

-४२७-

ॐ दाशरथिप्रपूजितायै स्वाहा

oṁ dāśarathiprapūjitāyai svāhā
427. To she who is worshiped by Daśarath

-४२८-

ॐ दशाननारिसम्पूज्यायै स्वाहा

oṁ daśānanārisampūjyāyai svāhā
428. To she who is worshiped as the circumstances of humanity

-४२९-

ॐ दशाननारिदेवतायै स्वाहा

oṁ daśānanāridevatāyai svāhā
429. To she who is the goddess of the circumstances of humanity

-४३०-

ॐ दशाननारिप्रमदायै स्वाहा

oṁ daśānanāripramadāyai svāhā
430. To she who is the giver of love in the circumstances of humanity

-४३१-

ॐ दशाननारिजन्मभ्वे स्वाहा

oṁ daśānanārijanmabhve svāhā
431. To she who gives birth to all beings born in the circumstances of humanity

-४३२-

ॐ दशाननारिरतिदायै स्वाहा

oṁ daśānanāriratidāyai svāhā
432. To she who gives affection in the circumstances of humanity

-४३३-

ॐ दशाननारिसेवितायै स्वाहा

oṁ daśānanārisevitāyai svāhā
433. To she who serves the circumstances of humanity

-४३४-

ॐ दशाननारिसुखदायै स्वाहा

oṁ daśānanārisukhadāyai svāhā
434. To she who gives happiness in the circumstances of humanity

-४३५-

ॐ दशाननारिवैरिहृते स्वाहा

oṁ daśānanārivairihṛte svāhā

435. To she who gives joy even to the enemies of the circumstances of humanity

-४३६-

ॐ दशाननारीष्टदेव्यै स्वाहा

oṁ daśānanārīṣṭadevyai svāhā

436. To she who is the goddess who is the chosen form of worship for the circumstances of humanity

-४३७-

ॐ दशग्रीवारिवन्दितायै स्वाहा

oṁ daśagrīvārivanditāyai svāhā

437. To she who is praised by the enemies of the one with ten necks (Rāvaṇa had ten necks, which support his ten heads)

-४३८-

ॐ दशग्रीवारिजनन्यै स्वाहा

oṁ daśagrīvārijananyai svāhā

438. To she who is the mother of the enemies of the one with ten necks

-४३९-

ॐ दशग्रीवारिभाविन्यै स्वाहा

oṁ daśagrīvāribhāvinyai svāhā

439. To she who creates the attitude of the enemies of the one with ten necks

-४४०-

ॐ दशग्रीवारिसहितायै स्वाहा

oṁ daśagrīvārisahitāyai svāhā

440. To she who is written about in the literature of the enemies of the one with ten necks

-४४१-

ॐ दशग्रीवसभाजितायै स्वाहा

oṁ daśagrīvasabhājitāyai svāhā
441. To she is extolled by the one with ten necks

-४४२-

ॐ दशग्रीवारिरमण्यै स्वाहा

oṁ daśagrīvāriramaṇyai svāhā
442. To she who is romanced by the enemies of the one with ten necks

-४४३-

ॐ दशग्रीववधूरप्यै स्वाहा

oṁ daśagrīvavadhūrapyai svāhā
443. To she is near to the daughter-in-law of the one with ten necks

-४४४-

ॐ दशग्रीवनाशकर्त्र्यै स्वाहा

oṁ daśagrīvanāśakartryai svāhā
444. To she who is the cause of the destruction of the one with ten necks

-४४५-

ॐ दशग्रीववरप्रदायै स्वाहा

oṁ daśagrīvavarapradāyai svāhā
445. To she who gave the boon to the one with ten necks

-४४६-

ॐ दशग्रीवपुरस्थायै स्वाहा

oṁ daśagrīvapurasthāyai svāhā
446. To she who resides in the city of the one with ten necks

-४४७-

ॐ दशग्रीववधोत्सुकायै स्वाहा

oṁ daśagrīvavadhotsukāyai svāhā
447. To she who receives the greatest delight from the slaying of the one with ten necks

-४४८-

ॐ दशग्रीवप्रीतिदात्र्यै स्वाहा

oṁ daśagrīvaprītidātryai svāhā
448. To she who is the creator of the beloved of the one with ten necks

-४४९-

ॐ दशग्रीवविनाशिन्यै स्वाहा

oṁ daśagrīvavināśinyai svāhā
449. To she who is the destroyer of the one with ten necks

-४५०-

ॐ दशग्रीवहवकर्यै स्वाहा

oṁ daśagrīvahavakaryai svāhā
450. To she who is the cause of the offering of the one with ten necks

-४५१-

ॐ दशग्रीवानपायिन्यै स्वाहा

oṁ daśagrīvānapāyinyai svāhā
451. To she who removes all the obstacles from the one with ten necks

-४५२-

ॐ दशग्रीवप्रियावन्द्यायै स्वाहा

oṁ daśagrīvapriyāvandyāyai svāhā
452. To she who is praised as the beloved of the one with ten necks

-४५३-

ॐ दशग्रीवाहृतायै स्वाहा

oṁ daśagrīvāhṛtāyai svāhā
453. To she who causes the displeasure of the one with ten necks

-४५४-

ॐ दशग्रीवाहितकर्यै स्वाहा

oṁ daśagrīvāhitakaryai svāhā
454. To she who causes detriment to the one with ten necks

-४५५-

ॐ दशग्रीवेश्वरप्रियायै स्वाहा

oṁ daśagrīveśvarapriyāyai svāhā
455. To she who is the beloved of the lord of the one with ten necks

-४५६-

ॐ दशग्रीवेश्वरप्राणायै स्वाहा

oṁ daśagrīveśvaraprāṇāyai svāhā
456. To she who is the life force of the lord of the one with ten necks

-४५७-

ॐ दशग्रीववरप्रदायै स्वाहा

oṁ daśagrīvavarapradāyai svāhā
457. To she who gives the boon to the one with ten necks

-४५८-

ॐ दशग्रीवेश्वररतायै स्वाहा

oṁ daśagrīveśvararatāyai svāhā
458. To she who is the ultimate of the lord of the one with ten necks

-४५९-

ॐ दशवर्षीयकन्यकायै स्वाहा

oṁ daśavarṣīyakanyakāyai svāhā
459. To she who is the manifestation of the greatness of the ten young girls

-४६०-

ॐ दशवर्षीयबालायै स्वाहा

oṁ daśavarṣīyabālāyai svāhā
460. To she who is the greatness of the ten children

-४६१-

ॐ दशवर्षीयवासिन्यै स्वाहा

oṁ daśavarṣīyavāsinyai svāhā
461. To she who resides in the greatness of the ten

-४६२-

ॐ दशपापहरायै स्वाहा

oṁ daśapāpaharāyai svāhā
462. To she who takes away the ten kinds of sin

-४६३-

ॐ दम्यायै स्वाहा

oṁ damyāyai svāhā
463. To she who has self-control

-४६४-

ॐ दशहस्तविभूषितायै स्वाहा

oṁ daśahastavibhūṣitāyai svāhā
464. To she who displays ten hands

-४६५-

ॐ दशशस्त्रलसद्दोष्कायै स्वाहा

oṁ daśaśastralasaddoṣkāyai svāhā
465. To she who wields ten weapons against all defects

-४६६-

ॐ दशदिक्पालवन्दितायै स्वाहा

oṁ daśadikpālavanditāyai svāhā
466. To she who is praised by the protectors of the ten directions

-४६७-

ॐ दशावताररूपायै स्वाहा

oṁ daśāvatārarūpāyai svāhā

467. To she who is the form of the ten avatars, incarnations of god

-४६८-

ॐ दशावताररूपिण्यै स्वाहा

oṁ daśāvatārarūpiṇyai svāhā

468. To she who is the intrinsic nature of the form of the ten avatars

-४६९-

ॐ दशविद्याभिन्नदेव्यै स्वाहा

oṁ daśavidyābhinnadevyai svāhā

469. To she who is the goddess who distinguishes the ten forms of knowledge

-४७०-

ॐ दशप्राणस्वरूपिण्यै स्वाहा

oṁ daśaprāṇasvarūpiṇyai svāhā

470. To she who is the intrinsic nature of the form of the life force of the ten

-४७१-

ॐ दशविद्यास्वरूपायै स्वाहा

oṁ daśavidyāsvarūpāyai svāhā

471. To she who is the intrinsic nature of the ten forms of knowledge

-४७२-

ॐ दशविद्यामय्यै स्वाहा

oṁ daśavidyāmayyai svāhā

472. To she is the embodiment of the ten forms of knowledge

-४७३-

ॐ दृक्स्वरूपायै स्वाहा

oṁ dṛksvarūpāyai svāhā

473. To she who is the intrinsic nature of the form of respect

-४७४-

ॐ दृक्प्रदात्र्यै स्वाहा

oṁ dṛkpradātryai svāhā
474. To she who gives respect

-४७५-

ॐ दृग्रूपायै स्वाहा

oṁ dṛgrūpāyai svāhā
475. To she who is the form of respect

-४७६-

ॐ दृक्प्रकाशिन्यै स्वाहा

oṁ dṛkprakāśinyai svāhā
476. To she who illuminates respect

-४७७-

ॐ दिगन्तरायै स्वाहा

oṁ digantarāyai svāhā
477. To she who is the ultimate in all directions

-४७८-

ॐ दिगन्तरस्थायै स्वाहा

oṁ digantarasthāyai svāhā
478. To she who is established as the ultimate in all directions

-४७९-

ॐ दिगम्बरविलासिन्यै स्वाहा

oṁ digambaravilāsinyai svāhā
479. To she who desires to be clothed by all directions, or wearing space as a garment

-४८०-

ॐ दिगम्बरसमाजस्थायै स्वाहा

oṁ digambarasamājasthāyai svāhā
480. To she who is established in the assembly wearing space as a garment

-४८१-

ॐ दिगम्बरप्रपूजितायै स्वाहा

oṁ digambaraprapūjitāyai svāhā
481. To she who is worshiped wearing space as a garment

-४८२-

ॐ दिगम्बरसहचर्यै स्वाहा

oṁ digambarasahacaryai svāhā
482. To she who is the companion of the one wearing space as a garment

-४८३-

ॐ दिगम्बरकृतास्पदायै स्वाहा

oṁ digambarakṛtāspadāyai svāhā
483. To she who walks with the one wearing space as a garment

-४८४-

ॐ दिगम्बरहृताचित्तायै स्वाहा

oṁ digambarahṛtācittāyai svāhā
484. To she who brings joy to the consciousness of the one wearing space as a garment

-४८५-

ॐ दिगम्बरकथाप्रियायै स्वाहा

oṁ digambarakathāpriyāyai svāhā
485. To she who loves the words of the one wearing space as a garment

-४८६-

ॐ दिगम्बरगुणरतायै स्वाहा

oṁ digambaraguṇaratāyai svāhā
486. To she who is the ultimate quality of the one wearing space as a garment

-४८७-

ॐ दिगम्बरस्वरूपिण्यै स्वाहा

oṁ digambarasvarūpiṇyai svāhā

487. To she who is the intrinsic nature of the one wearing space as a garment

-४८८-

ॐ दिगम्बरशिरोधार्यायै स्वाहा

oṁ digambaraśirodhāryāyai svāhā

488. To she who holds high the head of she who wears space as a garment

-४८९-

ॐ दिगम्बरहृताश्रयायै स्वाहा

oṁ digambarahṛtāśrayāyai svāhā

489. To she who takes refuge in the delight of she who wears space as a garment

-४९०-

ॐ दिगम्बरप्रेमरतायै स्वाहा

oṁ digambarapremaratāyai svāhā

490. To she who is the ultimate love of she who wears space as a garment

-४९१-

ॐ दिगम्बररतातुरायै स्वाहा

oṁ digambararatāturāyai svāhā

491. To she who has abundant displeasure with the one who wears space as a garment

-४९२-

ॐ दिगम्बरीस्वरूपायै स्वाहा

oṁ digambarīsvarūpāyai svāhā

492. To she who is the intrinsic nature of the one who wears space as a garment

-४९३-

ॐ दिगम्बरीगणार्चितायै स्वाहा

oṁ digambarīgaṇārcitāyai svāhā

493. To she who receives offerings from the followers of the one who wears space as a garment

-४९४-

ॐ दिगम्बरीगणप्राणायै स्वाहा

oṁ digambarīgaṇaprāṇāyai svāhā

494. To she who is the life force of the followers of the one who wears space as a garment

-४९५-

ॐ दिगम्बरीगणप्रियायै स्वाहा

oṁ digambarīgaṇapriyāyai svāhā

495. To she who is the beloved of the followers of the one who wears space as a garment

-४९६-

ॐ दिगम्बरीगणाराध्यायै स्वाहा

oṁ digambarīgaṇārādhyāyai svāhā

496. To she who is the success of the followers of the one who wears space as a garment

-४९७-

ॐ दिगम्बरगणेश्वर्यै स्वाहा

oṁ digambaragaṇeśvaryai svāhā

497. To she who is the supreme goddess of the followers of the one who wears space as a garment

-४९८-

ॐ दिगम्बरगणस्पर्शामदिरापानविह्वलायै स्वाहा

oṁ digambaragaṇasparśāmadirāpānavihvalāyai svāhā

498. To she who is the intoxication from drinking alcoholic beverages which touches the followers of the one who wears space as a garment

-४९९-

ॐ दिगम्बरीकोटिवृतायै स्वाहा

oṁ digambarīkoṭivṛtāyai svāhā

499. To she who is the ten million changes or modifications of the one who wears space as a garment

-५००-

ॐ दिगम्बरीगणावृतायै स्वाहा

oṁ digambarīgaṇāvṛtāyai svāhā

500. To she who is the unchanging nature of the followers of the one who wears space as a garment

-५०१-

ॐ दुरन्तायै स्वाहा

oṁ durantāyai svāhā

501. To she who is the end of all wickedness

-५०२-

ॐ दुष्कृतिहरायै स्वाहा

oṁ duṣkṛtiharāyai svāhā

502. To she who takes away all wicked behavior

-५०३-

ॐ दुर्ध्येयायै स्वाहा

oṁ durdhyeyāyai svāhā

503. To she who is the contemplation of wickedness

-५०४-

ॐ दुरतिक्रमायै स्वाहा

oṁ duratikramāyai svāhā

504. To she who is the step-by-step order of the events to move beyond wickedness

-५०५-

ॐ दुरन्तदानवद्वेष्ट्यै स्वाहा

oṁ durantadānavadveṣṭyai svāhā
505. To she whose enmity brings an end to the wickedness of the dānavas

-५०६-

ॐ दुरन्तदनुजान्तकृते स्वाहा

oṁ durantadanujāntakṛte svāhā
506. To she who brings an end to the wickedness of the children of Danu

-५०७-

ॐ दुरन्तपापहन्त्र्यै स्वाहा

oṁ durantapāpahantryai svāhā
507. To she who slays and ends the sins of the wicked

-५०८-

ॐ दस्रनिस्तारकारिण्यै स्वाहा

oṁ dasranistārakāriṇyai svāhā
508. To she who is the cause of the means of success for accomplishing wonderful things

-५०९-

ॐ दस्रमानससंस्थानायै स्वाहा

oṁ dasramānasasaṁsthānāyai svāhā
509. To she who is situated in the thoughts of accomplishing wonderful things

-५१०-

ॐ दस्रज्ञानविवर्द्धिन्यै स्वाहा

oṁ dasrajñānavivarddhinyai svāhā
510. To she who disseminates wisdom for accomplishing wonderful things

-५११-

ॐ दस्रसम्भोगजनन्यै स्वाहा

oṁ dasrasambhogajananyai svāhā
511. To she who is the mother who unites in accomplishing wonderful things

-५१२-

ॐ दस्रसम्भोगदायिन्यै स्वाहा

oṁ dasrasambhogadāyinyai svāhā
512. To she who gives union with wonderful things

-५१३-

ॐ दस्रसम्भोगभवनायै स्वाहा

oṁ dasrasambhogabhavanāyai svāhā
513. To she who has her existence in union with wonderful things

-५१४-

ॐ दस्रविद्याविधायिन्यै स्वाहा

oṁ dasravidyāvidhāyinyai svāhā
514. To she who is the teacher of the knowledge of wonderful things

-५१५-

ॐ दस्रोद्वेगहरायै स्वाहा

oṁ dasrodvegaharāyai svāhā
515. To she who takes away enmity with wonderful things

-५१६-

ॐ दस्रजनन्यै स्वाहा

oṁ dasrajananyai svāhā
516. To she who is the mother of wonderful things

-५१७-

ॐ दस्रसुन्दर्यै स्वाहा

oṁ dasrasundaryai svāhā
517. To she who is the beauty of wonderful things

-५१८-

ॐ दस्रभक्तविधाज्ञानायै स्वाहा

oṁ dasrabhaktavidhājñānāyai svāhā
518. To she who is the wisdom of offering devotion to wonderful things

-५१९-

ॐ दस्रद्विष्टविनाशिन्यै स्वाहा

oṁ dasradviṣṭavināśinyai svāhā
519. To she who destroys all enmity with wonderful things

-५२०-

ॐ दस्रापकारदमन्यै स्वाहा

oṁ dasrāpakāradamanyai svāhā
520. To she who diminishes the effects of un-beneficial or negative actions for wonderful things

-५२१-

ॐ दस्रसिद्धिविधायिन्यै स्वाहा

oṁ dasrasiddhividhāyinyai svāhā
521. To she who exhibits the perfection of wonderful things

-५२२-

ॐ दस्रताराराधितायै स्वाहा

oṁ dasratārārādhitāyai svāhā
522. To she who gives the auspicious or prosperous illumination of wonderful things

-५२३-

ॐ दस्रमातृप्रपूजितायै स्वाहा

oṁ dasramātṛprapūjitāyai svāhā
523. To she who is worshiped as mother of wonderful things

-५२४-

ॐ दस्रदैन्यहरायै स्वाहा

oṁ dasradainyaharāyai svāhā
524. To she who takes away the duality from wonderful things

-५२५-

ॐ दस्रतातनिषेवितायै स्वाहा

oṁ dasratātaniṣevitāyai svāhā
525. To she who is a servant of That in wonderful things

-५२६-

ॐ दस्रपितृशतज्योतिषे स्वाहा

oṁ dasrapitṛśatajyotiṣe svāhā
526. To she who is the light of truth of the father in wonderful things

-५२७-

ॐ दस्रकौशल्दायिन्यै स्वाहा

oṁ dasrakauśaladāyinyai svāhā
527. To she who gives the welfare of wonderful things

-५२८-

ॐ दशशीर्षारिसहितायै स्वाहा

oṁ daśaśīrṣārisahitāyai svāhā
528. To she who is extolled in the literature of the enemies of the one with ten heads, Rāvaṇa, who stole Sītā

-५२९-

ॐ दशशीर्षारिकामिन्यै स्वाहा

oṁ daśaśīrṣārikāminyai svāhā
529. To she who is the desire of the enemies of the one with ten heads

-५३०-

ॐ दशशीर्षपुर्यै स्वाहा

oṁ daśaśīrṣapuryai svāhā
530. To she who dwells in the city of the one with ten heads

-५३१-

ॐ देव्यै स्वाहा

oṁ devyai svāhā
531. To she who is the goddess

-५३२-

ॐ दशशीर्षसभाजितायै स्वाहा

oṁ daśaśīrṣasabhājitāyai svāhā
532. To she who is victorious over the assembly of the one with ten heads

-५३३-

ॐ दशशीर्षारिसुप्रीतायै स्वाहा

oṁ daśaśīrṣārisuprītāyai svāhā
533. To she who is the beloved of the enemies of the one with ten heads

-५३४-

ॐ दशशीर्षवधूप्रियायै स्वाहा

oṁ daśaśīrṣavadhūpriyāyai svāhā
534. To she who is the beloved daughter-in-law of the one with ten heads

-५३५-

ॐ दशशीर्षशिरश्छेत्र्यै स्वाहा

oṁ daśaśīrṣaśiraśchetryai svāhā
535. To she who cuts the heads from the one with ten heads

-५३६-

ॐ दशशीर्षनितम्बिन्यै स्वाहा

oṁ daśaśīrṣanitambinyai svāhā
536. To she whose beautiful hips and buttocks are loved by the one with ten heads

-५३७-

ॐ दशशीर्षहरप्राणायै स्वाहा

oṁ daśaśīrṣaharaprāṇāyai svāhā

537. To she who takes away the life force from the one with ten heads

-५३८-

ॐ दशशीर्षहरात्मिकायै स्वाहा

oṁ daśaśīrṣaharātmikāyai svāhā

538. To she who takes away the capacity of the soul to manifest from the one with ten heads

-५३९-

ॐ दशशीर्षहराराध्यायै स्वाहा

oṁ daśaśīrṣaharārādhyāyai svāhā

539. To she who takes away prosperity from the one with ten heads

-५४०-

ॐ दशशीर्षारिवन्दितायै स्वाहा

oṁ daśaśīrṣārivanditāyai svāhā

540. To she who is praised by the enemies of the one with ten heads

-५४१-

ॐ दशशीर्षारिसुखदायै स्वाहा

oṁ daśaśīrṣārisukhadāyai svāhā

541. To she who gives happiness to the enemies of the one with ten heads

-५४२-

ॐ दशशीर्षकपालिन्यै स्वाहा

oṁ daśaśīrṣakapālinyai svāhā

542. To she who gives protection to the one with ten heads

-५४३-

ॐ दशशीर्षज्ञानदात्र्यै स्वाहा

oṁ daśaśīrṣajñānadātryai svāhā
543. To she who gives wisdom to the one with ten heads

-५४४-

ॐ दशशीर्षारिदेहितायै स्वाहा

oṁ daśaśīrṣāridehitāyai svāhā
544. To she who gives a body to the enemies of the one with ten heads

-५४५-

ॐ दशशीर्षवधोपात्तश्रीरामचन्द्ररूपतायै स्वाहा

oṁ daśaśīrṣavadhopāttaśrīrāmacandrarūpatāyai svāhā
545. To she who gives the form of the respected Rāma in order to slay the one with ten heads

-५४६-

ॐ दशशीर्षराष्ट्रदेव्यै स्वाहा

oṁ daśaśīrṣarāṣṭradevyai svāhā
546. To she who is the goddess of the kingdom of the one with ten heads

-५४७-

ॐ दशशीर्षारिसारिण्यै स्वाहा

oṁ daśaśīrṣārisāriṇyai svāhā
547. To she who is the confidant of the one with ten heads

-५४८-

ॐ दशशीर्षभ्रातृतुष्टायै स्वाहा

oṁ daśaśīrṣabhrātṛtuṣṭāyai svāhā
548. To she who gives satisfaction to the brother of the one with ten heads

-५४९-

ॐ दशशीर्षवधूप्रियायै स्वाहा

oṁ daśaśīrṣavadhūpriyāyai svāhā

549. To she who is the beloved daughter-in-law of the one with ten heads

-५५०-

ॐ दशशीर्षवधूप्राणायै स्वाहा

oṁ daśaśīrṣavadhūprāṇāyai svāhā

550. To she who is the life force of the beloved daughter-in-law of the one with ten heads

-५५१-

ॐ दशशीर्षवधूरतायै स्वाहा

oṁ daśaśīrṣavadhūratāyai svāhā

551. To she who is the ultimate of the beloved daughter-in-law of the one with ten heads

-५५२-

ॐ दैत्यगुरुरतासाध्व्यै स्वाहा

oṁ daityagururatāsādhvyai svāhā

552. To she who is the ultimate efficient ascetic (sadhu) who is guru of those of duality

-५५३-

ॐ दैत्यगुरुप्रपूजितायै स्वाहा

oṁ daityaguruprapūjitāyai svāhā

553. To she who is worshiped by the guru of those of duality

-५५४-

ॐ दैत्यगुरूपदेष्ट्यै स्वाहा

oṁ daityagurūpadeṣṭyai svāhā

554. To she who gives instructions to the guru of those of duality

-५५५-

ॐ दैत्यगुरुनिषेवितायै स्वाहा

oṁ daityagurunișevitāyai svāhā

555. To she who is served by the guru of those of duality

-५५६-

ॐ दैत्यगुरुगतप्राणायै स्वाहा

oṁ daityagurugataprāṇāyai svāhā

556. To she who exists as the life force of the guru of those of duality

-५५७-

ॐ दैत्यगुरुतापनाशिन्यै स्वाहा

oṁ daityagurtāpanāśinyai svāhā

557. To she who destroys the purifying austerities of the guru of those of duality

-५५८-

ॐ दुरन्तदुःखशमन्यै स्वाहा

oṁ durantaduḥkhaśamanyai svāhā

558. To she who gives peace to the pain of the end of wickedness

-५५९-

ॐ दुरन्तदमनीतम्यै स्वाहा

oṁ durantadamanītamyai svāhā

559. To she whose beautiful hips and buttocks bring the end of wickedness

-५६०-

ॐ दुरन्तशोकशमन्यै स्वाहा

oṁ durantaśokaśamanyai svāhā

560. To she who gives peace to grief at the end of wickedness

-५६१-

ॐ दुरन्तरोगनाशिन्यै स्वाहा

oṁ durantaroganāśinyai svāhā
561. To she who destroys disease at the end of wickedness

-५६२-

ॐ दुरन्तवैरिदमन्यै स्वाहा

oṁ durantavairidamanyai svāhā
562. To she who mitigates the effects of enemies at the end of wickedness

-५६३-

ॐ दुरन्तदैत्यनाशिन्यै स्वाहा

oṁ durantadaityanāśinyai svāhā
563. To she who destroys duality at the end of wickedness

-५६४-

ॐ दुरन्तकलुशघ्नयै स्वाहा

oṁ durantakaluśaghnyai svāhā
564. To she who destroys impurities at the end of wickedness

-५६५-

ॐ दुष्कृतिस्तोमनाशिन्यै स्वाहा

oṁ duṣkṛtistomanāśinyai svāhā
565. To she who destroys the performing of evil hymns

-५६६-

ॐ दुराशयायै स्वाहा

oṁ durāśayāyai svāhā
566. To she who does not take rest with wickedness

-५६७-

ॐ दुराधारायै स्वाहा

oṁ durādhārāyai svāhā
567. To she who does not support wickedness

-५६८-

ॐ दुर्जयायै स्वाहा

oṁ durjayāyai svāhā

568. To she who conquers wickedness

-५६९-

ॐ दुष्टकामिन्यै स्वाहा

oṁ duṣṭakāminyai svāhā

569. To she who is in the desires of the wicked

-५७०-

ॐ दर्शनीयायै स्वाहा

oṁ darśanīyāyai svāhā

570. To she who can be seen through intuitive perception

-५७१-

ॐ दृश्यायै स्वाहा

oṁ dṛśyāyai svāhā

571. To she who is perceived

-५७२-

ॐ अदृश्यायै स्वाहा

oṁ adṛśyāyai svāhā

572. To she who is imperceptible

-५७३-

ॐ दृष्टिगोचरायै स्वाहा

oṁ dṛṣṭigocarāyai svāhā

573. To she who is within the range of perception

-५७४-

ॐ दूतीयागप्रियायै स्वाहा

oṁ dūtīyāgapriyāyai svāhā

574. To she who loves the sacrifice of the Ambassador

-५७५-

ॐ दूत्यै स्वाहा

oṁ dūtyai svāhā

575. To she who is the Ambassador

-५७६-

ॐ दूतीयागकरप्रियायै स्वाहा

oṁ dūtīyāgakarapriyāyai svāhā

576. To she who loves the performance of sacrifice by the Ambassador

-५७७-

ॐ दूतीयागकरानन्दायै स्वाहा

oṁ dūtīyāgakarānandāyai svāhā

577. To she who is the bliss in the performance of sacrifice by the Ambassador

-५७८-

ॐ दूतीयागसुखप्रदायै स्वाहा

oṁ dūtīyāgasukhapradāyai svāhā

578. To she who gives happiness in the sacrifice of the Ambassador

-५७९-

ॐ दूतीयागकरायातायै स्वाहा

oṁ dūtīyāgakarāyātāyai svāhā

579. To she who causes the performance of sacrifice by the Ambassador

-५८०-

ॐ दूतीयागप्रमोदिन्यै स्वाहा

oṁ dūtīyāgapramodinyai svāhā

580. To she who gives delight in the sacrifice of the Ambassador

-५८१-

ॐ दुर्वासःपूजितायै स्वाहा

oṁ durvāsaḥpūjitāyai svāhā

581. To she who is worshiped by Durvāsa Muni, (literally, who has controlled evil; an incarnation of Shiva)

-५८२-

ॐ दुर्वासोमुनिभावितायै स्वाहा

oṁ durvāsomunibhāvitāyai svāhā

582. To she who is the attitude of Durvāsa Muni

-५८३-

ॐ दुर्वासोऽर्चितपादायै स्वाहा

oṁ durvāso-rcitapādāyai svāhā

583. To she who is presented offerings by Durvāsa Muni

-५८४-

ॐ दुर्वासोमुनिभावितायै स्वाहा

oṁ durvāsomunibhāvitāyai svāhā

584. To she who is the attitude of Durvāsa Muni

-५८५-

ॐ दुर्वासोमुनिवन्द्यायै स्वाहा

oṁ durvāsomunivandyāyai svāhā

585. To she who is praised by Durvāsa Muni

-५८६-

ॐ दुर्वासोमुनिदेवतायै स्वाहा

oṁ durvāsomunidevatāyai svāhā

586. To she who is the goddess of Durvāsa Muni

-५८७-

ॐ दुर्वासोमुनिमातायै स्वाहा

oṁ durvāsomunimātāyai svāhā

587. To she who is the mother of Durvāsa Muni

-५८८-

ॐ दुर्वासोमुनिसिद्धिदायै स्वाहा

oṁ durvāsomunisiddhidāyai svāhā

588. To she who gives perfection to Durvāsa Muni

-५८९-

ॐ दुर्वासोमुनिभावस्थायै स्वाहा

oṁ durvāsomunibhāvasthāyai svāhā

589. To she who resides within the attitude of Durvāsa Muni

-५९०-

ॐ दुर्वासोमुनिसेवितायै स्वाहा

oṁ durvāsomunisevitāyai svāhā

590. To she who serves Durvāsa Muni

-५९१-

ॐ दुर्वासोमुनिचित्तस्थायै स्वाहा

oṁ durvāsomunicittasthāyai svāhā

591. To she who resides in the consciousness of Durvāsa Muni

-५९२-

ॐ दुर्वासोमुनिमण्डितायै स्वाहा

oṁ durvāsomunimaṇḍitāyai svāhā

592. To she who resides in the ornaments or decorations of Durvāsa Muni

-५९३-

ॐ दुर्वासोमुनिसञ्चारायै स्वाहा

oṁ durvāsomunisañcārāyai svāhā

593. To she who is in the transition of Durvāsa Muni

-५९४-

ॐ दुर्वासोहृदयङ्गमायै स्वाहा

oṁ durvāsohṛdayaṅgamāyai svāhā

594. To she who manifests in the heart and limbs of Durvāsa Muni

-५९५-

ॐ दुर्वासोहृदयाराध्यायै स्वाहा

oṁ durvāsohṛdayārādhyāyai svāhā

595. To she who is prosperity in the heart of Durvāsa Muni

-५९६-

ॐ दुर्वासोहृत्सरोजगायै स्वाहा

oṁ durvāsohṛtsarojagāyai svāhā

596. To she who is the foundation of the lotus which delights Durvāsa Muni

-५९७-

ॐ दुर्वासस्तापसाराध्यायै स्वाहा

oṁ durvāsastāpasārādhyāyai svāhā

597. To she who is prosperity in the purifying austerities of Durvāsa Muni

-५९८-

ॐ दुर्वासस्तापसाश्रयायै स्वाहा

oṁ durvāsastāpasāśrayāyai svāhā

598. To she who takes refuge in the purifying austerities of Durvāsa Muni

-५९९-

ॐ दुर्वासस्तापसरतायै स्वाहा

oṁ durvāsastāpasaratāyai svāhā

599. To she who is ultimate of the purifying austerities of Durvāsa Muni

-६००-

ॐ दुर्वासस्तापसेश्वर्यै स्वाहा

oṁ durvāsastāpaseśvaryai svāhā

600. To she who is the supreme goddess in the purifying austerities of Durvāsa Muni

-६०१-

ॐ दुर्वासोमुनिकन्यायै स्वाहा

oṁ durvāsomunikanyāyai svāhā
601. To she who is the daughter of Durvāsa Muni

-६०२-

ॐ दुर्वासोत्भूतसिद्धिदायै स्वाहा

oṁ durvāsotbhūtasiddhidāyai svāhā
602. To she who makes perfect the elements of Durvāsa Muni

-६०३-

ॐ दररात्र्यै स्वाहा

oṁ dararātryai svāhā
603. To she who is the fear of night

-६०४-

ॐ दरहरायै स्वाहा

oṁ daraharāyai svāhā
604. To she who takes away fear

-६०५-

ॐ दरयुक्तायै स्वाहा

oṁ darayuktāyai svāhā
605. To she who is one with fear

-६०६-

ॐ दरापहायै स्वाहा

oṁ darāpahāyai svāhā
606. To she who repels fear

-६०७-

ॐ दरघ्नयै स्वाहा

oṁ daraghnyai svāhā
607. To she who destroys fear

-६०८-

ॐ दरहन्त्र्यै स्वाहा

oṁ darahantryai svāhā
608. To she who slays fear

-६०९-

ॐ दरयुक्तायै स्वाहा

oṁ darayuktāyai svāhā
609. To she who is one with fear

-६१०-

ॐ दराश्रयायै स्वाहा

oṁ darāśrayāyai svāhā
610. To she who takes refuge in fear

-६११-

ॐ दरस्मेरायै स्वाहा

oṁ darasmerāyai svāhā
611. To she who is remembered in fear

-६१२-

ॐ दरापाङ्ग्यै स्वाहा

oṁ darāpāṅgyai svāhā
612. To she who is fear which has not yet manifested

-६१३-

ॐ दयादात्र्यै स्वाहा

oṁ dayādātryai svāhā
613. To she who is the giver of compassion

-६१४-

ॐ दयाश्रमायै स्वाहा

oṁ dayāśramāyai svāhā
614. To she who gives refuge with compassion

-६१५-

ॐ दस्रपूज्यायै स्वाहा

oṁ dasrapūjyāyai svāhā

615. To she who is worshiped by those who accomplish wonderful deeds

-६१६-

ॐ दस्रमातायै स्वाहा

oṁ dasramātāyai svāhā

616. To she who is the mother of those who accomplish wonderful deeds

-६१७-

ॐ दस्रदेव्यै स्वाहा

oṁ dasradevyai svāhā

617. To she who is the goddess of those who accomplish wonderful deeds

-६१८-

ॐ दुरोन्मदायै स्वाहा

oṁ duronmadāyai svāhā

618. To she who becomes crazy with the wicked

-६१९-

ॐ दस्रसिद्धायै स्वाहा

oṁ dasrasiddhāyai svāhā

619. To she who gives perfection to those who accomplish wonderful deeds

-६२०-

ॐ दस्रसंस्थायै स्वाहा

oṁ dasrasaṁsthāyai svāhā

620. To she who is established with those who accomplish wonderful deeds

-६२१-

ॐ दस्रातापविमोचिन्यै स्वाहा

oṁ dasrātāpavimocinyai svāhā
621. To she who nullifies the lack of austerities for those who accomplish wonderful deeds

-६२२-

ॐ दस्रक्षोभहरानित्यायै स्वाहा

oṁ dasrakṣobhaharānityāyai svāhā
622. To she who always takes away the agitation from those who accomplish wonderful deeds

-६२३-

ॐ दस्रलोकगतात्मिकायै स्वाहा

oṁ dasralokagatātmikāyai svāhā
623. To she who is the capacity of the soul to travel through the worlds of those who accomplish wonderful deeds

-६२४-

ॐ दैत्यगुर्वङ्गनावन्द्यायै स्वाहा

oṁ daityagurvaṅganāvandyāyai svāhā
624. To she who is praised as being worthy of respect even by the Daityas, beings of duality

-६२५-

ॐ दैत्यगुर्वङ्गनाप्रियायै स्वाहा

oṁ daityagurvaṅganāpriyāyai svāhā
625. To she who is loved as being worthy of respect even by the Daityas

-६२६-

ॐ दैत्यगुर्वङ्गनासिद्धायै स्वाहा

oṁ daityagurvaṅganāsiddhāyai svāhā
626. To she who has attained perfection as being worthy of respect even by the Daityas

-६२७-

ॐ दैत्यगुर्वङ्गनोत्सुकायै स्वाहा

oṁ daityagurvaṅganotsukāyai svāhā

627. To she who is eagerness as being worthy of respect even by the Daityas

-६२८-

ॐ दैत्यगुरुप्रियतमायै स्वाहा

oṁ daityagurupriyatamāyai svāhā

628. To she who is beloved by the guru of the Daityas

-६२९-

ॐ दैत्यगुरुनिषेवितायै स्वाहा

oṁ daityaguruniṣevitāyai svāhā

629. To she who is served by the guru of the Daityas

-६३०-

ॐ देवगुरुप्रसूरूपायै स्वाहा

oṁ devaguruprasūrūpāyai svāhā

630. To she who is the excellent form of the guru of the gods

-६३१-

ॐ देवगुरुकृतार्हणायै स्वाहा

oṁ devagurukṛtārhaṇāyai svāhā

631. To she who is honored with worship by the guru of the gods

-६३२-

ॐ देवगुरुप्रेमयुतायै स्वाहा

oṁ devagurupremayutāyai svāhā

632. To she who is the recipient of love from the guru of the gods

-६३३-

ॐ देवगुर्वनुमानितायै स्वाहा

oṁ devagurvanumānitāyai svāhā

633. To she who has received approval from the guru of the gods

-६३४-

ॐ देवगुरुप्रभावज्ञायै स्वाहा

oṁ devaguruprabhāvajñāyai svāhā

634. To she who gives honored wisdom to the guru of the gods

-६३५-

ॐ देवगुरुसुखप्रदायै स्वाहा

oṁ devagurusukhapradāyai svāhā

635. To she who gives happiness to the guru of the gods

-६३६-

ॐ देवगुरुज्ञानदात्र्यै स्वाहा

oṁ devagurujñānadātryai svāhā

636. To she who gives wisdom to the guru of the gods

-६३७-

ॐ देवगुरुप्रमोदिन्यै स्वाहा

oṁ devagurupramodinyai svāhā

637. To she who gives delight to the guru of the gods

-६३८-

ॐ दैत्यस्त्रीगणसम्पूज्यायै स्वाहा

oṁ daityastrīgaṇasampūjyāyai svāhā

638. To she who worships with the women of the Daityas

-६३९-

ॐ दैत्यस्त्रीगणप्रपूजितायै स्वाहा

oṁ daityastrīgaṇaprapūjitāyai svāhā

639. To she who is worshiped by the women of the Daityas

-६४०-

ॐ दैत्यस्त्रीगणरूपायै स्वाहा

oṁ daityastrīgaṇarūpāyai svāhā

640. To she who is the form of the women of the Daityas

-६४१-

ॐ दैत्यस्त्रीचित्तहारिण्यै स्वाहा

oṁ daityastrīcittahāriṇyai svāhā

641. To she who takes away the consciousness of the women of the Daityas

-६४२-

ॐ देवस्त्रीगणपूज्यायै स्वाहा

oṁ devastrīgaṇapūjyāyai svāhā

642. To she who is worshiped by the women of the gods

-६४३-

ॐ देवस्त्रीगणवन्दितायै स्वाहा

oṁ devastrīgaṇavanditāyai svāhā

643. To she who is praised by the women of the gods

-६४४-

ॐ देवस्त्रीगणचित्तस्थायै स्वाहा

oṁ de vastrīgaṇacittasthāyai svāhā

644. To she who is established in the consciousness of the women of the gods

-६४५-

ॐ देवस्त्रीगणभूषितायै स्वाहा

oṁ devastrīgaṇabhūṣitāyai svāhā

645. To she who illuminates the women of the gods

-६४६-

ॐ देवस्त्रीगणसंसिद्धायै स्वाहा

oṁ devastrīgaṇasaṁsiddhāyai svāhā

646. To she who has attained perfection among the women of the gods

-६४७-

ॐ देवस्त्रीगणतोषितायै स्वाहा

oṁ devastrīgaṇatoṣitāyai svāhā

647. To she who is the satisfaction of the women of the gods

-६४८-

ॐ देवस्त्रीगणहस्तस्थ चारुचामर बीजितायै स्वाहा

oṁ devastrīgaṇahastastha cārucāmara bījitāyai svāhā

648. To she who is the primary cause of the beautiful yakas tail in the hands of the women of the gods

-६४९-

ॐ देवस्त्रीगणहस्तस्थ चारुगन्ध विलेपितायै स्वाहा

oṁ devastrīgaṇahastastha cārugandha vilepitāyai svāhā

649. To she who is the beautiful scent applied by the hands of the women of the gods

-६५०-

ॐ देवाङ्गनाधृतादर्श दृष्ट्यर्त्थमुखचन्द्रमायै स्वाहा

oṁ devāṅganādhṛtādarśa dṛṣṭyartthamukhacandramāyai svāhā

650. To she who is the intuitive vision which is perceived like the beautiful radiant countenance of the moon shining without restraint upon the bodies of the gods

-६५१-

ॐ देवाङ्गनोत्सृष्टनागवल्लीदलकृतोत्सुकायै स्वाहा

oṁ devāṅganotsṛṣṭanāgavallīdalakṛtotsukāyai svāhā

651. To she who is the eagerness of the multitude of snake like creepers to emerge from the earth as limbs of the gods

-६५२-

ॐ देवस्त्रीगणहस्तस्थदीपमालाविलोकनायै स्वाहा

oṁ devastrīgaṇahastasthadīpamālāvilokanāyai svāhā

652. To she who is the illumination of the garlands of light situated in the hands of the women of the gods

-६५३-

ॐ देवस्त्रीगणहस्तस्थधूपघ्राणविनोदिन्यै स्वाहा

oṁ devastrīgaṇahastasthadhūpaghrāṇavinodinyai svāhā
653. To she who is the delight of the fragment scents of incense situated in the hands of the women of the gods

-६५४-

ॐ देवनारीकरगतवासकासवपायिन्यै स्वाहा

oṁ devanārīkaragatavāsakāsavapāyinyai svāhā
654. To she who establishes the abodes of the home-makers of the women of the gods

-६५५-

ॐ देवनारीकङ्कतिकाकृत्तकेशनिमार्जनायै स्वाहा

oṁ devanārīkaṅkatikākṛttakeśanimārjanāyai svāhā
655. To she who washes the hair which protects the women of the gods

-६५६-

ॐ देवनारीरुष्ट्यगात्रायै स्वाहा

oṁ devanārīruṣṭyagātrāyai svāhā
656. To she who pursues those who cause injury to the women of the gods

-६५७-

ॐ देवनारिकृतोत्सुकायै स्वाहा

oṁ devanārikṛtotsukāyai svāhā
657. To she who is the eagerness in the actions of the women of the gods

-६५८-

ॐ देवनारीविरचितापुष्पमालाविराजितायै स्वाहा

oṁ devanārīviracitāpuṣpamālāvirājitāyai svāhā
658. To she who is present in the flower garland prepared by the women of the gods

-६५९-

ॐ देवनारीविचित्राङ्ग्यै स्वाहा

oṁ devanārīvicitrāṅgyai svāhā

659. To she who is the various limbs of the women of the gods

-६६०-

ॐ देवस्त्रीदत्तभोजनायै स्वाहा

oṁ devastrīdattabhojanāyai svāhā

660. To she who is the food of the Ambassador of the women of the gods

-६६१-

ॐ देवस्त्रीगणगीतायै स्वाहा

oṁ devastrīgaṇagītāyai svāhā

661. To she who gives (sings or writes) the song of the multitude of the women of the gods

-६६२-

ॐ देवस्त्रीगीतनोत्सुकायै स्वाहा

oṁ devastrīgītanotsukāyai svāhā

662. To she who is the eagerness in the song of the women of the gods

-६६३-

ॐ देवस्त्रीनृत्यसुखिन्यै स्वाहा

oṁ devastrīnṛtyasukhinyai svāhā

663. To she who is the happiness in the dance of the women of the gods

-६६४-

ॐ देवस्त्रीनृत्यप्रदर्शिन्यै स्वाहा

oṁ devastrīnṛtyapradarśinyai svāhā

664. To she who sees the dance of the women of the gods

-६६५-

ॐ देवस्त्रीयोजितलसद्रत्नपादुपदाम्बुजायै स्वाहा

oṁ devastrīyojitalasadratnapādupadāmbujāyai svāhā
665. To she who is the jewel connecting together all the petals of the lotus of the women of the gods

-६६६-

ॐ देवस्त्रीगणविस्तीर्णचारुतल्पनिषेदुष्यै स्वाहा

oṁ devastrīgaṇavistīrṇacārutalpaniṣeduṣyai svāhā
666. To she who prohibits the pleasurable evils which could be performed on the beds of the women of the gods

-६६७-

ॐ देवनारीचारुकराकलिताङ्घ्र्यादिदेहिकायै स्वाहा

oṁ devanārīcārukarākalitāṅghryādidehikāyai svāhā
667. To she who is the cause of the physical manifestation in bodies of widespread darkness which could perturb the women of the gods

-६६८-

ॐ देवनारीकरव्यग्रऽतालवृत्तऽमरुत्सुखायै स्वाहा

oṁ devanārīkaravyagra-tālavṛtta-marutsukhāyai svāhā
668. To she who is the happiness of the unchanging rhythm focussed upon by the women of the gods

-६६९-

ॐ देवनारीवेणुवीणाऽनादसोत्कण्ठमानसायै स्वाहा

oṁ devanārīveṇuvīṇā-nādasotkaṇṭhamānasāyai svāhā
669. To she who is the thoughts of longing for the subtle vibrations and melodies of the vina and the flute played by the women of the gods

-६७०-

ॐ देवकोटिस्तुतिनुतायै स्वाहा

oṁ devakoṭistutinutāyai svāhā
670. To she who is praised in ten million songs of the gods

-६७१-

ॐ देवकोटिकृतार्हणायै स्वाहा

oṁ devakoṭikṛtārhaṇāyai svāhā
671. To she who is worthy of ten million praises by the gods

-६७२-

ॐ देवकोटिगीतगुणायै स्वाहा

oṁ devakoṭigītaguṇāyai svāhā
672. To she whose qualities are sung of in ten million songs of the gods

-६७३-

ॐ देवकोटिकृतस्तुत्यै स्वाहा

oṁ devakoṭikṛtastutyai svāhā
673. To she who has been sung of in ten million songs of the gods

-६७४-

ॐ दन्तदृष्ट्योद्वेगफलायै स्वाहा

oṁ dantadṛṣṭyodvegaphalāyai svāhā
674. To she who makes the fruits to flow from seeing the one with ivory tusks (Ganesh)

-६७५-

ॐ देवकोलाहलाकुलायै स्वाहा

oṁ devakolāhalākulāyai svāhā
675. To she who is the confused sound for the gods from those of lowly birth

-६७६-

ॐ द्वेषरागपरित्यक्तायै स्वाहा

oṁ dveṣarāgaparityaktāyai svāhā
676. To she who has left behind the feeling of enmity

-६७७-

ॐ द्वेषरागविवर्जितायै स्वाहा

oṁ dveṣarāgavivarjitāyai svāhā

677. To she who has excluded the feeling of enmity

-६७८-

ॐ दामपूज्यायै स्वाहा

oṁ dāmapūjyāyai svāhā

678. To she who worships the generous giver

-६७९-

ॐ दामभूषायै स्वाहा

oṁ dāmabhūṣāyai svāhā

679. To she who illuminates the generous giver

-६८०-

ॐ दामोदरविनाशिन्यै स्वाहा

oṁ dāmodaravināśinyai svāhā

680. To she who is the ultimate destruction of the generous giver

-६८१-

ॐ दामोदरप्रेमरतायै स्वाहा

oṁ dāmodarapremaratāyai svāhā

681. To she who is the ultimate love of the generous giver

-६८२-

ॐ दामोदरभगिन्यै स्वाहा

oṁ dāmodarabhaginyai svāhā

682. To she who is the good fortune of the generous giver

-६८३-

ॐ दामोदरप्रस्वे स्वाहा

oṁ dāmodaraprasve svāhā

683. To she who is the comfortable rest of the generous giver

-६८४-

ॐ दामोदरपत्न्यै स्वाहा

oṁ dāmodarapatnyai svāhā

684. To she who is the wife of the generous giver

-६८५-

ॐ दामोदरपतिव्रतायै स्वाहा

oṁ dāmodarapativratāyai svāhā

685. To she who is the wife who keeps the vow of fidelity to the generous giver

-६८६-

ॐ दामोदराऽभिन्नदेहायै स्वाहा

oṁ dāmodarā-bhinnadehāyai svāhā

686. To she whose body is not different from that of the generous giver

-६८७-

ॐ दामोदररतिप्रियायै स्वाहा

oṁ dāmodararatipriyāyai svāhā

687. To she who loves affection with the generous giver

-६८८-

ॐ दामोदराऽभिन्नतनवे स्वाहा

oṁ dāmodarā-bhinnatanave svāhā

688. To she who manifests in the various bodies of the generous giver

-६८९-

ॐ दामोदरकृतास्पदायै स्वाहा

oṁ dāmodarakṛtāspadāyai svāhā

689. To she who performs actions equal to the generous giver

-६९०-

ॐ दामोदरकृतप्राणायै स्वाहा

oṁ dāmodarakṛtaprāṇāyai svāhā
690. To she who exists as the life force of the generous giver

-६९१-

ॐ दामोदरगतात्मिकायै स्वाहा

oṁ dāmodaragatātmikāyai svāhā
691. To she who is the path by which the soul can manifest the generous giver

-६९२-

ॐ दामोदरकौतुकाढ्यायै स्वाहा

oṁ dāmodarakautukāḍhyāyai svāhā
692. To she who rides upon the curiosity about the generous giver

-६९३-

ॐ दामोदरकलाकलायै स्वाहा

oṁ dāmodarakalākalāyai svāhā
693. To she who is the art of the attributes of the generous giver

-६९४-

ॐ दामोदरालिङ्गिताङ्ग्यै स्वाहा

oṁ dāmodarāliṅgitāṅgyai svāhā
694. To she who is the trembling of those who pretend to be the generous giver

-६९५-

ॐ दामोदरकुतूहलायै स्वाहा

oṁ dāmodarakutūhalāyai svāhā
695. To she who is the curiosity about the generous giver

-६९६-

ॐ दामोदरकृताह्लादायै स्वाहा

oṁ dāmodarakṛtāhlādāyai svāhā
696. To she who gives the delight of the generous giver

-६९७-

ॐ दामोदरसुचुम्बितायै स्वाहा

oṁ dāmodarasucumbitāyai svāhā

697. To she who gives excellent kisses to the generous giver

-६९८-

ॐ दामोदरसुताकृष्टायै स्वाहा

oṁ dāmodarasutākṛṣṭāyai svāhā

698. To she who cultivates the children of the generous giver

-६९९-

ॐ दामोदरसुखप्रदायै स्वाहा

oṁ dāmodarasukhapradāyai svāhā

699. To she who gives happiness to the generous giver

-७००-

ॐ दामोदरसहाढ्यायै स्वाहा

oṁ dāmodarasahāḍhyāyai svāhā

700. To she who rides with the generous giver

-७०१-

ॐ दामोदरसहायिन्यै स्वाहा

oṁ dāmodarasahāyinyai svāhā

701. To she who is alone only with the generous giver

-७०२-

ॐ दामोदरगुणज्ञायै स्वाहा

oṁ dāmodaraguṇajñāyai svāhā

702. To she who knows the qualities of the generous giver

-७०३-

ॐ दामोदरवरप्रदायै स्वाहा

oṁ dāmodaravarapradāyai svāhā

703. To she who grants the boons of the generous giver

-७०४-

ॐ दामोदरानुकूलायै स्वाहा

oṁ dāmodarānukūlāyai svāhā

704. To she who acts favorably to the generous giver

-७०५-

ॐ दामोदरनितम्बिन्यै स्वाहा

oṁ dāmodaranitambinyai svāhā

705. To she who has beautiful hips and buttocks loved by the generous giver

-७०६-

ॐ दामोदरजलक्रीडाकुशलायै स्वाहा

oṁ dāmodarajalakrīḍākuśalāyai svāhā

706. To she who causes the rain of happiness for the generous giver

-७०७-

ॐ दर्शनप्रियायै स्वाहा

oṁ darśanapriyāyai svāhā

707. To she who loves intuitive perception

-७०८-

ॐ दामोदराबलक्रीडात्यक्तस्वजनसौहृदायै स्वाहा

oṁ dāmodarābalakrīḍātyaktasvajanasauhṛdāyai svāhā

708. To she who resides in the loving hearts of those who have left weakness behind for the generous giver

-७०९-

ॐ दामोदरलसद्रासकेलीकौतुकिन्यै स्वाहा

oṁ dāmodaralasadrāsakelīkautukinyai svāhā

709. To she who has a keen desire for amorous play with the generous giver

-७१०-

ॐ दामोदरभ्रातृकायै स्वाहा

oṁ dāmodarabhrātṛkāyai svāhā
710. To she who is brothers and sisters of the generous giver

-७११-

ॐ दामोदरपरायणायै स्वाहा

oṁ dāmodaraparāyaṇāyai svāhā
711. To she who is the last resort of the generous giver

-७१२-

ॐ दामोदरधरायै स्वाहा

oṁ dāmodaradharāyai svāhā
712. To she who supports the generous giver

-७१३-

ॐ दामोदरवैरिविनाशिन्यै स्वाहा

oṁ dāmodaravairivināśinyai svāhā
713. To she who destroys the enemies of the generous giver

-७१४-

ॐ दामोदररोपजायायै स्वाहा

oṁ dāmodararopajāyāyai svāhā
714. To she who has engendered the generous giver

-७१५-

ॐ दामोदरनिमन्त्रितायै स्वाहा

oṁ dāmodaranimantritāyai svāhā
715. To she who is invited by the generous giver

-७१६-

ॐ दामोदरपराभूतायै स्वाहा

oṁ dāmodaraparābhūtāyai svāhā
716. To she who is the supreme elements of the generous giver

-७१७-

ॐ दामोदरपराजितायै स्वाहा

oṁ dāmodaraparājitāyai svāhā
717. To she who undefinable by the generous giver

-७१८-

ॐ दामोदरसमाक्रान्तायै स्वाहा

oṁ dāmodarasamākrāntāyai svāhā
718. To she who does not allow any rebellion against the generous giver

-७१९-

ॐ दामोदरहताशुभायै स्वाहा

oṁ dāmodarahatāśubhāyai svāhā
719. To she who removes all impurities from the generous giver

-७२०-

ॐ दामोदरोत्सवरतायै स्वाहा

oṁ dāmodarotsavaratāyai svāhā
720. To she who is the ultimate festival of the generous giver

-७२१-

ॐ दामोदरोत्सवावहायै स्वाहा

oṁ dāmodarotsavāvahāyai svāhā
721. To she who invites to the festival of the generous giver

-७२२-

ॐ दामोदरस्तन्यदात्र्यै स्वाहा

oṁ dāmodarastanyadātryai svāhā
722. To she who gives her breasts of nourishment to the generous giver

-७२३-

ॐ दामोदरगवेषितायै स्वाहा

oṁ dāmodaragaveṣitāyai svāhā
723. To she who offers her milk to the generous giver

-७२४-

ॐ दमयन्तीसिद्धिदात्र्यै स्वाहा

oṁ damayantīsiddhidātryai svāhā

724. To she who gives perfection to those who are self-controlled

-७२५-

ॐ दमयन्तीप्रसाधितायै स्वाहा

oṁ damayantīprasādhitāyai svāhā

725. To she who gives the consecrated offering to those who are self-controlled

-७२६-

ॐ दमयन्तीष्टदेव्यै स्वाहा

oṁ damayantīṣṭadevyai svāhā

726. To she who is the chosen form of worship for those who are self-controlled

-७२७-

ॐ दमयन्तीस्वरूपिण्यै स्वाहा

oṁ damayantīsvarūpiṇyai svāhā

727. To she who is the intrinsic nature of those who are self-controlled

-७२८-

ॐ दमयन्तीकृतार्चायै स्वाहा

oṁ damayantīkṛtārcāyai svāhā

728. To she who makes the offering to those who are self-controlled

-७२९-

ॐ दमनर्षिविभावितायै स्वाहा

oṁ damanarṣivibhāvitāyai svāhā

729. To she who is the attitude of the seer who is self-controlled

-७३०-

ॐ दमनर्षिप्राणतुल्यायै स्वाहा

oṁ damanarṣiprāṇatulyāyai svāhā
730. To she who is the like the life force of the seer who is self-controlled

-७३१-

ॐ दमनर्षिस्वरूपिण्यै स्वाहा

oṁ damanarṣisvarūpiṇyai svāhā
731. To she who is the intrinsic nature of the seer who is self-controlled

-७३२-

ॐ दमनर्षिस्वरूपायै स्वाहा

oṁ damanarṣisvarūpāyai svāhā
732. To she who is the actual form of the seer who is self-controlled

-७३३-

ॐ दम्भपूरितविग्रहायै स्वाहा

oṁ dambhapūritavigrahāyai svāhā
733. To she who is at war with those who are filled with hypocrisy

-७३४-

ॐ दम्भहन्त्र्यै स्वाहा

oṁ dambhahantryai svāhā
734. To she who slays hypocrisy

-७३५-

ॐ दम्भदात्र्यै स्वाहा

oṁ dambhadātryai svāhā
735. To she who gives hypocrisy

-७३६-

ॐ दम्भलोकविमोहिन्यै स्वाहा

oṁ dambhalokavimohinyai svāhā
736. To she who fills the worlds with the ignorance of hypocrisy

-७३७-

ॐ दम्भशीलायै स्वाहा

oṁ dambhaśīlāyai svāhā

737. To she who is habituated to hypocrisy

-७३८-

ॐ दम्भहरायै स्वाहा

oṁ dambhaharāyai svāhā

738. To she who removes hypocrisy

-७३९-

ॐ दम्भवत्परिमर्दिन्यै स्वाहा

oṁ dambhavatparimardinyai svāhā

739. To she who slays those who are hypocrites

-७४०-

ॐ दम्भरूपायै स्वाहा

oṁ dambharūpāyai svāhā

740. To she who is the form of hypocrisy

-७४१-

ॐ दम्भकर्यै स्वाहा

oṁ dambhakaryai svāhā

741. To she who is the cause of hypocrisy

-७४२-

ॐ दम्भसन्तानदारिण्यै स्वाहा

oṁ dambhasantānadāriṇyai svāhā

742. To she who gives the continuous succession of hypocrisy

-७४३-

ॐ दत्तमोक्षायै स्वाहा

oṁ dattamokṣāyai svāhā

743. To she who is the liberation of the Ambassador

-७४४-

ॐ दत्तधनायै स्वाहा

oṁ dattadhanāyai svāhā
744. To she who is the wealth of the Ambassador

-७४५-

ॐ दत्तरोग्याथायै स्वाहा

oṁ dattarogyāthāyai svāhā
745. To she who is in accordance with the illness of the Ambassador

-७४६-

ॐ दाम्भिकायै स्वाहा

oṁ dāmbhikāyai svāhā
746. To she who is a hypocrite

-७४७-

ॐ दत्तपुत्रायै स्वाहा

oṁ dattaputrāyai svāhā
747. To she who is the child of the Ambassador

-७४८-

ॐ दत्तदारायै स्वाहा

oṁ dattadārāyai svāhā
748. To she who is a child of the Ambassador

-७४९-

ॐ दत्तहारायै स्वाहा

oṁ dattahārāyai svāhā
749. To she who takes the Ambassador across

-७५०-

ॐ दारिकायै स्वाहा

oṁ dārikāyai svāhā
750. To she who splits apart

-७५१-

ॐ दत्तभोगायै स्वाहा

oṁ dattabhogāyai svāhā
751. To she who enjoys with the Ambassador

-७५२-

ॐ दत्तशोकायै स्वाहा

oṁ dattaśokāyai svāhā
752. To she who grieves with the Ambassador

-७५३-

ॐ दत्तहस्त्यादिवाहनायै स्वाहा

oṁ dattahastyādivāhanāyai svāhā
753. To she who is the conveyance of the laughter of the Ambassador

-७५४-

ॐ दत्तमत्यै स्वाहा

oṁ dattamatyai svāhā
754. To she who is the idea or opinion of the Ambassador

-७५५-

ॐ दत्तभार्यायै स्वाहा

oṁ dattabhāryāyai svāhā
755. To she who is the wife of the Ambassador

-७५६-

ॐ दत्तशास्त्रावबोधिकायै स्वाहा

oṁ dattaśāstrāvabodhikāyai svāhā
756. To she who knows all the weapons of the Ambassador

-७५७-

ॐ दत्तपानायै स्वाहा

oṁ dattapānāyai svāhā
757. To she who is the drink of the Ambassador

-७५८-

ॐ दत्तदानायै स्वाहा

oṁ dattadānāyai svāhā
758. To she who gives to the Ambassador

-७५९-

ॐ दत्तदारिद्रनाशिनि स्वाहा

oṁ dattadāridranāśini svāhā
759. To she who destroys the affliction of the Ambassador

-७६०-

ॐ दत्तसौधावनीवासायै स्वाहा

oṁ dattasaudhāvanīvāsāyai svāhā
760. To she who resides in the palace of the Ambassador

-७६१-

ॐ दत्तस्वर्गायै स्वाहा

oṁ dattasvargāyai svāhā
761. To she who is the heaven of the Ambassador

-७६२-

ॐ दासदायै स्वाहा

oṁ dāsadāyai svāhā
762. To she who is the servant

-७६३-

ॐ दास्यतुष्टायै स्वाहा

oṁ dāsyatuṣṭāyai svāhā
763. To she who is the servant who gives satisfaction

-७६४-

ॐ दास्यहरायै स्वाहा

oṁ dāsyaharāyai svāhā
764. To she who takes away servitude

-७६५-

ॐ दासदासीशतप्रदायै स्वाहा

oṁ dāsadāsīśatapradāyai svāhā
765. To she who gives a hundred male and female servants

-७६६-

ॐ दाररूपायै स्वाहा

oṁ dārarūpāyai svāhā
766. To she who is the form of she who tears apart obstacles

-७६७-

ॐ दारवासायै स्वाहा

oṁ dāravāsāyai svāhā
767. To she who resides as she who tears apart obstacles

-७६८-

ॐ दारवासिहृदास्पदायै स्वाहा

oṁ dāravāsihṛdāspadāyai svāhā
768. To she whose feet reside in the heart of she who tears apart obstacles

-७६९-

ॐ दारवासिजनाराध्यायै स्वाहा

oṁ dāravāsijanārādhyāyai svāhā
769. To she who gives birth to prosperity in the heart of she who tears apart obstacles

-७७०-

ॐ दारवासिजनप्रियायै स्वाहा

oṁ dāravāsijanapriyāyai svāhā
770. To she who loves she who tears apart obstacles

-७७१-

ॐ दारवासिविनिर्मीतायै स्वाहा

oṁ dāravāsivinirmītāyai svāhā
771. To she who has created she who tears apart obstacles

-७७२-

ॐ दारवासिसमर्चितायै स्वाहा

oṁ dāravāsisamarcitāyai svāhā
772. To she who offers to she who tears apart obstacles

-७७३-

ॐ दारवास्याहृतप्राणायै स्वाहा

oṁ dāravāsyāhṛtaprāṇāyai svāhā
773. To she who is the delightful life force of she who tears apart obstacles

-७७४-

ॐ दारवास्यारिनाशिन्यै स्वाहा

oṁ dāravāsyārināśinyai svāhā
774. To she who destroys the enemies of she who tears apart obstacles

-७७५-

ॐ दारवासिविघ्नहरायै स्वाहा

oṁ dāravāsivighnaharāyai svāhā
775. To she who removes all obstacles from she who tears apart obstacles

-७७६-

ॐ दारवासिविमुक्तिदायै स्वाहा

oṁ dāravāsivimuktidāyai svāhā
776. To she who gives liberation to she who tears apart obstacles

-७७७-

ॐ दाराग्निरूपिण्यै स्वाहा

oṁ dārāgnirūpiṇyai svāhā
777. To she who is the intrinsic nature of the fire of she who tears apart obstacles

-७७८-

ॐ दारायै स्वाहा

oṁ dārāyai svāhā
778. To she who is she who tears apart obstacles

-७७९-

ॐ दारकार्यरिनाशिन्यै स्वाहा

oṁ dārakāryarināśinyai svāhā
779. To she who destroys the activities of the enemies of she who tears apart obstacles

-७८०-

ॐ दम्पत्यै स्वाहा

oṁ dampatyai svāhā
780. To she who is the master of the house

-७८१-

ॐ दम्पतीष्टायै स्वाहा

oṁ dampatīṣṭāyai svāhā
781. To she who is the chosen one of the master of the house

-७८२-

ॐ दम्पतीप्राणरूपिकायै स्वाहा

oṁ dampatīprāṇarūpikāyai svāhā
782. To she who is the manifestation of the form of the life force of the master of the house

-७८३-

ॐ दम्पतिस्नेहनिरतायै स्वाहा

oṁ dampatisnehaniratāyai svāhā
783. To she who is the ultimate love of the master of the house

-७८४-

ॐ दाम्पत्यसाधनप्रियायै स्वाहा

oṁ dāmpatyasādhanapriyāyai svāhā

784. To she who loves the spiritual discipline of the master of the house

-७८५-

ॐ दाम्पत्यसुखसेनायै स्वाहा

oṁ dāmpatyasukhasenāyai svāhā

785. To she who is the happy army of the master of the house

-७८६-

ॐ दाम्पत्यसुखदायिन्यै स्वाहा

oṁ dāmpatyasukhadāyinyai svāhā

786. To she who is the giver of happiness to the master of the house

-७८७-

ॐ दम्पत्याचारनिरतायै स्वाहा

oṁ dampatyācāraniratāyai svāhā

787. To she who is the ultimate which does not move from the master of the house

-७८८-

ॐ दम्पत्यामोदमोदितायै स्वाहा

oṁ dampatyāmodamoditāyai svāhā

788. To she who is the pleasure of all pleasures of the master of the house

-७८९-

ॐ दम्पत्यामोदसुखिन्यै स्वाहा

oṁ dampatyāmodasukhinyai svāhā

789. To she who is the happiness or pleasure for the master of the house

-७९०-

ॐ दाम्पत्याह्लादकारिण्यै स्वाहा

oṁ dāmpatyāhlādakāriṇyai svāhā

790. To she who is the cause of delight for the master of the house

-७९१-

ॐ दम्पतीष्टपादपद्मायै स्वाहा

oṁ dampatīṣṭapādapadmāyai svāhā

791. To she who is the petals of the lotus of the chosen form of worship of the master of the house

-७९२-

ॐ दाम्पत्यप्रेमरूपिण्यै स्वाहा

oṁ dāmpatyapremarūpiṇyai svāhā

792. To she who is the intrinsic nature of love for the master of the house

-७९३-

ॐ दाम्पत्यभोगभवनायै स्वाहा

oṁ dāmpatyabhogabhavanāyai svāhā

793. To she who is the existence of enjoyment of the master of the house

-७९४-

ॐ दाडिमीफलभोजिन्यै स्वाहा

oṁ dāḍimīphalabhojinyai svāhā

794. To she who eats the pomegranate fruit

-७९५-

ॐ दाडिमीफलसन्तुष्टायै स्वाहा

oṁ dāḍimīphalasantuṣṭāyai svāhā

795. To she who is satisfied with the pomegranate fruit

-७९६-

ॐ दाडिमीफलमानसायै स्वाहा

oṁ dāḍimīphalamānasāyai svāhā
796. To she who is the idea of the pomegranate fruit

-७९७-

ॐ दाडिमीवृक्षसंस्थानायै स्वाहा

oṁ dāḍimīvṛkṣasaṁsthānāyai svāhā
797. To she who is established in the pomegranate fruit tree

-७९८-

ॐ दाडिमीवृक्षवासिन्यै स्वाहा

oṁ dāḍimīvṛkṣavāsinyai svāhā
798. To she who resides in the pomegranate fruit tree

-७९९-

ॐ दाडिमीवृक्षरूपायै स्वाहा

oṁ dāḍimīvṛkṣarūpāyai svāhā
799. To she who is the form of the pomegranate fruit tree

-८००-

ॐ दाडिमीवनवासिन्यै स्वाहा

oṁ dāḍimīvanavāsinyai svāhā
800. To she who resides in the forest of pomegranate fruit trees

-८०१-

ॐ दाडिमीफलसाम्योरुपयोधरसमन्वितायै स्वाहा

oṁ dāḍimīphalasāmyorupayodharasamanvitāyai svāhā
801. To she who puts together the various means of peace like the seeds of a pomegranate fruit

-८०२-

ॐ दक्षिणायै स्वाहा

oṁ dakṣiṇāyai svāhā
802. To she who has ability

-८०३-

ॐ दक्षिणारूपायै स्वाहा

oṁ dakṣiṇārūpāyai svāhā
803. To she who is the form of ability

-८०४-

ॐ दक्षिणारूपधारिण्यै स्वाहा

oṁ dakṣiṇārūpadhāriṇyai svāhā
804. To she who supports the form of ability

-८०५-

ॐ दक्षकन्यायै स्वाहा

oṁ dakṣakanyāyai svāhā
805. To she who is the daughter of ability

-८०६-

ॐ दक्षपुत्र्यै स्वाहा

oṁ dakṣaputryai svāhā
806. To she who is the daughter of ability

-८०७-

ॐ दक्षमातायै स्वाहा

oṁ dakṣamātāyai svāhā
807. To she who is the mother of ability

-८०८-

ॐ दक्षस्वे स्वाहा

oṁ dakṣasve svāhā
808. To she who dwells with ability

-८०९-

ॐ दक्षगोत्रायै स्वाहा

oṁ dakṣagotrāyai svāhā
809. To she who is the progenitor of the lineage of ability

-८१०-

ॐ दक्षसुतायै स्वाहा

oṁ dakṣasutāyai svāhā

810. To she who is the daughter of ability

-८११-

ॐ दक्षयज्ञविनाशिन्यै स्वाहा

oṁ dakṣayajñavināśinyai svāhā

811. To she who destroyed the sacrifice of ability

-८१२-

ॐ दक्षयज्ञनाशकर्त्र्यै स्वाहा

oṁ dakṣayajñanāśakartryai svāhā

812. To she who caused the destruction of the sacrifice of ability

-८१३-

ॐ दक्षयज्ञान्तकारिण्यै स्वाहा

oṁ dakṣayajñāntakāriṇyai svāhā

813. To she who is the cause of the end of the sacrifice of ability

-८१४-

ॐ दक्षप्रसूत्यै स्वाहा

oṁ dakṣaprasūtyai svāhā

814. To she who gave birth to ability

-८१५-

ॐ दक्षेज्यायै स्वाहा

oṁ dakṣejyāyai svāhā

815. To she who is the mother of ability

-८१६-

ॐ दक्षवंशैकपावन्यै स्वाहा

oṁ dakṣavaṁśaikapāvanyai svāhā

816. To she who alone purified the family of ability

-८१७-

ॐ दक्षात्मजायै स्वाहा

oṁ dakṣātmajāyai svāhā
817. To she who gave birth to the soul of ability

-८१८-

ॐ दक्षसूनवे स्वाहा

oṁ dakṣasūnave svāhā
818. To she who was born from ability

-८१९-

ॐ दक्षजायै स्वाहा

oṁ dakṣajāyai svāhā
819. To she who is the child of ability

-८२०-

ॐ दक्षजातिकायै स्वाहा

oṁ dakṣajātikāyai svāhā
820. To she who was born from ability

-८२१-

ॐ दक्षजन्मायै स्वाहा

oṁ dakṣajanmāyai svāhā
821. To she who is the mother of ability

-८२२-

ॐ दक्षजनुषे स्वाहा

oṁ dakṣajanuṣe svāhā
822. To she who is in the mother of ability

-८२३-

ॐ दक्षदेहसमुद्भवायै स्वाहा

oṁ dakṣadehasamudbhavāyai svāhā
823. To she who engenders the body of ability

-८२४-

ॐ दक्षजनुषे स्वाहा

oṁ dakṣajanuṣe svāhā
824. To she who is in the mother of ability

-८२५-

ॐ दक्षयागध्वंसिन्यै स्वाहा

oṁ dakṣayāgadhvaṁsinyai svāhā
825. To she who destroys the sacrifice of ability

-८२६-

ॐ दक्षकन्यकायै स्वाहा

oṁ dakṣakanyakāyai svāhā
826. To she who manifests as the daughter of ability

-८२७-

ॐ दक्षिणाचारनिरतायै स्वाहा

oṁ dakṣiṇācāraniratāyai svāhā
827. To she who is the ultimate behavior of perfection

-८२८-

ॐ दक्षिणाचारतुष्टिदायै स्वाहा

oṁ dakṣiṇācāratuṣṭidāyai svāhā
828. To she who gives satisfaction to those who perform the behavior of perfection

-८२९-

ॐ दक्षिणाचारसंसिद्धायै स्वाहा

oṁ dakṣiṇācārasaṁsiddhāyai svāhā
829. To she who gives perfection to those who perform the behavior of perfection

-८३०-

ॐ दक्षिणाचारभावितायै स्वाहा

oṁ dakṣiṇācārabhāvitāyai svāhā

830. To she who gives the attitude to those who perform the behavior of perfection

-८३१-

ॐ दक्षिणाचारसुखिन्यै स्वाहा

oṁ dakṣiṇācārasukhinyai svāhā

831. To she who is the happiness of those who perform the behavior of perfection

-८३२-

ॐ दक्षिणाचारसाधितायै स्वाहा

oṁ dakṣiṇācārasādhitāyai svāhā

832. To she who gives more than adequate to those who perform the behavior of perfection

-८३३-

ॐ दक्षिणाचारमोक्षाप्त्यै स्वाहा

oṁ dakṣiṇācāramokṣāptyai svāhā

833. To she who includes among the liberated those who perform the behavior of perfection

-८३४-

ॐ दक्षिणाचारवन्दितायै स्वाहा

oṁ dakṣiṇācāravanditāyai svāhā

834. To she who praises those who perform the behavior of perfection

-८३५-

ॐ दक्षिणाचारशरणायै स्वाहा

oṁ dakṣiṇācāraśaraṇāyai svāhā

835. To she who gives refuge to those who perform the behavior of perfection

-८३६-

ॐ दक्षिणाचारहर्षितायै स्वाहा

oṁ dakṣiṇācāraharṣitāyai svāhā
836. To she who is the delight of those who perform the behavior of perfection

-८३७-

ॐ द्वारपालप्रियायै स्वाहा

oṁ dvārapālapriyāyai svāhā
837. To she who loves the protector of the door

-८३८-

ॐ द्वारवासिन्यै स्वाहा

oṁ dvāravāsinyai svāhā
838. To she who resides inside the door

-८३९-

ॐ द्वारसंस्थितायै स्वाहा

oṁ dvārasaṁsthitāyai svāhā
839. To she who is established inside the door

-८४०-

ॐ द्वाररूपायै स्वाहा

oṁ dvārarūpāyai svāhā
840. To she who is the form of the door

-८४१-

ॐ द्वारसंस्थायै स्वाहा

oṁ dvārasaṁsthāyai svāhā
841. To she who is established at the door

-८४२-

ॐ द्वारदेशनिवासिन्यै स्वाहा

oṁ dvāradeśanivāsinyai svāhā
842. To she who is established in the place inside the door

-८४३-

ॐ द्वारकर्यै स्वाहा

oṁ dvārakaryai svāhā
843. To she who is the cause of the door

-८४४-

ॐ द्वारधात्र्यै स्वाहा

oṁ dvāradhātryai svāhā
844. To she who is the support of the door

-८४५-

ॐ दोषमात्रविवर्जितायै स्वाहा

oṁ doṣamātravivarjitāyai svāhā
845. To she who excludes limitations and faults

-८४६-

ॐ दोषकरायै स्वाहा

oṁ doṣakarāyai svāhā
846. To she who produces faults

-८४७-

ॐ दोषहरायै स्वाहा

oṁ doṣaharāyai svāhā
847. To she who takes away faults

-८४८-

ॐ दोषराशिविनाशिन्यै स्वाहा

oṁ doṣarāśivināśinyai svāhā
848. To she who destroys heaps of faults

-८४९-

ॐ दोषाकरविभूषाढ्यायै स्वाहा

oṁ doṣākaravibhūṣāḍhyāyai svāhā
849. To she who rides upon the illumination of the commission of no fault

-८५०-

ॐ दोषाकरकपालिन्यै स्वाहा

oṁ doṣākarakapālinyai svāhā
850. To she who protects those who commit no fault

-८५१-

ॐ दोषाकरसहस्राभायै स्वाहा

oṁ doṣākarasahasrābhāyai svāhā
851. To she who illuminates thousands who commit no fault

-८५२-

ॐ दोशाकरसमाननायै स्वाहा

oṁ dośākarasamānanāyai svāhā
852. To she who has peace with those who commit no fault

-८५३-

ॐ दोषाकरमुख्यै स्वाहा

oṁ doṣākaramukhyai svāhā
853. To she who is the leader of those who commit no fault

-८५४-

ॐ दिव्यायै स्वाहा

oṁ divyāyai svāhā
854. To she who is divine

-८५५-

ॐ दोषाकरकराग्रजायै स्वाहा

oṁ doṣākarakarāgrajāyai svāhā
855. To she who was born before those who commit no fault

-८५६-

ॐ दोषाकरसमज्योतिषे स्वाहा

oṁ doṣākarasamajyotiṣe svāhā
856. To she who shines her light equally upon those who commit no fault

-८५७-

ॐ दोषाकरसुशीतलायै स्वाहा

oṁ doṣākarasuśītalāyai svāhā
857. To she who wafts excellent cooling rays to those who commit no fault

-८५८-

ॐ दोषाकरश्रेण्यै स्वाहा

oṁ doṣākaraśreṇyai svāhā
858. To she who is a multitude of those who commit no fault

-८५९-

ॐ दोषसदृशापाङ्गवीक्षणायै स्वाहा

oṁ doṣasadṛśāpāṅgavīkṣaṇāyai svāhā
859. To she who perceives un-manifested faults

-८६०-

ॐ दोषाकरेष्टदेव्यै स्वाहा

oṁ doṣākareṣṭadevyai svāhā
860. To she who is the chosen form of the goddess of those who commit no fault

-८६१-

ॐ दोषाकरनिषेवितायै स्वाहा

oṁ doṣākaraniṣevitāyai svāhā
861. To she who is served by those who commit no fault

-८६२-

ॐ दोषाकरप्राणरूपायै स्वाहा

oṁ doṣākaraprāṇarūpāyai svāhā
862. To she who is the form of the life force of those who commit no fault

-८६३-

ॐ दोषाकरमरीचिकायै स्वाहा

oṁ doṣākaramarīcikāyai svāhā
863. To she who is like water in the desert for those who commit no fault

-८६४-

ॐ दोषाकरोल्लसद्भालायै स्वाहा

oṁ doṣākarollasadbhālāyai svāhā
864. To she who is the brilliant illumination of those who commit no fault

-८६५-

ॐ दोषाकरसुहर्षिण्यै स्वाहा

oṁ doṣākarasuharṣiṇyai svāhā
865. To she who is the excellent delight of those who commit no fault

-८६६-

ॐ दोषाकरशिरोभूषायै स्वाहा

oṁ doṣākaraśirobhūṣāyai svāhā
866. To she who illuminates the head of those who commit no fault

-८६७-

ॐ दोषाकरवधूप्रियायै स्वाहा

oṁ doṣākaravadhūpriyāyai svāhā
867. To she who is the beloved of the daughter-in-law of those who commit no fault

-८६८-

ॐ दोषाकरवधूप्राणायै स्वाहा

oṁ doṣākaravadhūprāṇāyai svāhā
868. To she who is the life force of the beloved daughter-in-law of those who commit no fault

-८६९-

ॐ दोषाकरवधूर्मतायै स्वाहा

oṁ doṣākaravadhūrmatāyai svāhā

869. To she who is the idea or opinion of the beloved daughter-in-law of those who commit no fault

-८७०-

ॐ दोषाकरवधूप्रीतायै स्वाहा

oṁ doṣākaravadhūprītāyai svāhā

870. To she who is the beloved daughter-in-law of those who commit no fault

-८७१-

ॐ दोषाकरवधूरप्यै स्वाहा

oṁ doṣākaravadhūrapyai svāhā

871. To she who is even the beloved daughter-in-law of those who commit no fault

-८७२-

ॐ दोषापूज्यायै स्वाहा

oṁ doṣāpūjyāyai svāhā

872. To she who is worshiped by those who commit no fault

-८७३-

ॐ दोषापूजितायै स्वाहा

oṁ doṣāpūjitāyai svāhā

873. To she who worships those who commit no fault

-८७४-

ॐ दोषहारिण्यै स्वाहा

oṁ doṣahāriṇyai svāhā

874. To she who takes away all faults

-८७५-

ॐ दोषाजापमहानन्दायै स्वाहा

oṁ doṣājāpamahānandāyai svāhā
875. To she who is great bliss for those who do not repeat committing faults

-८७६-

ॐ दोषाजापपरायणायै स्वाहा

oṁ doṣājāpaparāyaṇāyai svāhā
876. To she who is the final end for those who do not repeat committing faults

-८७७-

ॐ दोषापुरश्चाररतायै स्वाहा

oṁ doṣāpuraścāraratāyai svāhā
877. To she who moves to make faults incomplete

-८७८-

ॐ दोषापूजकपुत्रिण्यै स्वाहा

oṁ doṣāpūjakaputriṇyai svāhā
878. To she who is daughter of those who worship without fault

-८७९-

ॐ दोषापूजकवात्सल्यकारिणीजगदम्बिकायै स्वाहा

oṁ doṣāpūjakavātsalyakāriṇījagadambikāyai svāhā
879. To she who is the mother of the perceivable worlds, the cause of the devoted children who worship without fault

-८८०-

ॐ दोषापूजकवैरिघ्न्यै स्वाहा

oṁ doṣāpūjakavairighnyai svāhā
880. To she who destroys the enemies of those who worship without fault

-८८१-

ॐ दोषापूजकविघ्नहृते स्वाहा

oṁ doṣāpūjakavighnahṛte svāhā

881. To she who takes delight in the worship without fault

-८८२-

ॐ दोषापूजकसन्तुष्टायै स्वाहा

oṁ doṣāpūjakasantuṣṭāyai svāhā

882. To she who is satisfied by the worship without fault

-८८३-

ॐ दोषापूजकमुक्तिदायै स्वाहा

oṁ doṣāpūjakamuktidāyai svāhā

883. To she who gives liberation to those who worship without fault

-८८४-

ॐ दमप्रसूनसम्पूज्यायै स्वाहा

oṁ damaprasūnasampūjyāyai svāhā

884. To she who is worshiped with fruit by those of self-control

-८८५-

ॐ दमपुष्पप्रियायै स्वाहा

oṁ damapuṣpapriyāyai svāhā

885. To she who loves the flowers of those of self-control

-८८६-

ॐ दुर्योधनपूज्यायै स्वाहा

oṁ duryodhanapūjyāyai svāhā

886. To she who was worshiped by Duryodhan (who fought with Kṛṣṇa and Arjuna in the Mahābharat)

-८८७-

ॐ दुःशासनसमर्चितायै स्वाहा

oṁ duḥśāsanasamarcitāyai svāhā
887. To she who was offered to by Duḥśāsan (brother of Duryodhan)

-८८८-

ॐ दण्डपाणिप्रियायै स्वाहा

oṁ daṇḍapāṇipriyāyai svāhā
888. To she who is the beloved of the one with a staff in his hands (a name of Yama, the god of death)

-८८९-

ॐ दण्डपाणिमातायै स्वाहा

oṁ daṇḍapāṇimātāyai svāhā
889. To she who is the mother of the one with a staff in his hands

-८९०-

ॐ दयानिध्यै स्वाहा

oṁ dayānidhyai svāhā
890. To she who is the treasure of compassion

-८९१-

ॐ दण्डपाणिसमाराध्यायै स्वाहा

oṁ daṇḍapāṇisamārādhyāyai svāhā
891. To she who is the enjoyable offering of the one with a staff in his hands

-८९२-

ॐ दण्डपाणिप्रपूजितायै स्वाहा

oṁ daṇḍapāṇiprapūjitāyai svāhā
892. To she who worships the one with a staff in his hands

-८९३-

ॐ दण्डपाणिगृहासक्तायै स्वाहा

oṁ daṇḍapāṇigṛhāsaktāyai svāhā
893. To she who belongs to the household of the one with a staff in his hands

-८९४-

ॐ दण्डपाणिप्रियंवदायै स्वाहा

oṁ daṇḍapāṇipriyaṁvadāyai svāhā
894. To she who speaks pleasingly to the one with a staff in his hands

-८९५-

ॐ दण्डपाणिप्रियतमायै स्वाहा

oṁ daṇḍapāṇipriyatamāyai svāhā
895. To she who is the beloved of the one with a staff in his hands

-८९६-

ॐ दण्डपाणिमनोहरायै स्वाहा

oṁ daṇḍapāṇimanoharāyai svāhā
896. To she who shows mesmerising beauty to the one with a staff in his hands

-८९७-

ॐ दण्डपाणिहृतप्राणायै स्वाहा

oṁ daṇḍapāṇihṛtaprāṇāyai svāhā
897. To she who is the delightful life force of the one with a staff in his hands

-८९८-

ॐ दण्डपाणिसुसिद्धिदायै स्वाहा

oṁ daṇḍapāṇisusiddhidāyai svāhā
898. To she who grants the attainment of excellence to the one with a staff in his hands

-८९९-

ॐ दण्डपाणिपरामृष्टायै स्वाहा

oṁ daṇḍapāṇiparāmṛṣṭāyai svāhā

899. To she who has the supreme relationship with the one with a staff in his hands

-९००-

ॐ दण्डपाणिप्रहतार्षिंयै स्वाहा

oṁ daṇḍapāṇiprahatārṣiṁyai svāhā

900. To she who shines with the learning of the one with a staff in his hands

-९०१-

ॐ दण्डपाणिविघ्नहरायै स्वाहा

oṁ daṇḍapāṇivighnaharāyai svāhā

901. To she who takes away the obstacles from the one with a staff in his hands

-९०२-

ॐ दण्डपाणिशिरोधृतायै स्वाहा

oṁ daṇḍapāṇiśirodhṛtāyai svāhā

902. To she who gives constant splendor to the head of the one with a staff in his hands

-९०३-

ॐ दण्डपाणिप्राप्तचर्चायै स्वाहा

oṁ daṇḍapāṇiprāptacarcāyai svāhā

903. To she who has attained to discussions with the one with a staff in his hands

-९०४-

ॐ दण्डपाण्युन्मुख्यै स्वाहा

oṁ daṇḍapāṇyunmukhyai svāhā

904. To she whose face is looked upon by the one with a staff in his hands

-९०५-

ॐ दण्डपाणिप्राप्तपदायै स्वाहा

oṁ daṇḍapāṇiprāptapadāyai svāhā
905. To she whose feet have been attained by the one with a staff in his hands

-९०६-

ॐ दण्डपाणिवरोन्मुख्यै स्वाहा

oṁ daṇḍapāṇivaronmukhyai svāhā
906. To she whose boon is looked upon by the one with a staff in his hands

-९०७-

ॐ दण्डहस्तायै स्वाहा

oṁ daṇḍahastāyai svāhā
907. To she who holds a staff in her hands

-९०८-

ॐ दण्डपाण्यै स्वाहा

oṁ daṇḍapāṇyai svāhā
908. To she who disciplines with her hands

-९०९-

ॐ दण्डबाहवे स्वाहा

oṁ daṇḍabāhave svāhā
909. To she who disciplines with her arms

-९१०-

ॐ दरान्तकृते स्वाहा

oṁ darāntakṛte svāhā
910. To she who is the end of fear

-९११-

ॐ दण्डदोष्कायै स्वाहा

oṁ daṇḍadoṣkāyai svāhā
911. To she who disciplines those with faults

-९१२-

ॐ दण्डकरायै स्वाहा

oṁ daṇḍakarāyai svāhā
912. To she who manifests discipline

-९१३-

ॐ दण्डचित्तकृतास्पदायै स्वाहा

oṁ daṇḍacittakṛtāspadāyai svāhā
913. To she who moves through the objects of consciousness with discipline

-९१४-

ॐ दण्डविद्यायै स्वाहा

oṁ daṇḍavidyāyai svāhā
914. To she who learns with discipline

-९१५-

ॐ दण्डिमातायै स्वाहा

oṁ daṇḍimātāyai svāhā
915. To she who is the mother of those with discipline

-९१६-

ॐ दण्डिखण्डकनाशिन्यै स्वाहा

oṁ daṇḍikhaṇḍakanāśinyai svāhā
916. To she who destroys the limitations of those with discipline

-९१७-

ॐ दण्डिप्रियायै स्वाहा

oṁ daṇḍipriyāyai svāhā
917. To she who is the beloved of those with discipline

-९१८-

ॐ दण्डिपूज्यायै स्वाहा

oṁ daṇḍipūjyāyai svāhā
918. To she who is worshiped by those with discipline

-९१९-

ॐ दण्डिसन्तोषदायिन्यै स्वाहा

oṁ daṇḍisantoṣadāyinyai svāhā
919. To she who gives satisfaction to those with discipline

-९२०-

ॐ दस्युपूज्यायै स्वाहा

oṁ dasyupūjyāyai svāhā
920. To she who is worshiped by impious people

-९२१-

ॐ दस्युरतायै स्वाहा

oṁ dasyuratāyai svāhā
921. To she who is the ultimate of impious people

-९२२-

ॐ दस्युद्रविणदायिन्यै स्वाहा

oṁ dasyudraviṇadāyinyai svāhā
922. To she who gives things to impious people

-९२३-

ॐ दस्युवर्गकृतार्हायै स्वाहा

oṁ dasyuvargakṛtārhāyai svāhā
923. To she who performs actions in every category for impious people

-९२४-

ॐ दस्युवर्गविनाशिन्यै स्वाहा

oṁ dasyuvargavināśinyai svāhā
924. To she who destroys every category for impious people

-९२५-

ॐ दस्युनिर्नाशिन्यै स्वाहा

oṁ dasyunirnāśinyai svāhā
925. To she who expels impious people

-९२६-

ॐ दस्युकुलनिर्नाशिन्यै स्वाहा

oṁ dasyukulanirnāśinyai svāhā

926. To she who expels the families of impious people

-९२७-

ॐ दस्युप्रियकर्यै स्वाहा

oṁ dasyupriyakaryai svāhā

927. To she who is the cause of love for impious people

-९२८-

ॐ दस्युनृत्यदर्शनतत्परायै स्वाहा

oṁ dasyunṛtyadarśanatatparāyai svāhā

928. To she who is totally devoted to watching the dances of impious people

-९२९-

ॐ दुष्टदण्डकर्यै स्वाहा

oṁ duṣṭadaṇḍakaryai svāhā

929. To she who is the cause of discipline for the wicked

-९३०-

ॐ दुष्टवर्गविद्राविण्यै स्वाहा

oṁ duṣṭavargavidrāviṇyai svāhā

930. To she who defeats all of the categories of the wicked

-९३१-

ॐ दुष्टवर्गनिग्रहार्हायै स्वाहा

oṁ duṣṭavarganigrahārhāyai svāhā

931. To she who restrains the categories of the wicked

-९३२-

ॐ दूषकप्राणनाशिन्यै स्वाहा

oṁ dūṣakaprāṇanāśinyai svāhā

932. To she who destroys the life force of the wicked

-९३३-

ॐ दुषकोत्तापजनन्यै स्वाहा

oṁ duṣakottāpajananyai svāhā

933. To she who is the mother of the affliction of the wicked

-९३४-

ॐ दूषकारिष्टकारिण्यै स्वाहा

oṁ dūṣakāriṣṭakāriṇyai svāhā

934. To she who is the cause of the desires of the wicked

-९३५-

ॐ दूषकद्वेषणकर्यै स्वाहा

oṁ dūṣakadveṣaṇakaryai svāhā

935. To she who is the cause of enmity of the wicked

-९३६-

ॐ दाहिकायै स्वाहा

oṁ dāhikāyai svāhā

936. To she who is a burning conflagration

-९३७-

ॐ दहनात्मिकायै स्वाहा

oṁ dahanātmikāyai svāhā

937. To she who is the cause of the manifestation of the soul of fire

-९३८-

ॐ दारुकारिनिहन्त्र्यै स्वाहा

oṁ dārukārinihantryai svāhā

938. To she who slays the enemies of the deodhar tree (also a name of Shiva and Krishna's Charioteer)

-९३९-

ॐ दारुकेश्वरपूजितायै स्वाहा

oṁ dārukeśvarapūjitāyai svāhā

939. To she who is worshiped by the supreme lord of the deodhar tree

-९४०-

ॐ दारुकेश्वरमातायै स्वाहा

oṁ dārukeśvaramātāyai svāhā

940. To she who is the mother of the supreme lord of the deodhar tree

-९४१-

ॐ दारुकेश्वरवन्दितायै स्वाहा

oṁ dārukeśvaravanditāyai svāhā

941. To she who is praised by the supreme lord of the deodhar tree

-९४२-

ॐ दर्भहस्तायै स्वाहा

oṁ darbhahastāyai svāhā

942. To she who holds darbha or kusha grass in her hand

-९४३-

ॐ दर्भयूतायै स्वाहा

oṁ darbhayūtāyai svāhā

943. To she who is with a large quantity of darbha or kusha grass

-९४४-

ॐ दर्भकर्मविवर्जितायै स्वाहा

oṁ darbhakarmavivarjitāyai svāhā

944. To she who prohibits action with darbha or kusha grass

-९४५-

ॐ दर्भमयै स्वाहा

oṁ darbhamayai svāhā

945. To she who manifests as darbha or kusha grass

-९४६-

ॐ दर्भतनवे स्वाहा

oṁ darbhatanave svāhā

946. To she who is the embodiment of darbha or kusha grass

-९४७-

ॐ दर्भसर्वस्वरूपिण्यै स्वाहा

oṁ darbhasarvasvarūpiṇyai svāhā
947. To she who is the intrinsic nature of all darbha or kusha grass

-९४८-

ॐ दर्भकर्माचाररतायै स्वाहा

oṁ darbhakarmācāraratāyai svāhā
948. To she who is the ultimate movement of action with darbha or kusha grass

-९४९-

ॐ दर्भहस्तकृतार्हणायै स्वाहा

oṁ darbhahastakṛtārhaṇāyai svāhā
949. To she who makes worship with her own hands with darbha or kusha grass

-९५०-

ॐ दर्भानुकूलायै स्वाहा

oṁ darbhānukūlāyai svāhā
950. To she who acts in a friendly or agreeable way with darbha or kusha grass

-९५१-

ॐ दार्भर्यायै स्वाहा

oṁ dārbharyāyai svāhā
951. To she who is present in a large quantity of darbha or kusha grass

-९५२-

ॐ दर्वीपात्रानुदामिन्यै स्वाहा

oṁ darvīpātrānudāminyai svāhā
952. To she who methodically controls drinking from a ladle

-९५३-

ॐ दमघोषप्रपूज्यायै स्वाहा

oṁ damaghoṣaprapūjyāyai svāhā
953. To she who is worshiped by those who practice self-control

-९५४-

ॐ दमघोषवरप्रदायै स्वाहा

oṁ damaghoṣavarapradāyai svāhā
954. To she who gives the boon to those who practice self-control

-९५५-

ॐ दमघोषसमाराध्यायै स्वाहा

oṁ damaghoṣasamārādhyāyai svāhā
955. To she who is pleased with offerings by those who practice self-control

-९५६-

ॐ दावाग्निरूपिण्यै स्वाहा

oṁ dāvāgnirūpiṇyai svāhā
956. To she who has the capacity to become the form of a fire in the forest

-९५७-

ॐ दावाग्निरूपायै स्वाहा

oṁ dāvāgnirūpāyai svāhā
957. To she who is the form of a fire in the forest

-९५८-

ॐ दावाग्निनिर्नाशितमहाबलायै स्वाहा

oṁ dāvāgninirnāśitamahābalāyai svāhā
958. To she who has the great strength of destruction of a fire in the forest

-९५९-

ॐ दन्तदंष्ट्रासुरकलायै स्वाहा

oṁ dantadaṁṣṭrāsurakalāyai svāhā
959. To she who is the bite of the teeth of the demons of duality

-९६०-

ॐ दन्तचर्चितहस्तिकायै स्वाहा

oṁ dantacarcitahastikāyai svāhā
960. To she who is contemplated of as the tusks of an elephant

-९६१-

ॐ दन्तदंष्ट्रस्यन्दनायै स्वाहा

oṁ dantadaṁṣṭrasyandanāyai svāhā
961. To she who is the rings which binds the teeth, tusks, or feet of an elephant

-९६२-

ॐ दन्तनिर्णाशितासुरायै स्वाहा

oṁ dantanirṇāśitāsurāyai svāhā
962. To she who destroys the teeth of the demons of duality

-९६३-

ॐ दधिपूज्यायै स्वाहा

oṁ dadhipūjyāyai svāhā
963. To she who is worshiped with yogurt

-९६४-

ॐ दधिप्रीतायै स्वाहा

oṁ dadhiprītāyai svāhā
964. To she who is loved with yogurt

-९६५-

ॐ दधीचिवरदायिन्यै स्वाहा

oṁ dadhīcivaradāyinyai svāhā

965. To she who gives the boon to Dadhīci, (who is as pure as yogurt, whose bones became the weapon with which Indra slay Vritrasura)

-९६६-

ॐ दधीचीष्टदेवतायै स्वाहा

oṁ dadhīcīṣṭadevatāyai svāhā

966. To she who is the chosen goddess of Dadhīci

-९६७-

ॐ दधीचिमोक्षदायिन्यै स्वाहा

oṁ dadhīcimokṣadāyinyai svāhā

967. To she who gives liberation to Dadhīci

-९६८-

ॐ दधीचिदैन्यहन्त्र्यै स्वाहा

oṁ dadhīcidainyahantryai svāhā

968. To she who takes away the duality for Dadhīci

-९६९-

ॐ दधीचिदरदारिण्यै स्वाहा

oṁ dadhīcidaradāriṇyai svāhā

969. To she who splits apart fear for Dadhīci

-९७०-

ॐ दधीचिभक्तिसुखिन्यै स्वाहा

oṁ dadhīcibhaktisukhinyai svāhā

970. To she who gives the happiness of devotion to Dadhīci

-९७१-

ॐ दधीचिमुनिसेवितायै स्वाहा

oṁ dadhīcimunisevitāyai svāhā

971. To she who serves Dadhīci Muni

-९७२-

ॐ दधीचिज्ञानदात्र्यै स्वाहा

oṁ dadhīcijñānadātryai svāhā
972. To she who gives wisdom to Dadhīci

-९७३-

ॐ दधीचिगुणदायिन्यै स्वाहा

oṁ dadhīciguṇadāyinyai svāhā
973. To she who gives all qualities to Dadhīci

-९७४-

ॐ दधीचिकुलसम्भूषायै स्वाहा

oṁ dadhīcikulasambhūṣāyai svāhā
974. To she who causes the family to shine for Dadhīci

-९७५-

ॐ दधीचिभुक्तिमुक्तिदायै स्वाहा

oṁ dadhīcibhuktimuktidāyai svāhā
975. To she who gives enjoyment and liberation to Dadhīci

-९७६-

ॐ दधीचिकुलदेव्यै स्वाहा

oṁ dadhīcikuladevyai svāhā
976. To she who is the family deity of Dadhīci

-९७७-

ॐ दधीचिकुलदेवतायै स्वाहा

oṁ dadhīcikuladevatāyai svāhā
977. To she who is the family deities of Dadhīci

-९७८-

ॐ दधीचिकुलगम्यायै स्वाहा

oṁ dadhīcikulagamyāyai svāhā
978. To she who is the family intended destination for Dadhīci

-९७९-

ॐ दधीचिकुलपूजितायै स्वाहा

oṁ dadhīcikulapūjitāyai svāhā

979. To she who is worshiped by the family of Dadhīci

-९८०-

ॐ दधीचिसुखदात्र्यै स्वाहा

oṁ dadhīcisukhadātryai svāhā

980. To she who gives happiness to Dadhīci

-९८१-

ॐ दधीचिदीनहारिण्यै स्वाहा

oṁ dadhīcidīnahāriṇyai svāhā

981. To she who takes away lowliness from Dadhīci

-९८२-

ॐ दधीचिदुःखहन्त्र्यै स्वाहा

oṁ dadhīciduḥkhahantryai svāhā

982. To she who slays pain for Dadhīci

-९८३-

ॐ दधीचिकुलसुन्दर्यै स्वाहा

oṁ dadhīcikulasundaryai svāhā

983. To she who is the beauty of the family for Dadhīci

-९८४-

ॐ दधीचिकुलसम्भूतायै स्वाहा

oṁ dadhīcikulasambhūtāyai svāhā

984. To she who is the judge for the family of Dadhīci

-९८५-

ॐ दधीचिकुलपालिन्यै स्वाहा

oṁ dadhīcikulapālinyai svāhā

985. To she who is the protector for the family of Dadhīci

-९८६-

ॐ दधीचिदानगम्यायै स्वाहा

oṁ dadhīcidānagamyāyai svāhā

986. To she who is the intended destination for the gifts of Dadhīci

-९८७-

ॐ दधीचिदानमानिन्यै स्वाहा

oṁ dadhīcidānamāninyai svāhā

987. To she who is respect for the gifts of Dadhīci

-९८८-

ॐ दधीचिदानसन्तुष्टायै स्वाहा

oṁ dadhīcidānasantuṣṭāyai svāhā

988. To she who is satisfaction for the gifts of Dadhīci

-९८९-

ॐ दधीचिदानदेवतायै स्वाहा

oṁ dadhīcidānadevatāyai svāhā

989. To she who is the deity of the gifts of Dadhīci

-९९०-

ॐ दधीचिजयसम्प्रीतायै स्वाहा

oṁ dadhīcijayasamprītāyai svāhā

990. To she who loves the victory of Dadhīci

-९९१-

ॐ दधीचिजपमानसायै स्वाहा

oṁ dadhīcijapamānasāyai svāhā

991. To she who is the thought most repeated by Dadhīci

-९९२-

ॐ दधीचिजपपूजाढ्यायै स्वाहा

oṁ dadhīcijapapūjāḍhyāyai svāhā

992. To she who rides upon the worship most repeated by Dadhīci

-९९३-

ॐ दधीचिजपमालिकायै स्वाहा

oṁ dadhīcijapamālikāyai svāhā
993. To she who is the garland of mantras most repeated by Dadhīci

-९९४-

ॐ दधीचिजपसन्तुष्टायै स्वाहा

oṁ dadhīcijapasantuṣṭāyai svāhā
994. To she who gives satisfaction for the mantras most repeated by Dadhīci

-९९५-

ॐ दधीचिजपतोषिण्यै स्वाहा

oṁ dadhīcijapatoṣiṇyai svāhā
995. To she who is the satisfaction for the mantras most repeated by Dadhīci

-९९६-

ॐ दधीचितापसाराध्यायै स्वाहा

oṁ dadhīcitāpasārādhyāyai svāhā
996. To she who is pleased by the purifying austerities performed by Dadhīci

-९९७-

ॐ दधीचिशुभदायिन्यै स्वाहा

oṁ dadhīciśubhadāyinyai svāhā
997. To she who gives pure illumination to Dadhīci

-९९८-

ॐ दूर्वायै स्वाहा

oṁ dūrvāyai svāhā
998. To she who is durbha grass

-९९९-

ॐ दूर्वादलश्यामायै स्वाहा

oṁ dūrvādalaśyāmāyai svāhā

999. To she who is sprouting durbha grass

-१०००-

ॐ दूर्वादलसमद्युते स्वाहा

oṁ dūrvādalasamadyute svāhā

1000. To she who is the newly created sprouts of durbha grass

इति दुर्गाया दकारादिसहस्रनामावल्याः स्वाहाकारः समाप्तः

iti durgāyā dakārādisahasranāmāvalyāḥ svāhākāraḥ samāptaḥ

Thus ends the Song for Durgā of a Thousand Names beginning with the letter D offered with "svāhā"

श्री दुर्गा चालीसा
Śrī Durgā Cālīsā

दोहा
dohā

जय श्री दुर्गा अम्बिका । जगत्पालिनी मात ।
तुम्हरो चालीसा रचहुँ । कीजै मोहि सनाथ ॥
jaya śrī durgā ambikā, jagatpālinī māta |
tumharo cālīsā racahuṁ, kījai mohi sanātha ||
Victory to the Respected Reliever of Difficulties, Mother of the Universe, the Mother who protects the world. I elucidate your song of praise. Please eradicate all ignorance.

चौपाई
caupāī

नमो नमो दुर्गे सुख करनी । नमो नमो अम्बे दुख हरनी ॥
namo namo durge sukha karanī |
namo namo ambe dukha haranī ||
I bow, I bow, to the Reliever of Difficulties, Cause of Happiness. I bow, I bow, to the Mother who takes away all pain.

निरंकार है ज्योति तुम्हारी । तिहूँ लोक फैली उजियारी ॥
niraṁkāra hai jyoti tumhārī | tihūṁ loka phailī ujiyārī ||
Your light illuminates all darkness, your brightness extends over the three worlds.

शशि ललाट मुख विशाला । नेत्र लाल भृकुटी विकराला ॥
śaśi lalāṭa mukha viśālā | netra lāla bhṛkuṭī vikarālā ||
With the moon on your forehead your face is tremendous. When you frown with red eyes it is terribly frightening.

रूप मातु को अति सुहवै ।
दरश करत जन अति सुख पावै ॥

rūpa mātu ko ati suhavai |
daraśa karata jana ati sukha pāvai ||

In the form of Mother it is extremely pleasing, and those who see you thusly receive the greatest pleasure.

तुम संसार शक्ति लै कीन्हा । पालन हेतु अन्नधन दीन्हा ॥

tuma saṁsāra śakti lai kīnhā |
pālana hetu annadhana dīnhā ||

You move all the energy amongst all objects and relationships. You protect all, and are the Giver of grains and wealth.

अन्नपूर्णा तुम जग पाला । तुमहीं आदि सुन्दरी बाला ॥

annapūrṇā tuma jaga pālā |
tumahīṁ ādi sundarī bālā ||

As the Goddess who is full of grains and food you protect the world. You are the foremost and most beautiful being.

प्रलयकाल सब नाशन हारी ।
तुम गौरी शिव शंकर प्यारी ॥

pralayakāla saba nāśana hārī |
tuma gaurī śiva śaṁkara pyārī ||

At the time of total dissolution you destroy all. You are the Goddess who is Rays of Light, beloved of Śiva, Śankar, the Cause of Peace.

शिव योगी तुम्हरे गुण गावें । ब्रह्मा विष्णु तुम्हें नित ध्यावें ॥

śiva yogī tumhare guṇa gāveṁ |
brahmā viṣṇu tumheṁ nita dhyāveṁ ||

Śiva and all yogis sing of your qualities. Brahma and Viṣṇu always meditate upon you.

रूप सरस्वति का तुम धारा ।
दै सुबुद्धि ऋषि मुनिन उवारा ॥

rūpa sarasvati kā tuma dhārā |
dai subuddhi ṛṣi munina uvārā ||

You wear the form of Sarasvati, Goddess of Knowledge. You give excellent knowledge which liberates the ṛṣis and munis.

धर्‌यो रूप नरसिंह को अम्बा ।
प्रकट भईं विदारि कै खम्बा ॥

dharyo rūpa narasiṁha ko ambā |
prakaṭa bhaīṁ vidāri kai khambā ||

You gave the form for Narasingha to wear, Mother, which manifested with the crumbling of the pillar.

रक्षा करि प्रहलाद बचायो ।
हिरण्यकशिपु को स्वर्ग पठायो ॥

rakṣā kari prahlāda bacāyo |
hiraṇyakaśipu ko svarga paṭhāyo ||

Oh Protector, you saved Prahlad, and sent Hiraṇyakaśipu to heaven.

लक्ष्मी रूप धर्‌यो जगमाँही । श्री नारायण अङ्ग समाहीं ॥

lakṣmī rūpa dharyo jagamāṁhī |
śrī nārāyaṇa aṅga samāhīṁ ||

You wear the form of Lakṣmi, Oh Mother of the Universe, which is regarded the same as the body of the Respected Nārāyaṇa.

क्षीरसिन्धु में करत बिलासा । दयासिन्धु दीजै मन आसा ॥

kṣīrasindhu meṁ karata bilāsā |
dayāsindhu dījai mana āsā ||

You are delighted in the ocean of milk. Oh Ocean of Compassion, please grant the mind's wish.

हिंगुलाज में तुम्ही भवानी ।
महिमा अमित न जात बखानी ॥

hiṁgulāja meṁ tumhī bhavānī |
mahimā amita na jāta bakhānī ||

In the Hiṅgulaj you are Bhavānī, the Mother of Existence. No one who is born can describe your greatness.

मातंगी धूमावति माता । भुवनेश्वरि बंगला सुखदाता ॥

mātaṁgī dhūmāvati mātā |
bhuvaneśvari baṁgalā sukhadātā ||

You are Mātaṅgī and Mother Dhūmāvati. As Bhuvaneśvari and Baṅgala you grant comfort and happiness.

श्री भैरवी जगत की तारिणी ।
छिन्न भाल भव दुःख निवारिणी ॥

śrī bhairavī jagata kī tāriṇī |
chinna bhāla bhava duḥkha nivāriṇī ||

As the respected fearful Bhairavī you deliver all the worlds. As Chinnamaṣṭa you prohibit pain in the all the worlds.

लाँगुर बीर करत अगबानी । केहरि बाहन सोह भवानी ॥

lāṁgura bīra karata agabānī |
kehari bāhana soha bhavānī ||

The excellent among the monkeys went to welcome you, oh Bhavānī, you who ride upon the lion.

कर महे खप्पर खड्ग विराजे ।
जाहि विलोकि काल भय भाजे ॥

kara mahe khappara khaṅga virāje |
jāhi viloki kāla bhaya bhāje ||

In your hands are the sword and a beggar's bowl. The Seer experiences the fear of Time, the Great Destroyer.

कर शोभित तब मातु त्रिशूला । जाते उठत शत्रु हिय शूला ॥

kara śobhita taba mātu triśūlā |
jāte uṭhata śatru hiya śūlā ||

Then in Mother's hand is seen the trident by which She abolishes the enemy's spear.

नगरकोट में तुम्हीं विराजत ।

तिंहूँ लोक में डंका वाजत ॥

nagarakoṭa meṁ tumhīṁ virājata |
tiṁhūṁ loka meṁ ḍaṁkā vājata ||

In Nagarkoṭ you are known as Virāja, and the people of the three worlds beat on the drums to celebrate you.

शुंभ निशुंभ दैत्य तुम मारे । रक्तबीज अगनित संहारे ॥

śuṁbha niśuṁbha daitya tuma māre |
raktabīja aganita saṁhāre ||

You slayed the demons Self-Conceit and Self-Deprecation. You dissolved the innumerable Seeds of Desire.

महिषासुर नृप अति अभिमानी ।

जेहि अघ भार मही अकुलानी ॥

mahiṣāsura nṛpa ati abhimānī |
jehi agha bhāra mahī akulānī ||

The King Great Ego was extremely proud. The burden of his guilt for sins brought him down low.

रूप कराल कालिका धारा ।

सैन्य सहित तुम ताहि सँहारा ॥

rūpa karāla kālikā dhārā |
sainya sahita tuma tāhi saṁhārā ||

As Kālī you wear an immense form. You destroyed the entire army in battle.

परी भीर सन्तन पै जब जब ।

भई सहाय मातु तुम तब तब ॥

parī bhīra santana pai jaba jaba |
bhaīṁ sahāya mātu tuma taba taba ||

Whenever your children are burdened with perplexity, then and there you manifest, Oh Mother, to render assistance.

अमरपुरी अरु बासव लोका ।

तब महिमा सब रहहि अशोका ॥

amarapurī aru bāsava lokā |
taba mahimā saba rahahi aśokā ||

Again and again you lead people to dwell in immortality. Then all elucidate your greatness with great joy and tranquility.

वाला में है ज्योति तुम्हारी । पूजहिं तुमहिं सदा नर नारी ॥

vālā meṁ hai jyoti tumhārī |
pūjahiṁ tumahiṁ sadā nara nārī ||

In all the inhabitants your light is burning. Men and women always perform your worship.

प्रेम भक्तियुत जो यश गावहिं ।

दुख दारिद्र निकट नहिं आवहिं ॥

prema bhaktiyuta jo yaśa gāvahiṁ |
dukha dāridra nikaṭa nahiṁ āvahiṁ ||

Whoever will sing this praise with love and devotion, pain and discomfort will not come close to them.

ध्यावहिं तुम्हें जो नर मनलाई ।

जान्म मरण ते सो छुटि जाई ॥

dhyāvahiṁ tumheṁ jo nara manalāī |
jānma maraṇa te so chuṭi jāī ||

Whatever man will meditate on you with full concentration, will escape from the cycle of birth and death.

जोगी सुर मुनि कहत पुकारी ।
योग न हो बिनु शक्ति तुम्हारी ॥

jogī sura muni kahata pukārī |
yoga na ho binu śakti tumhārī ||
The yogis, Gods, and munis all call out, "Without your energy union is impossible!"

शिवशंकर अचरज तप कीन्हा ।
काम क्रोध कहैं बस करि लीन्हा ॥

śivaśaṁkara acaraja tapa kīnhā |
kāma krodha kahaiṁ basa kari līnhā ||
Śiva Śankar performed a most wonderful tapasya by which He defeated Anger and Passion.

निशिदिन ध्यान धरहु शंकर को ।
काहु काल नहिं सुमिरो तुमको ॥

niśidina dhyāna dharahu śaṁkara ko |
kāhu kāla nahiṁ sumiro tumako ||
Even though one meditates upon Śiva every day, he can never reach to the heights of your attainment.

शक्ति रूप को मरम न पायो ।
शक्ति गई तब मन पछितायो ॥

śakti rūpa ko marama na pāyo |
śakti gaī taba mana pachitāyo ||
The form of energy is never destroyed. Who sings in praise of Energy, his mind will endure.

शरणागत हुई कीर्ति बखानी ।
जय जय जय जगदम्ब भवानी ॥

śaraṇāgata huī kīrti bakhānī |
jaya jaya jaya jagadamba bhavānī ||

Who takes refuge in you, fame will increase. Victory, victory, victory to the Divine Mother of the Universe, Mother of Existence!

भई प्रसन्न आदि जगदम्बा ।
दीन्ह शक्ति नहिं कीन्ह विलम्बा ॥

bhaīṁ prasanna ādi jagadambā |
dīnha śakti nahiṁ kīnha vilambā ||

Please be pleased, Oh Mother of the Universe. Give me energy without further delay.

मोको मातु कष्ट अति घेरो । तुम बिनु कौन हरे दुःख मेरो ॥

moko mātu kaṣṭa ati ghero |
tuma binu kauna hare duḥkha mero ||

Oh Mother, I am surrounded by difficulties. Other than you, who can take away my pain?

आशा तृषणा निपट सतावै ।
रिपु मूरख मोहि अति डरपावै ॥

āśā tṛṣṇā nipaṭa satāvai |
ripu mūrakha mohi ati ḍarapāvai ||

Wishes and desires are extremely tormenting. The ignorance caused by foolish limitations is extremely fearful.

शत्रु नाश कीजै महारानी ।
सुमिराहु एक चित तुमहि भवानी ॥

śatru nāśa kījai mahārānī |
sumirāhu eka cita tumahi bhavānī ||

Oh Great Queen, please destroy all enemies. Let me recollect One Consciousness, and let that be You, Oh Mother of Existence.

करहु कृपा हे मातु दयाला । ऋद्धि सिद्धि दै करहु निहाला ॥

karahu kṛpā he mātu dayālā |
ṛddhi siddhi dai karahu nihālā ||

Give me your Grace, Oh Compassionate Mother. Give increase to perfection causing Supreme Happiness.

जब लगि जियहुँ दया फल पाऊँ ।

तुम्हारो जस मैं सदा सुनाऊँ ॥

jaba lagi jiyahuṁ dayā phala pāūṁ |
tumhāro jasa maiṁ sadā sunāūṁ ||

When the fruit of Compassion touches my heart, I only want to always sing your praises.

दुर्गा चालीसा जो नर गावैं ।

सब सुख भोगि परम पद पावैं ॥

durgā cālīsā jo nara gāvaiṁ |
saba sukha bhogi parama pada pāvaiṁ ||

Whatever man sings this Durgā Cālīsā, Praise of the Divine Mother, will enjoy the highest happiness and attain the most exalted respect.

मो कहँ निज शरणागत जानी ।

करहु कृपा जगदम्ब भवानी ॥

mo kahaṁ nija śaraṇāgata jānī |
karahu kṛpā jagadamba bhavānī ||

Where will I find my own refuge? Please give me your Grace, Oh Mother of the Universe, Mother of Existence.

दोहा

dohā

सिंहावाहिनी मातु तुम । मुदमंगल दातार ।

करहु कृपा जनि जानिके । पर्‍यो तुम्हारे द्वार ॥

siṁhāvāhinī mātu tuma, mudamaṁgala dātāra |
karahu kṛpā jani jānike, paryo tumhāre dvāra ||

Mother, you ride upon a lion, Grantor of Delight and Welfare. Oh Mother of all beings, give Grace to your children, who have fallen at your door.

shree maa pūjā

worship of shree maa

ॐ सनातनी माया विद्महे ज्ञान प्रकाशायै धीमहे ।

तन्नो श्री माँ प्रचोदायत् ॥

oṁ sanātanī māyā vidmahe
jñāna prakāśāyai dhīmahe
tanno śrī mām̐ pracodāyat

Oṁ we meditate on the Eternal Measurement of Consciousness, we contemplate She who illuminates wisdom. May that Shree Maa grant us increase.

ॐ श्री सनातनी मायै नमो नमः

oṁ śrī sanātanī māyai namo namaḥ

oṁ again and again I bow to the Eternal Shree Maa.

मन्त्रपुष्पाङ्जली समर्पयामि

mantrapuṣpāñjalī samarpayāmi

I offer these handfuls of flowers with mantras and the highest respect.

puṣpāñjalī
offer flowers

सर्वमङ्गल मङ्गल्ये शिवे सर्वार्थ साधिके ।
शरण्ये त्र्यम्बके गौरि नारायणि नमोऽस्तु ते ॥

sarvamaṅgala maṅgalye śive sarvārtha sādhike
śaraṇye tryambake gauri nārāyaṇi namo-stu te

To the Auspicious of all Auspiciousness, to the Good, to the Accomplisher of all Objectives, to the Source of Refuge, to the Mother of the Three Worlds, to the Goddess Who Is Rays of Light, Exposer of Consciousness, we bow to you.

ॐ ह्रीं श्रीं दुं दुर्गायै नमः मन्त्रपुष्पाञ्जली समर्पयामि

oṁ hrīṁ śrīṁ duṁ durgāyai namaḥ mantrapuṣpāñjalī samarpayāmi

I offer these handfuls of flowers with mantras and the highest respect Oṁ I bow to the Goddess, Durgā, the Grantor of Increase, who Removes all Difficulties.

सृष्टिस्थितिविनाशानां शक्तिभूते सनातनि ।
गुणाश्रये गुणमये नारायणि नमोऽस्तु ते ॥

sṛṣṭisthitivināśānāṁ śaktibhūte sanātani
guṇāśraye guṇamaye nārāyaṇi namo-stu te

You are the Eternal Energy of Creation, Preservation and Destruction in all existence; that on which all qualities depend, that which limits all qualities, Exposer of Consciousness, we bow to you.

ॐ ह्रीं श्रीं दुं दुर्गायै नमः मन्त्रपुष्पाञ्जली समर्पयामि

oṁ hrīṁ śrīṁ duṁ durgāyai namaḥ mantrapuṣpāñjalī samarpayāmi

I offer these handfuls of flowers with mantras and the highest respect Oṁ I bow to the Goddess, Durgā, the Grantor of Increase, who Removes all Difficulties.

शरणागतदीनार्त परित्राण परायणे ।
सर्वस्यार्ति हरे देवि नारायणि नमोऽस्तु ते ॥

śaraṇāgatadīnārta paritrāṇa parāyaṇe
sarvasyārti hare devi nārāyaṇi namo-stu te

For those who are devoted to you and take refuge in you, you save from all discomfort and unhappiness. All worry you take away, Oh Goddess, Exposer of Consciousness, we bow to you.

ॐ ह्रीं श्रीं दुं दुर्गायै नमः मन्त्रपुष्पाञ्जली समर्पयामि

oṁ hrīṁ śrīṁ duṁ durgāyai namaḥ mantrapuṣpāñjalī samarpayāmi

I offer these handfuls of flowers with mantras and the highest respect Oṁ I bow to the Goddess, Durgā, the Grantor of Increase, who Removes all Difficulties.

praṇām

दुर्गां शिवां शान्तिकरीं ब्रह्माणीं ब्रह्मणः प्रियाम् ।
सर्वलोक प्रणेत्रीञ्च प्रणमामि सदा शिवाम् ॥

durgāṁ śivāṁ śāntikarīṁ brahmāṇīṁ brahmaṇaḥ priyām
sarvaloka praṇetrīñca praṇamāmi sadā śivām

The Reliever of Difficulties, Exposer of Goodness, Cause of Peace, Infinite Consciousness, Beloved by Knowers of Consciousness, all the inhabitants of all the worlds always bow to Her, and I am bowing to Goodness Herself.

मङ्गलां शोभनां शुद्धां निष्कलां परमां कलाम् ।
विश्वेश्वरीं विश्वमातां चण्डिकां प्रणमाम्यहम् ॥

maṅgalāṁ śobhanāṁ śuddhāṁ niṣkalāṁ paramāṁ kalām
viśveśvarīṁ viśvamātāṁ caṇḍikāṁ praṇamāmyaham

Welfare, Radiant Beauty, Completely Pure, Without Limitations, the Ultimate Limitation, the Lord of the Universe, the Mother of the Universe, to you Caṇḍi, to the Energy that Tears Apart Thought, I bow in submission.

सर्वदेवमयीं देवीं सर्वरोगभयापहाम् ।
ब्रह्मेशविष्णुनमितां प्रणमामि सदा शिवाम् ॥

sarvadevamayīṁ devīṁ sarvarogabhayāpahām
brahmeśaviṣṇunamitāṁ praṇamāmi sadā śivām

Composed of all the Gods, removing all sickness and fear, Brahma, Maheśwara and Viṣṇu bow down to Her, and I always bow down to the Energy of Infinite Goodness.

विन्ध्यस्थां विन्ध्यनिलयां दिव्यस्थाननिवासिनीम् ।
योगिनीं योगजननीं चण्डिकां प्रणमाम्यहम् ॥

vindhyasthāṁ vindhyanilayāṁ divyasthānanivāsinīm
yoginīṁ yogajananīṁ caṇḍikāṁ praṇamāmyaham

The dwelling place of Knowledge, residing in Knowledge, Resident in the Place of Divine Illumination, the Cause of Union, the Knower of Union, to the Energy that Tears Apart Thought we constantly bow.

ईशानमातरं देवीमीश्वरीमीश्वरप्रियाम् ।
प्रणतोऽस्मि सदा दुर्गां संसारार्णवतारिणीम् ॥

īśānamātaraṁ devīmīśvarīmīśvarapriyām
praṇato-smi sadā durgāṁ saṁsārārṇavatāriṇīm

The Mother of the Supreme Consciousness, the Goddess Who Is the Supreme Consciousness, beloved by the Supreme Consciousness, we always bow to Durgā, the Reliever of Difficulties, who takes aspirants across the difficult sea of objects and their relationships.

ॐ महादेव महात्रान महायोगि महेश्वर ।
सर्वपाप हरां देव मकाराय नमो नमः ॥

oṁ mahādeva mahātrāna mahāyogi maheśvara
sarvapāpa harāṁ deva makārāya namo namaḥ

Oṁ The Great God, the Great Reliever, the Great Yogi, Oh Supreme Lord, Oh God who removes all Sin, in the form of the letter "M," which dissolves creation, we bow to you again and again.

ॐ नमः शिवाय शान्ताय कारणत्राय हेतवे ।
निवेदायामि चात्मानं त्वं गति परमेश्वर ॥

oṁ namaḥ śivāya śāntāya kāraṇatrāya hetave
nivedāyāmi cātmānaṁ tvaṁ gati parameśvara

Oṁ I bow to the Consciousness of Infinite Goodness, to Peace, to the Cause of the three worlds, I offer to you the fullness of my soul, Oh Supreme Lord.

ॐ नमः शिवाय

oṁ namaḥ śivāya

oṁ I bow to the Consciousness of Infinite Goodness.

aśīrbād
blessings

ॐ श्रीर्वर्चस्वमायुष्यमारोग्यमाविधात् पवमानं महीयते ।
धान्यं धनं पशुं बहुपुत्रलाभंशतसंवत्सरं दीर्घमायुः ॥

oṁ śrīrvarcasvamāyuṣyamārogyamāvidhāt pavamānaṁ mahīyate
dhānyaṁ dhanaṁ paśuṁ bahuputralābhaṁ śatasaṁvatsaraṁ dīrghamāyuḥ

Oṁ You are blessed with the Highest Respect, with Wealth, with Life, with Freedom from disease and freedom to be One with the Greatness; with food, with wealth, with animals and with many children, and with a long life of one hundred years.

मन्त्रार्थाः सफलाः सन्तु पूणाः सन्तु मनोरथाः ।
शत्रूणां बुद्धिनाशोऽस्तु मित्राणामुदयस्तव ॥

mantrārthāḥ saphalāḥ santu pūṇāḥ santu manorathāḥ
śatrūṇāṁ buddhināśo-stu mitrāṇāmudayastava

May the meanings of the mantras bring excellent fruit, and may the journey of your mind be full and complete. May all enmity be removed from your intellect, and may friendship continuously rise.

आयुष्कामो यशस्कामो पुत्र-पौत्रस्तथैव च ।
आरोग्यं धनकामश्च सर्वे कामा भवन्तु मे ॥

āyuṣkāmo yaśaskāmo putra-pautrastathaiva ca
ārogyaṁ dhanakāmaśca sarve kāmā bhavantu me

May you enjoy life; may you enjoy fame, children and grandchildren throughout the generations; may you all live without disease, with abundance of wealth; and may all your disires be fulfilled.

visārjaṇa

removing the divine energy to the unmanifest

ॐ इतः पूर्व प्राणबुद्धिदेह धर्माधिकारतो ।

जाग्रत् स्वप्नशुषुप्त्यवस्थाशु मनसा ॥

oṁ ītaḥ pūrva prāṇabuddhideha dharmādhikārato jāgrat svapnaśuṣuptyavasthāśu manasā

Oṁ Thus the full and complete intelligence of the Life Force, the Cause of Dharma, the Way of Truth to Perfection, has been given. Waking Consciousness, Dreaming (or thinking) Consciousness, and Consciousness in Dreamless Sleep (intuitive Consciousness) in which all thoughts are situated.

वाचा कर्मणा हस्ताभ्यां पध्भ्यामूदरेण शिश्ना ।

यत् कृतं यदुक्तं यत् स्मृतं तत् सर्वं ब्रह्मार्पणं भवतु स्वाहा ॥

vācā karmaṇā hastābhyāṁ padhbhyāmūdareṇa śiśnā yat kṛtaṁ yaduktaṁ yat smṛtaṁ tat sarvaṁ brahmārpaṇaṁ bhavatu svāhā

All speech has been offered with folded hands raised in respect while bowing to the lotus feet. That activity, that union, that memory, all of that has been offered to the Supreme Divinity. I am One with God!

मां मदीयञ्च सकलं श्री चण्डिका चरणे समर्पये ।

ॐ तत् सत् ॥

māṁ madīyañca sakalaṁ śrī caṇḍikā caraṇe samarpaye oṁ tat sat

All of me and all that belongs to me entirely, I surrender to the feet of the respected caṇḍikā, She Who Tears Apart Thought. The Infinite, That is Truth.

ॐ ब्रह्मार्पणं ब्रह्म हविर्ब्रह्माग्नौ ब्रह्मणा हुतम् ।
ब्रह्मैव तेन गन्तव्यं ब्रह्मकर्मसमाधिना ॥

oṁ brahmārpaṇaṁ brahma havirbrahmāgnau
brahmaṇā hutam
brahmaiva tena gantavyaṁ brahmakarmasamādhinā

Oṁ The Supreme Divinity makes the offering; the Supreme Divinity is the offering; offered by the Supreme Divinity, in the fire of the Supreme Divinity. By seeing the Supreme Divinity in all actions, one realizes that Supreme Divinity.

ॐ पूर्णमदः पूर्णमिदं पूर्णात् पूर्णमुदच्यते ।
पूर्णस्य पूर्णमादाय पूर्णमेवावशिश्यते ॥

oṁ pūrṇamadaḥ pūrṇamidaṁ
pūrṇāt pūrṇamudacyate
pūrṇasya pūrṇamādāya pūrṇamevāva śiśyate

Oṁ That is whole and perfect. This is whole and perfect. From the whole and perfect, the whole and perfect becomes manifest. If the whole and perfect issue forth from the whole and perfect, even still only the whole and perfect remain.

ॐ शान्तिः शान्तिः शान्तिः

oṁ śāntiḥ śāntiḥ śāntiḥ

Oṁ Peace, Peace, Peace

क्षमास्य (visārjaṇ mudrā)

kṣamāsya

Please forgive me.

Appendix

चण्डी यज्ञ पद्धोति

Caṇḍī Yajña Paddhoti

The System of Worship of the Sacred Fire
for the Goddess Caṇḍī

वौषाट्

vauṣāṭ
Ultimate Purity!

open hands face up over havan kund

फट् फट् फट्

phaṭ phaṭ phaṭ
Purify! Purify! Purify!

abhishek - sprinkle water

फट् फट् फट्

phaṭ phaṭ phaṭ
Purify! Purify! Purify!

clap

हूं

hūṁ
Cut the Ego!

aṅkuśa mudrā

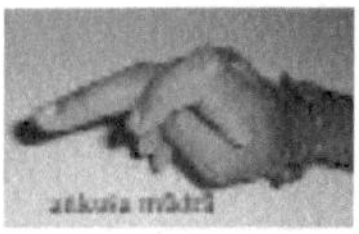

वं

vaṁ
Liberate!

dhenu mudrā

रं

raṁ
Purifying Consciousness!

yoni mudrā

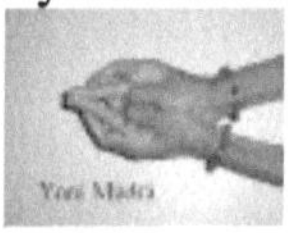

नमः

namaḥ
I bow!

praksạn

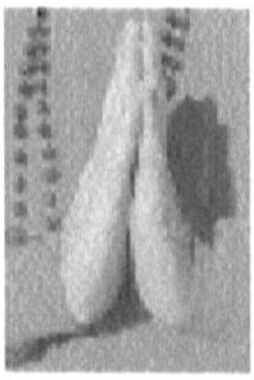

एते गन्धपुष्पे वह्नेर्योगपीठाय नमः

ete gandhapuṣpe vahneryogapīṭhāya namaḥ
With these scented flowers we bow to the place of union with the divine fire.

एते गन्धपुष्पे वह्निचैतन्याय नमः

ete gandhapuṣpe vāhnicaitanyāya namaḥ
With these scented flowers we bow to the Consciousness of the Divine Fire.

एते गन्धपुष्पे ॐ अग्नि मूर्त्तये नमः

ete gandhapuṣpe oṁ agni mūrttaye namaḥ
With these scented flowers we bow to deified image of the Divine Fire.

सोभयस्यास्य देवस्य विग्रहो यन्त्र कल्पणा ।
विना यन्त्रेण चेत्पूजा देवता न प्रसीदति ॥

sobhayasyāsya devasya vigraho yantra kalpaṇā
vinā yantreṇa cetpūjā devatā na prasīdati
We contemplate the form of the yantra which depicts the radiance of the Gods. Without using the yantra in the worship of consciousness the Gods are not as pleased.

यन्त्र मन्त्रमयं प्रहुर्देवता मन्त्ररूपिणी ।
यन्त्रेणापूजितो देवः सहसा न प्रसीदति ।
सर्वेषामपि मन्त्रणां यन्त्र पूजा प्रशस्यते ॥

yantra mantramayaṁ prahurdevatā mantrarūpiṇī
yantreṇāpūjito devaḥ sahasā na prasīdati
sarveṣāmapi mantraṇāṁ yantra pūjā praśasyate

The yantra conveys the objective meaning of the mantra, while the deity is the form of the mantra. By worshiping the deity by means of the yantra, the deity is completely satisfied. To attain all the bliss of the mantra, the worship of the yantra is highly recommended.

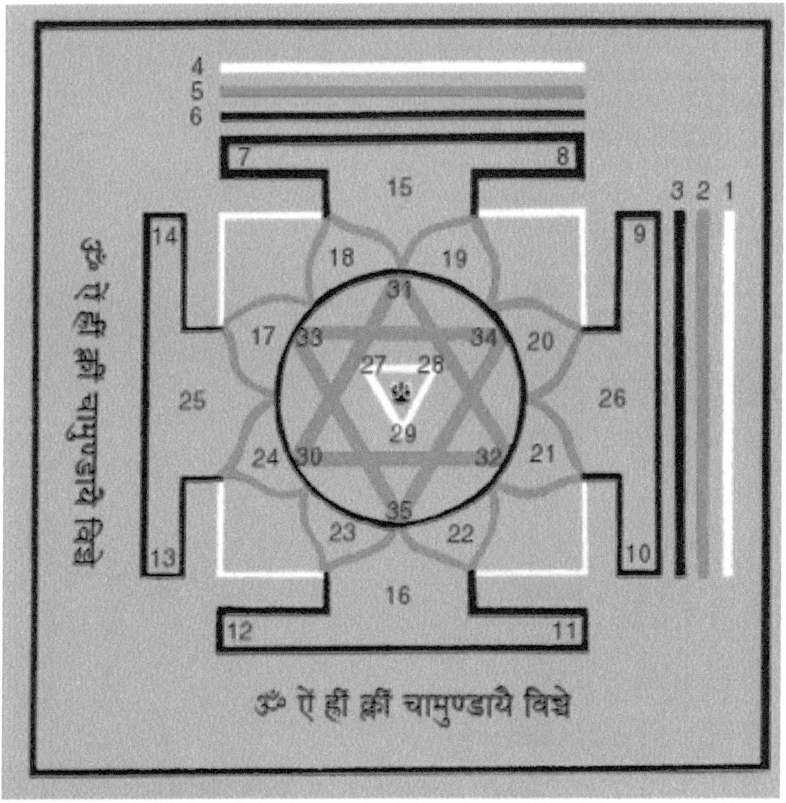

ततः स्थण्डिलमध्ये तु हसौःगर्भं त्रिकोणकम् ।
षट्कोणं तद्वहिर्वृत्तां ततोऽष्टदलपङ्कजम् ।
भूपुरं तद्वहिर्विद्वान् विलिखेद्यन्त्रमुत्तमम् ॥

**tataḥ sthaṇḍilamadhye tu hasauḥgarbhaṁ trikoṇakam
ṣaṭkoṇaṁ tadvahirvṛttāṁ tato-ṣṭadalapaṅkajam
bhūpuraṁ tadvahirvidvān vilikhedhyantramuttamam**

In the center of the place of worship is the single point which contains ha and sauḥ, Śiva and Śakti without distinction. Thereafter comes the three cornered equalateral triangle. Then six angles, outside of which is a circle, followed by eight lotus petals. The four doors are outside, and in this way the wise will draw the most excellent yantra.

- 1 -

ॐ मुकुन्दाय नमः

oṁ mukundāya namaḥ

oṁ I bow to the Giver of Liberation.

- 2 -

ॐ ईशनाय नमः

oṁ īśanāya namaḥ

oṁ I bow to the Ruler of All.

- 3 -

ॐ पुरन्दराय नमः

oṁ purandarāya namaḥ

oṁ I bow to the Giver of Completeness.

- 4 -

ॐ ब्रह्मणे नमः

oṁ brahmaṇe namaḥ

oṁ I bow to the Creative Consciousness.

- 5 -

ॐ वैवस्वताय नमः

oṁ vaivasvatāya namaḥ

oṁ I bow to the Universal Radiance.

- 6 -

ॐ इन्दवे नमः

oṁ indave namaḥ
oṁ I bow to the Ruler of Devotion.

- 7 -

ॐ आधारशक्तये नमः

oṁ ādhāraśaktaye namaḥ
oṁ I bow to the primal energy which sustains existence.

- 8 -

ॐ कुर्म्माय नमः

oṁ kurmmāya namaḥ
oṁ I bow to the Tortoise which supports creation.

- 9 -

ॐ अनन्ताय नमः

oṁ anantāya namaḥ
oṁ I bow to Infinity (personified as a thousand hooded snake who stands upon the Tortoise holding aloft the worlds).

- 10 -

ॐ पृथिव्यै नमः

oṁ pṛthivyai namaḥ
oṁ I bow to the Earth.

- 11 -

ॐ क्षीरसमूद्राय नमः

oṁ kṣīrasamūdrāya namaḥ
oṁ I bow to the milk ocean, or ocean of nectar, the infinite expanse of existence from which all manifested.

- 12 -

ॐ श्वेतद्वीपाय नमः

oṁ śvetadvīpāya namaḥ
oṁ I bow to the Island of Purity, which is in the ocean.

- 13 -

ॐ मणिमन्दपाय नमः

oṁ maṇimandapāya namaḥ
oṁ I bow to the Palace of Gems, which is on the island, the home of the Divine Mother.

- 14 -

ॐ कल्पवृक्षाय नमः

oṁ kalpavṛkṣāya namaḥ
oṁ I bow to the Tree of Fulfillment, which satisfies all desires, growing in the palace courtyard.

- 15 -

ॐ मणिवेदिकायै नमः

oṁ maṇivedikāyai namaḥ
oṁ I bow to the altar containing the gems of wisdom.

- 16 -

ॐ रत्नसिंहासनाय नमः

oṁ ratnasiṁhāsanāya namaḥ
oṁ I bow to the throne of the jewel.

- 17 -

ॐ धर्म्माय नमः

oṁ dharmmāya namaḥ
oṁ I bow to the Way of Truth and Harmony.

- 18 -

ॐ ज्ञानाय नमः

oṁ jñānāya namaḥ
oṁ I bow to Wisdom.

- 19 -

ॐ वैराग्याय नमः

oṁ vairāgyāya namaḥ
oṁ I bow to Detachment.

- 20 -

ॐ ऐश्वर्याय नमः

oṁ aiśvaryāya namaḥ
oṁ I bow to the Imperishable Qualities.

- 21 -

ॐ अधर्म्माय नमः

oṁ adharmmāya namaḥ
oṁ I bow to Disharmony.

- 22 -

ॐ अज्ञानाय नमः

oṁ ajñānāya namaḥ
oṁ I bow to Ignorance.

- 23 -

ॐ अवैराग्याय नमः

oṁ avairāgyāya namaḥ
oṁ I bow to Attachment.

- 24 -

ॐ अनैश्वर्याय नमः

oṁ anīśvaryāya namaḥ
oṁ I bow to the Transient.

- 25 -

ॐ अनन्ताय नमः

oṁ anantāya namaḥ
oṁ I bow to the Infinite.

- 26 -

ॐ पद्माय नमः

oṁ padmāya namaḥ
oṁ I bow to the Lotus.

- 27 -

अं अर्कमण्डलाय द्वादशकलात्मने नमः

aṁ arkamaṇḍalāya dvādaśakalātmane namaḥ
"A" we bow to the twelve aspects of the realm of the sun. Tapinī, Tāpinī, Dhūmrā, Marīci, Jvālinī, Ruci, Sudhūmrā, Bhoga-dā, Viśvā, Bodhinī, Dhāriṇī, Kṣamā; Containing heat, Emanating heat, Smoky, Ray-producing, Burning, Lustrous, Purple or Smoky-red, Granting enjoyment, Universal, Which makes known, Productive of Consciousness, Which supports, Which forgives.

- 28 -

उं सोममण्डलाय षोडशकलात्मने नमः

uṁ somamaṇḍalāya ṣoḍaśakalātmane namaḥ

"U" we bow to the sixteen aspects of the realm of the moon. Amṛtā, Prāṇadā, Puṣā, Tuṣṭi, Puṣṭi, Rati, Dhṛti, Śaśinī, Candrikā, Kānti, Jyotsnā, Śrī, Prīti, Aṅgadā, Pūrṇā, Pūrṇāmṛtā; Nectar, Which sustains life, Which supports, Satisfying, Nourishing, Playful, Constancy, Unfailing, Producer of Joy, Beauty enhanced by love, Light, Grantor of Prosperity, Affectionate, Purifying the body, Complete, Full of Bliss.

- 29 -

मं वह्निमण्डलाय दशकलात्मने नमः

maṁ vahnimaṇḍalāya daśakalātmane namaḥ

"M" we bow to the ten aspects of the realm of fire: Dhūmrā, Arciḥ, Jvalinī, Śūkṣmā, Jvālinī, Visphuliṅginī, Suśrī, Surūpā, Kapilā, Havya-Kavya-Vahā; Smoky Red, Flaming, Shining, Subtle, Burning, Sparkling, Beautiful, Well-formed, Tawny, The Messenger to Gods and Ancestors.

- 30 -

ॐ सं सत्त्वाय नमः

oṁ saṁ sattvāya namaḥ

oṁ I bow to activity, execution, light, knowledge, being.

- 31 -

ॐ रं रजसे नमः

oṁ raṁ rajase namaḥ

oṁ I bow to desire, inspiration, becoming.

- 32 -

ॐ तं तमसे नमः

oṁ taṁ tamase namaḥ

oṁ I bow to wisdom, to the darkness which exposes light, to rest.

- 33 -

ॐ आं आत्मने नमः

oṁ āṁ ātmane namaḥ

oṁ I bow to the Soul.

- 34 -

ॐ अं अन्तरात्मने नमः

oṁ aṁ antarātmane namaḥ
oṁ I bow to the Innermost Soul.

- 35 -

ॐ पं परमात्मने नमः

oṁ paṁ paramātmane namaḥ
oṁ I bow to the Universal Soul, or the Consciousness which exceeds manifestation.

- 36 -

ॐ ह्रीं ज्ञानात्मने नमः

oṁ hrīṁ jñānātmane namaḥ
oṁ I bow to the Soul of Infinite Wisdom.

सर्वतो भद्रमण्डल देवता स्थापनम

sarvato bhadramaṇḍala devatā sthāpanam

Establishment of the Excellent Circle of Deities

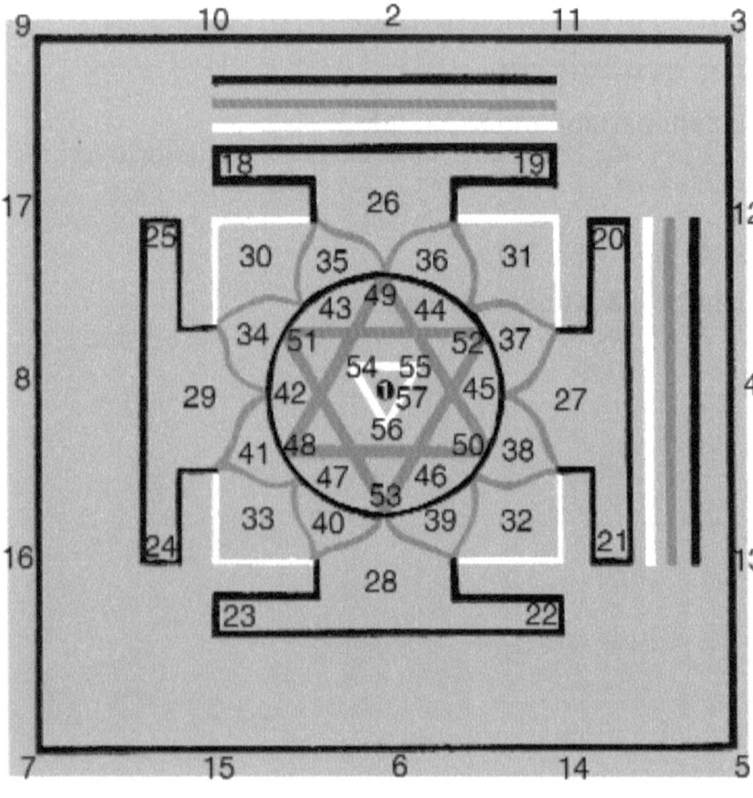

- 1 -

ॐ भूर्भुवः स्वः ब्रह्मणे नमः ब्रह्मणमावाहयामि स्थापयामि

oṁ bhūrbhuvaḥ svaḥ brahmaṇe namaḥ brahmaṇamāvāhayāmi sthāpayāmi

oṁ the Infinite Beyond Conception, the gross body, the subtle body and the causal body, we bow to the Creative Consciousness (Center). We invoke you, invite you and establish your presence.

- 2 -

ॐ भूर्भुवः स्वः सोमाय नमः सोममावाहयामि स्थापयामि

oṁ bhūrbhuvaḥ svaḥ somāya namaḥ somamāvāhayāmi sthāpayāmi

oṁ the Infinite Beyond Conception, the gross body, the subtle body and the causal body, we bow to the Lord of Devotion (N). We invoke you, invite you and establish your presence.

- 3 -

ॐ भूर्भुवः स्वः ईशानाय नमः ईशानमावाहयामि स्थापयामि

oṁ bhūrbhuvaḥ svaḥ īśānāya namaḥ īśānamāvāhayāmi sthāpayāmi

oṁ the Infinite Beyond Conception, the gross body, the subtle body and the causal body, we bow to the Ruler of All (NE). We invoke you, invite you and establish your presence.

- 4 -

ॐ भूर्भुवः स्वः इन्द्राय नमः इन्द्रमावाहयामि स्थापयामि

oṁ bhūrbhuvaḥ svaḥ indrāya namaḥ indramāvāhayāmi sthāpayāmi

oṁ the Infinite Beyond Conception, the gross body, the subtle body and the causal body, we bow to the Rule of the Pure (E). We invoke you, invite you and establish your presence.

- 5 -

ॐ भूर्भुवः स्वः अग्नये नमः अग्निमावाहयामि स्थापयामि

oṁ bhūrbhuvaḥ svaḥ agnaye namaḥ agnimāvāhayāmi sthāpayāmi

oṁ the Infinite Beyond Conception, the gross body, the subtle body and the causal body, we bow to the Divine Fire (SE). We invoke you, invite you and establish your presence.

- 6 -

ॐ भूर्भुवः स्वः यमाय नमः यममावाहयामि स्थापयामि

oṁ bhūrbhuvaḥ svaḥ yamāya namaḥ yamamāvāhayāmi sthāpayāmi

oṁ the Infinite Beyond Conception, the gross body, the subtle body and the causal body, we bow to the Supreme Controller (S). We invoke you, invite you and establish your presence.

\- 7 -

ॐ भूर्भुवः स्वः निर्ऋतये नमः निर्ऋतिमावाहयामि स्थापयामि

oṁ bhūrbhuvaḥ svaḥ nirṛtaye namaḥ nirṛtimāvāhayāmi sthāpayāmi

oṁ the Infinite Beyond Conception, the gross body, the subtle body and the causal body, we bow to the Destroyer (SW). We invoke you, invite you and establish your presence.

\- 8 -

ॐ भूर्भुवः स्वः वरुणाय नमः वरुणमावाहयामि स्थापयामि

oṁ bhūrbhuvaḥ svaḥ varuṇāya namaḥ varuṇamāvāhayāmi sthāpayāmi

oṁ the Infinite Beyond Conception, the gross body, the subtle body and the causal body, we bow to the Lord of Equilibrium (W). We invoke you, invite you and establish your presence.

\- 9 -

ॐ भूर्भुवः स्वः वायवे नमः वायुमावाहयामि स्थापयामि

oṁ bhūrbhuvaḥ svaḥ vāyave namaḥ vāyumāvāhayāmi sthāpayāmi

oṁ the Infinite Beyond Conception, the gross body, the subtle body and the causal body, we bow to the Lord of Liberation (NW). We invoke you, invite you and establish your presence.

\- 10 -

ॐ भूर्भुवः स्वः अष्टवसुभ्यो नमः अष्टवसुन् आवाहयामि स्थापयामि

oṁ bhūrbhuvaḥ svaḥ aṣṭavasubhyo namaḥ aṣṭavasun āvāhayāmi sthāpayāmi

oṁ the Infinite Beyond Conception, the gross body, the subtle body and the causal body, we bow to the Eight Lords of Benificence. We invoke you, invite you and establish your presence.

\- 11 -

ॐ भूर्भुवः स्वः एकादशरुद्रेभ्यो नमः
एकादशरुद्रानावाहयामि स्थापयामि

oṁ bhūrbhuvaḥ svaḥ ekādaśarudrebhyo namaḥ ekādaśarudrānāvāhayāmi sthāpayāmi

oṁ the Infinite Beyond Conception, the gross body, the subtle body and the causal body, we bow to the Eleven Relievers from Sufferings. We invoke you, invite you and establish your presence.

\- 12 -

ॐ भूर्भुवः स्वः द्वादशादित्येभ्यो नमः
द्वादशादित्यानावाहयामि स्थापयामि

oṁ bhūrbhuvaḥ svaḥ dvādaśādityebhyo namaḥ dvādaśādityānāvāhayāmi sthāpayāmi

oṁ the Infinite Beyond Conception, the gross body, the subtle body and the causal body, we bow to the Twelve Sons of Light. We invoke you, invite you and establish your presence.

\- 13 -

ॐ भूर्भुवः स्वः अश्विभ्यां नमः अश्विनौ आवाहयामि स्थापयामि

oṁ bhūrbhuvaḥ svaḥ aśvibhyāṁ namaḥ aśvinau āvāhayāmi sthāpayāmi

oṁ the Infinite Beyond Conception, the gross body, the subtle body and the causal body, we bow to the Two Horses of Pure Desire. We invoke you, invite you and establish your presence.

\- 14 -

ॐ भूर्भुवः स्वः सपैतृकविश्वेभ्यो देवेभ्यो नमः सपैतृकविश्वान् देवानावाहयामि स्थापयामि

oṁ bhūrbhuvaḥ svaḥ sapaitṛkaviśvebhyo devebhyo namaḥ sapaitṛkaviśvān devānāvāhayāmi sthāpayāmi

oṁ the Infinite Beyond Conception, the gross body, the subtle body and the causal body, we bow to the Ancestors along with the Shining Ones of the Universe. We invoke you, invite you and establish your presence.

- 15 -

ॐ भूर्भुवः स्वः सप्तयक्षेभ्यो नमः सप्तयक्षानावाहयामि स्थापयामि

oṁ bhūrbhuvaḥ svaḥ saptayakṣebhyo namaḥ saptayakṣānāvāhayāmi sthāpayāmi

oṁ the Infinite Beyond Conception, the gross body, the subtle body and the causal body, we bow to the Energy which brings the good and bad of wealth. We invoke you, invite you and establish your presence.

- 16 -

ॐ भूर्भुवः स्वः अष्टकुलनागेभ्यो नमः अष्टकुलनागानावाहयामि स्थापयामि

oṁ bhūrbhuvaḥ svaḥ aṣṭakulanāgebhyo namaḥ aṣṭakulanāgānāvāhayāmi sthāpayāmi

oṁ the Infinite Beyond Conception, the gross body, the subtle body and the causal body, we bow to the Family of eight snakes. We invoke you, invite you and establish your presence.

- 17 -

ॐ भूर्भुवः स्वः गन्धर्वाऽप्सरोभ्यो नमः गन्धर्वाऽप्सरसः आवाहयामि स्थापयामि

oṁ bhūrbhuvaḥ svaḥ gandharvā-psarobhyo namaḥ gandharvā-psarasaḥ āvāhayāmi sthāpayāmi

oṁ the Infinite Beyond Conception, the gross body, the subtle body and the causal body, we bow to the celestial musicians and heavenly maidens. We invoke you, invite you and establish your presence.

- 18 -

ॐ भूर्भुवः स्वः स्कन्दाय नमः स्कन्दमावाहयामि स्थापयामि

oṁ bhūrbhuvaḥ svaḥ skandāya namaḥ skandamāvāhayāmi sthāpayāmi

oṁ the Infinite Beyond Conception, the gross body, the subtle body and the causal body, we bow to the God of War. We invoke you, invite you and establish your presence.

- 19 -

ॐ भूर्भुवः स्वः वृषभाय नमः वृषभमावाहयामि स्थापयामि

oṁ bhūrbhuvaḥ svaḥ vṛṣabhāya namaḥ vṛṣabhamāvāhayāmi sthāpayāmi

oṁ the Infinite Beyond Conception, the gross body, the subtle body and the causal body, we bow to the Bull of Discipline, Conveyance of Śiva - Nandi. We invoke you, invite you and establish your presence.

- 20 -

ॐ भूर्भुवः स्वः शूलाय नमः शूलमावाहयामि स्थापयामि

oṁ bhūrbhuvaḥ svaḥ śūlāya namaḥ śūlamāvāhayāmi sthāpayāmi

oṁ the Infinite Beyond Conception, the gross body, the subtle body and the causal body, we bow to the Spear of Concentration. We invoke you, invite you and establish your presence.

- 21 -

ॐ भूर्भुवः स्वः महाकालाय नमः महाकालमावाहयामि स्थापयामि

oṁ bhūrbhuvaḥ svaḥ mahākālāya namaḥ mahākālamāvāhayāmi sthāpayāmi

oṁ the Infinite Beyond Conception, the gross body, the subtle body and the causal body, we bow to the Great Time. We invoke you, invite you and establish your presence.

- 22 -

ॐ भूर्भुवः स्वः दक्षादि सप्तगणेभ्यो नमः दक्षादि सप्तगणानावाहयामि स्थापयामि

oṁ bhūrbhuvaḥ svaḥ dakṣādi saptagaṇebhyo namaḥ dakṣādi saptagaṇānāvāhayāmi sthāpayāmi

oṁ the Infinite Beyond Conception, the gross body, the subtle body and the causal body, we bow to Ability and the other seven qualities. We invoke you, invite you and establish your presence.

\- 23 -

ॐ भूर्भुवः स्वः दुर्गायै नमः दुर्गामावाहयामि स्थापयामि

oṁ bhūrbhuvaḥ svaḥ durgāyai namaḥ durgāmāvāhayāmi sthāpayāmi

oṁ the Infinite Beyond Conception, the gross body, the subtle body and the causal body, we bow to the Reliever of Difficulties. We invoke you, invite you and establish your presence.

\- 24 -

ॐ भूर्भुवः स्वः विष्णवे नमः विष्णुमावाहयामि स्थापयामि

oṁ bhūrbhuvaḥ svaḥ viṣṇave namaḥ viṣṇumāvāhayāmi sthāpayāmi

oṁ the Infinite Beyond Conception, the gross body, the subtle body and the causal body, we bow to the All-Pervading Consciousness. We invoke you, invite you and establish your presence.

\- 25 -

ॐ भूर्भुवः स्वः स्वधायै नमः स्वधामावाहयामि स्थापयामि

oṁ bhūrbhuvaḥ svaḥ svadhāyai namaḥ svadhāmāvāhayāmi sthāpayāmi

oṁ the Infinite Beyond Conception, the gross body, the subtle body and the causal body, we bow to the Ancestors. We invoke you, invite you and establish your presence.

\- 26 -

ॐ भूर्भुवः स्वः मृत्युरोगेभ्यो नमः मृत्युरोगानावाहयामि स्थापयामि

oṁ bhūrbhuvaḥ svaḥ mṛtyurogebhyo namaḥ mṛtyurogānāvāhayāmi sthāpayāmi

oṁ the Infinite Beyond Conception, the gross body, the subtle body and the causal body, we bow to the Spirit of deadly illnesses. We invoke you, invite you and establish your presence.

- 27 -

ॐ भूर्भुवः स्वः गणपतये नमः गणपतिमावाहयामि स्थापयामि

oṁ bhūrbhuvaḥ svaḥ gaṇapataye namaḥ gaṇapatimāvāhayāmi sthāpayāmi

oṁ the Infinite Beyond Conception, the gross body, the subtle body and the causal body, we bow to the Lord of the Multitudes. We invoke you, invite you and establish your presence.

- 28 -

ॐ भूर्भुवः स्वः अद्भ्यो नमः अपः आवाहयामि स्थापयामि

oṁ bhūrbhuvaḥ svaḥ adbhyo namaḥ apaḥ āvāhayāmi sthāpayāmi

oṁ the Infinite Beyond Conception, the gross body, the subtle body and the causal body, we bow to Acts of Sacrifice. We invoke you, invite you and establish your presence.

- 29 -

ॐ भूर्भुवः स्वः मरुद्भ्यो नमः मरुतः आवाहयामि स्थापयामि

oṁ bhūrbhuvaḥ svaḥ marudbhyo namaḥ marutaḥ āvāhayāmi sthāpayāmi

oṁ the Infinite Beyond Conception, the gross body, the subtle body and the causal body, we bow to the Shining Ones. We invoke you, invite you and establish your presence.

- 30 -

ॐ भूर्भुवः स्वः पृथिव्यै नमः पृथ्वीमावाहयामि स्थापयामि

oṁ bhūrbhuvaḥ svaḥ pṛthivyai namaḥ pṛthvīmāvāhayāmi sthāpayāmi

oṁ the Infinite Beyond Conception, the gross body, the subtle body and the causal body, we bow to the Earth. We invoke you, invite you and establish your presence.

- 31 -

ॐ भूर्भुवः स्वः गङ्गादिनदीभ्यो नमः गङ्गादिनदीः आवाहयामि स्थापयामि

oṁ bhūrbhuvaḥ svaḥ gaṅgādinadībhyo namaḥ gaṅgādinadīḥ āvāhayāmi sthāpayāmi

oṁ the Infinite Beyond Conception, the gross body, the subtle body and the causal body, we bow to the Ganges and other rivers. We invoke you, invite you and establish your presence.

- 32 -

ॐ भूर्भुवः स्वः सप्तसागरेभ्यो नमः सप्तसागरानावाहयामि स्थापयामि

oṁ bhūrbhuvaḥ svaḥ saptasāgarebhyo namaḥ saptasāgarānāvāhayāmi sthāpayāmi

oṁ the Infinite Beyond Conception, the gross body, the subtle body and the causal body, we bow to the Seven Seas. We invoke you, invite you and establish your presence.

- 33 -

ॐ भूर्भुवः स्वः मेरवे नमः मेरुमावाहयामि स्थापयामि

oṁ bhūrbhuvaḥ svaḥ merave namaḥ merumāvāhayāmi sthāpayāmi

oṁ the Infinite Beyond Conception, the gross body, the subtle body and the causal body, we bow to Mount Meru. We invoke you, invite you and establish your presence.

- 34 -

ॐ भूर्भुवः स्वः गदाय नमः गदामावाहयामि स्थापयामि

oṁ bhūrbhuvaḥ svaḥ gadāya namaḥ gadāmāvāhayāmi sthāpayāmi

oṁ the Infinite Beyond Conception, the gross body, the subtle body and the causal body, we bow to the Club. We invoke you, invite you and establish your presence.

- 35 -

ॐ भूर्भुवः स्वः त्रिशूलाय नमः त्रिशूलमावाहयामि स्थापयामि

oṁ bhūrbhuvaḥ svaḥ triśūlāya namaḥ triśūlamāvāhayāmi sthāpayāmi

oṁ the Infinite Beyond Conception, the gross body, the subtle body and the causal body, we bow to the Trident. We invoke you, invite you and establish your presence.

- 36 -

ॐ भूर्भुवः स्वः वज्राय नमः वज्रमावाहयामि स्थापयामि

oṁ bhūrbhuvaḥ svaḥ vajrāya namaḥ vajramāvāhayāmi sthāpayāmi

oṁ the Infinite Beyond Conception, the gross body, the subtle body and the causal body, we bow to the Thunderbolt. We invoke you, invite you and establish your presence.

- 37 -

ॐ भूर्भुवः स्वः शक्तये नमः शक्तिमावाहयामि स्थापयामि

oṁ bhūrbhuvaḥ svaḥ śaktaye namaḥ śaktimāvāhayāmi sthāpayāmi

oṁ the Infinite Beyond Conception, the gross body, the subtle body and the causal body, we bow to Energy. We invoke you, invite you and establish your presence.

- 38 -

ॐ भूर्भुवः स्वः दण्डाय नमः दण्डमावाहयामि स्थापयामि

oṁ bhūrbhuvaḥ svaḥ daṇḍāya namaḥ daṇḍamāvāhayāmi sthāpayāmi

oṁ the Infinite Beyond Conception, the gross body, the subtle body and the causal body, we bow to the Staff. We invoke you, invite you and establish your presence.

- 39 -

ॐ भूर्भुवः स्वः खड्गाय नमः खड्गमावाहयामि स्थापयामि

oṁ bhūrbhuvaḥ svaḥ khaḍgāya namaḥ khaḍgamāvāhayāmi sthāpayāmi

oṁ the Infinite Beyond Conception, the gross body, the subtle body and the causal body, we bow to the Sword. We invoke you, invite you and establish your presence.

- 40 -

ॐ भूर्भुवः स्वः पाशाय नमः पाशमावाहयामि स्थापयामि

oṁ bhūrbhuvaḥ svaḥ pāśāya namaḥ pāśamāvāhayāmi sthāpayāmi

oṁ the Infinite Beyond Conception, the gross body, the subtle body and the causal body, we bow to the Net. We invoke you, invite you and establish your presence.

- 41 -

ॐ भूर्भुवः स्वः अङ्कुशाय नमः अङ्कुशमावाहयामि स्थापयामि

oṁ bhūrbhuvaḥ svaḥ aṅkuśāya namaḥ aṅkuśamāvāhayāmi sthāpayāmi

oṁ the Infinite Beyond Conception, the gross body, the subtle body and the causal body, we bow to the Goad. We invoke you, invite you and establish your presence.

- 42 -

ॐ भूर्भुवः स्वः गौतमाय नमः गौतममावाहयामि स्थापयामि

oṁ bhūrbhuvaḥ svaḥ gautamāya namaḥ gautamamāvāhayāmi sthāpayāmi

oṁ the Infinite Beyond Conception, the gross body, the subtle body and the causal body, we bow to Ṛṣi Gautam. We invoke you, invite you and establish your presence.

- 43 -

ॐ भूर्भुवः स्वः भरद्वाजाय नमः भरद्वाजमावाहयामि स्थापयामि

oṁ bhūrbhuvaḥ svaḥ bharadvājāya namaḥ bharadvājamāvāhayāmi sthāpayāmi

oṁ the Infinite Beyond Conception, the gross body, the subtle body and the causal body, we bow to Ṛṣi Bharadvāj. We invoke you, invite you and establish your presence.

- 44 -

ॐ भूर्भुवः स्वः विश्वामित्राय नमः विश्वामित्रमावाहयामि स्थापयामि

oṁ bhūrbhuvaḥ svaḥ viśvāmitrāya namaḥ viśvāmitramāvāhayāmi sthāpayāmi

oṁ the Infinite Beyond Conception, the gross body, the subtle body and the causal body, we bow to Ṛṣi Viśvāmitra we invoke you, invite you and establish your presence.

- 45 -

ॐ भूर्भुवः स्वः कश्यपाय नमः कश्यपमावाहयामि स्थापयामि

oṁ bhūrbhuvaḥ svaḥ kaśyapāya namaḥ kaśyapamāvāhayāmi sthāpayāmi

oṁ the Infinite Beyond Conception, the gross body, the subtle body and the causal body, we bow to Ṛṣi Kaśyapa.
We invoke you, invite you and establish your presence.

- 46 -

ॐ भूर्भुवः स्वः जमदग्नये नमः जमदग्निमावाहयामि स्थापयामि

oṁ bhūrbhuvaḥ svaḥ jamadagnaye namaḥ jamadagnimāvāhayāmi sthāpayāmi

oṁ the Infinite Beyond Conception, the gross body, the subtle body and the causal body, we bow to Ṛṣi Jamadagni. We invoke you, invite you and establish your presence.

- 47 -

ॐ भूर्भुवः स्वः वसिष्ठाय नमः वसिष्ठमावाहयामि स्थापयामि

oṁ bhūrbhuvaḥ svaḥ vasiṣṭhāya namaḥ vasiṣṭhamāvāhayāmi sthāpayāmi

oṁ the Infinite Beyond Conception, the gross body, the subtle body and the causal body, we bow to Ṛṣi Vaṣiṣṭha. We invoke you, invite you and establish your presence.

- 48 -

ॐ भूर्भुवः स्वः अत्रये नमः अत्रिमावाहयामि स्थापयामि

oṁ bhūrbhuvaḥ svaḥ atraye namaḥ atrimāvāhayāmi sthāpayāmi

oṁ the Infinite Beyond Conception, the gross body, the subtle body and the causal body, we bow to Ṛṣi Atri. We invoke you, invite you and establish your presence.

- 49 -

ॐ भूर्भुवः स्वः अरुन्धत्यै नमः अरुन्धतीमावाहयामि स्थापयामि

oṁ bhūrbhuvaḥ svaḥ arundhatyai namaḥ arundhatīmāvāhayāmi sthāpayāmi

oṁ the Infinite Beyond Conception, the gross body, the subtle body and the causal body, we bow to Devi Arundati, wife of Vaṣiṣṭha, example of purity. We invoke you, invite you and establish your presence.

- 50 -

ॐ भूर्भुवः स्वः ऐन्द्र्यै नमः ऐन्द्रीमावाहयामि स्थापयामि

oṁ bhūrbhuvaḥ svaḥ aindryai namaḥ aindrīmāvāhayāmi sthāpayāmi

oṁ the Infinite Beyond Conception, the gross body, the subtle body and the causal body, we bow to Aindri, the energy of the Rule of the Pure. We invoke you, invite you and establish your presence.

- 51 -

ॐ भूर्भुवः स्वः कौमार्य्यै नमः कौमारीमावाहयामि स्थापयामि

oṁ bhūrbhuvaḥ svaḥ kaumāryyai namaḥ kaumārīmāvāhayāmi sthāpayāmi

oṁ the Infinite Beyond Conception, the gross body, the subtle body and the causal body, we bow to Kumari, the energy of the ever pure one. We invoke you, invite you and establish your presence.

- 52 -

ॐ भूर्भुवः स्वः ब्राह्म्यै नमः ब्राह्मीमावाहयामि स्थापयामि

oṁ bhūrbhuvaḥ svaḥ brāhmyai namaḥ brāhmīmāvāhayāmi sthāpayāmi

oṁ the Infinite Beyond Conception, the gross body, the subtle body and the causal body, we bow to Brahmi, the energy of Creative Consciousness. We invoke you, invite you and establish your presence.

- 53 -

ॐ भूर्भुवः स्वः वाराह्यै नमः वाराहीमावाहयामि स्थापयामि

oṁ bhūrbhuvaḥ svaḥ vārāhyai namaḥ vārāhīmāvāhayāmi sthāpayāmi

oṁ the Infinite Beyond Conception, the gross body, the subtle body and the causal body, we bow to Varāhi, the energy of the Boar of Sacrifice. We invoke you, invite you and establish your presence.

- 54 -

ॐ भूर्भुवः स्वः चामुण्डायै नमः चामुण्डामावाहयामि स्थापयामि

oṁ bhūrbhuvaḥ svaḥ cāmuṇḍāyai namaḥ cāmuṇḍāmāvāhayāmi sthāpayāmi

oṁ the Infinite Beyond Conception, the gross body, the subtle body and the causal body, we bow to Camuṇḍa, the Conquerer of Passion and Meaness. We invoke you, invite you and establish your presence.

- 55 -

ॐ भूर्भुवः स्वः वैष्णव्यै नमः वैष्णवीमावाहयामि स्थापयामि

oṁ bhūrbhuvaḥ svaḥ vaiṣṇavyai namaḥ vaiṣṇavīmāvāhayāmi sthāpayāmi

oṁ the Infinite Beyond Conception, the gross body, the subtle body and the causal body, we bow to Vaiṣṇāvi, the energy of All-Pervading Consciousness. We invoke you, invite you and establish your presence.

- 56 -

ॐ भूर्भुवः स्वः माहेश्वर्यै नमः माहेश्वरीमावाहयामि स्थापयामि

oṁ bhūrbhuvaḥ svaḥ māheśvaryai namaḥ māheśvarīmāvāhayāmi sthāpayāmi

oṁ the Infinite Beyond Conception, the gross body, the subtle body and the causal body, we bow to Maheśvarī, the energy of the Supreme Sovereign. We invoke you, invite you and establish your presence.

- 57 -

ॐ भूर्भुवः स्वः वैनायक्यै नमः वैनायकीमावाहयामि स्थापयामि

oṁ bhūrbhuvaḥ svaḥ vaināyakyai namaḥ vaināyakīmāvāhayāmi sthāpayāmi

oṁ the Infinite Beyond Conception, the gross body, the subtle body and the causal body, we bow to Vaināki, the energy of excellent conduct. We invoke you, invite you and establish your presence.

सं गच्छध्वं

saṁ gacchadhvaṁ

ॐ सं गच्छध्वं सं वद्ध्वं सं वो मनांसि जानताम्

देवा भागं यथा पूर्वे संजानाना उपासते

oṁ saṁ gacchadhvaṁ saṁ vadadhvaṁ
saṁ vo manāṁsi jānatām
devā bhāgaṁ yathā pūrve saṁjānānā upāsate

Let all assemble together. Let all speak together. Let all minds be in harmony. The Shining Ones of ancient times all proceeded by this worship.

समानो मन्त्रः समितिः समानी समानं मनः सह चित्तमेषाम

समानं मन्त्रमभि मन्त्रये वः समानेन वो हविषा जुहोमि

samāno mantraḥ samitiḥ samānī
samānaṁ manaḥ saha cittameṣām
samānaṁ mantramabhi mantraye vaḥ
samānena vo haviṣā juhomi

When all thoughts are absorbed in mantra, then consciousness becomes fixed in the recollection most glorious. When all thoughts become absorbed in mantra, then by means of mantra all thoughts are poured as oblations into the divine fire.

समानी व आकूतिः समाना हृदयानि वः

समानमस्तु वो मनो यथा वः सुसहासति

samānī va ākūtiḥ samānā hṛdayāni vaḥ
samānamastu vo mano yathā vaḥ susahāsati

This place is common. These thoughts are common. So let our hearts be shared as well. Let all thoughts, all minds, be united so that all may enjoy peace and contentment.

Set Wood

ॐ ऐं चण्डिकायै विद्महे त्रिपुरायै धीमहे ।

तन्नो गौरी प्रचोदयात् क्लीं ॥

oṁ aiṁ caṇḍikāyai vidmahe tripurāyai dhīmahe |
tanno gaurī pracodayāt klīṁ ||
Oṁ Wisdom we meditate upon the Goddess Caṇḍi, She Who Tears Apart All Thoughts, contemplate She Who occupies the three cities (gross perception, subtle conception, and intuitivee cognition). May that Goddess Who is Rays of Light grant us increase klīṁ (the cause of dissolution of the gross body into the causal body in perfection.)

Light torches with Gayatri

ॐ भूर्भुवः स्वः ।

तत् सवितुर्वरेण्यम् भर्गो देवस्य धीमहि ।

धियो यो नः प्रचोदयात् ॥

oṁ bhūr bhuvaḥ svaḥ
tat savitur vareṇyam bhargo devasya dhīmahi
dhiyo yo naḥ pracodayāt
oṁ the Infinite Beyond Conception, the gross body, the subtle body and the causal body; we meditate upon that Light of Wisdom which is the Supreme Wealth of the Gods. May it grant to us increase in our meditations.

Encircle howan kuṇḍa three times, and set fire on right side.

वौषाट्

open hands face up

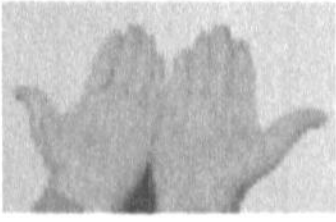

vauṣāṭ
Ultimate Purity!

फट् फट् फट्

abhishek - sprinkle water

phaṭ phaṭ phaṭ
Purify! Purify! Purify!

फट् फट् फट्
phaṭ phaṭ phaṭ
Purify! Purify! Purify!

clap

हूं
hūṁ
Cut the Ego!

aṅkuśa mudrā

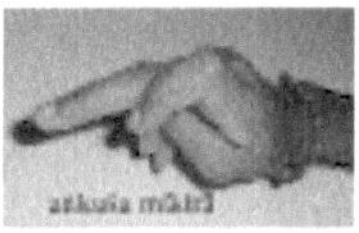

वं
vaṁ
Liberate!

dhenu mudrā

रं
raṁ
Purifying Consciousness!

yoni mudrā

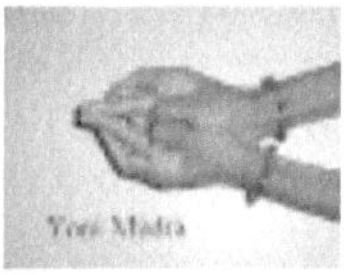

नमः
namaḥ
I bow!

prakṣan

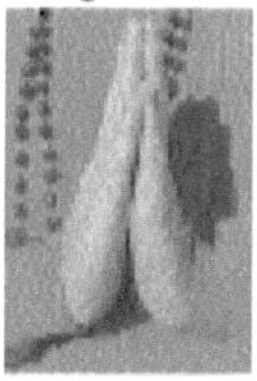

हुं फट् क्रव्यादिभ्यो नमः
huṁ phaṭ krayādibhyo namaḥ
Cut the Ego! Purify all evil beings!

one stick to side

three times fire sticks encircle howan kund:

सर्वमङ्गलमङ्गल्ये शिवे सर्वार्थसाधिके ।

शरण्ये त्र्यम्बके गौरि नारायणि नमोऽस्तु ते ॥

sarvamaṅgala maṅgalye śive sarvārtha sādhike
śaraṇye tryambake gauri nārāyaṇi namo-stu te

To the Auspicious of all Auspiciousness, to the Good, to the Accomplisher of all Objectives, to the Source of Refuge, to the Mother of the three worlds, to the Goddess Who is Rays of Light, Exposer of Consciousness, we bow to you.

सृष्टिस्थितिविनाशानां शक्तिभूते सनातनि ।

गुणाश्रये गुणमये नारायणि नमोऽस्तु ते ॥

sṛṣṭisthitivināśānāṁ śaktibhūte sanātani
guṇāśraye guṇamaye nārāyaṇi namo-stu te

You are the Eternal Energy of Creation, Preservation and Destruction in all existence; that upon which all qualities depend, that which limits all qualities, Exposer of Consciousness, we bow to you.

शरणागतदीनार्तपरित्राणपरायणे ।

सर्वस्यार्तिहरे देवि नारायणि नमोऽस्तु ते ॥

śaraṇāgatadīnārta paritrāṇa parāyaṇe
sarvasyārti hare devi nārāyaṇi namo-stu te

For those who are devoted to you and take refuge in you, you save from all discomfort and unhappiness. All worry you take away, Oh Goddess, Exposer of Consciousness, we bow to you.

Place Sticks to Enkindle Fire

जयन्ती मङ्गला काली भद्रकाली कपालिनी ।

दुर्गा क्षमा शिवा धात्री स्वाहा स्वधा नमोऽस्तु ते ॥

jayantī maṅgalā kālī bhadra-kālī kapālinī |
durgā kṣamā śivā dhātrī svāhā svadhā namo-stu te ||

She Who Conquers Over All, All-Auspicious, the Remover of Darkness, the Excellent One Beyond Time, the Bearer of the Skulls of Impure Thought, the Reliever of Difficulties, Loving Forgiveness, Supporter of the Universe, Oblations of I am One with God, Oblations of Ancestral Praise, to You, we bow.

upasaṁhara mudrā

ह्वयाम्यग्निं प्रथमं स्वस्तये ।

ह्वयामि मित्रावरुणाविहावसे ।

ह्वयामि रात्रीं जगतो निवेशनीं ।

ह्वयामिदेवं सवितारमूतये ॥

hvayāmyagniṁ prathamaṁ svastaye
hvayāmi mitrā varuṇā vihāvase
hvayāmi rātrīṁ jagato niveṣanīṁ
hvayāmi devaṁ savitāramūtaye

I am calling you, Agni, the Divine Fire, the Light of Meditation, first to grant success. I am calling you Friendship and the Continuous Flow of Equilibrium also to receive this offering. I am calling the Night of Duality who covers the universe. I am calling the Light of Wisdom, the Divine Being, to rise up within us.

हिरण्यगर्भः समवर्त्तताग्रे भूतस्य जातः पतिरेक आसीत्।
स दाधार पृथिवीं द्यामुतेमां कस्मै देवाय हविषा विधेम ॥

hiranyagarbhaḥ samavartatāgre
bhūtasya jātaḥ patireka āsīt
sa dādhāra pṛthivīṁ dyāmutemāṁ
kasmai devāya haviṣā vidhema

Oh Golden Womb, You are the One Eternal Existence from which all beings born on the earth have come forth. You always bear the earth and all that rises upon it. (You tell us) to which God shall we offer our knowledge and attention?

यथा विद्वां अरंकरद् विश्वेभ्यो यजतेभ्यः।
अयमग्ने त्वे अपि यं यज्ञं चकृमा वयम् ॥

yathā vidvāṁ araṁkarad viśvebhyoḥ yajatebhyaḥ
ayamagne tve api yaṁ yajñaṁ cakṛmā vayam

Through knowledge of this Eternal Cause, all beings born in the universe have come forth. It is in you, Oh Agni, Oh Light of Meditation, in the flame of sacrifice, that this constant movement will find rest.

त्वमग्ने प्रथमो अङ्गिरा ऋषिर्देवो देवानामभवः शिवः सखा।
तव व्रते कवयो विद्मनापसोऽजायन्त मरुतो भ्राजदृष्टयः ॥

tvamagne prathamo aṇgirā ṛṣirdevo
devānāmabhavaḥ śivaḥ sakhā
tava vrate kavayo vidmanāpaso-
jāyanta maruto bhrājadṛṣṭayaḥ

You, Oh Divine Light of Meditation, are the first among the performers of spiritual discipline, a Seer, a God; your name became one with all the Gods. You are the friend of Śiva, the Consciousness of Infinite Goodness. Through devotion to you, all the inspired poets (Ṛṣis who propound Vedic Knowledge, or Wisdom of Universality) come to Divine Knowledge, as did the Maruts (the 49 Gods of severe penance) did come forth from your worship.

त्वं मुखं सर्वदेवानां सप्तार्चिर्हविरद्मते ।
आगच्छ भगवनग्ने यज्ञेऽस्मिन् सन्निधा भव ॥

tvaṁ mukhaṁ sarvadevānāṁ saptārcirhaviradmate
āgaccha bhagavanagne yajñe-smin sannidhā bhava

You are the mouth of all the Gods, with your seven tongues you accept the offerings. Come here, Oh Lord Divine Fire, and take your seat in the midst of our sacrifice.

ॐ वैश्वानर जातवेद इहावह लोहिताक्ष सर्व कर्माणि
साधय स्वाहा ॥

oṁ vaiśvānara jātaveda ihāvaha lohitākṣa sarva karmāṇi
sādhaya svāhā

oṁ Oh Universal Being, Knower of All, come here with your red eyes. All of our Karma burn it! I AM ONE WITH GOD!

ॐ अग्नीमिळे पुरोहितं यज्ञस्य देवमृत्विजम् ।
होतारं रत्न धातमम् ॥

oṁ agnīmiḷe purohitaṁ yajñasya devamṛtvijam
hotāraṁ ratna dhātamam

Oh Agni, Light of Meditation, you are the Priest of Sacrifice, serving the offering of the divine nectar of Immortality. You give jewels to those who offer.

ॐ अग्नि प्रज्वलितं वन्दे जातवेदं हुताशनम् ।
सुवर्णवर्णममलं समिद्धं विश्वतो मुखम्

oṁ agni prajvalitaṁ vande jātavedaṁ hutāśanam
suvarṇavarṇamamalaṁ samiddhaṁ viśvato mukham

We lovingly adore the Divine Fire, Light of Meditation, sparkling, flaming brightly, knower of all, recipient of our offerings. With His excellent golden color, everywhere His omnipresent mouths are devouring oblations.

ॐ अग्नये नमः

oṁ agnaye namaḥ
oṁ We bow to the Divine Fire.

अग्ने त्वं चण्डिकानामसि

agne tvaṁ caṇḍikānāmasi
Oh Divine Fire, we are now calling you by the name Caṇḍi, She who Tears Apart Thoughts.

ॐ वागीश्वरी मृतुस्नातां नीलेन्दीवरलोचनाम् ।
वागीश्वरेण संयुक्तां क्रीडाभाव समन्विताम् ॥

oṁ vāgīśvarī mṛtu-snātāṁ nīlendīvaralocanām
vāgīśvareṇa saṁyuktaṁ krīḍābhāva samanvitam
The Supreme Goddess of Speech, dear Mother Saraswati, has just completed Her bath following Her monthly course of menstruation. With eyes of blue, bestowing boons, She moves into union with Vāgīṣvara, Brahma, the Lord of All Vibrations, and together they create the bhāva or intensity of reality, the attitude which unites all.

एते गन्धपुष्पे ॐ ह्रीं वागीश्वर्यै नमः

ete gandhapuṣpe oṁ hrīṁ vāgīśvaryai namaḥ
With these scented flowers oṁ we bow to the Supreme Goddess of Speech, or all Vibrations.

एते गन्धपुष्पे ॐ ह्रीं वागीश्वराय नमः

ete gandhapuṣpe oṁ hrīṁ vāgīśvarāya namaḥ
With these scented flowers oṁ we bow to the Supreme Lord of Speech, or all Vibrations.

एते गन्धपुष्पे ॐ अग्नेर्हिरण्यादि सप्तजिह्वाभ्यो नमः

ete gandhapuṣpe oṁ agnerhiraṇyādi saptajihvābhyo namaḥ

With these scented flowers oṁ we bow to the seven tongues of the Divine Fire, like golden, etc.

1. Kālī	Black
2. Karālī	Increasing, formidable
3. Mano-javā	Swift as thought
4. Su-Lohitā	Excellent shine
5. Sudhūmra-Varnā	Purple
6. Ugrā or Sphulingīnī	Fearful
7. Pradīptā	Giving light

एते गन्धपुष्पे ॐ सहस्रार्चिषे हृदयाय नमः

ete gandhapuṣpe oṁ sahasrārciṣe hṛdayāya namaḥ

With these scented flowers oṁ we bow to the heart from which emanates a thousand rays.

इत्याद्यग्ने षदङ्गेभ्यो नमः

ityādyagne ṣadaṅgebhyo namaḥ

In this way establish the Divine Fire in the six centers of the body.

एते गन्धपुष्पे ॐ अग्नये जातवेदसे इत्यद्याष्टमूर्त्तिभ्यो नमः

ete gandhapuṣpe oṁ agnaye jātavedase ityadyaṣṭa mūrttibhyo namaḥ

With these scented flowers oṁ we bow to the Divine Fire, the Knower of All, etc, in His eight forms for worship.

1. Jāta-Veda	Knower of All
2. Sapta-Jihva	Seven tongued
3. Vaiśvānara	Universal Being
4. Havyā-Vāhana	Carrier of Oblations
5. Aśwodara-Ja	Fire of Stomach, lower areas
6. Kaumāra Tejaḥ	From which the son of Śiva is born
7. Viśva-Mukha	Which can devour the universe
8. Deva-Mukha	The mouth of the Gods

एते गन्धपुष्पे ॐ ब्राह्म्यद्यष्टशक्तिभ्यो नमः

ete gandhapuṣpe oṁ brāhmyadyaṣṭaśaktibhyo namaḥ

With these scented flowers oṁ we bow to the eight Śaktis or Energies, like Brāhmī, etc.

1. Brāhmī	Creative Energy
2. Nārāyaṇī	Exposer of Consciousness
3. Māheśvarī	Energy of the Seer of All
4. Cāmuṇḍā	Slayer of Passion & Meanness
5. Kaumārī	The Ever Pure One
6. Aparājitā	The Unconquerable
7. Vārāhī	The Boar of Sacrifice
8. Nārasiṁhī	The Man-lion of Courage

एते गन्धपुष्पे ॐ पद्माद्यष्टनिधिभ्यो नमः

ete gandhapuṣpe oṁ padmādyaṣṭa nidhibhyo namaḥ

With these scented flowers oṁ we bow to the eight Treasures of the Lord of Wealth, like Padma, etc.

1. Padma	The lotus of Peace
2. Mahā-Padma	The great lotus of universal Peace
3. Śaṅkha	The conch of all vibrations
4. Makara	The emblem of Love
5. Kacchapa	Tortoise, the emblem of support
6. Mukunda	The Crest gem
7. Nanda	Bliss
8. Nīla	The blue light within like a Sapphire

एते गन्धपुष्पे ॐ इन्द्रादि लोकपालेभ्यो नमः

ete gandhapuṣpe oṁ indrādi lokapālebhyo namaḥ

With these scented flowers oṁ we bow to Indra and the Protectors of the Ten Directions.

1. Indra	East
2. Agni	South-East
3. Yama	South
4. Nairrita	South-West
5. Varuṇa	West
6. Vāyu	North-West
7. Kuvera (Soma)	North
8. Īśāna	North-East
9. Brahmā	Above
10. Viṣṇu (Ananta)	Below

एते गन्धपुष्पे ॐ वज्राद्यस्त्रेभ्यो नमः

ete gandhapuṣpe oṁ vajrādyastrebhyo namaḥ
With these scented flowers oṁ we bow to the Thunderbolt and other weapons.

1. Vajra	Indra's thunderbolt
2. Śakti	Agni's spear, dart, energy
3. Daṇḍa	Yama's staff
4. Khaḍga	Nairrita's sword
5. Pāśa	Varuṇa's net or noose
6. Aṅkuśa	Vāyu's hook
7. Gadā	Kuvera's mace
8. Triśūla	Īśāna's trident
9. Padma or Kamaṇḍelu	Brahma's lotus or begging bowl
10. Cakra	Viṣṇu's discus

एते गन्धपुष्पे ॐ वह्निर्चैतन्याय नमः

ete gandhapuṣpe oṁ vahnir caintanyāya namaḥ
With these scented flowers oṁ we bow to the Consciousness of the Divine Fire.

एते गन्धपुष्पे ॐ अग्नि मूर्त्तये नमः

ete gandhapuṣpe oṁ agni mūrttaye namaḥ
With these scented flowers oṁ we bow to the Image of the Divine Fire, the Light of Meditation.

ॐ अग्नये नमः

oṁ agnaye namaḥ
oṁ we bow to the Divine Fire.

रं रं रं रं रं

raṁ raṁ raṁ raṁ raṁ
R The Subtle Body; a Consciousness ; ṁ Perfection
Raṁ The manifestation of Perfection in the Subtle Body of Consciousness.

japa

ॐ चित् पिङ्गल हन हन दह दह पच पच सर्व ज्ञापय ज्ञापय स्वाहा

oṁ cit piṅgala hana hana daha daha paca paca sarva jñāpaya jñāpaya svāhā

The Infinite Beyond Conception, Consciousness, the subtle canal which rises, purify, purify, burn, burn, bring to perfection, bring to perfection all wisdom, all wisdom, I am One with God!

establishment within

āvāhaṇi mudrā (I invite you, please come.)

ॐ ऐं ह्रीं क्लीं चामुण्डायै विच्चे इहागच्छ

oṁ aiṁ hrīṁ klīṁ cāmuṇḍāyai vicce ihāgaccha

Oṁ aiṁ hrīṁ klīṁ cāmuṇḍāyai vicce,
I invite you, please come.

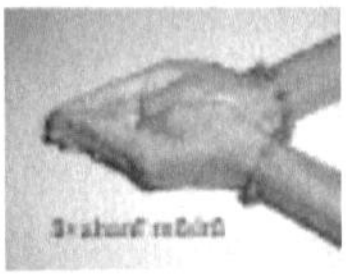

sthāpanī mudrā (I establish you within.)

इह तिष्ठ

iha tiṣṭha

I establish you within.

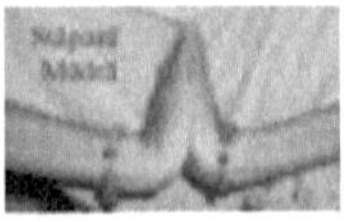

sannidhāpanī mudrā (I know you have many devotees who are requesting your attention, but I request that you pay special attention to me.)

इह सन्निरुध्यस्व

iha sannirudhyasva

I am binding you to remain here.

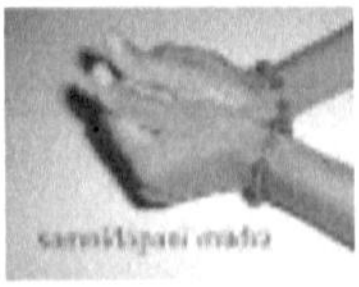

saṁrodhanī mudrā (I am sorry for any inconvenience caused.)

इह सनिहित भव

iha sanihita bhava

You bestow abundant wealth.

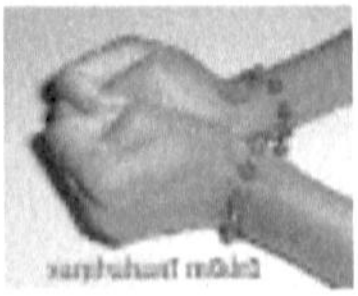

atmā samarpaṇa mudrā (I surrender my soul to you.)

अत्राधिष्ठानं कुरु

atrādhiṣṭhānaṁ kuru

I am depending upon you to forgive me in this matter.

prakṣan (I bow to you with devotion.)

देवि मम पूजां गृहाण

देवेशि भक्तशूलवे परित्राण करायिते ।

यावत् त्वं पूजयिष्यामि तावत् त्वं सुस्थिरा भव ।

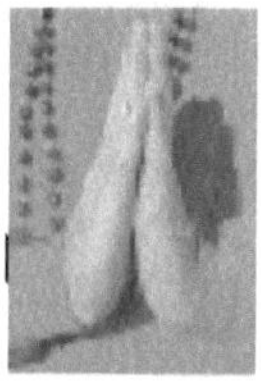

devi mama pūjāṁ gṛhāṇa
deveśi bhaktaśūlave paritrāṇa karāyite
yāvat tvaṁ pūjayiṣyāmi tāvat tvaṁ susthirā bhava

Oh Goddess, please accept my worship. Oh Goddess, remove all pain from your devotees. For so long as I worship you, please remain sitting still.

prāṇa pratiṣṭhā

establishment of life

ॐ अं आं ह्रीं क्रों यं रं लं वं शं षं सं हों हं सः

oṁ aṁ āṁ hrīṁ kroṁ yaṁ raṁ laṁ vaṁ śaṁ ṣaṁ saṁ hoṁ haṁ saḥ

oṁ The Infinite Beyond Conception, Creation (the first letter), Consciousness, Māyā, the cause of the movement of the subtle body to perfection and beyond; the path of fulfillment: control, subtle illumination, one with the earth, emancipation, the soul of peace, the soul of delight, the soul of unity (all this is I), perfection, Infinite Consciousness, this is I.

ॐ ऐं ह्रीं क्लीं चामुण्डायै विच्चे प्राणा इह प्राणाः

oṁ aiṁ hrīṁ klīṁ cāmuṇḍāyai vicce prāṇā iha prāṇāḥ

Oṁ aiṁ hrīṁ klīṁ cāmuṇḍāyai vicce. You are the life of this life!

ॐ अं आं ह्रीं क्रों यं रं लं वं शं षं सं हों हं सः

oṁ aṁ āṁ hrīṁ kroṁ yaṁ raṁ laṁ vaṁ śaṁ ṣaṁ saṁ hoṁ haṁ saḥ

oṁ The Infinite Beyond Conception, Creation (the first letter), Consciousness, Māyā, the cause of the movement of the subtle body to perfection and beyond; the path of fulfillment: control, subtle illumination, one with the earth, emancipation, the soul of peace, the soul of delight, the soul of unity (all this is I), perfection, Infinite Consciousness, this is I.

ॐ ऐं ह्रीं क्लीं चामुण्डायै विच्चे जीव इह स्थितः

oṁ aiṁ hrīṁ klīṁ cāmuṇḍāyai vicce jīva iha sthitaḥ

Oṁ aiṁ hrīṁ klīṁ cāmuṇḍāyai vicce. You are situated in this life (or individual consciousness).

ॐ अं आं ह्रीं क्रों यं रं लं वं शं षं सं हों हं सः

oṁ aṁ āṁ hrīṁ kroṁ yaṁ raṁ laṁ vaṁ śaṁ ṣaṁ saṁ hoṁ haṁ saḥ

oṁ The Infinite Beyond Conception, Creation (the first letter), Consciousness, Māyā, the cause of the movement of the subtle body to perfection and beyond; the path of fulfillment: control, subtle illumination, one with the earth, emancipation, the soul of peace, the soul of delight, the soul of unity (all this is I), perfection, Infinite Consciousness, this is I.

ॐ ऐं ह्रीं क्लीं चामुण्डायै विच्चे सर्वेन्द्रियाणि

oṁ aiṁ hrīṁ klīṁ cāmuṇḍāyai vicce sarvendriyāṇi

Oṁ aiṁ hrīṁ klīṁ cāmuṇḍāyai vicce. You are all these organs (of action and knowledge).

ॐ अं आं ह्रीं क्रों यं रं लं वं शं षं सं हों हं सः

oṁ aṁ āṁ hrīṁ kroṁ yaṁ raṁ laṁ vaṁ śaṁ ṣaṁ saṁ hoṁ haṁ saḥ

oṁ The Infinite Beyond Conception, Creation (the first letter), Consciousness, Māyā, the cause of the movement of the subtle body to perfection and beyond; the path of fulfillment: control, subtle illumination, one with the earth, emancipation, the soul of peace, the soul of delight, the soul of unity (all this is I), perfection, Infinite Consciousness, this is I.

ॐ ऐं ह्रीं क्लीं चामुण्डायै विच्चे वाग् मनस्त्वक्चक्षुः-श्रोत्र-घ्राण-प्राणा इहागत्य सुखं चिरं तिष्ठन्तु स्वाहा

oṁ aiṁ hrīṁ klīṁ cāmuṇḍāyai vicce vāg manastvakcakṣuḥ śrotra ghrāṇa prāṇā ihāgatya sukhaṁ ciraṁ tiṣṭhantu svāhā

Oṁ aiṁ hrīṁ klīṁ cāmuṇḍāyai vicce. You are all these vibrations, mind, sound, eyes, ears, tongue, nose and life force. Bring forth infinite peace and establish it forever, I am One with God!

kara nyāsa
establishment in the hands

ॐ ह्रां अंगुष्ठाभ्यां नमः

oṁ hrāṁ aṅguṣṭhābhyāṁ namaḥ thumb forefinger
Oṁ hrāṁ in the thumb I bow.

ॐ ह्रीं तर्जनीभ्यां स्वाहा

oṁ hrīṁ tarjanībhyāṁ svāhā thumb forefinger
Oṁ hrīṁ in the forefinger, I am One with God!

ॐ ह्रूं मध्यमाभ्यां वषट्

oṁ hrūṁ madhyamābhyāṁ vaṣaṭ thumb middlefinger
Oṁ hrūṁ in the middle finger, Purify!

ॐ ह्रैं अनामिकाभ्यां हुं

oṁ hraiṁ anāmikābhyāṁ huṁ thumb ring finger
Oṁ hraiṁ in the ring finger, Cut the Ego!

ॐ ह्रौं कनिष्ठिकाभ्यां बौषट्

oṁ hrauṁ kaniṣṭhikābhyāṁ vauṣaṭ thumb little finger
Oṁ hrauṁ in the little finger, Ultimate Purity!

Roll hand over hand forwards while reciting karatal kar,
and backwards while chanting pṛṣṭhābhyāṁ,
then clap hands when chanting astrāya phaṭ.

ॐ ह्रः करतल कर पृष्ठाभ्यां अस्त्राय फट् ॥

oṁ hraḥ karatal kar pṛṣṭhābhyāṁ astrāya phaṭ
Oṁ hraḥ I bow with the weapon of Virtue.

ॐ ऐं ह्रीं क्लीं चामुण्डायै विच्चे

oṁ aiṁ hrīṁ klīṁ cāmuṇḍāyai vicce
Oṁ aiṁ hrīṁ klīṁ cāmuṇḍāyai vicce.

aṅga nyāsa

establishment in the body

Holding tattva mudrā, touch heart.

ॐ ह्रां हृदयाय नमः

oṁ hrāṁ hṛdayāya namaḥ touch heart

Oṁ hrāṁ in the heart, I bow.

Holding tattva mudrā, touch top of head.

ॐ ह्रीं शिरसे स्वाहा

oṁ hrīṁ śirase svāhā top of head

Oṁ hrīṁ on the top of the head, I am One with God!

With thumb extended, touch back of head.

ॐ ह्रूं शिखायै वषट्

oṁ hrūṁ śikhāyai vaṣaṭ back of head

Oṁ hrūṁ on the back of the head, Purify!

Holding tattva mudrā, cross both arms.

ॐ ह्रैं कवचाय हुं

oṁ hraiṁ kavacāya huṁ cross both arms

Oṁ hraiṁ crossing both arms, Cut the Ego!

Holding tattva mudrā, touch two eyes and in between at once with three middle fingers.

ॐ ह्रौं नेत्रत्रयाय वौषट्

oṁ hrauṁ netratrayāya vauṣaṭ touch three eyes

Oṁ hrauṁ in the three eyes, Ultimate Purity!

Roll hand over hand forwards while reciting karatala kara and backwards while chanting pṛṣṭhābhyāṁ, then clap hands when chanting astrāya phaṭ.

ॐ ह्रः करतल कर पृष्ठाभ्यां अस्त्राय फट् ॥

oṁ hraḥ karatal kar pṛṣṭhābhyāṁ astrāya phaṭ

Oṁ hraḥ I bow with the weapon of Virtue.

ॐ ऐं ह्रीं क्लीं चामुण्डायै विच्चे

oṁ aiṁ hrīṁ klīṁ cāmuṇḍāyai vicce
Oṁ aiṁ hrīṁ klīṁ cāmuṇḍāyai vicce.

japa

hold flower to your heart

ॐ अम्बे ऽअम्बिकेऽम्बालिके न मा नयति कश्चन ।

ससस्त्यश्वकः सुभद्रिकां कापीलोवासिनीम् ॥

oṁ ambe-ambike-mbālike na mā nayati kaścana
sasastyaśvakaḥ subhadrikāṁ kāpīlovāsinīm
Mother of the Perceivable Universe, Mother of the Conceivable Universe, Mother of the Universe of Intuitive Vision, lead me to that True Existence. As excellent crops (or grains) are harvested, so may I be taken to reside with the Infinite Consciousness.

place flower in the fire

ॐ जयन्ती मङ्गला काली भद्रकाली कपालिनी ।

दुर्गा क्षमा शिवा धात्री स्वाहा स्वधा नमोऽस्तु ते ॥

oṁ jayantī maṅgalā kālī bhadra kālī kapālinī
durgā kṣamā śivā dhātrī svāhā svadhā namo-stu te
Oṁ. She Who Conquers Over All, All-Auspicious, She Who is Beyond Time, the Excellent One Beyond Time, the Bearer of the Skulls of Impure Thought, the Reliever of Difficulties, Loving Forgiveness, Supporter of the Universe, Oblations of I am One with God, Oblations of Ancestral Praise, to You, we bow.

upasaṁhara sthāpana mudrā

दुर्गां शिवां शान्तिकरीं ब्रह्माणीं ब्रह्मणः प्रियाम् ।
सर्वलोक प्रणेत्रीञ्च प्रणमामि सदा शिवाम् ॥

durgāṁ śivāṁ śāntikarīṁ brahmāṇīṁ brahmaṇaḥ priyām
sarvaloka praṇetrīñca praṇamāmi sadā śivām

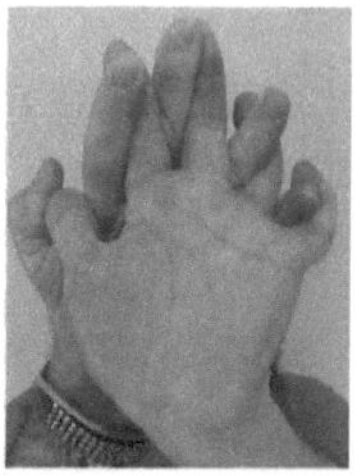

The Reliever of Difficulties, Exposer of Goodness, Cause of Peace, Infinite Consciousness, Beloved by Knowers of Consciousness; all the inhabitants of all the worlds always bow to Her, and I am bowing to Goodness Herself.

मङ्गलां शोभनां शुद्धां निष्कलां परमां कलाम् ।
विश्वेश्वरीं विश्वमातां चण्डिकां प्रणमाम्यहम् ॥

maṅgalāṁ śobhanāṁ śuddhāṁ niṣkalāṁ paramāṁ kalām
viśveśvarīṁ viśvamātāṁ caṇḍikāṁ praṇamāmyaham

Welfare, Radiant Beauty, Completely Pure, Without Limitations, the Ultimate Limitation, the Lord of the Universe, the Mother of the Universe, to you Caṇḍi, to the Energy that Tears Apart Thought, I bow in submission.

ॐ ऐं चण्डिकायै विद्महे त्रिपुरायै धीमहे ।
तन्नो गौरी प्रचोदयात् क्लीं ॥

oṁ aiṁ caṇḍikāyai vidmahe tripurāyai dhīmahe |
tanno gaurī pracodayāt klīṁ ||

Oṁ Wisdom we meditate upon the Goddess Caṇḍi, She Who Tears Apart All Thoughts, contemplate She Who occupies the three cities (gross perception, subtle conception, and intuitivee cognition). May that Goddess Who is Rays of Light grant us increase klīṁ (the cause of dissolution of the gross body into the causal body in perfection.)

āvāhaṇi mudrā (I invite you, please come.)

ॐ ह्रीं चण्डिके इहागच्छ

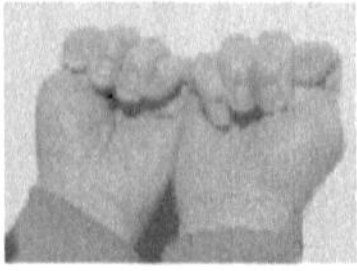

oṁ hrīṁ caṇḍike ihāgaccha
oṁ She Who Tears Apart Thought,
I invite you, please come.

sthāpanī mudrā (I establish you within.)

इह तिष्ठ

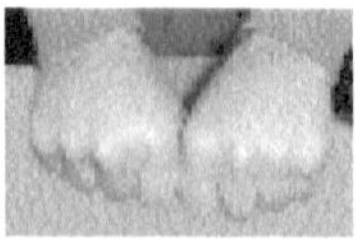

iha tiṣṭha
I establish you within.

sannidhāpanī mudrā (I know you have many devotees who are requesting your attention, but I request that you pay special attention to me.)

इह सन्निदेहि

iha sannidehi
I am binding you to remain here.

saṁrodhanī mudrā (I am sorry for any inconvenience caused.)

इह सनिहित भव

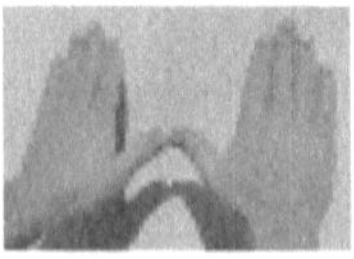

iha sanihita bhava
You bestow abundant wealth.

atmā samarpaṇa mudrā (I surrender my soul to you.)

अत्राधिष्ठानं कुरु

atrādhiṣṭhānaṁ kuru
I am depending upon you to forgive me in this matter.

prakṣan (I bow to you with devotion.)

देवि मम पूजां गृहाण

देवेशि भक्तशूल्वे परित्राण करायिते ।

यावत् त्वं पूजयिष्यामि तावत् त्वं सुस्थिरा भव ॥

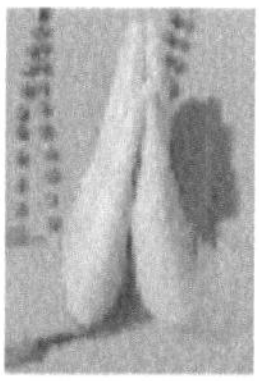

devi mama pūjāṁ gṛhāṇa
deveśi bhaktaśūlave paritrāṇa karāyite
yāvat tvaṁ pūjayiṣyāmi tāvat tvaṁ susthirā bhava

Oh Goddess, please accept my worship. Oh Goddess, remove all pain from your devotees. For so long as I worship you, please remain sitting still.

Pūjā

Worship of fire

ॐ वैश्वानर जातवेद इहावह लोहिताक्ष सर्व कर्माणि साधय स्वाहा ॥

oṁ vaiśvānara jātaveda ihāvaha lohitākṣa sarva karmāṇi sādhaya svāhā

Oh Universal Being, Knower of All, come here with your red eyes. All of our Karma burn it! I AM ONE WITH GOD!

dhūpam
dhīpam
arghyam
puṣpam
naivedyam
taṁbūlam

purify ghee container

open hands face up

वौषाट्

vauṣāṭ
Ultimate Purity!

फट् फट् फट्

abhishek - sprinkle water

phaṭ phaṭ phaṭ
Purify! Purify! Purify!

फट् फट् फट्

clap

phaṭ phaṭ phaṭ
Purify! Purify! Purify!

aṅkuśa mudrā

हूं

hūṁ
Cut the Ego!

dhenu mudrā

वं

vaṁ
Liberate!

yoni mudrā

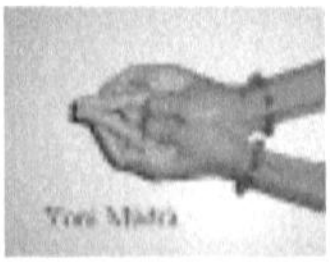

रं

raṁ
Purifying Consciousness!

prakṣan

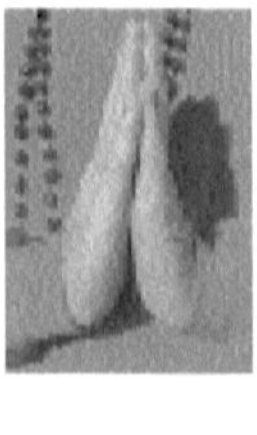

नमः

namaḥ
I bow!

Place three pieces of grass with the following mantras

ईड

īḍa

The subtle passage which brings the light of the sun.

पिङ्गल

piṅgala

The subtle passage which brings the light of the moon.

सुषुम्ना

suṣumnā

The subtle passage which brings the light of the fire.

place ghee container on the grass

फट्

phaṭ

Purify!

ghee oblations

ॐ अग्नये स्वाहा

oṁ agnaye svāhā

oṁ To the Divine Fire, I am One with God!

ॐ सोमाय स्वाहा

oṁ somāya svāhā

oṁ To the Moon, emblem of Devotion, I am One with God!

ॐ अग्नीषोमाभ्यां स्वाहा

oṁ agnīṣomābhyāṁ svāhā

oṁ To the Divine Fire and to the Moon, emblem of Devotion, I am One with God!

ॐ अग्नये स्विष्टकृते स्वाहा

oṁ agnaye sviṣṭakṛte svāhā

oṁ To the Divine Fire, to whom excellent honor is given, I am One with God!

ॐ भूः स्वाहा

oṁ bhūḥ svāhā
oṁ Gross Perception, I am One with God!

ॐ भुवः स्वाहा

oṁ bhuvaḥ svāhā
oṁ Subtle Perception, I am One with God!

ॐ स्वः स्वाहा

oṁ svaḥ svāhā
oṁ Intuitive Perception, I am One with God!

ॐ भूर्भुवः स्वः स्वाहा

oṁ bhūrbhuvaḥ svaḥ svāhā
oṁ Gross Perception; oṁ Subtle Perception; oṁ Intuitive Perception, I am One with God!

ॐ वैश्वानर जातवेद् इहावह लोहिताक्ष सर्व कर्माणि साधय स्वाहा ॥

oṁ vaiśvānara jātaveda ihāvaha lohitākṣa sarva karmāṇi sādhaya svāhā
Oh Universal Being, Knower of All, come here with your red eyes. All of our Karma burn it! I AM ONE WITH GOD!

ॐ चित् पिङ्गल हन हन दह दह पच पच सर्व ज्ञापय ज्ञापय स्वाहा

oṁ cit piṅgala hana hana daha daha paca paca sarva jñāpaya jñāpaya svāhā
The Infinite Beyond Conception, Consciousness, the subtle canal which rises, purify, purify, burn, burn, bring to perfection, bring to perfection all wisdom, all wisdom, I am One with God!

Perform Homa of Sankalpa

सर्वतो भद्रमण्डल देवता होम

sarvato bhadramaṇḍala devatā homa

Sacrificial Fire Offerings to the Excellent Circle of all the Gods

- 1 -

ॐ ब्रह्मणे नमः स्वाहा

oṁ brahmaṇe namaḥ svāhā

We bow to Creative Consciousness (Center), I am One with God.

- 2 -

ॐ सोमाय नमः स्वाहा

oṁ somāya namaḥ svāhā

We bow to Lord of Devotion (N), I am One with God.

- 3 -

ॐ ईशानाय नमः स्वाहा

oṁ īśānāya namaḥ svāhā

We bow to Ruler of All (NE), I am One with God.

- 4 -

ॐ इन्द्राय नमः स्वाहा

oṁ indrāya namaḥ svāhā

We bow to Rule of the Pure (E), I am One with God.

- 5 -

ॐ अग्नये नमः स्वाहा

oṁ agnaye namaḥ svāhā

We bow to Divine Fire (SE), I am One with God.

- 6 -

ॐ यमाय नमः स्वाहा

oṁ yamāya namaḥ svāhā

We bow to Supreme Controller (S), I am One with God.

- 7 -

ॐ निर्ऋतये नमः स्वाहा

oṁ nirṛtaye namaḥ svāhā

We bow to Destroyer (SW), I am One with God.

- 8 -

ॐ वरुणाय नमः स्वाहा

oṁ varuṇāya namaḥ svāhā
We bow to Lord of Equilibrium (W), I am One with God.

- 9 -

ॐ वायवे नमः स्वाहा

oṁ vāyave namaḥ svāhā
We bow to Lord of Liberation (NW), I am One with God.

- 10 -

ॐ अष्टवसुभ्यो नमः स्वाहा

oṁ aṣṭavasubhyo namaḥ svāhā
We bow to the Eight Lords of Benificence, I am One with God.

- 11 -

ॐ एकादशरुद्रेभ्यो नमः स्वाहा

oṁ ekādaśarudrebhyo namaḥ svāhā
We bow to the Eleven Relievers from Sufferings, I am One with God.

- 12 -

ॐ द्वादशादित्येभ्यो नमः स्वाहा

oṁ dvādaśādityebhyo namaḥ svāhā
We bow to the Twelve Sons of Light, I am One with God.

- 13 -

ॐ अश्विभ्यां नमः स्वाहा

oṁ aśvibhyāṁ namaḥ svāhā
We bow to the Two Horses of Pure Desire, I am One with God.

- 14 -

ॐ सपैतृकविश्वेभ्यो देवेभ्यो नमः स्वाहा

oṁ sapaitṛkaviśvebhyo devebhyo namaḥ svāhā
We bow to the Ancestors along with the Shining Ones of the Universe, I am One with God.

- 15 -

ॐ सप्तयक्षेभ्यो नमः स्वाहा

oṁ saptayakṣebhyo namaḥ svāhā

We bow to the Energy which brings the good and bad of wealth, I am One with God.

- 16 -

ॐ अष्टकुलनागेभ्यो नमः स्वाहा

oṁ aṣṭakulanāgebhyo namaḥ svāhā

We bow to the Family of eight snakes, I am One with God.

- 17 -

ॐ गन्धर्वाऽप्सरोभ्यो नमः स्वाहा

oṁ gandharvā-psarobhyo namaḥ svāhā

We bow to the celestial musicians and heavenly maidens, I am One with God.

- 18 -

ॐ स्कन्दाय नमः स्वाहा

oṁ skandāya namaḥ svāhā

We bow to the God of War, I am One with God.

- 19 -

ॐ वृषभाय नमः स्वाहा

oṁ vṛṣabhāya namaḥ svāhā

We bow to the Bull of Discipline, Conveyance of Śiva -- Nandi, I am One with God.

- 20 -

ॐ शूलाय नमः स्वाहा

oṁ śūlāya namaḥ svāhā

We bow to the Spear of Concentration, I am One with God.

- 21 -

ॐ महाकालाय नमः स्वाहा

oṁ mahākālāya namaḥ svāhā

We bow to the Great Time, I am One with God.

\- 22 -

ॐ दक्षादि सप्तगणेभ्यो नमः स्वाहा

oṁ dakṣādi saptagaṇebhyo namaḥ svāhā

We bow to to Ability and the other seven qualities, I am One with God.

\- 23 -

ॐ दुर्गायै नमः स्वाहा

oṁ durgāyai namaḥ svāhā

We bow to the Reliever of Difficulties, I am One with God.

\- 24 -

ॐ विष्णवे नमः स्वाहा

oṁ viṣṇave namaḥ svāhā

We bow to the All-Pervading Consciousness, I am One with God.

\- 25 -

ॐ स्वधायै नमः स्वाहा

oṁ svadhāyai namaḥ svāhā

We bow to the Ancestors, I am One with God.

\- 26 -

ॐ मृतयुरोगेभ्यो नमः स्वाहा

oṁ mṛtyurogebhyo namaḥ svāhā

We bow to the Spirit of deadly illnesses, I am One with God.

\- 27 -

ॐ गणपतये नमः स्वाहा

oṁ gaṇapataye namaḥ svāhā

We bow to the Lord of the Multitudes, I am One with God.

\- 28 -

ॐ अद्भ्यो नमः स्वाहा

oṁ adbhyo namaḥ svāhā

We bow to to Acts of Sacrifice, I am One with God.

\- 29 -

ॐ मरुद्भ्यो नमः स्वाहा

oṁ marudbhyo namaḥ svāhā

We bow to the Shining Ones, I am One with God.

- 30 -

ॐ पृथिव्यै नमः स्वाहा

oṁ pṛthivyai namaḥ svāhā

We bow to the Earth, I am One with God.

- 31 -

ॐ गङ्गादिनदीभ्यो नमः स्वाहा

oṁ gaṅgādinadībhyo namaḥ svāhā

We bow to the Ganges and other rivers, I am One with God.

- 32 -

ॐ सप्तसागरेभ्यो नमः स्वाहा

oṁ saptasāgarebhyo namaḥ svāhā

We bow to the Seven Seas, I am One with God.

- 33 -

ॐ मेरवे नमः स्वाहा

oṁ merave namaḥ svāhā

We bow to Mount Meru, I am One with God.

- 34 -

ॐ गदाय नमः स्वाहा

oṁ gadāya namaḥ svāhā

We bow to the Club, I am One with God.

- 35 -

ॐ त्रिशूलाय नमः स्वाहा

oṁ triśūlāya namaḥ svāhā

We bow to the Trident, I am One with God.

- 36 -

ॐ वज्राय नमः स्वाहा

oṁ vajrāya namaḥ svāhā

We bow to the thunderbolt, I am One with God.

- 37 -

ॐ शक्तये नमः स्वाहा

oṁ śaktaye namaḥ svāhā

We bow to Energy, I am One with God.

\- 38 -

ॐ दण्डाय नमः स्वाहा

oṁ daṇḍāya namaḥ svāhā
We bow to the Staff, I am One with God.

\- 39 -

ॐ खड्गाय नमः स्वाहा

oṁ khaḍgāya namaḥ svāhā
We bow to the Sword, I am One with God.

\- 40 -

ॐ पाशाय नमः स्वाहा

oṁ pāśāya namaḥ svāhā
We bow to the Net, I am One with God.

\- 41 -

ॐ अङ्कुशाय नमः स्वाहा

oṁ aṅkuśāya namaḥ svāhā
We bow to the Goad, I am One with God.

\- 42 -

ॐ गौतमाय नमः स्वाहा

oṁ gautamāya namaḥ svāhā
We bow to Ṛṣi Gautam, I am One with God.

\- 43 -

ॐ भरद्वाजाय नमः स्वाहा

oṁ bharadvājāya namaḥ svāhā
We bow to Ṛṣi Bharadvāj, I am One with God.

\- 44 -

ॐ विश्वामित्राय नमः स्वाहा

oṁ viśvāmitrāya namaḥ svāhā
We bow to Ṛṣi Viśvāmitra, I am One with God.

\- 45 -

ॐ कश्यपाय नमः स्वाहा

oṁ kaśyapāya namaḥ svāhā
We bow to Ṛṣi Kaśyapa, I am One with God.

- 46 -

ॐ जमदग्नये नमः स्वाहा

oṁ jamadagnaye namaḥ svāhā
We bow to Ṛṣi Jamadagni, I am One with God.

- 47 -

ॐ वसिष्ठाय नमः स्वाहा

oṁ vasiṣṭāya namaḥ svāhā
We bow to Ṛṣi Vaṣisṭha, I am One with God.

- 48 -

ॐ अत्रये नमः स्वाहा

oṁ atraye namaḥ svāhā
We bow to Ṛṣi Atri, I am One with God.

- 49 -

ॐ अरुन्धत्यै नमः स्वाहा

oṁ arundhatyai namaḥ svāhā
We bow to Devi Arundati, wife of Vaṣisṭha, example of purity, I am One with God.

- 50 -

ॐ ऐन्द्र्यै नमः स्वाहा

oṁ aindryai namaḥ svāhā
We bow to Aindri, the energy of the Rule of the Pure, I am One with God.

- 51 -

ॐ कौमार्य्यै नमः स्वाहा

oṁ kaumāryyai namaḥ svāhā
We bow to Kumarī, the energy of the Ever Pure One, I am One with God.

- 52 -

ॐ ब्राह्म्यै नमः स्वाहा

oṁ brāhmyai namaḥ svāhā
We bow to Brahmi, the energy of Creative Consciousness, I am One with God.

- 53 -

ॐ वाराह्यै नमः स्वाहा

oṁ vārāhyai namaḥ svāhā

We bow to Varāhi, the energy of the Boar of Sacrifice, I am One with God.

- 54 -

ॐ चामुण्डायै नमः स्वाहा

oṁ cāmuṅḍāyai namaḥ svāhā

We bow to Cāmuṇḍa, the Conquerer of Passion and Meaness, I am One with God.

- 55 -

ॐ वैष्णव्यै नमः स्वाहा

oṁ vaiṣṇavyai namaḥ svāhā

We bow to Vaiṣṇāvi, the energy of All-Pervading Consciousness, I am One with God.

- 56 -

ॐ माहेश्वर्यै नमः स्वाहा

oṁ māheśvaryai namaḥ svāhā

We bow to Maheśvarī, the energy of the Supreme Sovereign, I am One with God.

- 57 -

ॐ वैनायक्यै नमः स्वाहा

oṁ vaināyakyai namaḥ svāhā

We bow to Vainākī, the energy of excellent conduct, I am One with God.

food offering

ॐ सत्पात्रं शुद्धसुहविर्व्विविधानेकभक्षणम् ।
निवेदयामि देवेशि सर्वतृप्तिकरं परम् ॥

oṁ satpātraṁ śuddhasuhavirv vividhānekabhakṣaṇam
nivedayāmi deveśi sarvatṛptikaraṁ param

Oṁ This ever-present platter containing varieties of the purest offerings of food we are presenting to the Lord of Gods to cause all satisfaction, most excellent and transcendental.

ॐ अन्नपूर्णे सदा पूर्णे शङ्करप्राणवल्लभे ।
ज्ञानवैराग्यसिद्ध्यर्थं भिक्षां देहि नमोऽस्तु ते ॥

oṁ annapūrṇe sadā pūrṇe śaṅkara prāṇavallabhe
jñānavairāgyasiddhyarthaṁ bhikṣāṁ dehi namo-stu te

oṁ Goddess who is full, complete and perfect with food and grains, always full, complete and perfect, the strength of the life force of Śiva, the Cause of Peace. For the attainment of perfection in wisdom and renunciation, please give us offerings. We bow down to you.

माता च पार्वती देवी पिता देवो महेश्वरः ।
बान्धवाः शिवभक्ताश्च स्वदेशो भुवनत्रयम् ॥

mātā ca pārvatī devī pitā devo maheśvaraḥ
bāndhavāḥ śivabhaktāśca svadeśo bhuvanatrayam

Our Mother is the Goddess, Pārvatī, and our Father is the Supreme Lord, Maheśvara. The Consciousness of Infinite Goodness, Śiva, Lord of the three worlds, is being extolled by his devotees.

ॐ ऐं ह्रीं क्लीं चामुण्डायै विच्चे भोगनैवेद्यम् समर्पयामि

oṁ aiṁ hrīṁ klīṁ cāmuṇḍāyai vicce bhog-naivedyam samarpayāmi

With this presentation of food oṁ aiṁ hrīṁ klīṁ cāmuṇḍāyai vicce.

offer food to fire

सर्वमङ्गलमङ्गल्ये शिवे सर्वार्थसाधिके ।
शरण्ये त्र्यम्बके गौरि नारायणि नमोऽस्तु ते ॥

sarvamaṅgala maṅgalye śive sarvārtha sādhike
śaraṇye tryambake gauri nārāyaṇi namo-stu te

To the Auspicious of all Auspiciousness, to the Good, to the Accomplisher of all Objectives, to the Source of Refuge, to the Mother of the three worlds, to the Goddess Who is Rays of Light, Exposer of Consciousness, we bow to you.

ॐ ऐं ह्रीं क्लीं चामुण्डायै विच्चे भोगनैवेद्यम् समर्पयामि

oṁ aiṁ hrīṁ klīṁ cāmuṇḍāyai vicce bhog-naivedyam samarpayāmi

With this presentation of food oṁ aiṁ hrīṁ klīṁ cāmuṇḍāyai vicce.

सृष्टिस्थितिविनाशानां शक्तिभूते सनातनि ।
गुणाश्रये गुणमये नारायणि नमोऽस्तु ते ॥

sṛṣṭisthitivināśānāṁ śaktibhūte sanātani
guṇāśraye guṇamaye nārāyaṇi namo-stu te

You are the Eternal Energy of Creation, Preservation and Destruction in all existence; that upon which all qualities depend, that which limits all qualities, Exposer of Consciousness, we bow to you.

ॐ ऐं ह्रीं क्लीं चामुण्डायै विच्चे भोगनैवेद्यम् समर्पयामि

oṁ aiṁ hrīṁ klīṁ cāmuṇḍāyai vicce bhog-naivedyam samarpayāmi

With this presentation of food oṁ aiṁ hrīṁ klīṁ cāmuṇḍāyai vicce.

शरणागतदीनार्तपरित्राणपरायणे ।

सर्वस्यार्तिहरे देवि नारायणि नमोऽस्तु ते ॥

śaraṇāgatadīnārta paritrāṇa parāyaṇe
sarvasyārti hare devi nārāyaṇi namo-stu te

For those who are devoted to you and take refuge in you, you save from all discomfort and unhappiness. All worry you take away, Oh Goddess, Exposer of Consciousness, we bow to you.

ॐ ऐं ह्रीं क्लीं चामुण्डायै विच्चे भोगनैवेद्यम् समर्पयामि

oṁ aiṁ hrīṁ klīṁ cāmuṇḍāyai vicce bhog-naivedyam samarpayāmi

With this presentation of food oṁ aiṁ hrīṁ klīṁ cāmuṇḍāyai vicce.

drinking water

ॐ समस्तदेवदेवेशि सर्वतृप्तिकरं परम् ।

अखण्डानन्दसम्पूर्णं गृहाण जलमुत्तमम् ॥

ॐ ऐं ह्रीं क्लीं चामुण्डायै विच्चे पानार्थं जलम् समर्पयामि

oṁ samasta devadeveśi sarvatṛptikaraṁ param
akhaṇḍānanda sampūrṇaṁ gṛhāṇa jalamuttamam
oṁ aiṁ hrīṁ klīṁ cāmuṇḍāyai vicce pānārthaṁ jalam samarpayāmi

Oṁ Goddess of All the Gods and the fullness of Infinite Bliss, please accept this excellent drinking water. With this offering of drinking water oṁ aiṁ hrīṁ klīṁ cāmuṇḍāyai vicce.

betel nuts

पूगीफलं महद्दिव्यं नागवल्ली दलैर्युतम् ।
एलादिचूर्णसंयुक्तं ताम्बूलं प्रतिगृह्यताम् ॥
ॐ ऐं ह्रीं क्लीं चामुण्डायै विच्चे ताम्बूलं समर्पयामि

pūgīphalaṁ mahaddivyaṁ nāgavallī dalairyutam
elādicūrṇasaṁyuktaṁ tāmbūlaṁ pratigṛhyatām
oṁ aiṁ hrīṁ klīṁ cāmuṇḍāyai vicce tāmbūlaṁ samarpayāmi

These betel nuts, which are great and divine, come from vines that creep like a snake. United with cardamom ground to a powder, please accept this offering of mouth-freshening betel nuts. With this offering of mouth freshening betel nuts oṁ aiṁ hrīṁ klīṁ cāmuṇḍāyai vicce.

dakṣiṇā

ॐ पूजाफलसमृद्ध्यर्थं तवाग्रे स्वर्णमीश्वरि ।
स्थापितं तेन मे प्रीता पूर्णान् कुरु मनोरथान् ॥

oṁ pūjāphalasmṛddhyarthaṁ tavāgre svarṇamīśvari
sthāpitaṁ tena me prītā pūrṇān kuru manorathān

Oṁ For the purpose of increasing the fruits of worship, Oh Supreme Goddess of all Wealth, we establish this offering of that which is dear to me. Bring to perfection the journey of my mind.

हिरण्यगर्भगर्भस्थं हेमबीजं विभावसोः ।
अनन्तपुण्यफलदमतः शान्तिं प्रयच्छ मे ॥

hiraṅyagarbhagarbhasthaṁ hemabījaṁ vibhāvasoḥ
anantapuṇyaphaladamataḥ śāntiṁ prayaccha me

Oh Golden Womb, in whom all wombs are situated, shining brightly with the golden seed. Give infinite merits as fruits, we are wanting for peace.

ॐ ऐं ह्रीं क्लीं चामुण्डायै विच्चे दक्षिणां समर्पयामि

oṁ aiṁ hrīṁ klīṁ cāmuṇḍāyai vicce dakṣiṇāṁ samarpayāmi

Oṁ With this offering of wealth oṁ aiṁ hrīṁ klīṁ cāmuṇḍāyai vicce.

flower

मल्लिकादि सुगन्धीनि मालित्यादीनि वै प्रभो ।
मयाऽहृतानि पूजार्थं पुष्पाणि प्रतिगृह्यताम् ॥
ॐ ऐं ह्रीं क्लीं चामुण्डायै विच्चे पुष्पम् समर्पयामि

mallikādi sugandhīni mālityādīni vai prabho
mayā-hṛtāni pūjārthaṁ puṣpāṇi pratigṛhyatām
oṁ aiṁ hrīṁ klīṁ cāmuṇḍāyai vicce puṣpam samarpayāmi

Various flowers, such as mallikā and others of excellent scent, are being offered to you, Our Lord. All these flowers have come from the devotion of our hearts for your worship. Please accept them. With this offering of a flower oṁ aiṁ hrīṁ klīṁ cāmuṇḍāyai vicce.

पूर्णहुति
Pūrṇahuti

ॐ इतः पूर्व प्राणबुद्धिदेह धर्माधिकारतो ।
जाग्रत् स्वप्नशुषुप्तयवस्थाशु मनसा ॥

oṁ ītaḥ pūrva prāṇabuddhideha dharmādhikārato jāgrat svapnaśuṣuptyavasthāśu manasā

Oṁ Thus the full and complete intelligence of the Life Force, the Cause of Dharma, the Way of Truth to Perfection, has been given. Waking Consciousness, Dreaming (or thinking) Consciousness, and Consciousness in Dreamless Sleep (intuitive Consciousness) in which all thoughts are situated.

वाचा कर्मणा हस्ताभ्यां पध्भ्यामूदरेण शिश्ना ।
यत् कृतं यदुक्तं यत् स्मृतं तत् सर्वं ब्रह्मार्पणं भवतु स्वाहा ॥

vācā karmaṇā hastābhyāṁ padhbhyāmūdareṇa śiśnā yat kṛtaṁ yaduktaṁ yat smṛtaṁ tat sarvaṁ brahmārpaṇaṁ bhavatu svāhā

All speech has been offered with folded hands raised in respect while bowing to the lotus feet. That activity, that union, that memory, all of that has been offered to the Supreme Divinity, I am One with God.

मां मदीयञ्च सकलं श्री चण्डिका चरणे समर्पये ।
ॐ तत् सत् ॥

māṁ madīyañca sakalaṁ śrī caṇḍikā caraṇe samarpaye oṁ tat sat

All of me and all that belongs to me entirely, I surrender to the feet of the respected caṇḍikā, She Who Tears Apart Thought. The Infinite, That is Truth.

ॐ ब्रह्मार्पणं ब्रह्म हविर्ब्रह्माग्नौ ब्रह्मणा हुतम् ।
ब्रह्मैव तेन गन्तव्यं ब्रह्मकर्मसमाधिना ॥

oṁ brahmārpaṇaṁ brahma havir
brahmāgnau brahmaṇā hutam
brahmaiva tena gantavyaṁ brahmakarmasamādhinā

oṁ The Supreme Divinity makes the offering; the Supreme Divinity is the offering; offered by the Supreme Divinity, in the fire of the Supreme Divinity. By seeing the Supreme Divinity in all actions, one realizes that Supreme Divinity.

ॐ पूर्णमदः पूर्णमिदं पूर्णात् पूर्णमुदुच्यते ।
पूर्णस्य पूर्णमादाय पूर्णमेवावशिश्यते ॥

oṁ pūrṇamadaḥ pūrṇamidaṁ
pūrṇāt pūrṇamuducyate
pūrṇasya pūrṇamādāya pūrṇamevāva śiṣyate

oṁ That is whole and perfect; this is whole and perfect. From the whole and perfect, the whole and perfect becomes manifest. If the whole and perfect issue forth from the whole and perfect, even still only the whole and perfect will remain.

ॐ शान्तिः शान्तिः शान्तिः ॥

oṁ śāntiḥ śāntiḥ śāntiḥ

oṁ Peace, Peace, Peace

क्षमास्य (visārjaṇ mudrā)

kṣamāsya

Please forgive me.

प्रणाम्
praṇām

सर्वमङ्गलमङ्गल्ये शिवे सर्वार्थसाधिके ।
शरण्ये त्र्यम्बके गौरि नारायणि नमोऽस्तु ते ॥

sarvamaṅgala maṅgalye śive sarvārtha sādhike
śaraṇye tryambake gauri nārāyaṇi namo-stu te
To the Auspicious of all Auspiciousness, to the Good, to the Accomplisher of all Objectives, to the Source of Refuge, to the Mother of the three worlds, to the Goddess Who is Rays of Light, Exposer of Consciousness, we bow to you.

सृष्टिस्थितिविनाशानां शक्तिभूते सनातनि ।
गुणाश्रये गुणमये नारायणि नमोऽस्तु ते ॥

sṛṣṭisthitivināśānāṁ śaktibhūte sanātani
guṇāśraye guṇamaye nārāyaṇi namo-stu te
You are the Eternal Energy of Creation, Preservation and Destruction in all existence; that upon which all qualities depend, that which limits all qualities, Exposer of Consciousness, we bow to you.

शरणागतदीनार्तपरित्राणपरायणे ।
सर्वस्यार्तिहरे देवि नारायणि नमोऽस्तु ते ॥

śaraṇāgatadīnārta paritrāṇa parāyaṇe
sarvasyārti hare devi nārāyaṇi namo-stu te
For those who are devoted to you and take refuge in you, you save from all discomfort and unhappiness. All worry you take away, Oh Goddess, Exposer of Consciousness, we bow to you.

दुर्गां शिवां शान्तिकरीं ब्रह्माणीं ब्रह्मणः प्रियाम् ।
सर्वलोकप्रणेत्रीञ्च प्रणमामि सदा शिवाम् ॥

durgāṁ śivāṁ śāntikarīṁ
brahmāṇīṁ brahmaṇaḥ priyām
sarvaloka praṇetrīñca praṇamāmi sadā śivām

The Reliever of Difficulties, Exposer of Goodness, Cause of Peace, Infinite Consciousness, Beloved by Knowers of Consciousness; all the inhabitants of all the worlds always bow to Her, and I am bowing to Goodness Herself.

मङ्गलां शोभनां शुद्धां निष्कलां परमां कलाम् ।
विश्वेश्वरीं विश्वमातां चण्डिकां प्रणमाम्यहम् ॥

maṅgalāṁ śobhanāṁ śuddhāṁ
niṣkalāṁ paramāṁ kalām
viśveśvarīṁ viśvamātāṁ
caṇḍikāṁ praṇamāmyaham

Welfare, Radiant Beauty, Completely Pure, without limitations, the Ultimate Limitation, the Lord of the Universe, the Mother of the Universe, to you Caṇḍi, to the Energy which Tears Apart Thought, I bow in submission.

सर्वदेवमयीं देवीं सर्वरोगभयापहाम् ।
ब्रह्मेशविष्णुनमितां प्रणमामि सदा शिवाम् ॥

sarvadevamayīṁ devīṁ sarvarogabhayāpahām
brahmeśaviṣṇunamitāṁ praṇamāmi sadā śivām

Composed of all the Gods, removing all sickness and fear, Brahma, Maheśvara and Viṣṇu bow down to Her, and I always bow down to the Energy of Infinite Goodness.

विन्ध्यस्थां विन्ध्यनिलयां दिव्यस्थाननिवासिनीम् ।
योगिनीं योगजननीं चण्डिकां प्रणमाम्यहम् ॥

vindhyasthāṁ vindhyanilayāṁ divyasthānanivāsinīm
yoginīṁ yogajananīṁ caṇḍikāṁ praṇamāmyaham
The dwelling place of Knowledge, residing in Knowledge, Resident in the place of Divine Illumination, the Cause of Union, the Knower of Union, to the Energy Which Tears Apart Thought we constantly bow.

ईशानमातरं देवीमीश्वरीमीश्वरप्रियाम् ।
प्रणतोऽस्मि सदा दुर्गां संसारार्णवतारिणीम् ॥

īśānamātaraṁ devīmīśvarīmīśvarapriyām
praṇato-smi sadā durgāṁ saṁsārārṇavatāriṇīm
The Mother of the Supreme Consciousness, the Goddess Who is the Supreme Consciousness, beloved by the Supreme Consciousness, we always bow to Durgā, the Reliever of Difficulties, who takes aspirants across the difficult sea of objects and their relationships.

ॐ महादेव महात्राण महायोगि महेश्वर ।
सर्वपापहरां देव मकाराय नमो नमः ॥

oṁ mahādeva mahātrāṇa mahāyogi maheśvara
sarvapāpaharāṁ deva makārāya namo namaḥ
oṁ The Great God, the Great Reliever, the Great Yogi, Oh Supreme Lord, Oh God who removes all Sin, in the form of the letter "M" which dissolves creation, we bow to you again and again.

ॐ नमः शिवाय शान्ताय कारणत्रय हेतवे ।
निवेदयामि चात्मानं त्वं गतिः परमेश्वर ॥

oṁ namaḥ śivāya śāntāya kāraṇatraya hetave
nivedayāmi cātmānaṁ tvaṁ gatiḥ parameśvara
oṁ I bow to the Consciousness of Infinite Goodness, to Peace, to the Cause of the three worlds, I offer to you the fullness of my soul, Oh Supreme Lord.

त्वमेव माता च पिता त्वमेव त्वमेव बन्धुश्च सखा त्वमेव ।
त्वमेव विद्या द्रविणं त्वमेव त्वमेव सर्वम् मम देवदेव ॥

tvameva mātā ca pitā tvameva
tvameva bandhuśca sakhā tvameva
tvameva vidyā draviṇaṁ tvameva
tvameva sarvam mama deva deva

You alone are Mother and Father, you alone are friend and relative. You alone are knowledge and wealth, Oh my God of Gods, you alone are everything.

कायेन वाचा मनसेन्द्रियैर्वा बुद्ध्यात्मानवप्रकृतस्वभावत् ।
करोमि यद्यत् सकलम् परस्मै नारायणायेति समर्पयामि ॥

kāyena vācā manasendriyairvā
buddhyātmā nava prakṛta svabhavat
karomi yadyat sakalam parasmai
nārāyaṇāyeti samarpayāmi

Body, speech, mind, the five organs of knowledge (five senses) and the intellect; these nine are the natural condition of human existence. In their highest evolution, I move beyond them all, as I surrender completely to the Supreme Consciousness.

ॐ पापोऽहं पापकर्माहं पापात्मा पापसम्भव ।
त्राहि मां पुण्डरीकाक्षं सर्वपापहरो हरिः ॥

oṁ pāpo-haṁ pāpakarmāhaṁ pāpātmā pāpasambhava
trāhi māṁ puṇḍarīkākṣaṁ sarvapāpa haro hariḥ

oṁ I am of sin, confusion, duality; my actions are of duality; this entire existence is of duality. Oh Savior and Protector, Oh Great Consciousness, take away all sin, confusion, duality.

ॐ मन्त्रहीनं क्रियाहीनं भक्तिहीनं सुरेश्वरि ।
यत्पूजितं मया देवि परिपूर्णं तदस्तु मे ॥

oṁ mantrahīnaṁ kriyāhīnaṁ bhaktihīnaṁ sureśvari
yatpūjitaṁ mayā devi paripūrnaṁ tadastu me

oṁ I know nothing of mantras. I do not perform good conduct. I have no devotion, Oh Supreme Goddess. But Oh my God, please accept the worship that I offer.

त्वमेव प्रत्यक्षम् ब्रह्माऽसि ।
त्वामेव प्रत्यक्षम् ब्रह्म वदिष्यामि ।
ऋतम् वदिष्यामि, सत्यम् वदिष्यामि ।
तन मामवतु, तद वक्तारमवतु ।
अवतु माम्, अवतु वक्तारम् ॥

tvameva pratyakṣam brahmā-si
tvāmeva pratyakṣam brahma vadiṣyāmi
ṛtam vadiṣyāmi, satyam vadiṣyāmi
tana māmavatu, tada vaktāramavatu
avatu mām, avatu vaktāram

You alone are the Perceivable Supreme Divinity. You alone are the Perceivable Supreme Divinity, so I shall declare. I shall speak the nectar of immortality. I shall speak Truth. May this body be your instrument. May this mouth be your instrument. May the Divine always be with us. May it be thus.

ॐ सह नाववतु सह नौ भुनक्तु । सह वीर्यं करवावहै ।
तेजस्विनावधीतमस्तु । मा विद्विषावहै ॥

oṁ saha nāvavatu, saha nau bhunaktu
saha vīryam karavāvahai tejasvināvadhītamastu
mā vidviṣāvahai

oṁ May the Lord protect us. May the Lord grant us enjoyment of all actions. May we be granted strength to work together. May our studies be thorough and faithful. May all disagreement cease.

ॐ असतो मा सद् गमय । तमसो मा ज्योतिर्गमय ।
मृत्योर्मा अमृतं गमय ॥

oṁ asatomā sad gamaya tamasomā jyotirgamaya
mṛtyormā amṛtaṁ gamaya
oṁ From untruth lead us to Truth. From darkness lead us to the Light. From death lead us to Immortality.

ॐ सर्वेषां स्वस्तिर्भवतु । सर्वेषां शान्तिर्भवतु । सर्वेषां पूर्णं भवतु । सर्वेषां मङ्गलं भवतु सर्वे भवन्तु सुखिनः । सर्वे सन्तु निरामयाः । सर्वे भद्राणि पश्यन्तु । मा कश्चिद् दुःख भाग्भवेत् ॥

oṁ sarveṣāṁ svastir bhavatu sarveṣāṁ śāntir bhavatu
sarveṣāṁ pūrṇaṁ bhavatu sarveṣaṁ maṅgalaṁ bhavatu
sarve bhavantu sukhinaḥ
sarve santu nirāmayāḥ sarve bhadrāṇi paśyantu mā kaścid duḥkha bhāgbhavet
oṁ May all be blessed with the highest realization. May all be blessed with Peace. May all be blessed with Perfection. May all be blessed with Welfare. May all be blessed with comfort and happiness. May all be free from misery. May all perceive auspiciousness. May all be free from infirmities.

गुरुर्ब्रह्मा गुरुर्विष्णुः गुरुर्देवो महेश्वरः ।
गुरुः साक्षात् परं ब्रह्म तस्मै श्रीगुरवे नमः ॥

gurur brahmā gururviṣṇuḥ gururdevo maheśvaraḥ
guruḥ sākṣāt paraṁ brahma tasmai śrīgurave namaḥ
The Guru is Brahmā, Guru is Viṣṇu, Guru is the Lord Maheśvara. The Guru is actually the Supreme Divinity, and therefore we bow down to the Guru.

ॐ ब्रह्मार्पणं ब्रह्म हविर्ब्रह्माग्नौ ब्रह्मणा हुतम् ।
ब्रह्मैव तेन गन्तव्यं ब्रह्मकर्मसमाधिना ॥

oṁ brahmārpaṇaṁ brahma havir
brahmāgnau brahmaṇā hutam
brahmaiva tena gantavyaṁ
brahmakarma samādhinā

oṁ The Supreme Divinity makes the offering; the Supreme Divinity is the offering; offered by the Supreme Divinity, in the fire of the Supreme Divinity. By seeing the Supreme Divinity in all actions, one realizes that Supreme Divinity.

ॐ पूर्णमदः पूर्णमिदं पूर्णात् पूर्णमुदच्यते ।
पूर्णस्य पूर्णमादाय पूर्णमेवावशिष्यते ॥

oṁ pūrṇamadaḥ pūrṇamidaṁ
pūrṇāt pūrṇamudacyate
pūrṇasya pūrṇamādāya pūrṇamevāva śiṣyate

oṁ That is whole and perfect; this is whole and perfect. From the whole and perfect, the whole and perfect becomes manifest. If the whole and perfect issue forth from the whole and perfect, even still only the whole and perfect will remain.

ॐ शान्तिः शान्तिः शान्तिः

oṁ śāntiḥ śāntiḥ śāntiḥ

oṁ Peace, Peace, Peace

tilak

त्र्यायुषञ्जमदग्ने कश्यपस्यत्र्यायुषम् ।
यद्देवेषुत्र्यायुषन्तन्नोऽअस्तुत्र्यायुषम् ॥

tryāyuṣañjamadagne kaśyapasyattryāyuṣam
yaddeveṣuttryāyuṣantanno-astuttryāyuṣam

Three lifetimes filled with Peace is the blessing of Jamadagni (Literally, He who gives birth to Fire). From the muni, Kaśyapa, three lifetimes filled with Peace. From all the Gods three lifetimes filled with Peace, so let that be unto you, three lifetimes filled with Peace.

More Books by Shree Maa and Swami Satyananda Saraswati

Annapurna Sahasranam
Before Becoming This
Bhagavad Gita
Chandi Path
Cosmic Puja
Cosmic Puja Bengali
Devi Gita
Devi Mandir Songbook
Durga Puja Beginner
Ganesh Puja
Hanuman Puja
Kali Dhyanam
Kali Puja
Lakṣmī Sahasranam
Sahib Sadhu, The White Sadhu
Shiva Puja Beginner
Shiva Puja and Advanced Yajna
Shree Maa Cookbook
Shree Maa: The Guru and the Goddess
Shree Maa: The Life of a Saint
Sundar Kanda
Swami Purana

CDs and Cassettes

Chandi Path
Dark Night Mother
Durga Puja Beginner (Instructional)
Goddess is Everywhere
Lalita Trishati
Mahamrtyunjaya Mantra
Mantras of the Nine Planets
Navarna Mantra
Om Mantra
Sadhu Stories from the Himalayas
Shiva is in My Heart
Shiva Puja Beginner (Instructional)
Shiva Puja & Advanced Yajna
Shree Maa in the Temple of the Heart
Shree Maa on Tour 1998
Songs of Ramprasad
Thousand Names of Kali

Videos

Across the States with Shree Maa & Swamiji
Meaning and Method of Worship
Shree Maa: Meeting a Modern Saint
Visiting India with Shree Maa and Swamiji

Please visit us at www.shreemaa.org
Our email is infóshreemaa.org

www.ingramcontent.com/pod-product-compliance
Lightning Source LLC
Chambersburg PA
CBHW021050080526
44587CB00010B/194
* 9 7 8 1 8 7 7 7 9 5 1 5 2 *